Savaging the Civilized

OXFORD
UNIVERSITY PRESS

YMCA Library Building, Jai Singh Road, New Delhi 110 001

Oxford University Press is a department of the University of Oxford. It furthers the University's objective of excellence in research, scholarship, and education by publishing worldwide in

Oxford New York
Athens Auckland Bangkok Bogota Buenos Aires Calcutta
Cape Town Chennai Dar es Salaam Delhi Florence Hong Kong Istanbul
Karachi Kuala Lumpur Madrid Melbourne Mexico City Mumbai
Nairobi Paris Sao Paolo Singapore Taipei Tokyo Toronto Warsaw

with associated companies in

Berlin Ibadan

First published by Oxford University Press 1999
Second impression 1999

ISBN 0 19 564781 5

For sale only in South Asia

Printed in India at Pauls Press, New Delhi
and published by Manzar Khan, Oxford University Press
YMCA Library Building, Jai Singh Road, New Delhi 110 001

SAVAGING THE CIVILIZED

Verrier Elwin, His Tribals, and India

RAMACHANDRA GUHA

OXFORD
UNIVERSITY PRESS

Verrier Elwin, *c.* 1954 (Sunil Janah)

for Sujata

We tend to think of an Age in terms of the man we take as representative of it, and forget that equally a part of the man's significance may be his battle with his Age.

T. S. Eliot

What makes a man change his nationality, abjure civilization and, in the upshot, become a blend of Schweitzer in Africa and Gauguin in Tahiti?

W. G. Archer on Verrier Elwin

PROLOGUE

The Other Side of the Raj

In July 1943, as the Second World War was moving towards a climax, two American journalists raced each other deep into the Indian forest. They were Sonia Tamara of the *New York Herald Tribune* and Herbert Matthews of the rival *New York Times*, and their quarry was a forty-year-old Englishman, Verrier Elwin, an Oxford scholar and renegade priest who had made his home with the Gond tribals of the Maikal hills.

It was Sonia Tamara who reached Elwin first. She spent a week with him before rushing off to the nearest post office—in the town of Jabalpur, 150 miles from Elwin's own village of Patangarh. Her telegrams spoke of the scholar's 'simple, truthful manner' and of his work, amidst tigers, bears and malaria, for the 'primitivest, ancientest tribes' that offered 'one more aspect of the complexest Indian problem.' The man had gone native in the most emphatic sense, by marrying a 'pretty dark Gond girl with lithe limbs tiny hands everready smile,' their union confirmed by 'millenary old Gond rites.'

The American reporter found that these tribals spoke to the anthropologist without reticence, allowing him to record 'their lifestories their customs rites intimatest habits.' The affection the Gond and Baiga had for Elwin was manifest: when their car stopped in a village, wired Tamara, 'men women children outpoured talked volubly smiled babies put into his lap.'[1]

The breathlessness marks this out as an authentic scoop, the testimony of the 'first reporter whos reached Central Indias aboriginal tribes.' And yet, more sober commentators were equally impressed by the singularity of Elwin's life in the forest. They included the two greatest Indians of modern times, Jawaharlal Nehru and Mahatma Gandhi, and the French writer Romain Rolland. It was Rolland who wrote in 1936: 'In Africa, Albert Schweitzer, the philosopher; in India, Verrier Elwin, the poet'—a pairing that remains an intriguing one.[2] Fourteen years later, the *Times Literary Supplement* celebrated Elwin as a 'man of great culture and originality of thought,' a 'poet and translator as well as social worker, explorer and ethnologist, and in every branch of his work he is first-rate.' He was, it concluded, 'one of the best contributions this country ever made to India.'[3]

Thus the *TLS* in 1950; but I suspect few readers of that journal will recognize Elwin's name any more. For now, in the nineteen nineties, most British people know of their encounter with India mostly through books and films about sahibs and memsahibs. Their libraries are awash with studies of viceroys and explorers, of a Younghusband who was the first (white) man to reach Lhasa and a Mountbatten who gallantly lowered the Union Jack. Their television sets are peppered with retrospective celebrations of households, set in heat and dust, which defied death and disease to 'stay on.'

We Indians meanwhile know of our colonial experience through lenses tinted black. Our economists compute the drain of wealth to London and Manchester, our historians memorialize acts of resistance, big or small. An earlier generation of 'nationalists' wrote of campaigns visible and public, from the great revolt of 1857 down to Gandhi's triumphant satyagrahas of the thirties and forties. The present generation of 'subalternists' seek to recover voices silenced by the nationalists, the unnamed peasants and tribals whose protests against imperial authority were frequently more radical than the schemes of the Indian National Congress. But the new historians adhere likewise to the colour bar, the too easy division of the social world of colonial India between dominant whites and discontented browns.

Both British nostalgist and Indian nationalist cannot easily account for men like Verrier Elwin, or women like Annie Besant who was a socialist and suffragette in London before becoming a spiritualist and freedom-fighter in Madras. Elwin and Besant were exemplars of what the sociologist Shiv Visvanathan has called the 'other side of the Raj.' This other side also includes the saintly Charles Freer Andrews, the friend of Gandhi and of

Indian plantation workers from Fiji to Guyana; the brilliant if inconstant Philip Spratt, a communist who came to blow up India in 1927 but ended up a passionate free-marketeer and analyst of the 'Hindu personality;' and the missionary Edward J. Thompson, biographer of Tagore, novelist of rural India and, in the words of his son, the great historian E. P. Thompson, 'a courier between cultures who wore the authorized livery of neither.'[4] Nor must one forget the women, who—judging by the readiness with which they changed their names—were more inclined to discard the culture they were born into. I think, for example, of Sister Nivedita (Margaret Noble), the Irishwoman who joined and led a Hindu religious order; and of Mira Behn (Madeleine Slade), the British admiral's daughter who adopted Gandhi and after years in his service left India to seek out the spirit of Beethoven in Austria.

In 1961 an American scholar published a study titled *The Nine Lives of Annie Besant*, comprising two 500-page volumes titled, respectively, *The First Five Lives* and *The Next Four Lives.* At about the same time Elwin was writing his autobiography. When he asked his publisher to suggest a title, the man came up with twenty-five alternatives. How could one adequately illustrate, in four or five words, a life so varied? 'From Merton to Nongthymai' would mark only the place he came from and the place he ended up in; 'Khadi, Cassock, and Gown' mechanically matched dress to vocation; 'Into the Forests, Over the Hills' said something of the terrain he went through on the way but nothing of what he did therein; 'Anthropologist at Large' and 'Philanthropologist' only indicated his last professional affiliation (and might invite unwelcome jokes about the 'philanderopologist'!); 'No Tribal Myth' and 'My Passage to Tribal India' focused only on the people with whom he had made his home.[5]

Verrier Elwin was as eccentric as Annie Besant, as inclined to rebel, as willing to throw up one career and campaign for another. He was also a better writer and, in the circumstances of his life, luckier. Besant, who came to Madras in 1893 and died there in 1932, knew only one kind of India; but Elwin, who came in 1927 and stayed on till his death in 1964, knew both the India of the Raj and the India of the Congress, and made notable contributions to both. We are fortunate, too, that the richness of experience is equalled by the richness of the oeuvre. For Elwin was a novelist, pamphleteer, poet, anthropologist, and autobiographer, an author in many genres of works that were influential in their day and are not unread in ours.

To write about Verrier Elwin is to throw fresh light on men of influence like Gandhi and Nehru, to focus once more on forgotten and oppressed peoples, to travel through all parts of India, to anticipate (by decades) current ideas of religious dialogue and cultural pluralism, to explore the practice of governments colonial and nationalist. In his life, and more so in his work, some of the great debates of the twentieth century find eloquent expression. A book on a man as public and controversial as Elwin shades the difference between self and society, biography and history. That said, this study stays close to its central character. I have not suppressed fact or been coy with opinion, but the interpretation is in the telling: for to intervene with currently fashionable theory would spoil the integrity of the narrative, indeed the integrity of life as it was lived by Verrier Elwin.

Contents

List of Illustrations

Copyright owners have been credited below within brackets.

CHAPTER ONE

Evangelical Ghetto

In fetid slums, in tiny hamlets, in fashionable watering-places, [late-nineteenth-century] Evangelicals were 'foremost in every scheme for propagating the gospel.' But their proselytism fell with greatest force on their closest relatives. Indoctrination, like philanthropy, began at home.

Clive Dewey

Verrier was the first of the Elwins to depart from the strict and narrow path of orthodoxy in religion and politics since the family began four hundred years ago.

Shamrao Hivale

Verrier Elwin's life was marked by a series of departures, by lively espousals and vigorous rejections of one way of life and belief for another. His first and in some ways most surprising move was away from the pious and resolutely imperialist background of the family into which he was born. The career of this rebel and controversialist begins in humdrum circumstances which are retrospectively interesting, so to say, inasmuch as they seem to contrast so precisely with the astonishing volcanic eruptions of his later life.

Harry Verrier Holman Elwin, to provide a full name he rarely used, was born in Dover on 29 August 1902. The Elwins were an Anglo-Saxon family of genteel but not aristocratic background, archetypes of what George Orwell once called the 'lower-upper-middle-class.' The men worked for the most part as solicitors, clergymen and officials. Two of Verrier's uncles, and two of his cousins, served in the Indian Civil Service.

Verrier's father, Edmund Henry Elwin, was born in 1871, the fifth son in a family of twelve. He studied at Merton College, Oxford, graduating in the summer of 1893 with a third-class honours degree in theology. He then joined the evangelical seminary, Wycliffe Hall, founded in 1877 to train graduates who wanted holy orders and be made 'God's men, Christian gentlemen in the finest and best sense of the word.'[1]

Ordained in 1894, E. H. Elwin was appointed curate of the Oxford parish of St Peter-le-Bailey. But Wycliffe Hall encouraged its men to take the gospel overseas, and in 1896 Elwin joined a party of Oxbridge men going out to the Church Missionary Society's station in Sierra Leone, a colony known with reason as the 'White Man's Grave.' In ninety years of work the CMS lost half its men to disease, but not before winning 50,000 converts in and around the capital, Freetown. The city was founded in 1787 by four hundred slaves dispatched to West Africa on a ship paid for by London philanthropists, who helpfully sent along 'eighty white women of loose character to keep them company.' The settlers, long since removed from their ancestral faith, were rich pickings for the missionaries. When the elder Elwin arrived in Freetown it already had a thriving Christian life: eighty working branches of a Bible-Reading Union, packed Sunday schools, churches with congregations of a thousand and more. Evangelical work now focused on an unclaimed and as yet largely unknown hinterland dominated by Muslim and 'heathen' communities.[2]

Edmund Elwin's first appointment was as vice-principal of Fourah Bay College, an institution affiliated to the University of Durham which allowed 'Africa's sons, without leaving African soil, [to] qualify for English degrees on equal terms with Englishmen.' On graduation most students of Fourah Bay were gathered into the fold of the CMS. The college sent forth a steady stream of pastors and teachers into the heart of West Africa, a territory that could scarcely be evangelized by Europeans alone.[3]

In the first months of 1898 Sierra Leone was convulsed by a popular rebellion. The immediate provocation was a new hut tax, to be paid in 'sterling coin' by every African who dwelt in his own home. The tax brought to a climax a more general disaffection with alien rule, and the response was explosive. As one eyewitness recalled, the uprising was 'really an attempt to cast off British rule, sweep away everything English, and drive the Sierra Leonean back to [Freetown]. There is not the slightest evidence that any discrimination was exercised, or any special spleen vented. Government quarters, trading centres, mission stations, were all equally assailed; and in every case where defense was inadequate, they raided, looted and murdered to their heart's content.'[4]

One victim of the rising was the principal of Fourah Bay, Reverend W. J. Humphrey, who was caught by the rebels and executed while on a tour of missions in the interior. Towards the end of the year, with the insurgency crushed and the hut tax withdrawn, pastors were allowed to return to their stations. In August 1899 their work was inspected afresh by Reverend Elwin, who had succeeded Humphrey both as principal of Fourah Bay and as secretary of the Sierra Leone Mission. In less than a week Elwin travelled 200 miles by row-boat, on horseback, and by foot, while plagued by rats and mosquitoes in the rudimentary dwellings where he passed the nights. Starting one afternoon from the college wharf, his boat reached Port Lokkoh after four hours of 'monotonous pulling of the oars.' The next day he set off with a colleague for the bush village of Funknin. Arriving at the mission after a twelve-hour trek, Elwin 'set to work, examined the log-book, the itinerating-book, the accounts, the service-book, and the school register; handed them a letter from the finance committee, talked it over and made suggestions:' an examination conducted at every station thereafter.

But routine was also accompanied by ritual, as the priest exhorted his juniors to claim Africans for their church. At Rogbere he assembled the pastors for Communion, and as they 'knelt round His Table right away in the heathen country, [they] learnt a little more really what Christ dying for the whole world meant, and what it means to follow in His steps as missionaries.' Victories were few and far between, but the evangelist hoped for the miraculous mass conversion, the single spark that would light a collective fire. A Temne youth in Makomp showed a striking interest in the Bible; prepared by a catechist, he was ready to be baptised by the visitor from Freetown. One morning Reverend Elwin led the boy down to the river and, in the presence of most of the village baptised him in the water with the name of Yusufu Koma. 'It was a touching sight,' affirmed the priest:

> His father and mother were there and all his people, and it must have made an impression far more than baptism with sprinkling would have done to a people well trained in parables to see this boy thus saying good-bye to the past and rising to a new life in the risen Christ. I addressed the people after, and then Koma, telling him to be a brave 'krugba ka Christ' (warboy of

> Christ). We had the Communion together, and then I started [back] for Port Lokkoh.[5]

E. H. Elwin's faith was described by his son, years later, as 'one of the dullest types of religion in the world.'[6] A student at Fourah Bay put it more neutrally; the principal, he said, 'forcibly emphasized the necessity for a life of saintliness and self-consecration to God.'[7] A photograph reproduced in the college jubilee volume shows the principal seated amidst his students: balding, bespectacled, an expression of grim resolution on his face. There is no gainsaying his commitment, for the number of graduates from Fourah Bay more than doubled during his tenure, while his energetic secretaryship helped restore the faith of a Mission badly shaken by the uprising of 1898. Hard work found its reward in preferment and in 1901, when the Bishop of Sierra Leone was appointed Chaplain-General of the British forces, Elwin was the obvious choice as his successor.

In the last week of December 1901 Edmund Elwin sailed with his wife for Liverpool. A month later, on 25 January 1902, he was consecrated along with the newly appointed Bishop of Likoma at a ceremony held at Westminster Abbey. The Archbishop of Canterbury, presiding, chose his text from the Book of Matthew: 'Lo, I am with you always, even unto the end of the world.' These words, said the archbishop, were 'especially appropriate for such an occasion as this, when they were sending forth ministers of the Gospel to preach the Word in distant parts, in countries which could not be called Christian, to heathens who knew nothing of the revealed word of God.' Even as he spoke, the spread of the Word was aided by the spread of the telegraph, the steamboat and the Union Jack. Characteristically, the Anglican pontiff saw the hand of providence in the consolidation of British imperialism. 'Not half the human race had yet learnt what the Gospel was,' he concluded, 'and the Lord was calling them. He was making it day by day easier to reach the places where His work was to be done wherever they might be on the whole surface of the globe.'[8]

An interested spectator at Westminster Abbey was the new bishop's wife: a disinterested one (so to say) was their son, a struggling foetus conceived, by my calculations, on the ship that carried his parents from Freetown to Liverpool. When the boy was born in August, the bishop was back at his post in West Africa, where he would be for most of Verrier's infancy. Growing up in a fatherless household, Verrier's first important relationships were with women. The family consisted of Verrier, his sister Eldyth, who was a year-and-a-half younger, and their brother Basil, who was four years younger still. Brother and sister were natural playmates, with the baby kept at a distance from the very beginning.[9] But it was their mother who was unquestionably the central figure in his early life. Verrier's portrait of his mother, in his later writings and especially in his memoirs, mixes genuine affection with a sardonic assessment of her fanatical faith. Evangelical families rested on a unanimity of opinion between husband and wife: no trouble here, for Minnie Elwin was devoted to the bishop and his religion. A renowned beauty (the looks were passed on to Verrier), she was also a forceful character, being described by one of her son's friends as 'the most powerful woman I have met,' by another as 'strongly Protestant and Fundamentalist,' by a third as 'a rather dominating possessive woman, but gracious in a distant missionary way.'[10]

To the Evangelical faith in the literalness of the Bible Minnie Elwin added a messianic belief in the Second Coming. The family, recalled Verrier, could not go 'to a theatre, cinema, circus or other place of entertainment, for it would have been rather embarrassing if Jesus had arrived in the middle of the programme.' God was the unseen member of the Elwin home, a more-than-adequate substitute for the father away in Africa. His Son, however, was the cause of sibling dispute. At the age of seven Verrier announced that he had given his heart to Jesus; when Eldyth insisted that she had done likewise, her brother hit her on the head with a celluloid doll, declaring: 'I am the only member of the family who has done it.'[11]

The renegade in the family was Minnie's mother, Flora Holman. She didn't go to church, never opened her Bible, and took regular swigs from a bottle of brandy hidden underneath her dress. Verrier and Eldyth knew Grandma Holman to be marked for Hell, but meanwhile she was the source of stories more fanciful than any to be found in the Bible. Her tales of northern India, where her father had been a soldier, began with Sitapur in Awadh, where 'wolves were very plentiful and very bold, and were accustomed to a good supply of Indian babies.' The canines came in search of a white baby, the Colonel's child, no less, to be thwarted by a devoted pie-dog who 'slept by the cot-side and accompanied the child everywhere.' At Agra, their next posting, thieves entered the house at night; by the time father emerged from the bedroom, sword in hand, the gang had made its getaway, leaving behind a 'grinning nude wretch' who tormented the soldier 'by playing around the dining-table in the most elastic and aggravating manner.' From Agra they moved on to Phillaur, a town (they had been warned) known for 'cholera, white ants, dust storms and a sprinkling of mad dogs.' What hit them instead was a terrific cyclone, with hailstones large enough to stun horses and kill crows. The wind 'lifted the tiles off the roof like biscuits,' their carriage was 'turned inside out and smashed to pieces, and our sleepy coachman was blown down a well.'[12]

Granny Holman's tales transported Verrier and Eldyth from the murky fog of England to the burning plains of India. Their father laboured on in Africa, confirming converts, raising money for a new cathedral in Freetown (left by his predecessor without a roof), rebuilding stations gutted in the 1898 rising and staffing them with fresh recruits. The policy of Africanization lay discredited after the troubles, but the bishop thought that only native pastors could be sent as 'pioneers to the unevangelized parts of our Hinterland' to meet the challenge of the other faith with universalist aspirations. 'It is high time,' remarked the bishop to a representative of the journal *Great Thoughts*, 'that the Christian Church everywhere awoke to the most earnest consideration of the question whether in the near future Africa is to be dominated by Islam or by Christianity.' He admitted that a pagan village won over to Islam exchanged 'its dirt and squalor for neatness and cleanliness,' he acknowledged that what 'it teaches of God is also a great advance on fetishism:' nonetheless, Islam encouraged polygamy and slavery, evils the African had to be delivered from. Islam, declared the bishop, 'cannot elevate any race beyond a certain level, and that a low one—higher than barbarism, it is true, but far below Christianity. Only the Gospel of Christ can bring hope to the Dark Continent.'[13]

This was spoken in April 1909; in November Bishop Elwin was dead, claimed, like so many of his fellows, by a deadly fever that ran its course within a week. He was buried at the Kissy Road cemetery in Freetown. One of Verrier's clearest childhood memories was news of his father's death reaching the family in England. Minnie Elwin shut herself in the lavatory but her son crept up to hear her weep.[14]

'Had the Bishop lived Verrier's life would have been very different,' remarks Elwin's early hagiographer;[15] but so of course would have been his mother's. E. H. Elwin was elevated to the episcopate at thirty, the minimum age: with years of service in the tropics he would assuredly been rewarded with a sinecure at home, preparatory to a steady march up the hierarchy of the Church of England. Minnie Elwin might have anticipated becoming the wife of the Bishop of Durham or Norwich, opening fairs, awarding prizes, contentedly raising her children in a financially secure and stable home.

Her husband's death left a gap which Minnie Elwin filled with renewed devotion to her religion and her family. There was little money; where once they might have hoped to live in a spacious home in Cathedral Close, the Elwins now had to make do with tiny rented quarters: two rooms and a bathroom shared with other lodgers. Mrs Elwin fought continually with her landladies, the children grew up in 'an atmosphere of catastrophic rows with these formidable women.' The rows meant they were often on the move: between the ages of six and ten Verrier lived in and attended schools in the towns of Reigate, Eastbourne and London.

As the eldest child, a boy of precocious intelligence to boot, Verrier was the centre of his mother's affections and ambitions. Her family rallied around to help send him to a 'public' school: which one would it be? In their choice Mrs Elwin and her advisers were dominated, it seems, 'by the desire to keep [the boy] untainted by the Church of Rome and the infidelity which they believed to come from the application of modern scholarship to the Bible.' Westminster in London was a day school whose expenses could more easily be managed, but it was found to be soft on Catholicism. Rugby was considered next, but its headmaster was an admirer of Charles Darwin who admitted that he could think of the Book of Genesis as true only in a 'symbolic' sense. The choice finally settled on Dean Close Memorial School in Cheltenham, of a lineage scarcely as distinguished as the others but with a reassuringly Evangelical cast.[16]

The Cheltenham school was named for Francis Close, the Evangelical publicist and bitter opponent of the Anglo-Catholic or High Church faction in the Church of England. Born in 1797, Close was emphatically Low Church, a Tory who condemned Anglo-Catholics for their love of ritual and their greater tolerance of other religions. 'The Bible is conservative,' he said, 'the Prayer Book conservative, the Liturgy conservative, the Church conservative, and it is impossible for a minister to open his mouth without being conservative.' His dogmatism was awesome. The poet Alfred Tennyson spoke of Cheltenham as a 'polka, parson-worshipping place of which Francis Close is Pope,' while the London *Times* dismissed him as an 'ignorant, meddling claptrap preacher' who held in thrall an 'equally ignorant congregation.'[17]

Tennyson and *The Times* represented the intellectual party; however, the professionals and tradesmen who followed Francis Close were not lacking in number, money, influence or faith. In 1886 this supposedly ignorant congregation started a school in the preacher's name, choosing as its first headmaster a man of similar conviction and force of character. H. W. Flecker, born in 1859 into a family of Austrian Jewish converts, was a graduate of the University of Durham who had 'raised himself in the world solely by his brilliant intellectual gifts and his inexhaustible capacity for hard work.' Remembered by a younger colleague as a man of 'immensely strong will' who 'would not tolerate incompetence or halfheartedness,' Flecker created a school in line with the founders' intentions. His distrust of Anglo-Catholics would have pleased Close. As his grandson writes, 'A prayer book with a cross on the cover was disapproved of in the family as savouring of the near-idolatrous practices of the Ritualists.' Many of the students at Flecker's school were sons of Evangelical clergy. They could not have been left in safer hands, for (his biographer remarks) 'the great tradition of conversion, of bringing souls to God, lay behind—say within—the whole of Flecker's life and career.'[18]

Dean Close School was run more or less as a family enterprise. The headmaster taught mathematics and literature, his wife took on German and Hebrew, a son taught classics and a daughter science. The domination of the patriarch was confirmed by the layout of the place. The school is tiny in comparison with the typical English public school, its eight-acre campus built up with dorms and offices and classrooms and auditoria. This smallness might have fostered a feeling of intimacy, or more likely a sense of being closed in. The headmaster's study was at one end of the main corridor: when summoned, boys would walk nervously down the long passage, the door closing behind them as they entered to be spoken to, chastised or, as was sometimes the case, caned.

Verrier Elwin joined the school in September 1915 when Dr Flecker had been in control for almost thirty years. In that time he had made of Dean Close a respectable public school, if not yet of the first rank. But his powers were now on the decline. To the toll of age had been added the difficulties of war and the alienation of a greatly loved son. This was the poet James Elroy Flecker, author of *Hassan* and other works, and the only member of the family with no connection to Dean Close. Sent to another and better school, Uppingham, James Elroy had rebelled against his parents' faith, which he variously described as hypocritical, a farce, 'intolerably narrow,' merely a set of 'episcopal enlargements on Biblical platitudes.' At Oxford James Elroy fell in with the Anglo-Catholics, observing of the Evangelical undergraduates that their 'collective brain-power would not suffice to run a tuck-shop.' Before long he wrote to his father professing agnosticism, thus 'cutting the last thread of the double life.' On leaving university he married a Greek girl. His wife was never acknowledged by his parents, for whom the Greeks and their church were dangerously allied to Catholicism.[19]

James Elroy Flecker died of consumption in January 1915, unreconciled with his parents. In any case, the poet's spirit was quite alien to the atmosphere of their school. When Verrier arrived later in the year, militarism had been joined to Evangelicalism. With his Austrian ancestry, Dr Flecker had ambivalent feelings about the war, but he could not fight the mood of bellicose nationalism within and without the school. Afternoon games gave way to parades and marches conducted by a mock Officers Training Corps, in preparation for mass recruitment on graduation. A pacifist master remarked that 'the place isn't a school, it's a depot,' but his complaint went unacknowledged. The school magazine, the *Decanian*, printed with pride long lists of the serving and the dead. Some 700 Old Decanians enlisted in the army, of which as many as 120 perished in the trenches. A War Memorial Chapel was erected at the end of hostilities from a fund subscribed to by Old Boys and their parents, the impecunious Mrs Elwin contributing one pound, the minimum acceptable donation.

The war concluded, Dean Close returned with vigour to its principles. 'The evangelisation of the world in this generation' was a slogan on the lips of parents and teachers alike, and in the last weeks of 1919 the school was visited by a succession of missionaries working overseas. Verrier and his class heard the Reverend C. E. Tyndale-Biscoe speak on his work in Kashmir, Dr W. Miller on his school in northern Nigeria, and the Reverend J. A. F. Warner on missionary prospects in the United Provinces of India. The *Decanian* meanwhile was reproducing letters written to Dr Flecker by L. W. Smith, an old student currently working with the Punjab Government. Smith was viewing, from the sidelines, Gandhi's first non-cooperation movement against the Raj, which he thought a 'foolish thing altogether,' supplied 'with plenty of money and an unlimited quantity of ill-will.' In Gujranwala, where Smith was posted, a procession marched defiantly through the town, carrying an effigy of the king-emperor. This was then cremated according to Hindu rites, with the ashes immersed in the Chenab river. One of the Old Decanian's duties was to identify sites for punitive police pickets to forestall further trouble.

Two classes ahead of Verrier Elwin was Stephen Neill, regarded as the school's star student. The son of the vicar of St Mark's Church in Cheltenham, Neill had a phenomenal aptitude for languages and a near-photographic memory. He was also very pious. For years after he left school—with a scholarship to Trinity College, Cambridge—the Classics teacher would correct answers by saying 'Stephen Neill would never have written this.' In school Verrier shadowed Neill honour for honour, winning, like the elder boy, the three prestigious prizes for history, literature and scripture. But the divergences in their paths were also becoming apparent. When in 1918 a Crusaders Bible Class was founded by Neill (at the time Senior Prefect), Verrier was content to stay put in the Literary Society.[20]

Verrier's interest in English literature was kindled by Dr Flecker himself who, unusually for an Anglican, was an admirer of the poetry of John Donne. When a senior teacher left for the front the headmaster appointed two boys, Verrier being one, to look after the library. Other masters introduced him to Horace and Pope, and some writers he discovered on his own. A lasting recollection of life at school was of 'getting up at five in the morning to go in stockinged feet down the steps—put shoes on—and out into the grounds to read Wordsworth.'[21]

Verrier's wide and probably indiscriminate reading bore fruit in a series of papers read at the Lit. Soc. In three years his choice of subjects moved from the carefully conventional to the daringly heterodox. In 1919 he spoke on Hebrew poetry and on Thackeray; the next year on Swinburne and Tennyson, and more controversially on Wordsworth. *The Decanian* reported that 'H. V. Elwin read an enthusiastic, and in the opinion of many, a very misguided paper on Wordsworth. People who had preserved a dignified silence for terms, unlocked their hearts and expressed their utmost abhorrence of, or their entire agreement with, Wordsworth's nature-philosophy.' His advocacy of the poet's pantheism had divided the ranks, but Verrier was to go further still. In the summer of 1921 this secretary of the Literary Society brought his duties to a close by reading a paper on the anti-Christian thinker Samuel Butler. 'By his sympathetic treatment of the subject,' remarked *The Decanian*, 'H. V. Elwin showed us that he was not in complete disagreement with the rather grotesque views expressed in "Erewhon" and Butler's other works.'

Verrier Elwin left Dean Close in 1921. When I visited the school seventy-five years later I found it had diluted but by no means abandoned the principles on which it was founded. A kindly and helpful archivist, Humphrey Osmond, introduced me in the staff room as someone 'working on Verrier Elwin, a younger contemporary of Stephen Neill.' The headmaster, pleased, explained the credo of the school as 'trying to build on our traditions—the heritage of Stephen Neill and your chap.' The chaplain, more astute, seemed to have realized that mentioning Neill and Elwin in the same breath was an injustice to at least one of them, so after the formalities he put it this way: 'We have a tradition of producing rugged individualists—Richard St Barbe Baker (famous for planting trees to stop the spread of the African desert), George Adamson (the lion tamer, husband of Joy) and your chap.'

Stephen Neill is still venerated in Dean Close as the prize pupil whose future career most fully embodied the aspirations of the Evangelical party of the Church of England. Neill held high office—as Bishop of Tirunelvelli in southern India and Professor of Theology in Hamburg—and his contributions to scholarship include the standard histories of Anglicanism and of Christianity in South Asia. On returning to England he served for many years on Dean Close's board of governors. Neill, I was told, had donated a huge chunk of his book royalties to the school. He had also delivered the commemoration address before he died. Sadly, he didn't live long enough to write the foreword to the *Centenary Volume.* There now hangs a portrait of Stephen Neill in the school, the only Old Decanian so honoured, the pupil described by a loving *alma mater* as 'Evangelist, Missionary, Statesman, Scholar, Teacher and Benefactor.'

Anticipating my arrival, the archivist had taken out old issues of the *Decanian* with entries on Elwin already flagged. The photocopier was in the same room as the computers. At one terminal sat the chaplain, typing out the question paper for the 'Sykes and Charles and Elizabeth Prize,' the scripture prize once won both by my chap and theirs. As Mr Osmond photocopied the pages I slyly noted down the first and last questions of the question paper. The first was 'Write down Psalm 103 from memory;' the last: ' "Being a Christian at school is quite easy. But how will I manage when I leave?" Write a letter giving advice to an imaginary friend who has asked this question.'

The kind of letter Stephen Neill would have written Verrier Elwin, perhaps?

CHAPTER TWO

Oxford Rebellion

But in case you think my education was wasted
I hasten to explain
That having once been to the University of Oxford
You can never really again
Believe anything than anyone says and that of course is an asset
In a world like ours;
Why bother to water a garden
That is planted with paper flowers?

Louis Macniece (Merton 1925–8)

My path, thank God, led me through Oxford, but it also, thank God, led me away from it.

George Santayana

In the summer of 1921 Mrs Minnie Elwin acquired a new and semi-permanent home. For the not insubstantial sum of a thousand pounds she bought a two-storeyed house on Warnborough Road in north Oxford, just beyond the perimeter of what counts as university territory. The family were living in a rented cottage in the town of Worthing, but with Verrier's admission to Merton College his mother had thought to move closer. At Dean Close her son's education was reliably supervised by Dr Flecker, but it now seemed necessary to resume direct responsibility for his instruction.

Mrs Elwin's worries were not misplaced. The freedoms of the university are in contrast to the rule-bound regimen of an English public school—'the problems of life that confront one here,' wrote a Merton contemporary of Verrier, were: '1. How to find time to do any work. 2. How to get to bed before one . . . 3. How to get drunk cheaply. 4. How to be rude first. 5. How to sign one's name.' A typical day ran like this:

> Roll-call 5 to 8—bath after or before. Breakfast by fire 8.45. May or may not be lecture from 10 to 12. Lunch at 1.15. Afternoon spent in Darrell's motor or antique shops—I hope to play hockey occasionally. Tea at Fuller's or Ellison and Cavell's as cheap there as in college: may or may not be an hour's tutorial in the evening. Dine in hall at 7. 30—or dine out. Cinema or orgy afterwards. Gates shut at 12—a life, as you perceive, so fitted to prepare one for the thorny paths of the world. I am making the best of it and have bought some very nice suede shoes for 32/6. Never again, I am convinced, shall I have such comfort or such a beautiful room to live in—it is well then to enjoy it while one can.[1]

The freedoms of college are temporal, social, intellectual, spatial: the boy fresh from school is all at once free to do what he wants with his time, go where he wishes, decide what he shall read and argue about, whom he shall befriend and whom avoid. To move from Dean Close to Merton was to enter a more variegated world, a hetereogeneity of belief, race and nationality. True, there were few students from working-class backgrounds, but plenty from the other end of the spectrum, the Anglo-Catholic or agnostic products of Eton and Harrow little known to a boy from a middle-class and Evangelical home. Moreover, with the Rhodes scholarship scheme in place, one in ten students came from overseas; many from the USA and the white dominions, but an increasing number from British India.

Tucked away in a quiet lane behind the busy High Street, Merton is one of the smaller and less visible of Oxford's colleges. Founded in 1264, it is by one reckoning the oldest in the university. It is a proud college and a very pretty one. The historian A. L. Rowse, an exact contemporary of Elwin (at Christ Church), wrote feelingly of 'the beauty of Merton, the high midsummer pomps, honeyed light on stone, the garden within the city walls, the limes and roses, the outlook on Christ Church Meadows.'[2] Merton has a reputation for gaiety that goes back to the Civil War, and a kitchen once deemed to be the best in Oxford, its pleasures recorded in this anonymous ditty:

> Within those walls, where through the glimmering shade,
> Appear the pamphlets in a moulding heap,

Each in his narrow bed till morning laid,
The peaceful Fellows of the College sleep.
No chattering females crowd their social fire,
No dread of discord have they or of strife;
Unknown the names of Husband and of sire,
Unfelt the plagues of matrimonial life.
Oft have they basked along the sunny walls,
Oft have the benches bowed beneath their weight.
How fecund are their looks when dinner calls!
How smoke the cutlets on their crowded plates!

This was written in the 1870s; by the 1920s the Fellows were married and, if not, more inclined to read books and write them. Merton's reputation for indolence was dealt a decisive blow by the philosopher A. C. Bradley, a Fellow of the college from 1870 to 1924. Bradley's influence was to reach out into the wider world through T. S. Eliot, whom he tutored when the poet was in residence in 1914–15. When Verrier entered Merton a few years later, the Age of Bradley was coming to a close, to be superseded by the equally long-lived Age of Garrod.

H. W. Garrod joined Merton in 1901, as a tutor in Literature and Classics. He was an authority on Keats and Wordsworth, Horace and Charlemagne, and also the author of a famous 'depreciation' of Jane Austen. He was a lifelong bachelor, devoted to his studies and his students. In *Who's Who* he listed his recreations as 'none,' a typical Garrod joke. He wore a battered hat and had at his heels a succession of blue spaniels, always called Chips. Books, dogs and undergraduates took up most of Garrod's time: he loved playing chess and bowls with students.[3] All in all, he set a standard of collegiality that other Fellows strove nobly to fulfil. George Mallaby, who entered Merton the year before Verrier, remembered the bond between teachers and students:

> Between boys and schoolmasters there must always be some reserve, some barrier of disciplined respect, a certain lack of easy candour and relaxed manners. Between dons and undergraduates this need not be so and in the Merton of 1920 it certainly was not so . . . It was not only the weekly tutorial—it was the constant, daily contact with dons, not only your own tutor, but dons of all kinds, theologians, scientists, philosophers, historians who stopped you in the quad for a chat, who spoke at your debates, read papers at your literary societies, watched your games and invited you to meals.[4]

Reading English literature, Verrier had much to do with Garrod and with David Nicol Smith, a Scotsman with an equally versatile mind and range of interests. Nicol Smith's books included studies of Dryden, Hazlitt, and Johnson: he was also a noted Shakespeare scholar. However, the English School's syllabi was rather antiquated; a later student, John Betjeman, described it as 'really Anglo-Saxon, Northumbrian dialect and tedious medieval poems.'[5] Verrier himself most enjoyed the solitary 'modern' paper, on the eighteenth century, the period in which both his teachers were acknowledged specialists. Outside the classroom he assisted Nicol Smith with his *Oxford Anthology of Eighteenth Century English Verse*. He also helped Garrod with an essay on the seventeenth-century dramatist Middleton, learning a lesson about the essential loneliness of the scholar's vocation. When the student's sections were passed by the professor without any alterations, Verrier worried that readers would notice the decline in style. 'There are no two human beings, Mr Elwin,' answered Garrod, 'who will read this article with the same attention which you and I have given it.'[6]

Garrod also presided with indulgent wit over the Bodley Club, a literary discussion group which met in his rooms three or four times a term. Both dons and undergraduates were in attendance: while the former 'dealt each other shrewd blows with Latin quotations,' the latter were encouraged to present papers and speak up in any case.[7] In Verrier's first year, papers were read on Kipling's jingoism, socialism and literature, the Celtic tradition, and the 'Case for Contemporary Poetry.' The Bodley Club partook of its patron's qualities: witty, iconoclastic, inclusive, moving beyond 'the insularity of England into the internationalism of the Kingdom of Letters.'[8]

The Oxford of the twenties has been memorialized by literary historians as the decade of the aesthete, the cultivated, fun-loving upper-class and homoerotic student for whom university was 'a sort of passionate party all the time.' The picture has been drawn and redrawn in a slew of adoring biographies, self-serving memoirs (as in *Memoirs of an Aesthete* by Harold Acton), and novels (pre-eminently Evelyn Waugh's *Brideshead Revisited*). These accounts all centre on the aesthete; when another point of view is allowed, it is that of the 'hearty,' the rugged rugger-playing athlete with whom the dandy was in ideological and occasionally physical combat.[9]

A prominent aesthete at Merton was the Etonian Robert Byron, later to win renown as a travel writer. Byron hung out with sons of prime ministers and with prospective lords and earls, collected paintings and antique furniture, and printed a card which read:

> Mr Robert Byron
> At Home
> Eight o'clock to midnight
> For the remainder of the Term.

The hearties of Merton, who were more numerous, gathered in the Myrmidon Club. The Myrmidons were wealthy and well connected, but also dissolute and daring, in the habit of breaking college windows and college rules. A leading Myrmidon was the mountaineer A. C. Irvine who, in June 1924 when still an undergraduate, 'most tragically yet most gloriously lost his life in this year's expedition to ascend Mount Everest.' Irvine was last seen with George Mallory a thousand feet below the summit; at Merton (where he had been elected to serve as secretary of the club for the following year) they were sure he had climbed the highest mountain in the world. Affecting a certain style, the Myrmidons smoked Turkish cigarettes in packets stamped with the club's monograms, tipped into silver ashtrays. Once a year the club hosted a seven-course dinner in one of Oxford's most famous restaurants. Guest speakers in Verrier's time (not that he was a member) included the well-known Tory politician Lord Birkenhead.[10]

Evelyn Waugh's biographer Christopher Sykes, writing of the time when both he and his subject were up at Oxford, remarks that it was 'portrayed with popular inaccuracy for years after its cessation as a town populated by aesthetes in flowing hair in perpetual strife with exasperated athletes.'[11] In truth, aesthetes and athletes together made up only a small proportion of undergraduates. A good many other were taken up with studies, scholarship and, perhaps more surprisingly, faith. 'There can surely be no spot in Christendom, with the possible exception of Malta, which is exposed to such a concentration of clerics:' So remarks the *Oxford Magazine* as late as 1946. Then, and for some time previously, the university had been marked by a rich diversity of Christian traditions. Unitarians, Congregationalists and Baptists all ran Oxford colleges. There was also a Roman Catholic chaplaincy whose incumbent in the nineteen-twenties was the formidable Ronald Knox, a man who wrote detective novels in his spare time, the royalties accruing to his church.[12]

The university's official faith, Anglicanism, was a house divided. In the nineteenth century Oxford had spawned the Tractarian movement which split the Church of England into High and Low Church factions. The High Church tradition was carried forward by Keble College, founded in 1872, and in Pusey House, established twelve years later. Anglo-Catholicism was at the peak of its influence in Oxford in the 1920s, attracting converts by its social activities—it sought actively to reclaim working-class communities 'lost' to non-conformism—and through the beauty of its rituals: the 'altar with its candle-sticks and tapers, its censer and its *lavabo* dish, its copes and its wafers and its services so beautiful that "some that had been there desired to end their days in the Bishop's chapel." ' Borrowing the mass and confession from Rome, the Anglo-Catholics provided a grandeur and mystery altogether lacking in the arid pieties of the Evangelical tradition.[13]

The apostle of Anglo-Catholicism at Merton was the college chaplain, F. W. Green. Born in 1884, educated at King Edward VI School, Norwich, and at Brasenose College, Oxford, Green was a High Churchman in politics and a post-Gladstonian Liberal in politics, a radical who deplored the excesses of capitalism and imperialism without going quite so far as to call himself a 'socialist.' A formative influence had been the four years he spent as a curate of St Anne's, Limehouse, in London's East End. Green's chief literary work was a commentary on St Matthew in the Clarendon Bible. Although he published little he read widely; fluent in German, he was also well versed in Continental scholarship (he did not agree with Cardinal Newman that the best defense against rationalist criticism was 'the shield of the Holy Spirit combined with an ignorance of the German language'). Green was devoted to a college in which both his sons studied—so did a nephew, while one of his daughters married a Merton man.[14]

In 1924 Verrier Elwin graduated with a first class, one of only three such in Merton that year. The college gifted him one hundred pounds to support his next degree, which in family tradition was to be in theology.[15] The move from literature to theology implied a shift in allegiance from Garrod to Green. Already, in the latter part of his first degree, Verrier had been noticed absenting himself from meetings of the Bodley Club. One supposes that the discussions in Garrod's rooms were reported back to Warnborough Road, as for instance a talk on the parallels between pagan and Christian myths which concluded: 'So God in great good humour declared himself a rumour.' Through Verrier's erratic attendance—his presence/absence duly noted in the minutes—one senses a *real* tussle, the love of words and dispute set against a fuller immersion in this irreverent and heterodox group, in which priests were habitually referred to as 'Gents with Dog-Collars' and socialism was defended. Eventually caution (or mother) prevailed; elected secretary of the Bodley Club for 1923–4, 'Mr Elwin was unfortunately compelled to refuse the office.' Shortly afterwards he resigned his membership of the club.[16]

Intellectually and otherwise Oxford made Verrier—as he was to remark in very general terms in his autobiography. The frustration for the biographer is that for this period we have no direct self-testimonies: no diaries or letters or printed essays, only a few poems of uncertain quality. When I visited Merton in search of material from the 'twenties that might still be around, the lady librarian, a new arrival, stiffly pointed out that I had come without an appointment—and did I not understand it was getting to the end of term, with Finals approaching? She suggested I go back to Germany (where I was then living) and write afresh to Dr Stephen Gunn, Fellow in History and College Archivist, seeking permission and asking him to suggest a suitable date when I might next come. I walked out in ill temper, followed by a student who had overheard the conversation. In the sunny quad outside he told me he would take me to 'Steve's room.' Contrary to the impression carried in the librarian's voice, Steve turned out to be absurdly young and highly approachable. The student introduced me to his history tutor, I explained my mission, and the three of us then went down into the college vault to fish out some massive and magnificently bound volumes of the *Registrium College Mertonensis*, the Governor's Minutes. The volume I needed, covering the years 1915 to 1936, was duly found and the student instructed to carry it up to the tutor's room.

By now it was time for Steve's next tutorial. He seated me at his desk while he lounged with the students on sofas. They discussed the problem of dearth in Tudor England while I scanned the Governor's Minutes. Verrier Elwin's name popped in and out, as the recipient of this award or that stipend, but of his voice and opinions there was not a sign. I noted, with interest, that the month he entered Merton, June 1921, two women servants were engaged to work in the Fellows' Quadrangle at wages 'not exceeding 27/6 a week.' A little later the Fellows adopted the report of a committee it had appointed, on the 'Sale of Wine to Undergraduates,' which had recommended that the practice not be introduced. All this was helpful as background but it was not what I had hoped to find.

When the tutorial ended and the students left, I told my fellow historian of the poverty of my find. 'Let me ask Dr Highfield's advice,' he answered, and was on the phone to his predecessor as College Archivist. Other sources were identified and instructions as to their location conveyed. We returned to the library whose keeper, noting the company I was now keeping, was an altogether different person. Steve asked her for the keys to the old library, built in the fourteenth century and, according to Benn's *Blue Guide*, 'perhaps the most interesting medieval library in England,' but no longer used on a day-to-day basis. We went up, passing the rows of first editions, towards a cupboard where our quarry lay. When this was opened volumes tumbled out, lots of them, smaller and more modestly bound than the ones I had previously seen. They were the minute-books of the undergraduate societies.

One must be thankful for the British attention to record-keeping, and for cracks in the system which allow interlopers to peep. From the records kept in the old library at Merton we can track Verrier's intellectual and, more hesitantly, his emotional development. We know thus that he did not join the Myrmidons, for he had not the status. We know also that he joined the Bodley Club out of interest, leaving when its deliberations seemed to clash with what he heard at home. And we know too that he both joined and stayed with a third society, run by F. W. Green, to attend whose meetings Mrs Elwin might more readily have assented. This was the Merton College Church Society, founded in 1875, the most animated of its kind in Oxford, celebrating its 600th meeting in October 1924. It met four or five times a term in the chaplain's rooms; starting soon after dinner, meetings broke for Evensong and resumed thereafter. Members were required to be 'communicants of the Church of England, accepting their creeds and formularies,' no such condition obtaining for the other clubs in the college.

The syllabus for the theology degree was in itself dull and conventional: the study of the Old and New Testaments, and of Greek commentaries up to the time of St Augustine. 'While it may no longer be possible to study theology as if the world came into existence in 4004 BC,' remarked one modernist cleric, 'it is still possible in Oxford to do so as if the world went out of existence in AD 461.'[17] The scriptures and very early ecclestiastical history were in, the philosophy and comparative sociology of religion out. The latter omissions were, however, made up by F. W. Green through the speakers he brought in to the Merton College Church Society. Green sought to expose his wards to a wide range of lecturers and topics. The first meeting that Verrier attended, while still an Eng. Lit. student, was addressed by a priest who worked on the road with tramps; the second featured a talk on 'retreats,' another aspect of the religious life that would scarcely have been discussed at home or in Dean Close.

A vocal undergraduate member of the Society was Alston Dix, already moving towards the monastic Catholicism he was to embrace after leaving Merton. (As Dom Gregory, Dix lived in Nashdom Abbey from 1926, later becoming Prior: his published works include *The Image and Likeness of God.*) In March 1923, when another student read a paper on 'Christianity and Communism,' Dix commented that 'capitalism was an evil, and there was no hope of reform so long as Capital monopolized politics. The Church must cut loose from the secular power and work out a social policy based on Christian principles.' Two months later Dix read a paper which argued, with 'a shower of ecclesiastical epigrams,' that the Anglican Church should disestablish itself from the state. For the Church of England had sacrificed its liberty to criticize, sharing in the 'complicity of unjustifiable acts of state-craft;' only through disestablishment would it gain its freedom and a 'real advancement of respect in the heart of the ordinary citizen.' Dix promoted his own brand of catholicism, saying that 'we should be more Catholic in the sense of being inclusive [rather] than in the sense of being orthodox.'[18]

Verrier at first resisted the radicalism of Green and Dix. In June 1922, when a guest speaker urged an 'ultimate reunion' of the Church of England with Rome, Verrier 'defended the Evangelical position against its detractors;' he also spoke enthusiastically of the fruits of missionary work in Sierra Leone. The family heritage he was not prepared to disavow, at least not yet. But the Anglo-Catholics were at work led by Dix, and by Max Petitpierre, a chemistry student who was also to be a future monk of Nashdom Abbey. They used outrageous flattery—Verrier was 'far too good to waste his time on these unintelligent evangelicals'—and an abundance of affection. While Dix was arguing with Verrier in his rooms, Petitpierre would be on his knees, praying that his heart be touched.[19]

The conversion was slow but steady. Appointed President of the Oxford University Bible Union, a fundamentalist stronghold, Verrier made it into a wing of the ecumenical Students Christian Movement, from whose 'liberal wiles' it had hitherto been preserved.[20] By now he was acquiring a reputation as an orator. Bryan Beady, who was two years junior to Verrier at Merton, remembered him as being of 'medium height, with a crop of unruly hair, two searching blue eyes, and the pink and white complexion and bubbling enthusiasm of the schoolboy.' His personality 'combined to an amazing degree the abounding energy of an intensely practical Christian with the profound learning and strange, compelling power of the born mystic.' The conflict within him between a persisting Evangelical allegiance and an emerging Anglo-Catholic one only helped make his speeches more effective. 'It was worthwhile,' writes Beady,

> foregoing a dance to hear one of his addresses as president of the Oxford University Bible Union, for Elwin had a gift of speech which Demosthenes might have envied. Metaphors tumbled over each other as he passed in a breath—without the trace of a note—from fervent exhortation to simple

> pathos, or clinched a passage of inspired rhetoric with some humorous anecdote which brought a smile to the lips of his most solemn hearer.
>
> Keen Evangelical as he then was . . . he had already soared into realms beyond the ken of his simple-minded colleagues. He took a naive delight in startling them by casually remarking that he had just seen the ghost of Duns Scotus stalking through Mob Quad, or had fallen into a trance after gazing fixedly at an electric light bulb.[21]

In May 1923 Verrier proposed to the College Church Society that coffee and cigarettes no longer be provided at its meetings, and the money saved be sent to slums in London. He was in fact preparing to sacrifice more than these casual stimulants. 'Elwin likes mysticism,' minuted the secretary of the society in November, explaining some months later that he liked mystics even more. In a paper presented on 3 March 1924 Verrier celebrated the mystic as one who 'had a knowledge of the hidden unity of the Universe.' Although the twentieth century despised 'saints as being dreamy and impractical,' his study of medieval mystics showed that they 'combined a passion for God and for [the] Church with a very practical outlook on life.' The discussion that followed was animated and for the most part hostile. The distinguished theologian Gilbert Shaw reminded Verrier that 'all the widespread occult movements of today were the result of a desire for self-expression' akin to mysticism. A student attacked Richard Rolle, one of Verrier's exemplars, as 'immoral.' Even F. W. Green, in the chair, worried that mysticism might mean 'unbalanced practices in prayer,' an unfortunate 'surrendering to the Unknown.' Verrier stoutly stood his ground. The mystic, he said, must be admired for his capacity to suffer and come through times of spiritual darkness.[22]

In June 1924 Verrier was elected president of the College Church Society. Later that year the annual Church Congress was held at Oxford. At a session on 'What the Youth asks of the Church' Verrier was chosen to represent Oxford, Stephen Neill, Cambridge. The crafty Neill obtained a copy of Verrier's speech beforehand, allowing him to make some carefully prepared cracks at his expense.[23] The press reports, however, generously praised both men. In his talk Verrier challenged his elders to recognize the faith of his generation: it was not true, he said, that the young were only interested nowadays in 'Food, Football, and Felix' (the last a reference to a feline forerunner of Mickey Mouse). The *Church Times* wrote of Verrier that 'he was probably the most youthful-looking speaker who has ever addressed a Church Congress. He spoke vigorously and movingly of what the best youth of the day were looking to the Church for, and he pleaded eloquently for all that the Church should be offering them.' Both Neill and Elwin were 'on a high level, and their sincerity and earnestness shone through them with a poignancy almost wistful in its appeal.'[24]

The debate was chaired by a bishop; other bishops were in the audience, as were Verrier's mother and sister. His first public appearance was a triumph: noticed in the newspapers, the subject of an admiring comment by the Dean of St Paul's.[25] Mrs Elwin is likely to have seen the performance as a happy prelude to a successful career in the Church of England—at home rather than abroad, for she was not about to risk another life extinguished early in the tropics. But Verrier was not much attracted by the status of an establishment priest, and certainly not by the money. He was already showing signs of a lifelong disregard for money: he was never to have much of it. Bryan Beady writes of one sunny morning in 1924 or 1925, when he was punting with some friends on the river. They bought a basket of strawberries beforehand but later realized that this did not leave them enough money to pay for the punt. Spotting Verrier standing on Magdalen Bridge, Beady shouted out: 'Lend me seven-and-six.' 'Coming,' replied Verrier, and soon three half-crowns landed on the cushions of the punt as it passed below the bridge. When Beady later repaid the loan, Verrier wrote him a postcard likening the remittance to 'an unexpected gift from a rich uncle.'[26]

Verrier had taken from F. W. Green and Alston Dix the belief that God was, or at any rate should be, on the side of the poor. In October 1925 he read a paper to the Church Society which rehearsed his move away from the 'genteel inanities of conventional religion,' that 'set of dead, schematic rules,' that 'series of many formal syllogisms.' What he termed Public School religion implied a reduction of faith to 'a mere authority, compulsion and regulation,' with 'rebellion an expensive item on the budget.' Four years in Oxford had taught him, however, to

> measure life by loss, not gain . . . Christ speaks to us of the triumphant glories of Resurrection, but no less of the stumbling agonies of the Way of Sorrows. To follow Him literally—and logically—may mean poverty, ill-health, loss of friends, position, fame; it may mean misunderstanding; it is

> costly all the way along. And it means these things not only in the dim ideal future, when we become missionaries, or slum-parish priests, or monks, it must mean them here and now in Oxford.[27]

For Verrier, as for his mentors, Christ was not historical but contemporary. A poem written around this time, which reads now like an amalgam of Philip Larkin and Handel's *Messiah*, speaks of how

> In a motor garage the Christ is born,
> To-day! To-day!
> To the whirr of the wheels and the toot of the horn,
> To-day! To-day!
> Spanner and plug and bolt and tyre,
> Rolls and Ford and Taxi 'For Hire,'
> They hail in passionate desire
> The baby Christ, the God of the Road, the King,
> the King of Glory.[28]

'What a lot of time I wasted during my undergraduate years on religion,' recalled Verrier in his memoirs, adding: 'but religion was very exciting then and it also, I suppose, provided an alternative interest, taking the place of bridge or racing.' We know that he gave up all pretence of being an athlete after a brief tenure as captain of the soccer second eleven, in a season which was 'a disastrous one for the College, for my team lost every single match, usually by about fifteen goals to nil.'[29] We suspect also that his friendships were confined to his own sex. Dean Close was a boy's school; Merton had no girl students either, and though there were a few elsewhere in Oxford it seems the women Verrier got closest to were the two women servants who joined the college when he did. Nor, for reasons of finance and faith did he follow other undergraduates into London and return by the last train from Paddington—known as 'The Fornicator.'[30]

His studies, his friends, his inner life and his social life all revolved around religion. This wholehearted if narrow-minded engagement had its rewards, for in the summer of 1926 he was awarded a First in his Theology Finals. It now appeared, as one of his friends was to write, that Verrier had 'the world at his feet. Behind him was a brilliant career, before him golden opportunities of service and preferment.'[31] A fellowship in an Oxford college was there for the taking but his family pressed him to join the Church of England. When he was offered the vice-principal's job at his father's old seminary, Wycliffe Hall, there was strong pressure on him to accept. He joined, playing for time, further pleasing Mother when he was ordained in Christ Church Cathedral by the Bishop of Oxford. But unknown to her and his principal he was secretly attending mass at that bastion of Anglo-Catholicism, Pusey Hall. F. W. Green at Merton advised him to throw over Wycliffe Hall for a parish in the slums of London or Manchester. There was also the example of his friend Dix, who had withdrawn into a monastery.[32]

In August another option presented itself. With some friends Verrier attended a conference at Swanwick of the Students Christian Movement, where they met a visitor from India, looking for young men to take back with him. J. C. Winslow was a product of Eton and Balliol who had gone out to India in 1905 as a missionary of the Society for the Propagation of the Gospel (SPG). Disgusted by the barriers between British and Indian Christians, and deeply impressed by Mahatma Gandhi's movement of national renewal, Winslow decided to leave the SPG and strike out on his own. One of his models was the radical priest Charles Freer Andrews, intimate of Gandhi and a theologian notably sympathetic to eastern religions: Christ, said Andrews, had come to India not to destroy but to fulfil. Winslow himself would not believe that 'Hinduism, with its astonishing richness of spiritual and cultural heritage, is meant simply to be swept away by the religion of Christ.' Rather, Jesus would 'take all those elements in it which are of permanent value, and bring them to a richer completion than they could have attained without Him.'[33]

In 1920 Winslow founded the Christa Seva Sangh (CSS), which drew inspiration from the traditional ashram ideal of Hindus, as well as from its more recent reinterpretation by Gandhi, whose ashram at Sabarmati was at once a centre of the religious life and of service to the poor. The members of the CSS wore the homespun cotton (khadi) promoted by Gandhi, ate vegetarian food, Indian-style (with their fingers, while squatting on the floor), and used Indian motifs in their chapel and in their homes.

The CSS was at first based near Ahmednagar, in the Deccan countryside. Working in low-caste neighbourhoods, Winslow and his men presented the story of Christ in Marathi and through the traditional verse forms, the *bhajan* and *kirtan.* Conversions were few, so in 1925 they moved—on the advice of the Bishop of Bombay, E. J. Palmer, another Balliol man—to the great Maratha city of Poona, as yet 'almost untouched by Christian influence.' Winslow hoped here to expose the brilliant young students of the city's colleges to the richness and power of the Christian tradition.[34]

Winslow was a man of great charm and charisma, with the appearance and style of a man who might yet bring India to Christ where all before him had failed. Tall and bearded, he wore a cassock made of white khadi but with a girdle in saffron, the Hindu colour of renunciation. He was an able speaker and singer, in English as well as Marathi. Prefacing and ending his speech with Marathi hymns, he made a powerful impression on the students at Swanwick. Two of these, Algy Robertson from Cambridge and Oliver Fielding-Clarke from Oxford, promised to join his ashram the next year. A third, Verrier Elwin, was keenly impressed but would not commit himself.[35]

At the time he met Winslow, Verrier had already begun to look eastwards. There was of course a family connection with the Raj, but elements of another India were being made known to him by an undergraduate at Jesus College, Bernard Aluwihare. A fervent anti-colonialist and later Law Minister of independent Ceylon, Aluwihare guided Verrier to the writings of Tagore and the work of Gandhi. He also effected a personal introduction to Sarvepalli Radhakrishnan, soon to be appointed Spalding Professor of Eastern Religions at Oxford. In the summer of 1926 the philosopher took Verrier and Bernard on a leisurely punt down the river, the three discussing comparative religion.[36] Radhakrishnan seems also to have handed out a reading list, for later that year Verrier published a poem, inspired by an Eastern text, on the solitariness of the spiritual life:

The Lantern
(After the Bhagavad Gita)

The silent soul is as a sheltered flame
　　That in a windless spot unwavering
Offers its light to God. Its hidden name
　　Fire-vested angels sing.

Around it blow the trade-winds of desire;
Breezes of passion, gusts of sudden dread,
But not a breath intruding stirs the fire,
By heaven's silence fed.

O Heart that stirreth with our loss,
Temple of silence built in pain
We light our lanterns at Thy Cross
A purer flame to gain.[37]

The subject of India and its faiths, meanwhile, had also featured in the meetings of the college Church Society. The Master of University College, Sir Michael Salter—who not long before had visited Rabindranath Tagore at his university in Santiniketan—read a paper on 'The Ancient Hindu Tradition and the Christian Faith.' This advocated an 'intellectual compromise' between the Hindu ideal of Rest and the Christian ideal of active and willing Service. The compromise was in fact being worked out by the Christa Seva Sangh in Poona, as explained by Winslow when he spoke in Merton, on Verrier's invitation, in October 1926. Winslow remarked that many Hindus admired Christ but loathed a church that clothed itself in English rites and English customs. The CSS, on the other hand, took heed of the warning of the Sikh-Christian mystic, Sadhu Sundar Singh, that if the water of life was offered in a Western cup, India would not drink it.

Other wise men came to Merton from the east. One such was Reverend W. E. S. Holland of the YMCA in Allahabad, a cleric sympathetic to Gandhi and his struggle. Speaking in May 1927 on 'Indian nationalism in relation to Christianity,' Holland suggested that the problems of the Church were chiefly of its own making. 'Whenever an Englishman went to India,' he remarked, 'the Indians always asked themselves one question, "Is this man out here for our interests or his own?" and if, as had so often been the case, they found it was his own, they then took no interest in him or what he said.' The message resonated with Winslow's and then, the next month, Green's wards were addressed by the first Indian Bishop of the Anglican Church, Azariah of Dornakal. Azariah talked of the new mood of humility in his church, of attempts to make it more relevant to Indian customs and methods of worship.[38]

Algy Robertson and Oliver Fielding-Clarke had booked their passage to Poona for September but Verrier was, it seems, not quite ready to take the plunge. Wycliffe Hall he knew he had to leave, but he was inclined at first towards a parish at home which might satisfy his theological inclinations without offending Mother. 'My mind anchored me to Oxford,' he remembered later, 'my spirit told me to go and throw my life into an unknown sea which might easily turn out to be a morass.'[39] Robertson and Fielding-Clarke took him on a tour of the lakes, and won him over. The 'call from India' came, if his sister is to be believed, in the grounds of the Royal Hotel, Capel Curig, looking over the waters at Snowdon peak beyond.[40] Why did he choose Winslow's experiment, an unknown quantity, over the tried and honourable paths laid before him by Green and Dix? In his memoirs Verrier wrote that he decided on India as an

> act of reparation, that from my family somebody should go to give instead of to get, to serve with the poorest people instead of ruling them, to become one with the country that we had helped to dominate and subdue. This idea became sufficiently important to break up my Oxford career and was the driving force that carried me through many difficult years in India.[41]

Such was the interpretation offered thirty-five years after the event: let us set against it a letter written to Green in July 1927, which suggested he was going out to India

> For these reasons:
>
> (i) It would greatly ease the situation at home. Mother has been wonderful, but we have had a few dreadful scenes, and I can see how deeply she feels it all.
>
> (ii) It will enable me to test both the missionary and religious vocation, not committing me for more than two years.
>
> (iii) It will enable me to settle down in a Liberal Catholic atmosphere. My mind is by no means settled; and I so dislike externals etc. that, if I stayed in England, I should fear one of two things—either a reaction away from organized religion altogether, or the acceptance of all these things on authority, and I doubt if the authority of the C. of E. would be sufficient.
>
> (iv) In Poona, we shall live under discipline: we shall have for 'directors' the neighbouring Cowley Fathers; we shall have a rule.
>
> (v) The Community is to be run on Indian lines, and its policy is precisely that which we have always applauded—great sympathy, the spirit of identification, the presentation of a Christian Consummator, not of an iconoclast.

> (vi) We shall do practical and manual work by the side of study, against a great background of prayer.
>
> (vii) The Bishop [of Oxford] approves. He was very much against a London parish. The doctor has passed me. My mother has acquiesced. And the witness of a great peace in my heart gives me hope that I have chosen rightly. . . .
>
> . . . You have always told me to do the unacceptable thing, and now I do hope you will be able to approve of the Indian plan.[42]

It seems that it was more than the idea of reparation which took Verrier to Poona. He was attracted by the personality and liberal catholic beliefs of Winslow, certainly, and by his experiment, its novel synthesis of the vocations of missionary, slum-parish priest, and monk. Most of all, though, India beckoned because of its distance from Oxford, the escape it offered from the scenes at home, the prospect it held for him to work out his faith without having continually to fight for it.

CHAPTER THREE

Between Christ and the Congress

But in the last event I must speak of the English rule in India apart from whence it comes and whither it goes. It stands by itself in history, proud and incomparable, a work of art, a treasure to be put against a velvet cloth in the world's gallery of politics. I am pleased that it is English; I can easily apply the molluscous objectivity of a Huxley or a Toynbee to India as to Shakespeare's sonnets or a well-known lawn. But it needs no patriotism to appreciate such a monument . . . To see a great race given scope for the exercise of its greatest strength, to see it conduct the art of government on a scale and with a perfection accomplished by no other race, is to achieve that sublime pleasure in the works of man which, ordinarily, is conferred only on the great artists.

Robert Byron, *An Essay on India* (1931)

Of all the western nations the English are the least capable of appreciating the qualities of Indian civilization, and the most capable of appreciating its defects. . . . Add to this that whereas all the other conquerors of India had migrated to the country, settled down and lived there, and become assimilated to Indian conditions, the English are, of all races, the least assimilable. They carried to India all their own habits and ways of life; squatted, as it were, in armed camps; spent as in exile twenty or twenty-five years; and returned home, sending out new men to take their place, equally imbued with English ideals and habits, equally unassimilable.

Goldsworthy Lowes Dickinson,
An Essay on India, China and Japan (1913)

On 18 October 1927, five Englishmen bound for India were given a splendid send-off in London. A dismissal service was held at St Matthew's in Westminster: attended by family and friends, and presided over by the legendary Bishop Gore 'mitred and vested in a cape of cloth of gold, to give his advice, his blessing and God-speed.' The Christa Seva Sangh had been described to the bishop as a 'sort of experiment.' 'Experiment!,' remarked Gore in his address, 'I would call it a whole complex of experiments.' Indeed, the occasion reminded him of a 'similar one fifty years ago, when four young priests like you set out for the Oxford Mission to Calcutta. But within a year one had joined the Church of Rome, one had gone out of his mind, and one was in his grave.'[1]

The levity was typical of the man: at a private audience beforehand Gore had wished the wayfarers good luck, adding, 'but you will all be out of the CSS in five years.' The church establishment showed a considerable interest in the volunteers; apart from Gore, the bishops of Salisbury and Kensington also chaired farewell meetings for them. Through two centuries of British rule most Indians had stubbornly stuck to their own faiths, but this new enterprise, which carried the Gospel in an eastern dress, might yet succeed where countless others had failed, more so as the messengers had half-a-dozen Oxbridge degrees between them. The *Church Times* wrote hopefully of the service in Westminster: 'Five young men, four of them priests, knelt before the golden altar of St Matthew's in the gathering gloom of an October afternoon, their last in England. Now they are on their way to India, their mission to reveal how akin the Christ is to the wise, meditative man of the East, far closer to him perhaps than to his bustling, thoughtless brother of the West, with his passion to do rather than to know.'[2]

The next morning Elwin and company took a boat to Paris, calling briefly at a Russian Orthodox academy before boarding the train to Rome. They toured the Vatican and St Peter's but were moved most at the principal Jesuit church, the Sesu, where one morning they saw streams of ordinary people receiving communion before going to work. Verrier was deeply impressed by an altar over which was inscribed, in Italian: 'From the tram-way men of Rome to the Sacred Heart.' That will be the day, he thought, when one can go to St Paul's and see an altar subscribed to by the 'London County Council's tram-drivers and conductors.'[3]

At Assissi, where they went next, the five men celebrated the Eucharist on the roof of their hotel, viewing with wonder 'the whole country over which St Francis roamed.' Travelling overland via Naples they boarded the *S. S. Oronsay* at Genoa on 23 October. They shared the third-class decks with 1100 others and made themselves at home in the way they knew best. Fielding-Clarke was elected superintendent of social activities, summoning people with a bell to chess and sing-song. Algy Robertson, the longest in holy orders, held confirmation classes for the young boys on ship. For Verrier the voyage was made happy and memorable by the 'thrill of landing at Port Said, the serenity of the Suez Canal, the lovely scenery of the Gulf of Suez, the exquisite off-shore breezes as we neared Ceylon.'[4]

The group reached Colombo on 5 November, their hosts the Bishop of Ceylon and the Principal of St Thomas' College, Kandy. Verrier spoke to students of the college while Algy and Bernard preached at churches nearby. Later, they were taken to the rock-temple of Derubulla and the Temple of the Tooth at Kandy. On the 10th they departed for southern India, the last lap of their ecclesiastical orienting journey. Verrier had not previously been out of England; exposed these past weeks to a dazzlingly varied fare of landscapes and faiths, he made his acquaintance now with the oldest of them all, the 'Syrian' Christians of Malabar, converted according to legend by the apostle St Thomas in the first century of the Christian era. They met several of their leaders and a day was taken up with a trek to the Wynaad hills, to see a monastery run by the Syrians on Franciscan lines. Malabar after the rains was glorious and green, its people well fed and well housed, with 'thousands of boys and girls pouring into the schools.' Verrier's first taste of the subcontinent was notably free of poverty, squalor and disease. There was to be plenty of all that later.[5]

From Malabar the party took an overnight bus to Bangalore, to stay there at Bishop Cotton School and learn about the problems of the Anglo-Indian community. They then travelled by train across the Deccan, arriving finally at Poona on 20 November, five weeks after they had started. They were met at the station by Winslow and three of his Indian Brothers, who immediately garlanded them with flowers. The group drove on to the ashram in an open horse-carriage, to receive, as Verrier wrote to his mother, 'the most amazing welcome from the Indian contractors working on our land. Garland after garland was hung around our necks, six or seven in all; bouquets were put into our hands; cuffs of flowers round our wrists; one Indian made a long speech; another sang a poem specially composed for the occasion. The flowers were simply wonderful, masses and masses of them—we were so laden we could hardly move.'[6]

The ashram of the Christa Seva Sangh was being built adjacent to the agricultural college in Shivaji Peth, on the outskirts of Poona. Through the eighteenth century Poona had been the capital of the Peshwas, the post-Mughal dynasty which once controlled huge chunks of central and western India. A home of traditional scholarship, it was more recently the centre of social reform movements against caste and for the emancipation of women. It was also a centre of nationalist propaganda; Bal Gangadhar Tilak and Gopalkrishna Gokhale, Gandhi's great predecessors in the Congress, had both lived and worked there. When Winslow's recruits reached Poona the city was sullenly contemplating the arrival of the Simon Commission, just appointed to enquire into India's future. The nationalists opposed the Commission because it was all-white and because its terms ruled out the granting of independence. Through all this it remained a solidly Hindu, even Brahmanical, city. As 'a strategic point Poona is of almost greater importance than Bombay,' remarked a 1918 report of the Free Church of Scotland; from the missionary point of view there was the hope that its 'quick, intelligent, restless desire for reform or even for change' might yet be 'a desire that should be brought to recognize the leadership and inspiration of Christ.'[7]

There was work to be done, but first an ashram to be built. In November 1927 the CSS was still housed in tents, its members working side by side with coolies, carrying baskets of earth to the building site. Winslow thought the failure of the Indian church had been as much of appearance as ideology. White missionaries mimicked the lifestyle of officials and planters, but the Hindus were to be won 'only by lives of penitential renunciation.' The Quaker and friend of Gandhi, Muriel Lester, wrote that the ideal of the Christian ashram rejected the 'ultra-European architecture and stiff pews' of the older churches in favour of chapels suited to squatting rather than sitting on raised seats, with wide verandahs where 'inquirers, passers-by and self-conscious people might stand, hearing and seeing all, while still preserving their aloofness.' The aim was to make the lives of missionaries as transparent as Gandhi's, such that 'distinctions of race and caste would be blotted out in the joy of serving Christ.'[8]

The priests of the Poona ashram lived in modest rooms shared with their brown brethren, eating, sleeping and praying on the floor. Aspects of

Indian tradition were incorporated in the building of their chapel, in its representations of Christ and its forms of worship. Life was truly Franciscan. The brothers' individual cells were tiny—eight feet by four feet—partitioned by gunny cloth slung across on a wire. A cotton mattress and an open bookshelf were the only items of 'furniture.' Once, when Winslow was away, the Archdeacon of Bombay introduced beds, but these were removed by the founder when he returned.[9]

The sincerity and simplicity of the CSS won ready admiration. Winslow and his men, recalled the distinguished socialist Kamaladevi Chattopadhyay, 'had something of the flavour of the ancient hermits of the early Christian Church.'[10] Another visitor, Jawaharlal Nehru, also marked the CSS as an exception to a 'conservative and reactionary' church whose members were 'usually wholly ignorant of India's past history and culture' and in any case 'more interested in pointing out the sins and failings of the heathen.' On the other hand, noted Nehru, 'the Christa Seva Sangh of Poona contains some fine Englishmen, whose religion has led them to understand and serve and not to patronise . . .'.[11]

The ashram of the Christa Seva Sangh still stands in Shivaji Peth, enclosed on all sides by the city that has grown to surround it. Its inmates are now elderly Englishwomen rather than young Englishmen. They courteously escort the outsider in search of old documents to the library. That room, as also the others, are much the same as they were in 1927. So is the food, the standard and humble ashram fare of saltless *daal* and spiceless curry. But the profile of those who live here has certainly changed. While I looked into old issues of the *Ashram Review*, on the table next to mine a young girl was studying for her law exams. She was a Christian from Kerala whose mother lived in the ashram—two young companions for three European ladies who were the wrong side of seventy.

To visit the Christa Seva Sangh today is to be powerfully reminded of the iron law of Indian institutional decay. The average life of a reasonably well-functioning institution is twenty years; none, it seems, remain in good health after the death or disappearance of the founder. Gandhi's own ashrams, Sabarmati and Sevagram, still function in a desultory and decrepit way, but for all the influence they now command they might as well be dead. Why should Winslow's ashram be any different? It requires an effort of the will to think of it as it once was, a centre of active and radical theological work, a bridge between the worlds of Anglican Christianity and an increasingly assertive Indian nationalism.

Whatever its present state, when the party of Englishmen reached Poona in November 1927 they found the Christa Seva Sangh brimming over with energy and inspiration. As Winslow had hoped, it threw down a gauntlet to the clergymen who ministered to the sahibs and lived like them in walled-in bungalows. To Verrier, out of Oxford, it offered a contrast to past experience that was sharp but not unwelcome. Three weeks after arriving in Poona he wrote to F. W. Green with relief and exultation:

> For once in my life not to be treated as a successful examinee! To have no flattery or attention from one week's end to another! To eat always the same food, largely Indian, and none of it very pleasant! To wear sandals, to be clothed in white, to sleep on hard ground! To eat with one's fingers! To dig and to cart mud about! To be bitten all over by mosquitos! To try and learn a language that looks like this [a line in the Marathi script followed]. It is very odd, and very wonderful. I am learning things about Yoga; and shall be visiting Hindu monasteries and ascetics from time to time. I am shortly to meet Mahatma Gandhi. I had a wonderful time with the Jacobite monks in Travancore, and some interesting talks with two Carmelites. And Rome—on the way—completed my conversion.[12]

In January 1928 Verrier was deputed by the CSS to attend a meeting of an International Fellowship of Religions, held at Gandhi's ashram on the banks of the Sabarmati river in Ahmedabad, a night's train journey from Poona. Addressing the delegates, the Mahatma said that 'all religions were true and also that all had some error in them.' From this it followed that 'we can only pray, if we are Hindus, or if we are Mussalmans, not that a Hindu or a Christian should become a Mussalman, nor should we even secretly pray that anyone should be converted, but our innermost prayer should be that a Hindu should be a better Hindu, a Muslim a better Muslim and a Christian a better Christian. That is the fundamental truth of fellowship.'[13]

That all religions were equally true or equally false: this was an argument that Verrier had not heard before, and at first he did not know what to make of it. One evening the Mahatma took the visiting priest aside for a chat, questioning him keenly about his brotherhood. He was pleased that the CSS men wore khadi—the insignia of national renewal—and also that they had observed a day's silence ('spiritual *hartal*,' as Verrier colourfully called it) on the day the Simon Commission arrived in India. Verrier seemed to recognize in Sabarmati a likely model for their own work, 'a simple arduous life of devoted service rooted in the supernatural world.' If this is 'the Heart of Aryavarta,' he remarked, 'never has a nation's heart beat with a purer passion or a more catholic love.'[14] But the priest also made something of an impression on his hosts. In a report he wrote on the fellowship, Gandhi's secretary Mahadev Desai singled out 'Mr Elwin,' a man 'just out of his teens and fresh from Oxford, come to India, as he said, to do some atonement for the sins of his countrymen in keeping India in chains.'[15]

Many years later Verrier was to write that the week in Sabarmati turned him from a fellow-traveller to an 'ardent disciple' of the Indian national movement: 'It was as if I had suddenly been reborn as an Indian on Indian soil.'[16] At the time, he seemed willing to follow Gandhi's politics, but measured his theological position more critically. On returning to Poona he plunged into Gandhi's writings, reading with fascination and not a little dismay the account of his disputes with Christians in South Africa. When an English friend wrote asking for an 'opinion,' Verrier could not quite make up his mind. Gandhi, he said, had certainly impressed him as a saint,

> with a saint's heroism, a saintly joy, and a saint's love; but [he is] something of the faddist, and *intellectually* singularly unsound. He is a born leader of conduct, but not of thought. His religious position struck me as deeply unsatisfactory (and you know how *very* liberal I am to Hinduism in general; I admire it immensely). But Gandhiji's outlook (as for instance that all religions are true) strikes me as neither genuinely Eastern or Hindu, nor genuinely modern in the best sense of the word. Its an amalgam of Ruskin, Tolstoi, Emerson and that gang—a type which I have never understood or liked. But when I think of Bapu, as we call him, the light of his life, his courtesy, his joy, his charm, his prayerfulness, his self-control, his peace, his sway over his noble splendid followers, I can only bow in reverence. Cut off his head, and I would mark him Xt. But his mind is far behind his life . . .

Follow the man, not his mind; in the beginning Verrier could afford to take Gandhi piecemeal. But his immediate mentor demanded unqualified loyalty, which had its own burdens. On the one side, Winslow followed F. W. Green in conveying Verrier into a realm of thought that was 'immensely deeper, richer, more fruitful' than his native Evangelicalism. 'How woefully inadequate Protestantism seems,' observed Verrier, 'specially here in India; a . . . rationalized faith over a deeply supernatural one; a prayer life haphazard and unorganized over against the grand and stately mechanism of the Yoga, . . . a mushroom growth over a venerable religion that makes even Rome look young.'

The problems lay not with Winslow's catholicism but the demands it made on the body. The Rule of the Ashram enjoined Poverty—through a 'hard, stern, inconvenient, exasperating discipline, a thing to be willed, accepted, loved and given to Him, but no light thing'—and Celibacy, which in Winslow's credo was not based 'on any anti-feminism, any homosexual absorption in our own sex,' but grounded rather 'on a tender reverent recognition of the glory and joy of married life,' a life 'deliberately set aside and offered up for the sake of souls.'

To be poor and celibate in Poona was always intended as a struggle. Indeed, in the first months of 1928 two great temptations crossed Verrier's path. The first was an offer to return to his beloved Oxford as Chaplain-fellow of Merton to succeed Green (who had been appointed Canon of Norwich). The second, indubitably more threatening, was the attraction of a lady described as 'a beautiful, holy, spiritual woman-soul who shows to one constantly all that must be left if by God's power I am able to persevere.'[17]

Race unknown, name unmentioned; this one fleeting reference is all we have of Verrier's first proper engagement with the other sex. But against the attractions of the woman-soul stood the Rule of the Sangha: for the moment, the latter triumphed. 'I have felt the brunt of these temptations through the whole territory of my being,' wrote Verrier to a friend, 'they have been hard, unbelievably hard to meet, deeply painful and humbling to feel at all; but they have been necessary to re-adjust and strengthen my outlook on these great, holy, and all-too-lightly-undertaken states of life.'[18]

To re-dedicate himself to Winslow's ideals Verrier indulged, as a colleague remembered, in 'rather exaggerated and unwise mortification.'[19] In his memoirs Verrier was more specific without mentioning the temptation these mortifications were designed to cast out. 'All through 1928,' he recalled, 'I was undoubtedly playing with my health. I not only sat and slept on the floor. I went a little further and sat and slept on a cement floor with nothing to protect me but a thin piece of sacking. I gave up my mattress and even my pillows in an ardour for self-discipline. I went barefoot, ate anything I was given.'[20]

Winslow had placed Verrier in charge of the library, whose growing collection was targeted by the resident rat. The creature's tastes were, in a word, catholic. 'After starting on the *Hibbert Journal*, he devoured several volumes of Copec, and then in mystical mood ate the Koran and the Folly of the Cross in a single night. We fancy the creature might be a Theosophist.'[21] While one Indian bug threatened his books, another less solitary bug made for his intestines. When his diet and sleeping habits, always injudicious, were carried through the hot weather into the monsoon, he suffered a violent attack of dysentery. He was admitted to the Sassoon Hospital and for some weeks hovered between life and death. Winslow cut short a tour of south India to be beside his most brilliant disciple, visiting him daily, a 'most wonderfully soothing and understanding soul.'[22] Bishop Palmer arrived from Bombay, some thought to adminster the last rites. Instead, displaying 'to the full the Oxford blend of idealism and commonsense,' he presented the patient with three bottles of champagne.[23]

The champagne helped but in the end his life was saved by the devoted labours of the doctor, Major Plumptree, and the nurse, Sister Hillsom (who had once ministered to Gandhi).[24] After a month in bed he recovered sufficiently to walk but remained much too weak to return to the ashram. The doctor advised him to go home to Oxford for a year, thence to examine afresh his fittedness, physical and otherwise, for India and the monastic vocation.

In October 1928 Verrier returned to his mother's home in Oxford. Rest did not rule out research and his days were spent for the most part in the Bodleian. As a student Verrier had been constrained by an antiquated syllabus, but now his theological horizons were wider. His reading focused on what might connect his native land with the adopted one: specifically, the parallels between the mystical traditions of medieval Christianity and Hinduism.

In six months Verrier produced two slim books, fine illustrations of what would now perhaps be called the dialogue of faiths. The first study, of a book by an unknown mystic of the fourteenth century, sought to make Christian mysticism intelligible to the Indian. The author of 'The Cloud of Unknowing,' wrote Verrier, interpreted the *sastras* or holy books in the vernacular, in the manner of the great Marathi Bhakti poets Tukaram and Ramdas. Religion was thus made more democratic, available to those who understood neither Latin or Sanskrit. Verrier thought 'The Cloud' provided a commentary on an old Indian debate, between the rival claims of *bhakti* (love) and *jnana* (knowledge). The latter was the way of the yogi, and 'The Cloud' was indeed the nearest thing there was to a Christian yoga, with the difference that it claimed to be the work of the supernatural, bringing the soul closer to God.[25]

The book was read and admired by Indian Christians searching themselves for points of convergence between a foreign faith and spiritual traditions native to Indian soil.[26] Its arguments are pursued further in Verrier's study of the theologian Richard Rolle, whom he called, in an inspired comparison, the leader of 'the bhakti movement in fifteenth century England.' For Rolle, as for the Bhakti poets, music and song were the perfect means to express communion with God. In his love of song, this Englishman is 'already an Oriental: he feels with Chaitanya and Kabir the rhythm of the Universe; with N. V. Tilak he would sing, not merely tell, the praise of Christ.' For Rolle and his fellow mystics religion was a 'natural, unsophisticated thing, a song of joy in the heart, the name of the Beloved on the lips, the spontaneous movement of the soul heavenway.' Their joyousness matched the spirit of Bhakti; indeed, these mystics 'would have been perfectly at home in India. How well Rolle would have understood Tukaram! How entirely Mirabai would have appreciated Mother Julian!'[27]

These books point to a now complete disenchantment with Evangelicalism, with its denial of mysticism and its refusal to listen to other faiths. In a bitter commentary on the Church of England as he knew it, Verrier wrote that for Rolle and company the Church was 'no tyrant forcing their originality into a single mould but a courteous and homely mother in whose arms they [found] security and strength.'[28] In writing these books Verrier had before him the example of Jack Winslow, whose intent was the softening of Christianity with doses of Hindu thought, and of Mahatma Gandhi, who sought to invigorate Hinduism with elements of the Christian tradition. By March he was ready to return to India, to test his ideas in practice, but the doctors would not clear him yet. Marking time, he chaired the third annual meeting of Anglican and Russian Orthodox priests. He saw this as carrying forward the CSS model of 'peace-making,' the open-ness to 'all creeds, sects, even religions.' He also spoke to Indian students of London University, finding to his disappointment that many were 'full of a secularist spirit.'[29]

In June 1929 the doctors passed him as fit for travel in a further three months, leaving him 'counting the days till I can return to my beloved country.'[30] He left finally on 29 September, accompanied by Leonard Schiff, another Oxford man bound for the Christa Seva Sangh. En route they spent a couple of days with the Orthodox outpost in Paris. Their hosts had been forced into exile by the godless Bolsheviks, but Verrier took heart in their deep love of Russia. It held a message for him; committed *to* India but in a religious and racial sense never to be *of* it. From Paris they carried on to Umbria, to spend some time with the nuns of the Eremo Franciscano, who were penfriends of Verrier's and fellow admirers of Mahatma Gandhi. 'I am sure,' he wrote to the Umbria nuns before boarding ship at Naples, 'that it is possible for a Christian and a priest to be a disciple of India, just as French or Russian religious [people are] passionately patriotic and truly wedded to their own culture.' Emboldened by his recent researches, he saw Christianity as the fulfilment of the religious history of India, taking the best of all the faiths it found there. God spoke

> through countless voices in the east, heralds of the Incarnation cry out to us through India's mystics and poets, The Eternal Word is uttered silently in her glorious art and sounds in her songs, the Creator is seen in the grand beauty of her woods and rivers and mountains. India is a land alive with thoughts of God, and as though dazzled by the profusion of His Witness, she has become the mother of religions. For here the path truly is from multiplicity to unity, from the diverse to the single, to the one Utterance and

> Truth of God in the Face of Jesus Christ. And yet that One is somehow not only the negation but the crown of all that multiplicity. You reach it not only by subtraction, but by *addition.*

The passage to India lay this time through the Holy Land. Verrier and Leonard did the rounds of Bethlehem and Jerusalem before going off to monasteries in the mountains. One was situated on the High Mountain of Temptation, overlooking the valley of the Jordan, its members working with their hands and worshipping in a cave chapel. Not far away was the fifteen-hundred-year-old monastery of Mar Saba, in the vale of Cedron, whose monks lived in rooms cut into the rock. Verrier was impressed. 'Such is the desert,' he remarked,

> the place where men are homeless and God alone at home. That such asceticism, such heroic pilgrimage, such simplicity and solitude of life and such valour of prayer, should still endure in our world which so hates extremes may well make us admire God for the courage of His saints and wonder at our own half-heartedness. [31]

When he reached Poona in November, Verrier found that in the ashram 'half-heartedness' was being measured in strictly political terms. The city and country were in ferment. Already during his first stint with the CSS the peasants of western India had begun a long struggle against land revenue. While he was away working in the Oxford libraries, the Congress met for its annual meeting, passing on 26 January 1929 a resolution demanding that *purna swaraj* (complete independence) be granted within the year. Meanwhile, the Simon Commission was met everywhere by black-flag demonstrations. The police came out in force, and in one clash in Lucknow the Lion of Punjab, Lala Lajpat Rai, suffered mortal injury. The Viceroy, Lord Irwin, rushed to London for consultations and returned with a promise of a conference to discuss 'Dominion Status,' in itself some way short of what was being demanded by Congress. The younger radicals in the Congress, such as Jawaharlal Nehru and Subhas Chandra Bose, were pressing Mahatma Gandhi to come out of his ashram and start civil disobedience once again.

The stage was set for the most dramatic chapter in India's independence struggle. On 2 March 1930 Gandhi gave notice to Irwin that he planned to march to the sea and break British laws prohibiting the making of salt by individuals. Irwin said nothing, so on the 12th the Mahatma took some eighty followers on a procession towards the sea. The 200 miles from Sabarmati to Dandi, the eventual destination, were covered in a leisurely twenty-four days, almost every step covered by the international press. Gandhi reached Dandi village on the evening of 5 April. The next morning he walked to the sea, picking up a fistful of salt with the words, 'With this I am shaking the foundations of the British Empire.' He was arrested soon afterwards but within weeks civil disobedience became an all-India affair. The salt laws, the forest laws, the liquor laws, all aspects of government policy that were seen as life-limiting or unjust, were violated in a thousand locations. The state bore down swiftly, filling the jails with Congress leaders and volunteers.[32]

By early 1930 the country was completely polarized. Some Indians sided with the Raj, many others stood with the Congress and courted arrest. Most unhappily placed was the Christa Seva Sangh, no doubt an extraordinary experiment but one whose inherent frailties were being daily exposed by the Salt Satyagraha and its aftermath. It now had squarely to face questions it preferred to keep buried under the mud. Was it an Indian ashram or a Western-style monastic order? Was it to be run autocratically by Winslow or democratically as a collective? Should it actively preach or merely set an example through exemplary conduct? Was its message addressed to high castes or to outcastes? When the crunch came would it side with the church establishment or with Indian nationalists?

When the crunch came the founder of the ashram left on furlough. In March Jack Winslow departed for England, apparently to raise money and look for new recruits. It is hard not to escape the conclusion that he did not want to decide one way or the other. That burden now fell on Verrier, appointed acting *acharya* (head) of the Sangh. One member, Algy Robertson, advised him to keep the ashram out of politics and work to make it a pure monastic order. On the other side were those who wanted to align straightaway with the Congress, such as Leonard Schiff, and especially an Indian member from Sholapur: this was Shamrao Hivale, who had joined the Sangh late in 1928, after graduating from Rajaram College in Kolhapur. Shamrao came from a family with a record of public service. His brother, B. P. Hivale, was a well-known educationist based first at Bombay's Wilson College and then at Ahmednagar College in the Deccan. Shamrao himself was a passionate nationalist, devoted equally to the politics of Gandhi and the songs of Tukaram. Short, dark, with wavy hair and sparkling black eyes, he was also a most personable character, with more friends, Christian and non-Christian, than any other member of the Sangh.

Leonard and Shamrao both impressed on Verrier the need to take a stand quickly: but he was inclined their way in any case. The rebel in him was drawn to the Congress (in its fight with the Raj very much the underdog), the follower in him to Gandhi, who was a far more substantial figure than Winslow or Green—the two men whose leadership he had previously acknowledged. True, there was the Mahatma's theological indeterminacy to consider; but at the time it seemed trifling when compared with the political indecisiveness of Father Jack.

For all his sincerity and desire for 'reconciliation,' Winslow always took care to stay on his side of the religious and racial divide. Verrier, by contrast, was already speaking and thinking of India as 'my motherland.' As the head of the Ashram he now put into practice a neat syllogism: the Christa Seva Sangh works for India and Indians, the Congress represents India and Indians, therefore the CSS must stand by Congress and Gandhi.

Verrier's decision to throw the ashram into the rebel camp was influenced by a incident in Bombay shortly after Gandhi's arrest. He was visiting some friends who lived in the Girgaum Back Road, close to Mani Bhavan, the city headquarters of the Congress. The Bhavan had been sealed by the authorities, and a group of Congress sympathizers were trying to work their way closer to the building. From a window high above he watched, feeling like 'one of the most miserable men in the world,' his

> fellow-countrymen delivering lathi charges on innocent and harmless passers-by. There was no demonstration; no shouting of slogans; no breaking of the law; not even such a crowd as would interfere with the traffic; only a number of people [who] wanted to look at their loved Congress House now in the

> hands of the police. A charming-looking student went up to one of the British sergeants and asked a question: the latter raised his club and struck him in the face. Four stories up I heard the crack of the blow. The sergeant hurled an old man to the ground. He chased and mercilessly beat a boy who was going along the road. He hustled a respectable businessman, knocking his morning paper out of his hand and contemptuously kicking it across the road. I lost all count of the number of people who were assaulted . . .
>
> No one who has ever watched a lathi charge, especially on innocent people, will ever forget it—those huge sticks whirling in the air, the thud and thwack of the blow falling on head or shoulder, the studied arrogance of those who strike, the amazing Christ-like patience of the sufferers.[33]

Jack Winslow in London had hoped that Verrier would steer 'the good barge "Christa Seva Sangh" clear of the fatal rock of unsympathetic aloofness without involving it in the vortex of political strife.'[34] Post-Dandi such neutrality was impossible, certainly in Poona, home to many Indian nationalists and home too to the jail in which some of them were housed. The good barge now had a Roll of Honour up in its chapel, prayers being offered daily for Gandhi, Nehru, Patel, Bajaj and others behind bars. Verrier himself had no doubt on which side justice and the Christian virtues lay. 'How infinitely pathetic it is' he remarked, 'to see Christianity armed and dominant against Hinduism seeking the Cross with Christ.'[35]

To show solidarity with Congress the ashram members resolved to spin daily, propagate khadi and join in the picketing of liquor shops. They also went about collecting instances of violence on the part of the police. Two Brothers even joined an 'illegal' procession to Yeravada, the jail just outside Poona where Gandhi was incarcerated. One was Leonard Schiff, feelingly described by the district magistrate of Poona as 'obviously a fanatical sympathizer with Gandhi and the present Congress movement.'[36] The Archdeacon of Bombay wrote to Verrier, as the head of the ashram, complaining that Leonard had been spotted in public wearing a Gandhi cap. The Brothers, in response, 'passed a vote of congratulation on [Leonard] for having worn a Gandhi cap.'[37]

In June the ashram was visited by Reginald Reynolds, a young Quaker deputed by the Society of Friends to visit Gandhi in Yeravada prison. Reynolds came to Poona from Ahmedabad, noticing the difference between an ashram solidly behind its leader and a Sabarmati mourning its absent Mahatma. He was charmed by Verrier, whom he had not previously met. 'He was very good-looking,' he remembered twenty years later, 'and in his white khaddar cassock gave an impression of having stepped straight off the streets of gold through one of those gates of pearl.' Reynolds was sure 'that no Hindu institution ever enjoyed so much laughter'. The visitor also recorded one characteristic Elwinism. A London writer had been pouring out figures on the 'benefits' of British rule in India; when Reynolds commented on his inaccuracies Verrier remarked: 'I thought he was no statistician when I found he had dismissed the Trinity in a footnote.'[38]

The CSS in the summer of 1930 was a happy and united band of brothers. When the Bishop of Bombay questioned Verrier's ability to guide the Sangh in Winslow's absence, the rebel's answer was to seek and get a unanimous vote of confidence 'in his dealing with the present political situation above all criticism.' The same meeting, held on 7 July, also 'most willingly' granted Verrier permission to address the Nationalist Christian Association of Bombay.[39] He was to speak on 'Christ and Satyagraha,' a choice of topic testifying to his growing willingness to assume a role outside the Ashram. The priest was becoming the publicist, 'Verrier' giving way to the more formal and more authoritative 'Father Elwin.'

Verrier's Bombay lecture, delivered before a packed audience at the Blavatsky Hall on 9 July, boldly attempted to reconcile Western Christianity with Indian nationalism. He said he spoke not as a member of the CSS, nor as an Englishman, but 'as one who would like to call himself an Indian and who tries to look at things from the Indian standpoint and to identify himself in every way with the country of his adoption.' But he spoke also as a priest, providing theological comfort to those Indians who wished to defy their bishops by following Gandhi.

Verrier began by acknowledging the traditions of civic obedience in Christianity, the injunctions to maintain the status quo and support the state, to render unto Caesar what is Caesar's. But he gave more weight to alternative traditions which justified resistance to the state: for instance, when authority is not just but usurped—as Indians regarded British rule; when the state brings into force unjust laws—such as forest laws and the salt tax in British India; or when rulers impoverish the spirit of fellowship—as the Raj had done by setting up barriers of race and class.

The Christian dissenter also had before him the figure of Jesus, who 'was certainly regarded by his contemporaries as a dangerous revolutionary in every sphere of life.'

As indeed was Gandhi, a man who took the principle of non-violence into politics, who suffused his struggle with prayer, who insisted on Truth, Discipline, Restraint, Patience and Love. No longer did Verrier think Gandhi to be theologically backward; on the contrary he seemed to him to be the unacknowledged Christ of Hinduism. 'On the whole,' said Father Elwin to his flock in Blavatsky Lodge, 'the campaign initiated by Mahatma Gandhi, both in its method and spirit, is more in accordance with the mind of Christ than any other similar campaign that the world has ever seen.'[40]

To an Indian friend who was likewise devoted to Christ and Gandhi, Verrier described his Bombay lecture as 'completely definite, but restrained.' In fact it was terribly provocative, with the printed pamphlet dedicated to 'All my friends in jail.' *Christ and Satyagraha* was reprinted within the month; when Verrier followed it with a devotional series on the Mahatma, published in the nationalist newspaper *Bombay Chronicle*, it was clear that he was 'perfectly willing, indeed anxious, for imprisonment in the cause of India.'[41] Meanwhile, back in the United Kingdom, Jack Winslow was summoned to a meeting at the India Office. The home secretary of the Government of India had posted to London a copy of *Christ and Satyagraha*, its offending passages marked, asking that the CSS's founder be shown the text 'with a view to impressing upon him the undesirability of members of the mission encouraging the Civil Disobedience movement in any way, either by speech or conduct.' On 29 September Winslow was interviewed by the under-secretary of state who told him sternly that his society was 'under the cloak of religion, lending its support to the avowed enemies of Government.' Father Jack 'fully realized the difficulty of the position and prejudice for the Brotherhood [from] tracts such as *Christ and Satyagraha*:' he thought his disciple had the license to speak on the subject, yet 'definitely disagreed' with his conclusions. Winslow then agreed to 'stiffen' up the CSS rule to limit the freedom of Brothers to give voice to their opinions in public.[42]

Winslow returned to Poona on 23 November, and immediately put out an appeal for reconciliation, the bringing in of 'our Lord's own spirit of loving and understanding sympathy to bear upon the issue in dispute, in place of the spirit of mutual recrimination and slander.'[43] But by now the disciple was out of control, going off in early December to join a fact-finding mission to report on allegations of police brutality in Gujarat. The mission was headed by the respected social worker A. V. Thakkar, like Verrier a man sympathetic to the Congress without actually being part of it.

The team spent two weeks in Gujarat, visiting some sixty villages in all. They stayed some nights at Hindu temples, other nights in peasant homes. Verrier went off one day on a side trip to Dandi, where Gandhi had been arrested in April. He saw there a tiny hut made of bamboo and thatch; this was the 'Palace of the real ruler of India,' a stunning contrast to 'the magnificence of the Viceregal Lodge in Delhi, built on the money of millions who hardly get enough to eat.'[44] He also called with the team on refugee camps in the chiefdom of Baroda, meant for peasants facing repression in British territory. In his report Verrier provided vivid illustrations of the beatings of men and women, the confiscation of property, the burning of homes, and the forcible closure of Gandhian ashrams. As he looked into the faces of greybeards insulted and beaten by the police, Verrier 'seemed to see the thorn crowned face of Jesus suffering in all the sorrows of His children.' As he spoke to widows who had been harassed, he thought of his 'own mother, and I wondered how I should feel if my quiet Oxford home were broken open and my mother and sister assaulted and insulted by the police.' This might all be the work of Indian subordinates, but Verrier believed 'the British officials cannot be exempted from responsibility as a word from higher authority could stop most of the abuses.' Would they not have acted if this tale of beating and insult had come from villages in the Cotswolds?[45]

His countrymen had let him down; so too had his church. At least in

India, he noted mournfully, the Church of England 'bears the appearance so largely of being allied to imperialist Britian.'[46] This 'Christian Priest whose duty is to humanity' (as he now spoke of himself) would take the side of free India in politics, and of Gandhi in person. The C of E had betrayed him; happily, he was wanted by all kinds of people outside it. In April alone he addressed the birthday celebrations of the saint Ramakrishna Paramhansa, spoke on Christianity to the Prarthana Samaj of Poona, and presided over a meeting of the Christian Nationalist Party which welcomed its leaders on their release from jail. Everywhere he went Verrier was shadowed by an intelligence agent whose job was to transcribe and transmit his speeches to the home department of the Government of India. The deputy inspector general of police, forwarding these reports to New Delhi, wrote disgustedly of 'Father Elwin's sickly adulation of Mr Gandhi whom he described as a kind of Messiah, the greatest socialist living who was endeavouring to establish a kingdom of the poor for the poor by the poor . . .' The agent's reports were faithful to the spirit if not always to the letter, as witness an account of a speech in Poona which had Verrier saying: 'I first became acquainted with the teachings of Mahatmaji when I was a student at Cambridge and in those days I used to get a portrait of Mahatmaji in my room in order that I may daily enjoy his sight.'[47]

Against those years of worship Verrier could boast of but one brief meeting with his idol, back in Sabarmati in the early weeks of 1928. In April 1931 Gandhi was out of jail and resting in Bombay; finding himself in the same city, Verrier requested Mahadev Desai to arrange an interview. Mahadev asked him to come at four o'clock the next morning. Arriving at the appointed hour, Verrier found his man brushing his teeth with a stick of *neem.* What was he to do? The occasion, he felt,

> demanded ceremony, obeisance; I longed to kiss his feet. But I have not yet quenched my wretched Western sense of humour. You can't touch the feet even of the greatest man in the world if he has a twig in his mouth and is holding a spittoon. So I made a deep but rather stupid bow, and Bapu, removing his twig, gave me one of those perfect radiant smiles which make a man his friend and follower for ever. He made a few remarks and then continued his ablutions. Presently he took his place for Prayers, and asked me to sit by him. Mirabehn sat on the other side, so that this 'Enemy of the British Empire' sat for his prayer between two Britishers!

Later in the day Verrier accompanied Gandhi to a meeting with mill-hands. A group of young communists heckled the Mahatma unmercifully, calling him a traitor for having signed a pact with the viceroy, as well as a tool of the capitalists who helped fund him. Unperturbed by the 'hissing, shouting and mocking laughter,' Gandhi reminded the young men that he had made the worker's cause his own from his South African days, living with them and sharing their sorrows. But he would not countenance the use of violence; rather, by means of his suffering he would awaken the mill-owners to their sense of duty. This approach to the worker–capitalist relation, thought Verrier, would do nicely for the India–British one, that other conflict subject to Gandhi's 'all-sided weapon of love, which will not overthrow and embitter the opponent, but change his heart.'[48]

In Bombay Verrier also met Vallabhbhai Patel, the Congress strongman and chief organizer of the peasant movements in Gujarat. Patel, who must have been greatly pleased by the priest's report on police atrocities, warmly embraced him. He also bumped into Jawaharlal Nehru but did not get a chance to talk to him. Nehru was forty-two and balding, but withal the hero of young India, and the most likely successor to Gandhi. He was also a very handsome man, Verrier writing home of his 'most beautiful face, the face of a dreamer and idealist, keenly intellectual, indomitable and courageous.'

There was in Verrier a great yearning to *belong*; now the Congress took possession of him, as the Anglo-Catholics and the Christian ashramites had previously. As ever, once he took sides he saw things starkly in black and white. In between meetings with Gandhi and Patel he called on the Bishop of Bombay. E. J. Palmer had been replaced by R. D. Acland, an orthodox priest not bound by ties of personal affection to the Brothers in Poona. In a circular letter which was in itself a massive act of insubordination, Verrier wrote sarcastically of the bishop and his position. Acland's bungalow was on Malabar Hill: the windows looked out over the bay, but down on the other side lay the real India, with its crowded bazaars and hot and stuffy third-class railway carriages. The bishop had made of his home on the hill a little piece of England: when Verrier visited him he was digesting lunch in the cushioned depths of his armchair. 'You are very young,' he told Verrier, flicking the ash off his cigar, 'you are inexperienced, you are very very foolish. You have greatly annoyed Government with your report on Gujerat. Personally I don't believe a word of it. I do not know of a single example where the authorities exceeded their duties. Even if they were brutal, they had to be . . . Where would we be if we did not rule by force?' Verrier did not answer back but thought as he went away, 'Yes my Lord, where will *you* be in a free India.'[49]

Back in Poona, Verrier spent the whole of Good Friday spinning. This, he wrote to Gandhi, was a real 'experience of purification;' the *charkha* itself he knew now to be a 'dual symbol of our union with the poor and with God.' He sent the yarn to Mirabehn (Madelene Slade), apologizing for its poor quality. Mira passed it on to Gandhi for inspection. The Master pronounced it 'quite weavable,' with 'the count somewhere near 20.' Nonetheless, he agreed that 'it is poor for the spirit of love and dedication that lay behind the sacrifical act.'[50] Verrier now longed to follow his yarn to Sabarmati. 'Is there any possibility of my spending a week with your party,' he wrote to Mira, the only English woman or man permitted into the Mahatma's inner circle: 'I do so want just to be able to watch Bapu and learn from him.'[51] Gandhi was then touring rural Gujarat, taking stock of the ashrams and schools set up in the wake of the peasant movement. Verrier caught up with him at the Swaraj Ashram in Bardoli and stayed a week. Bardoli was serving as the 'temporary court of one whom millions enshrine in their hearts as their uncrowned king,' yet Verrier found Gandhi extraordinarily accessible. 'You go to him,' wrote the newest of his followers, 'and for those few minutes he is yours—completely. He is thinking about you, and about nothing else. This great mind, which holds in its grasp the vexed problem of a continent, is for the time entirely directed to your little problem.'

It was most likely on this visit that Gandhi told Verrier that just as he regarded Mirabehn as his daughter, he, Verrier, would be his son.[52] But of course Verrier had already adopted the Mahatma as his stand-in father, successor to the chaplain of Merton and the acharya of the Christa Seva Sangh. Verrier's devotion was unconditional, in line with an Indian interpretation of the father–son relationship. While in Bardoli he washed Gandhi's famous loincloth, cleaned his vessels, and prepared his meal of fruits and nuts. In between the Mahatma found time for some 'heavenly conversations' with him.[53]

Bardoli was the hometown of Vallabhbhai Patel, who knew of Verrier's skills as writer and speaker and knew also the value to the Congress cause of this former Oxford don and still-serving priest. Verrier was thus whisked away from the Swaraj Ashram into the villages to speak on Congress' behalf. On 4 June he spoke at Rayan, in honor of forty-two volunteers released from jail, and two days later spoke at a similar meeting in Varad. In both places he deplored the police *zulum* (terror), praising the *satyagrahis* for meeting the state's weapons of violence and untruth with non-violence and truth. Verrier saw the 'spirit of Gandhi Raj' replacing 'Gunda Raj' (rule by hooligans) in Gujarat. Wherever he went he asked forgiveness for the crimes of his countrymen, not all of whom were, as he reminded his audience and himself, opposed to Indian freedom. Gandhi he saw as 'the friend of [the] good element and [the] enemy of the bad element in England.'[54]

By May 1931, still a good eighteen months short of the five years given him by Bishop Gore, Verrier knew that he must leave the Christa Seva Sangh. He was, and had been for some time now, a deep embarrassment to the CSS in the work it hoped to do within the Indian church. Equally, the CSS was an embarrassment to him in such work as he might do outside. He wanted to exchange the contemplative life—which in India seemed 'not only impossible, but a crime'—for an active one. Was he to go back to England and live the 'life of a second-rate scholar,' or was he to 'have another complete "conversion?"' In the Poona ashram he saw interesting things and met interesting people, but remained 'entirely apart from the suppressed and down-trodden.' So long as he was in the Sangh he would always be seen as a 'Padre-Sahib.' He had to cut himself from the foreign connection, to work more closely with Indians, perhaps even *under* them.[55]

Verrier felt a 'great inner urge away, to more complete poverty, more complete union with India, greater toil, fuller suffering.' He could not, he sensed, truly help the poor save by becoming one of them. This, in India, could mean only that he should 'find a little hut in the "untouchable" quarter of some village and live there as a poor man.' To his friends in Umbria, to whom he felt most akin theologically, Verrier described this as

> a step of faith at midnight. I have no material or financial resources of any kind. I do not know whether I shall have anyone with me. I have no idea what the future holds. But the vividly-present love of our most sweet Lord tells me that there is a tiny piece of work to do and I shall live to do it.[56]

Leaving the Christa Seva Sangh was unquestionably the most difficult step in a life already marked by departures. It would be a little easier, perhaps, if another inmate were to flee the Winslowian coop with him. Verrier wrote to the most likely volunteer, Shamrao Hivale, asking whether he would come too. Sham was at the time at Muirfield, training at its Benedictine seminary. While he awaited Sham's reply Verrier's education was 'beginning all over again.' He was now learning to cook, to wash, to spin faster and better, to do all the things that would allow him to live with the poor as they did.

By mutual consent Verrier and the CSS decided to part in November, leaving him five months to search for a home and prepare to live in it. In June he was invited by A. V. Thakkar to come on a tour of the ashrams he ran. Thakkar, who had befriended him in the Gujarat enquiry the previous December, was a sure and experienced guide to the poor of India. Born in 1869, two months after Mahatma Gandhi and in the same state of Gujarat, he had first been trained as an engineer. In 1914 he left his job in the Bombay Municipality to join the Servants of India Society, the social welfare organization founded by Gopalkrishna Gokhale. In 1921 he was sent to organize famine relief in the coastal districts of Maharashtra. This brought him face to face with the poverty of Bhil tribals: two years later he founded the Bhil Seva Mandal at Dahod, the first tribal welfare organization run and staffed by Indians. It ran schools and dispensaries for the Bhils, interceded on their behalf with moneylenders and officials, and promoted khadi and temperance.[57]

Mahatma Gandhi was once asked why he paid little attention to the tribes. He replied: 'I have entrusted that part of our work to A. V. Thakkar.'[58] Universally known as 'Bapa' (Father), Thakkar was undoubtedly a man of great integrity, courage and commitment. Thakkar Bapa, wrote an admirer in 1928, was

> a friend of the poor, the untouchable and the aborigine. The cry of torment, anguish and torture attracts him from one remote corner to the other. Whether it be a famine calamity or a flood devastation, official persecution

> or temperance work, khaddar organization or opening wells and tanks for untouchables, you cannot miss the mark and the guiding and unerring hand of Amritlal. The theatre of his activities is among the depressed and the oppressed in out-of-the-way places or among forest tribes in the hills.[59]

Before they left for Dahod and the Bhils, Thakkar took Verrier on a tour of the *bhangi* colonies of Bombay. The priest was shaken by the terrible conditions in which the scavengers lived. He described the typical bhangi quarter as 'no more a collection of tiny kennels, the houses built out of the sides of kerosene tins nailed together, without windows, on ground which, when the rain pours down, becomes a swamp exhaling poisonous vapours. Here live brothers and sisters of our own, condemned by a vile social custom to a life of degrading toil.' The sight of Indian poverty was not a pleasant experience, especially in the cities. 'The worst slums in London,' remarked Verrier, 'are nothing to these tenements, laden with humanity, dripping with filth.'

The Bhils, whom he visited next, were also desperately poor, but lived in altogether more attractive surroundings. Thakkar's ashrams he thought models of their kind: small, familial (not more than fifty Bhil boys and girls in each), teaching the three R's alongside vocational skills. He was delighted by the Bhils; unlike the bhangis not degraded and bowed-down, but with a rich culture still intact. They were, he wrote,

> an attractive people, very dark in colour, men with long hair and almost naked, the women covered with heavy brass bangles. They are primitive in their superstitions, offering clay horses, jars and beehive-shaped vessels to the spirits. They live in fear of ghosts and demons. They specially reverence the moon and the horse. They will eat almost any animal, but not the fowl, which is used by witches. They all carry bows and arrows which they use with great precision. They are strong and brave and you may see old men who have killed leopards and tigers with their hands.[60]

The Bhils would fascinate this student of religions; more so as their beliefs were not to be found in the bound volumes on Eastern religions that he had so assiduously studied in the Bodleian. The trip with Thakkar stimulated Verrier but also confused him. The tribes were as neglected as the untouchables—might not he work with them instead? Whatever he decided, he had first to learn to staff and run his own show. From Dahod he proceeded straight to the mother of all modern ashrams, the one in Ahmedabad. Verrier spent almost a month at Sabarmati, staying with Gandhi in his hut, accompanying him on his morning walks, less willingly submitting to the extraordinarily harsh regimen of a seventeen-hour day taken up with prayer, study, spinning, cooking, washing, language class and more prayer. He certainly enjoyed his conversations with Gandhi and learnt a great deal from them. When he asked the Mahatma why he didn't write a commentary on the Gospel, Gandhi replied: 'Hindus do not all accept my interpretation of my own religion, and I would not care to force on Christians my views on Christianity.' One could best serve one's religion, he was told, not by proselytizing but by merely being a better Christian, or better Hindu, or Mussalman or Buddhist. Verrier had heard this before, in January 1928, but he was now more prepared to accept an idea of theological tolerance that went much beyond even the most liberal of Christian traditions, all of which somewhere deep down still stuck to the idea that their superior Gospel must be made available to those who did not follow it.

At Sabarmati Verrier made some new friendships and renewed some old ones. He talked more to Mahadev Desai, Mirabehn, and Vallabhbhai Patel, and was freshly introduced to Acharya J. B. Kripalani, whom he immediately loved, this 'artist, philosopher, poet-turned-spinner.' Kripalani, like the others, had thrown away 'money, position, prospects' to join Gandhi and his movement. Verrier was struck by the idealism and sacrifice but couldn't help noticing that life in Sabarmati was somewhat one-sided. He noted with interest and possibly some nervousness that the strictest chastity was enjoined both within and outside marriage. The Mahatma himself, for the most part so sweet and reasonable, could be 'very stern in his dealings with those [followers] who have moral lapses, and his normal remedy is immediate expulsion from his ashram, always however with the possibility of a return after real penitence has been shown.' Verrier also complained of the lack of culture: the library was open only once a week, there was little interest in art (Kripalani excepted), and music was loved not for its own sake but rather for what it could give to the morning prayers. Then there was the food, which could only be described as 'ashramatic.' Verrier tried to imagine how that lovable epicurean idiot Bertie Wooster would have reacted on being given for lunch a 'steaming hell-brew served up in a great bucket.' Verrier himself offered, for private consumption, these

THOUGHTS OF A GOURMET ON BEING CONFRONTED
WITH AN ASHRAM MEAL

(after Francis Thompson)

O food inedible, we eat thee
O drink incredible, we greet thee.
Meal indigestible, we bless thee.
O naughty swear-word, we suppress thee.[61]

Verrier left Sabarmati undecided as to his future. One part of him wanted to go with Gandhi all the way; the other part wondered whether he was up to it, or even if it was worth it. Would he want to follow and enforce at his own ashram a timetable which went:

4.0.	Rising Bell
4.20	Prayer
6.0	Light Breakfast (cup of milk and piece of bread)
6.10–7.0	Study
7.0.–9.0	Spinning and Carding Class
9.15	Hindi Class
10.0	Bath, washing clothes, etc.
10.45	Mid-day meal of chapattis, boiled vegetables and curds
11.15–12.30	Rest
12.30	Lecture on Technique of Weaving
1.30–3.30	Weaving Shed
4.0–5.0	Spinning
5.0	Bathe in river
5.30	Evening meal of chapattis, boiled vegetables, a little rice, and milk. Some fruit.
6.15	Walk
7.30	Prayer
8.0–9.0	Recreation
9.0	Bed

On returning to Poona Verrier fell ill, the fever brought on one thinks by the uncertainty and the self-doubt. He spent a week in hospital, delirious and in strange company: 'other patients gambling till midnight, goats wandering through the wards, buffaloes walking unconcerned through the corridors.'[62] But by the time he was discharged he had made up his mind. He knew for certain that the Christians did not want him. He had not preached in a church for fourteen months and even the liberal-minded YMCA withdrew an invitation to speak because the secretary and his committee felt 'Father Elwin was undesirable,' because he was both too catholic and too Indian.[63] On the other side he was wanted by the Gandhians, including the youngest and most eccentric among them.

He took as symbolic the manner of his departure from Sabarmati. As he prepared to board the *tonga* that would take him to the station, he was surrounded by Mahadev Desai's little boy, Narayan, and three other children, with the secretary of the All India Cow Protection League. The boys hung on to his thin legs and arms, shouting 'Father Elwin, don't go away, Father Elwin don't go away.'[64]

CHAPTER FOUR

Breaking Ranks

Verrier's whole concern was, in one sense, a series of unconscious ways of rebelling against a dominant mother, a powerful Evangelical . . . Each stage of his life was one step further away from his mother. His greatest and most dangerous gift was his enchanting character. This was quite uncultivated and he was equally attractive to men and women. There was a light about him. He had humour, gentleness, depth and a great impressive intellect. If only he had a first-class spiritual director, which he never did, things might have been very different!

Leonard Schiff, once of the Christa Seva Sangh

As a missionary Elwin is probably excellent, but as a friend of India he is too credulous and sentimental to be anything but a dangerous nuisance.

Director, Intelligence Department, Government of India

In August 1931 Mahatma Gandhi sailed for London and the Round Table Conference to discuss India's political future. Meanwhile Verrier in Poona finished a book that stated the Congress case before the British public. Remarkably, he had persuaded his acharya to collaborate, Father Jack perhaps thinking that the conference represented a triumph of reconciliation over recrimination. The celebratory chapters, on 'The half-naked fakir' and 'The meaning of satyagraha,' appeared under Verrier's name, with Winslow appending his own signature to a high-sounding but politically innocuous essay on 'The Place of the Christian Church in a New India.' But the book appeared under both their names, Winslow's first, Verrier remarking maliciously that this was sure 'to get poor old Fr. Jack into great trouble.'[1]

The final parting with the Christa Seva Sangh, pushed forward to

September, was welcomed by both sides. Winslow was glad to be rid of his troublesome subordinate, Verrier relieved to be a 'free unfettered worker.' He was more relieved still when Shamrao Hivale wrote from England that he would come with him wherever they went. Shamrao had temporized for a while, for the principal of the Muirfield seminary assured him he would soon be a minister of the Church of England, with a British parish if he so wished. He had now to judge the prospects of a priesthood against an unlicensed life outside the church. As young Indians of the time would, he took his case before the court of Mahatma Gandhi. Boarding the night train from Leeds, Sham arrived at London early in the morning and made straight to Gandhi's temporary home in the East End. He met the Mahatma on his morning walk; Gandhi heard him out and advised him to join his party and return with them to India.[2]

Verrier was most pleased to know that Sham was coming home, that with him would be an Indian bridge to the poor. They would collect Hindu brothers, Muslim brothers, Christian brothers, in a truly inter-faith fellowship. 'I don't want a lot of theology about it,' wrote the leader, 'but I want so much love, divine, supernatural, holy, Christ-like love, that the [religious] differences will be submerged.'[3]

One senses in this freewheeling ecumenism the influence of those heavenly conversations in Bardoli and Sabarmati. Indeed Gandhi in London offered to old-style Christian imperialists the example of his disciple. Addressing a group of missionaries on 8 October he told them that, were he an English priest, he would 'go into [the poor] as Elwin has gone . . . He will establish Christian ashrams among the untouchables, with a church in a mud-hut for his own and his colleagues' use. He wants simply to live with them as God may guide his life.'[4]

Back in India, however, Verrier had started moving away from the untouchables. Vallabhbhai Patel told him the outcastes were not his problem; the Hindus, who had thrown them out of society, must themselves make 'reparation' for them. The argument made sense to Verrier, but Patel, a canny politician, must also not have wanted Hindus shown up by a Christian radical directing attention to the iniquities of the caste system. In any case, the priest himself began favouring the tribes. For one thing, they lived amidst woods and hills, not in festering city slums or beyond the boundaries of villages. For another, his Bhil experience showed that they had a rich and still-vigorous culture. With the tribes one had a real chance of doing *something*, helping them through schools and hospitals to make an honourable truce with the modern world.

It was another Congressman, Jamnalal Bajaj, who suggested that he work with the great Gond tribe of central India. Bajaj was a prosperous merchant and treasurer of the Congress, based in Wardha, in the Central Provinces. Wardha is close to being the exact geographical centre of India; this, and the proximity of Bajaj and the availability of his funds, was to make Gandhi move there from Sabarmati in 1936. 'Why don't you do something for a tribe,' Jamnalal now asked Verrier, 'which is almost entirely neglected both by national workers and by missionaries?'[5]

In the first week of November Verrier took a train from Bombay to the little market town of Betul, up on the Satpura plateau. From Betul two Congressmen accompanied him into the forest. They called at Banjaridhal where, that previous summer, the tribals had revolted against the forest restrictions. 'No lectures were given,' according to the intelligence report, but the Gonds were asked if they had any complaints to make. The party moved on to the adjoining district of Chhindwara, where Verrier's search took him to the village of Tamia, on the road to Pachmarhi. Tamia was pretty but its attractions had already been noted. Finding it the headquarters of a Swedish mission-centre and hospital, Verrier retreated in haste.

The Central Provinces tour of 'Father Elwin, a European dressed in khadi' was well covered by his faithful CID agent. We know thus that his final port of call was Wardha, where on 15 November he at last made a speech, its contents fancifully embroidered by his shadow. In this account the priest had learnt to make bombs and fire guns in the Great War. Then he read in the trenches a collection of Gandhi's speeches and decided to come to India 'to fight a different battle.' He apologized in person to the Mahatma, taking thereafter to khadi and the charkha, as a disciplined soldier of Indian freedom, or swaraj.[6]

The making of bombs might have not figured in Verrier's c.v., but his first commitment was undoubtedly to Gandhi and swaraj. A mark of this commitment is the fact that it was only after he decided to live with the Gonds that he made contact with Alex Wood, Bishop of Nagpur, in whose diocese the Central Provinces fell and who in the hierarchy of the church was his superior. Verrier finally wrote to the bishop on 12 December of their plans to buy land in Betul with the help of Jamnalal Bajaj, asking for his blessing and license. To write to Wood last, he said, was 'part of my whole scheme—of beginning at the opposite end, and working from the Indian standpoint.' The ashram he planned would be 'open to all religions; it would serve the people, but not be "Missionary" in the ordinary sense. The Christian members would try to express the spirit of Christ in love and service; that would be their sermon. Another thing in my mind was that I should only go where I was invited by the people of India themselves.'[7]

The bishop was not pleased with the timing of the letter, still less with its contents. To his superior, the Metropolitan of India, he communicated his anger at Verrier going to the Gonds at the invitation of Jamnalal Bajaj. Bajaj, he complained, 'has as much right to invite a Christian Mission to the Gonds as I would have to invite a Hindu Mission to start work in Italy.' He was also worried that Verrier was not going to 'cure souls.' He knew of his great gifts as writer and speaker, and doubtless hoped that with his spiritual direction the young man would come to proselytize among the Gonds. To that end he craftily suggested an alternative location. 'I am perfectly certain,' wrote the Bishop to Verrier, 'that you would be welcomed by the Gonds themselves in a certain portion of the Mandla District called Karanjia. This place has acquired more or less a sacred character from the fact that a band of German missionaries opened up work there in 1841 and four of the party died and are buried there. They have had no successors . . .' Karanjia, he said, was a first-class location because it was surrounded by Gond villages, yet was not far from a reservation of the Baigas, 'another people who have been practically untouched by Missions.' The village was also on the pilgrim route to the temple in Amarkantak, the source of the river Narmada, to which came devout Hindus from all over northern India.[8]

Betul, Chhindwara, or Mandla—the final decision would have to await his friend's return. Shamrao had booked himself on the same ship, the *S. S. Pilsna*, as the party coming home from the abortive Round Table Conference. When the *Pilsna* docked in Bombay, on 28 December, Verrier was in the huge crowd that assembled to greet Gandhi. First in line were members of the Congress Working Committee who took the great man away for an emergency meeting. Verrier saw Gandhi but was too shy to greet him. He felt bad about it afterwards, but 'it had to be,' he consoled himself, for the Mahatma 'was facing issues too momentous for any individual to claim him.'[9]

Shamrao Hivale met Verrier straight off the boat, the issues he faced being momentous only for the two of them. The friends left immediately for Matheran, a quiet town perched on top of the Western Ghats, sixty miles south of Bombay. Here they discussed Bajaj's proposal and Wood's, on occasion it seems in the presence of a woman-soul. Once more, all we have is a single reference in a letter written to the Italian sisters. On 2nd January he wrote to them that

> Next week we go out 'not knowing whither.' Government is preventing our getting land; we may remain homeless; we may be arrested . . . And just at this moment a crushing pain has come to me, the greatest trial of years I think—I cannot share it—I can only offer it to the Heart of Sorrow and of Love.[10]

Matheran, with its hills, lakes and long lonely walks along wooded paths, was the perfect setting for romance. At just this point of time, two other eccentrically gifted Englishmen were falling in love in Indian hill-stations. In Simla Malcolm Muggeridge was in the throes of a passionate affair with the Indo-Hungarian artist Amrita Sher-Gil; while in nearby Kulu the journalist Ian Stephens was worshipfully following Penelope Chetwode, daughter of the commander-in-chief of the Indian army, on horseback. One alliance across the racial barrier, the other across a social one, both abetted by the air of the mountains, neither designed to last.

Verrier's flame was not of this eminence. She was, judging from a later confession, a Parsi doctor named Ala Pocha, originally from Poona but now also a member of the Mahatma's outer circle. They met, they talked, they held hands and walked, but in the end it was Verrier who drew away in favour of the Gonds and the vow of celibacy by which he still felt bound.

At Matheran Verrier and Shamrao decided on Karanjia, but they were not to go there just yet. On the morning of the 3rd January a telegram arrived from Mahadev Desai in Bombay, asking them to come at once. The London conference not having yielded what he wanted, Gandhi announced a fresh round of civil disobedience. When Sham and Verrier reached Mani Bhavan that evening, they found a huge but peaceful crowd assembled outside. Inside, Gandhi was sitting on the floor, spinning. As it was his weekly day of silence he scribbled a note saying that Mahadev would give them 'instructions.' These were duly conveyed: a request to travel on behalf of the Congress to report on the political situation in the North-West Frontier Province.

Sham and Verrier slept that night with Gandhi's party, their beds laid out under a tent on the roof of Mani Bhavan. At the crack of dawn they were woken up by a whispered message: 'The police have come.' They got up to see a uniformed commissioner of police touching the Mahatma on his shoulder and saying, 'Mr Gandhi, it is my duty to arrest you.' The prisoner had half-an-hour to get himself ready. Five minutes is what it took to brush his teeth and put on a clean dhoti. Gandhi then led the singing of a Vaishnava hymn, and wrote a few last letters. One was a set of instructions to his partymen, another a message to Verrier which read

> My dear Elwyn [*sic*],
>
> I am so glad you have come. I would like you yourself to tell your countrymen that I love them even as I love my own countrymen. I have never done anything towards them in hatred or malice and God willing I shall never do anything in that manner in future. I am acting no differently towards them now from what I have done under similar circumstances towards my own kith and kin.
>
> with love
> yours
> M. K. Gandhi[11]

Also arrested in different parts of India were Nehru, Patel, Rajagopalachari, Bajaj and others. The lesser Congressmen, still at large, immediately got to work. Devadas Gandhi, the Mahatma's youngest son, called on some Congress-minded merchants who put up the money for the Frontier trip. Meanwhile Bernard Aluwihare, who was also sleeping on the Mani Bhavan terrace that night, lent his old Oxford friend his suit.

Verrier resorted to being a sahib, travelling under false pretences, else he would not have been allowed into the Frontier. In that province one of Gandhi's most remarkable followers, Khan Abdul Ghaffar Khan, had led a peaceful satyagraha among the gun-toting Pathans. This was known as the movement of Khudai Khitmatgars (Servants of God); at its height it commanded 100,000 volunteers. But in December there had been a massive crackdown which put the leaders and countless Khitmatgars into jail. The Congress leadership had little news from this distant province, and no journalists were allowed in either. Hence the dispatch of a sympathetic Englishman posing as a commercial traveller, the faithful Sham as his Indian 'assistant.'

Verrier and Sham left Bombay on the 6th by the Frontier Mail, stopping in Delhi en route. Here they met one of Mrs Elwin's friends, the wife of Sir Lancelot Graham, secretary to the legislature. When Verrier asked Lady Graham what the attitude of the CP government might be to their projected work with the Gonds, she arranged for him to meet the home secretary, H. W. Emerson. Verrier liked Emerson, a 'hard hitting straight man,' but was dismayed by his advice, which was that he was not likely to be allowed into the Gond country unless he gave an undertaking not to support the Congress in speech or in writing.[12]

Of course neither the Grahams nor Emerson knew why Verrier was in Delhi in the first place. The traveller and his assistant continued their northbound journey, reaching Peshawar on the 9th. In the Frontier, where the Raj was at its most reactionary, where white only talked down to brown, Sham was made to sleep in the verandah outside his friend's room. When they got their bill there were two items, marked 'Food for the Sahib' and 'Food for the Fellow,' the latter at half-price.

Peshawar itself was under curfew and the police were out in force. During the day Verrier stayed indoors while his servant went out into the bazaar to make contacts with Congress sympathizers—merchants, lawyers, students and others. Under cover of darkness some rebels crept into the hotel to pass on eyewitness accounts of the movement and its suppression. One day the visitors hired a car and went out into the hills, calling on the Afridi tribesmen. Then Verrier made the mistake of trying to obtain the other side of the story. He wrote to the deputy commissioner, revealing his mission and requesting an interview. He received in reply an order externing him from the province. The police came round to search their room and luggage; what they failed to find were their notes on the trip, hidden inside a packet of breakfast cereal placed boldy on the table. They left Peshawar by the next available train.[13]

Verrier's Frontier report put together the evidence they collected on state repression: the column marches, the aerial sorties, the massive arrests and beatings of Khudai Khitmatgars. He admitted that the Pathans had occasionally deviated from the path of non-violence, but in his view this did not justify the terror. The 'ordinary Englishman in the Frontier,' he noted, 'is callous and without imagination,' illustrating 'the old India at its worst.' But he was sure his side would win in the end. The spirit of peaceful revolution, among the Pathans and elsewhere, would not 'be crushed, and soon through truth, patience, love and suffering, it will lead the people to victory.'[14]

Verrier and Sham were removed from the Frontier on the 15 January; within a fortnight they were on their way to make their home in a village they had not previously set sight on. Not yet thirty, Verrier had already forsaken a comfortable career in England for an uncertain life overseas; cast his lost with a small, struggling sect rather than rest securely within the folds of the Anglican church; and gone on to become a camp follower and occasional cheerleader of a popular movement aimed at the overthrow of the British empire. But the move to Karanjia was more noteworthy still. There were at this time in India a few Englishmen, such as Jack Winslow, sincerely interested in intercultural dialogue; fewer still, like C. F. Andrews, willing to harness their Christian belief to the anti-imperialist struggle; but none who had actually identified with poor Indians to the extent of living with them.

The district of Mandla, in whose northern corner lay the village of Karanjia, was called, by a British civilian who had once served there, the 'Ultima Thule of civilization, the dreaded home of the tiger, the Gond, and the devil.'[15] Rugged and utterly beautiful, dominated by magnificent sal forests, the district is now crisscrossed by an all-weather road which touches Karanjia en route to Amarkantak. But in 1932 one had first to take a train to Pendra Road, thirty-five miles away, and then travel over jungle and ghat by foot, which took three days, or by bullock-cart, which took five. Laden with books, medicine and food, Verrier and Sham took the slower route. Karanjia, which they reached at noon on the 30th, they found to be a scattered collection of hamlets set in a wooded valley. The smallest of the hamlets, with the lovely name of Tikeri Tola, was situated on a hill at the edge of the forest with wonderful views all around.

The visitors had come unannounced and the villagers were at first downright hostile. Verrier later recalled, with some feeling, the moment of their arrival in Karanjia: 'We had been travelling with a buffalo cart for three days; we were very tired; none of the villagers would come near us; . . . the D.C. had ordered us out of the district—and I remember sitting down on a big stone, and its coolness reminded me of a stone seat in Merton Chapel where I used to sit on Sunday evenings and look at that glorious place lit dimly by candles and hear the organ—and I wished I was there.'[16]

Sham and Verrier were finally allowed to rent a room by a Mussalman, Hyder Ali, who was outside the caste system anyhow. At first no one was willing to sell milk and vegetables except an old woman out of caste 'on account of an irregular maidenhood.' It was when they were visited by the police that the Gonds decided they were men of standing and began coming round. It helped that Shamrao was able to treat men beaten up by other men or merely bitten by scorpions.[17] By late February Verrier was writing that Sham was already 'the adored of the village going on errands of love to the sick'—he was also his friend's 'delight and comrade and helper.'[18]

The police had come on the advice of the district magistrate of Mandla, alerted by his superiors in the Central Provinces administration, in turn put wise by Emerson in New Delhi. The home secretary thought 'Elwin's presence among the Gonds in present circumstances could hardly fail to be a disturbing influence and probably the cause of trouble.' The priest, he remarked, was 'a highly strung neurotic young man who believes he has a mission in India.' (Political disagreement, in the Raj's understanding, could stem only from an excess of nervous energy.) Unlike Emerson the chief secretary of the Central Provinces had not yet met Elwin, but after a close study of the Bombay Secret Proceedings decided he did not want him in his territory. He warned the commissioner of the Jabalpur division that 'Elwin is a young man with plenty of brains and is also capable of great self-denial and means well apparently, but is neurotic and imbued with that form of charity which sees good only in himself and those who play upon his vanity.'[19]

Like their colleagues in Peshawar the policemen who visited Karanjia failed to find the evidence to clinch their case. This was the manuscript of Verrier's book *Truth about India*, written in his first few weeks in the village and published in London later in the year. Here he drew attention once again to the chasm separating British precept from colonial practice. The 'champions of liberty,' he remarked, had turned the subcontinent 'into a vast prison-house.' Instead of forcing 'our alien, unwarranted, extravagant, irresponsible rule upon India by the sword,' the British should take heed of Gandhi's 'message of friendliness and hope' and depart before they were thrown out. A reviewer wrote of the book that 'though the author does not belong to the Congress, the case for the Congress could hardly be put with more convincing advocacy.'[20]

While Verrier wrote away, Shamrao organized the construction of their ashram. The site was atop Tikeri Tola; the labour, local men and women; the materials they worked with, bamboo, mud, and grass. By early March the building had come up, a little house with five little rooms in front, a chapel at the back, the two enclosed by a mud wall leaving an open courtyard in the centre. The wall was decorated Gond-style, with motifs of tigers, elephants and other animals; Verrier overriding Sham's objections that this would lend support to 'animist superstitions'—he answered that it was really a new zoo for St Francis, after whom the ashram was named. The ashram flew a saffron flag with the cross high above it and was approached by a long flight of steps, much like a temple. All told it had cost one hundred rupees, or seven pounds sterling.[21]

To better know the neighbourhood the two friends visited the source of the Narmada at Amarkantak. Walking round the river with Hindu pilgrims, Shamrao had a 'wonderful interior awakening, a kind of mystic conversion.' He had dreamt that something like this would happen if he were to visit the Holy Land, but God's ways were 'so strange' that, when his soul was touched, it was where thousands down the centuries had searched for other gods. He was now thinking of taking the saffron robe, of being a 'real brother' to everyone.[22]

Shamrao had, in any case, seen their move to the forest as a 'deliberate attempt to find reality away from the bustle and confusion of politics.'[23] But Verrier, poor fellow, remained confused, torn between social work and political work, quiet service or heroic martyrdom. On the one side he agreed with Shamrao that 'the turmoil of the political world made a cold and alien home for the spirit.' On the other side, as he wrote to Mirabehn, he would always 'be ready to go on an enquiry' for the Congress, hoping no doubt he would finally be arrested. One detects a tinge of envy—if Madelene Slade, the admiral's daughter, could be imprisoned several times in Gandhi's cause, why not this son of a bishop? 'How I long to go to jail,' he wrote, 'to show really that I love India.' This love shone through his dreams, too; one of these placed Queen Victoria in Purgatory, to remain there till the last Indian child gained its freedom.

The weekly visits from the police, a letter from the district magistrate stating that 'in view of your political record we do not want you in this district,' all seemed to point to an eventual arrest. As it happened it was not the political but the clerical establishment which took him on. The Bishop of Nagpur wrote saying that he would license him only if he took an oath of allegiance to the king-emperor and a further oath of canonical obedience to himself. Only this, the bishop felt, would separate Verrier 'absolutely from the Congress Party which has been declared an illegal association on account of its unconstitutional and unlawful methods of working.' A lively correspondence followed, with Verrier defending Congress as the 'mouthpiece and representative' of the Indian people and calling Gandhi the 'most sublime and Christ-like figure now living on the planet.' He handed his superior a lesson in theology, quoting St Augustine to the effect that the church would be a city which summons citizens from all tribes; which meant, in the present context, that it 'must enfold within its arms of love everyone in India, from the member of the European Association to the most extreme follower of Pandit Jawaharlal Nehru.' 'No one nowadays,' he loftily concluded, 'makes the unphilosophical and unCatholic separation of politics and religion, and it would be contrary to my whole thinking to do so.'[24]

Bishop Wood replied to the lesson more in sorrow than in anger. Gandhi, he said, far from being Christ-like, wanted 'the re-establishment of some form of the Vedic Religion and culture in India, when his party has the power.' But Verrier, in contrast, appeared to him to 'have gifts which might be of great value if used in the service of our Lord and for extending his Kingdom.' He could not believe that Verrier meant all that he said, and would come to Karanjia to interview him personally. 'I always believe in giving a man a fair chance,' said the bishop.[25]

Wood came to Karanjia on 8th April, accompanied by two of his priests, one of these an Ulsterman and fanatic imperialist. The next day the bishop penned a long account, for the Metropolitan, of what was 'on the whole a most interesting [but] unsatisfactory interview.'[26] He described Verrier as 'very fit and as charming as ever,' Shamrao merely as his 'protege.' The last time he saw them they wore khaddar cassocks in the CSS style, but now they were clad in kurta and dhoti. Verrier had a bare head and bare feet and a black umbrella, 'all signs of the priesthood gone. He looked like Bearse, our Indore Professor, who thinks he has become a Hindu.' The bishop was not much more impressed by the ashram. True, it was perched on a 'delightful little hill,' but it looked decidedly temporary. The roof was thatched; he thought 'the whole thing will go to pieces in the first heavy Monsoon shower.' The room had no furniture of any kind. There were blankets on the floor, though, to sit on. The chapel had an altar with a cross and candles. On its left was displayed a list of prisoners to be prayed for, headed by the Mahatma's name. On the right hung another and more palatable list which included the souls of the German missionaries buried in Karanjia.

A narrative of the interview followed. In response to Verrier's statement that the ashram would 'not be missionary in the ordinary sense,' and no one's religion would be interfered with, the bishop asked the question: 'Our Lord says go, teach and baptise. Gandhi says, go, teach but don't baptise. Whom would he follow?' Verrier became distressed and said their work would be their sermon, but no one would be definitely moved to become Christian. Wood dismissed this as the 'YMCA platform,' with 'all the privileges of Christianity but no urge to baptism.'

The talk then turned to politics. Verrier, in his own account, written three years later, remembers reminding Wood that the bishop served as a chaplain in the Great War, thus giving moral support to those whose job was to kill others. He had acted as a sort of chaplain too, but to a non-violent army using the weapons of non-violence and truth.[27] The bishop recalled it differently, with himself scoring the debating points. Verrier, he said, got 'very impassioned and said the best way to serve the King Emperor was to be the bitter enemy of the Government of India.' Wood rejoined that 'had it not been for the organization of the Government and the self-sacrifice of many of its officers and others during the famines of 1895–6–7 and 1899–1900 most of the Congress supporters would not now be alive to curse the Satanic Government that gave them life.' Even Shamrao, he said meaningfully, was a 'famine-child.'

The bishop finally asked Verrier what link he desired with the church. Did he want to follow C. F. Andrews in rejecting his orders and becoming a 'perjured priest?' The younger man said he didn't want to resign his orders but gave the example of the Bishop of London who had licensed a Bolshevik priest who flew the hammer-and-sickle with the cross atop his church (the priest was probably his old CSS mate, Oliver Fielding-Clarke). He then told Wood that his own clergy flew the Union Jack over their churches. The bishop said this was not with his approval; he only allowed the Red Cross of St George. At this point Shamrao, who had stayed silent, interjected with 'A Bloody Red Cross.' The bishop's seconds also entered the fray. The Ulsterman was boiling over, enraged that Verrier had 'blasphemed' the empire and the Union Jack. He called him a traitor, a renegade and a few other things besides. That ended the interview, the visitors going off without even drinking their tea.

Wood confessed that he couldn't help liking Verrier, 'though his opinions are utterly poisonous gall to me.' He would not license him in his present state of mind but hoped that he would come round to dedicating his prodigious powers to the extension of Christ's kingdom. 'If he would only put Christ before Congress and Khaddar,' he remarked wistfully, 'he would be a perfect missionary—perfectly wonderful.' 'I like the lad,' said Wood, 'but I don't like Shamrao. I think he is there to keep Elwin up to the mark. He is a hard rather stupid Maratha. The most persistent of Indian races.'

This was unfair to Sham who, for the most part, followed Verrier rather than led him. Actually both were quite shaken by the interview and the attitude of the bishop. If Wood did not license him, wrote Verrier to the Metropolitan, 'we shall not grumble. We have youth on our side, and we can afford to wait a decade or two for the recognition of our work. But whatever happens, you may be assured that nothing will shake my allegiance to the Church of my baptism and ordination.'[28] His resolve was strengthened by a moving and most understanding letter from Mahatma Gandhi. 'I wish you would not take to heart what the Bishop has been saying,' urged this veteran of many battles with the bishops of his own religion: 'Your pulpit is the whole earth. The blue sky is the roof of your own church.' The message of Jesus, declared Gandhi, 'is in the main denied in the churches, whether Roman or English, High or Low.' Gandhi thought that excommunication by the bishop was itself 'the surest sign that the truth is in you and with you.'[29] To underline that Christ did not belong only to his highly-salaried defenders, he took up an old suggestion of Verrier that they sing a Christian hymn in Sabarmati. They now sang 'Lead, Kindly, Light' in a Gujarati version every Friday evening at 7.40, wrote the Mahatma; maybe they could join them, at the same time, wherever they were.[30]

Verrier also took heart from the life of St Francis. He had been reading numerous biographies of the saint in preparation for a study commissioned by the Christian Literature Society of India. He found that Francis was much like Gandhi in his love of the poor and love of love, although he 'would not have cared for the Mahatma's food-rules nor had he any real interest in political affairs.' The life of the saint also recalled the life of the Marathi Bhakti poet Tukaram—born likewise into well-to-do stock but who, falling in love with poverty, 'wandered, God-intoxicated, from place to place, singing his songs of love.' Both Tukaram and Francis 'had the same tender love of animals; both were marked by an astonishing humility and a joy that triumphed over every obstacle; both were utterly unconventional and utterly lovable.' Writing the book in May 1932 the author unsurprisingly also found parallels between Francis and himself. The saint of Assissi, wrote this priest who would not be licensed by his own bishop, 'was a churchman who was also a free man. His churchmanship never impeded the onward-rushing splendour of his liberty.' Francis established his order without any reference to a Bishop, and freely preached while a layman. 'The fact that these irregularities were tolerated' was 'an indication that the medieval Church was not the steel-frame organisation of modern rationalist fancy.'[31]

Fighting with his Bishop, writing on St Francis, Verrier made little progress with the work of the ashram. Meanwhile Mrs Elwin, who had not seen her son in three years, wrote asking him to come home for the summer. He was at first worried that if he left India he would not be allowed to return. His passport was due to expire in July: as a precautionary move he visited the passport officer in Bombay. The official told him that due to a technicality it could not be renewed in India, but once he reached London he would have no difficulty in having it endorsed there. Reassured, Verrier made plans to spend four months in England, seeing mother, raising funds for their ashram and, not least, trying to 'stir the conscience of friends about what is happening in India.' There was also the 'prospect of some spiritual fellowship' in Europe, of finding Christians who were willing to talk to and be seen with him. While Verrier was away Shamrao would be learning the ashram trade at Thakkar's Bhil Seva Mandal and at a Christian ashram at Tirupattur in south India.[32]

The day before Verrier left for London he issued a statement denying rumours that by going to the Gonds he had lost faith in the Congress. It remained for him 'the only political organization that represents the masses of India,' while the 'advent of the political idealism of Mr Gandhi [was] the most important event of the twentieth century.' Out of the jungle, temporarily, Verrier plunged with relish into the maelstrom of politics. He stopped in Europe, calling on pro-Indian groups in Italy, France and Switzerland. He spent a day with the Mahatma's most famous biographer, Romain Rolland, at his home in Villeneuve. When he reached London, on 15th July, he was met by his family, but also by Agatha Harrison and Professor Horace Alexander, well-known Quaker admirers of Gandhi. His first public meeting, that same evening, was at the East End: he thought 'Bapu would like that.' In the chair was George Lansbury, leader of the Labour opposition in the House of Commons. The next morning he spoke at the Quaker headquarters, Friends House in Euston, the meeting convened by the India Conciliation Group, the India League and The Friends of India.[33]

In between 'rushing here and there, seeing people and addressing meetings,' Verrier spent time at his home in Oxford. His mother he found on the edge of a nervous breakdown because of his religious views: 'Mother is all with us over India, but religiously she talks a different language.' (She had been converted to his political views by Gandhi and Mahadev Desai when they called on her the previous year). He asked his friends to pray for her: 'her protestanism is such a barrier,' he complained, 'it is fanatical.' When his old director F. W. Green told him that the bishop's refusal to license him did not mean that he couldn't celebrate, he rushed off to the chapel of the APR house in London. But his mother then refused to take the sacraments from him because he had celebrated like a Catholic, in vestments.[34]

In the last week of July Verrier sent in his application for a new passport; it was countersigned by George Lansbury, a final provocation to add to all the others. It now came out that the passport officer in Bombay had lied; he had full authority to extend the document but was advised not to. British consuls in Rome, Paris, Naples, Lyons—wherever Verrier might call en route—had been telegraphed warning them not to give him what he wanted. The Government of India also communicated to the secretary of state in London their wish to see this trouble-maker safely out of India. But he was of that opinion anyhow. The week Verrier landed in England a journal brought out by British sympathizers of Gandhi published an essay by him where he characterized British rule in India as that 'of some hulking bully stamping on a lovely and defenceless bird.' The imagery deeply angered the secretary of state and his underlings: this was the kind of writing, they said, 'that set young Indians out to murder Englishmen.'[35]

On 29th July 1932 Verrier was informed he would be issued a fresh passport but it would be stamped 'invalid for India.' He could go anywhere in the world or the British empire (pretty much the same thing), except where he most wished to be. Verrier was devastated. The next day he wrote a long letter to the secretary of state, Sir Samuel Hoare, explaining that his work with the Gonds was purely non-political. In any event, he did not 'see how the presence of a follower of St Francis working for Christ in the remote jungles of the Central Provinces is going to disturb Law and Order in India.' He complained of the chicanery of the Bombay official; he would have cancelled his passage had he known the truth. For he

> could never have risked—even at serious cost to my health—the possibility of exile from India. My home is in India; my work, my books, my papers, are in India . . . There is a group of devoted Indian Christians who have left everything to join me in working for the poor for whom I am responsible. I have nothing to live on in England, and I have nothing to do in England.[36]

Verrier knew enough of the Raj to think this direct approach might not work. He thus contacted William Paton, secretary of the International Missionary Council, a liberal churchman with wide experience of India. Paton had several times visited the CSS ashram in Poona; indeed, in 1931 he was asked by the India Office to report on the Brothers' activities. He had then described Verrier as 'a very charming person and a considerable scholar' whom he would try and persuade to 'rein in his horns.' Paton was pained by the racial divide erected by British clergymen working in India. He remarked of Verrier and Leonard Schiff that 'foolish though they may be in certain of their words and actions, they have, at great cost to themselves, tried to cross that [racial] barrier and to identify themselves with Indians. In so far as they succeed, they are real instruments of goodwill.'[37]

This time around it was the rebel rather than the authorities who called upon Paton's services. Verrier told him that if only he was allowed to go back to the Gonds, he would give an undertaking to stay away from politics altogether. Conveying this to the India Office, Paton said he could not himself believe 'that so unselfish and manifestly Christian a person can in the long run do other than good by being in India, for his influence tends to make Indians better men and to demolish racial feeling.'[38]

Verrier, spreading his bets, had also approached another of his influential friends. On 31st July he wrote to Lady Graham, briefly in England, but preparing to return with her husband to Sind, of which province he had just been appointed governor. Verrier repeated the offer of an undertaking, for he only wanted to return to their work in Karanjia, which 'is just starting beautifully.' But were he made to remain in England he would be 'forced into all sorts of political activities!'

When Lady Graham wrote stating the government's case that he had been a 'very unfair and very uncharitable opponent,' Verrier answered that

'I see things from underneath and you see them from above, and they look completely different.' In any case all that was behind them, for God had now called him to the Gonds. Would not her husband ask the government to offer a 'honourable' undertaking? The threat he now unveiled was a more telling one. If he couldn't return, said Verrier, his co-workers would 'be miles away from any Church and cut off from the Sacraments which mean so much for them. For their sake so that they may have their communions—I am ready to agree to any conditions.'[39]

The euphemisms, the exaggerations, the threats subtly held out, all bear the mark of a writer who knew his audience and how best to move it. Sir Lancelot Graham sent the letters on to the India Office, adding his opinion that Verrier would honour any undertaking he signed. London consulted the Government of India, who were in no mood to relent. 'Whatever his assurances,' commented the chief secretary of the Central Provinces, 'his harmlessness cannot be taken for granted.' For his record showed 'him to be of so unbalanced a mind that it would be an undoubted relief to Government if he left India and did not return here.' 'It is clear,' added an official of the home department, that 'Mr Elwin was out in India for little more than fishing in troubled waters.' In any case 'he was not a dependable character, and it seems unlikely that any great reliance could be placed on any undertaking to be given by him.'[40]

These opinions were all forwarded to the home secretary, M. G. Hallett. On 23rd August Hallett wrote to the viceroy advising him not to allow Elwin to come back, this 'in his own interests as well as the interests of Government.' On the evidence put on his table, he thought it doubtful that the priest would 'really cut himself adrift' from the Congress. The next day he was visited by Sir Lancelot Graham, carrying copies of his wife's correspondence with Verrier, supported by his own recommendation. Placing this personal approach from a colleague against file notings by his inferiors, Hallett changed his mind. Graham had persuaded him that 'in the jungles of the Gond country [Elwin] will be fairly safe, and it certainly seems hard to keep a man from his mission in life.' Hallett now thought the Government could take the risk of allowing him back in; he would himself draft a foolproof undertaking to bind the priest should he stray back into politics.[41] The undertaking, as finally approved by the India Office, asked Verrier to

(i) confine himself entirely to missionary work among the Gonds;
(ii) take no part in civil disobedience or any other political movement;
(iii) refrain, as far as possible, from associating with any persons engaged in political agitation;
(iv) refrain from writing articles against the government.

Curiously, on the very day, 26th August, that Hallett changed his mind, Verrier was having misgivings about his offer of political abstinence. News came from India that Mirabehn had been arrested once more. 'How brave she is,' he thought,' 'how cowardly I am.'[42] But a month later, when the draft undertaking reached him, he was willing to sign. Ever the scholar, he would however improve and edit the text. Could the India Office please change 'missionary' to 'religious and social' in the first clause? This made no difference to its intent, being rather 'a technical theological point. I do not care to to use the word "missionary" in connection with my work because the word has come to imply an attitude to the problems of comparative religion that I do not myself hold.'[43]

The correction was allowed, Verrier signing the undertaking on 4th October and being issued a passport soon after. But he took it that he was not bound by the undertaking while still in England and worked hard in the days that remained. He first spoke on 'The Religious Philosophy of Mahatma Gandhi' at a crowded meeting at SCM House, applauded by most but heckled by 'some Leninist Negroes, a pietistic Swede, and two Communist Indians.' He repeated the lecture at Friends House, attacked this time by a drunken ex-deputy commissioner from the Central Provinces. While he could, Verrier advanced the Congress case in public and in private. He had tea with the Archbishop of York and urged on him the need for the church to play its part in bringing Indians and Englishmen together. He dined with the News Editor of Reuters and asked for proper and balanced coverage of Indian events. The man replied: 'We estimate things solely by their news-value. Mr Gandhi always has news-value. In USA, however, his news-value has declined since he came to London and parleyed with the British Government.'

Verrier also had a twenty-minute meeting with Lord Irwin in his mansion in Eaton Square, with Irwin's 'opulent-looking' dachschund in attendance. The former Viceroy told Verrier that 'the Government of India has the lowest possible opinion of you.' He also refused to criticize his successor, Lord Willingdon, who had made clear his desire to scotch Gandhi and direct action 'once and for all.'[44]

Back in New Delhi the Government of India was having third thoughts. The Bombay government, which had suffered most at Verrier's hands, passed on two letters it had intercepted: written to friends in the Sabarmati Ashram, and whose contents left one in no doubt of his continuing support for civil disobedience. It also forwarded a copy of *Truth about India*, seized by the Customs, as 'further evidence of the pro-Congress and subversive activities indulged in by this individual.' M. G. Hallett, once more in the hot spot, agreed that the book be banned in India, but felt that the man himself could be allowed back in. In his judgement Elwin seemed 'quite prepared to devote himself to the Gonds.' But his boss, the home member, definitely disagreed, noting that 'if at a moment when Father Elwin is profuse with his promises to us of good behaviour he is actively engaged in the Congress movement in England, I take leave to doubt his sincerity and at any rate his consistency.'

The home member prevailed; on 11th October 1932 the Government of India wired London expressing its 'serious misgivings about [Elwin's] good faith,' and requesting that the undertaking not be offered him. The secretary of state had to wire back saying it was unfortunately 'too late.' For the priest had claimed his passport, and booked his return journey aboard the *S. S. Victoria*.[45]

If a file had been put up earlier, or a few telegrams sent more promptly, Elwin might never have returned to India. It is a little disconcerting to discover that this is something he does not ever seem to have known.

CHAPTER FIVE

An Ashram of One's Own

To you this little village is dear as the moon,
And from the great city you have dragged me away
Here if you want paper you must tear up your clothes,
For ink you must use the kazal from your eyes,
Yet to you this little village is dear as the moon.

Gond folk song

Our company of workers [in the ashram] is now really representative. There are Christians, Hindus, a Brahmin, a Mussalman, Gonds; polygamists, henogamists, monogamists, celibates; polytheists, henotheists, monotheists, theists, animists, pantheists, monists; vegetarians, egg-eaters, rat-eaters, beef-eaters and those to whom even the dung of the cow is sacred; bacon-eaters and those to whom even the smell of the pig is anathema, all united. How nice it is!

Verrier Elwin, diary entry of 20 October 1934

'Father Elwin back in India' screamed a front page story in the *Bombay Chronicle* on the 4th of November 1932. The newspaper's reporter, down to meet Elwin by the quayside, found him carrying a stuffed mongoose and a statue of St Francis, his political beliefs firmly intact. Pressed for a statement on Civil Disobedience, Elwin would only say that Mahatma Gandhi's fast of September, in protest against communal electorates, had 'made a very deep impression on the minds of the English people.' Then he quickly added: 'I am not at liberty to make a statement regarding political matters.'[1] He had said enough; the journalist departed, reassured that the priest's heart still lay with the Congress. Others hoped his pen would be freed to push the nationalist case once more. Welcoming Verrier back, his friend Jamnalal Bajaj wrote: 'No one can doubt your great love for the cause which you have had to abjure—for a short while let us hope.'[2]

This was Verrier's hope too. Forbidden by the terms of his undertaking to follow the Mahatma in politics, he could yet follow him in the principles by which he ran his ashram. Two months after his return, with the buildings in place and a Montessori school opened for ten Gond children, Verrier wrote to his mentor that he and Shamrao felt 'entirely one with Sabarmati and Wardha [Gandhi's two ashrams] though a thousand miles behind.'[3]

This statement was put immediately to the test when, the next week, the Ashram of St Francis had its first visitor, Mary Gillet of the Christa Seva Sangh. A teacher trained in Roehampton, Mary was 'very keen on everything Indian, particularly the freedom struggle.' Through Verrier, whom she first met in England in 1929, she came out to Poona to join the CSS. A socialist of strong convictions, Mary thought the concern of most Christians with the personal application of religion 'has been responsible for the gradual but ever-quickening landslide of Western civilization towards catastrophe.' She wished in India to reaffirm and reinvigorate the social side of the Gospel, taking the side of subject nations against empires and slaves against masters. Soon after coming to Poona she started a play centre for low-caste children, inspired by Gandhi's movement against untouchability. 'Young, modern and brash,' she was apt to do things that others in the CSS disapproved of, such as riding a bicycle in a saree, her dress and brown hair flying in the wind.[4]

When Verrier and Shamrao left the CSS towards the end of 1931, Mary was much troubled. After they departed the Englishmen in charge of the Poona ashram turned it into a monastic order run on rather strict lines. Mary now faced the future with 'some trepidation.' She wasn't sure if 'what I ought to do is the same thing as what I want so much to do,' which was to join Verrier. Visiting Karanjia in January 1933 Mary found at once that

> This ashram of all places I have stayed in most nearly comes up to the Franciscan ideal. The whole countryside is rather like Italy—hills and valleys and blue skies and peasants singing. The ashram stands on the top of a little hill and the village is below. In the morning it is a great delight to sit for

> prayers on the hill-top, the sky growing bright with sunrise as the moon goes down and the Southern Cross standing over the hills in front of us.
>
> The chapel is the tiniest imaginable. It is full when four of us are in but I love its smallness and its mud walls. To be in it is to be part of the lovely earth all round. What I like very much about the ashram is that the villagers and anybody just walk in when they like as though it belongs to them—as it does, of course. The wild beast brothers, though rather less welcome, are not less familiar with the place.[5]

The evocation left unsaid the ashram's main attraction: its founder. Mary was in love, but Verrier, at least in the beginning, resisted. She wanted to defy all convention and join them, a lone Englishwoman living with men in the depths of the forest: she wished, as the *CSS Review* not so delicately put it, 'to give her many talents and gifts to Father Elwin and the Gonds.' But Verrier had been warned that admitting women members would take from them the 'heroic note.' She was persistent, perhaps remarkably so, for subsequent developments were swift. On the 25th of January, two weeks after she had arrived on a visit, Mary joined the ashram as 'Brother Mary,' to live with Shamrao and Verrier much as 'Mirabehn lives with Bapu and his brothers'—that is, in the purest platonic friendship.[6] Another fortnight and Verrier and Mary had written to friends that they would be married after Easter in their mud chapel of St Francis, this to be followed by a honeymoon tour by bullock cart through the jungle villages of the district. The marriage would unite them

> in love of Christ and of India, of ashram life and St Francis, of the life of poverty and of the poor. Our marriage therefore will mean little change in our way of life. We want to give our lives to India, to her poor and for her freedom. We shall continue to live as Tertiaries in the ashram, for we have always visualized the possibility of having here married as well as unmarried members. This is a quite normal thing in Indian ashrams.[7]

The last sentence was disingenuous. With the letter was enclosed a photograph of Mary sitting on a string-bed under a mango tree in the courtyard of the ashram. She is wearing a white cotton saree, a mode of dress to which she seems quite accustomed, and has a spinning wheel in front of her. Her head is turned towards Verrier's camera, showing her wavy hair and strong features: a woman of character, of pleasant if not striking appearance. Without question, Verrier and Mary were brought together by more than a devotion to Christ and the poor. They were much attracted to each other, determined to live a married life that was in fact not quite the normal thing in Indian ashrams, where even husband and wife were expected to live together in the purest chastity, in the state of *brahmacharya.*

The first person to react adversely was Shamrao. He thought he would lose his friend, but Verrier assured him he would always 'be the little brother of us and my own companion and dearest friend.' Shamrao soon got over his jealousy, but the couple knew that the opposition outside was likely to be more fierce. As Mary remarked, their decision would make 'a number of people whom I love, very disappointed and unhappy for a time.' 'Will the enclosed news [announcing the marriage] be too great a disappointment to you,' wrote Verrier to the Italian sisters: 'You will stand by us? We shall have much criticism and we shall lose many supporters. We are facing a future of real poverty but we have both wanted that always . . . But I am not sorry for what I am doing! I have found a friend who is the perfect companion in this lovely and difficult task.'[8]

A letter that passed through many drafts was posted to the final court of appeal in Sabarmati. Here Verrier anticipated Gandhi's objections by claiming that Mary and he, though chaste thus far, had not actually taken a pledge of celibacy. We have 'carefully considered our position,' he wrote, 'India is our home: our marriage will be the marriage of two poor people; our children would be the children of poor people.' Then he continued:

> You will be disappointed that we do not feel able at the moment to practice celibacy after marriage. I think I can truly say that the reason for this is not animal passion, but the fact that we have not sufficient intellectual conviction of its immediate necessity or of its wisdom in our own case to enable us to carry it out. I had hoped to be an ascetic, but you yourself have warned me that I must recognise my physical limitations.[9]

Gandhi might in fact have more easily understood a yielding to animal passion, but not, in one of his followers, a disagreement on the principle of brahmacharya. In his credo the conquest of desire was on par with the abolition of untouchability and the promotion of spinning. His own struggles in this respect, as recounted in *The Story of My Experiments with Truth,* had been long and arduous; in his ashram he was continually challenging himself and his followers to lead lives of exemplary purity in thought and action, mind and body. Husband and wife lived together as brother and sister, and sexual 'irregularities' were treated with the utmost severity. This attitude could be carried to excess. Verrier was once staying with some Gandhians in a house by the sea in Bombay, when Mirabehn shut the windows as soon as lunch was served. He protested, for it was a hot day, but Mira said severely: 'No, Verrier, the sea breeze will bring in particles of salt with it. This will fall on the food and make it more difficult for you to control your passions.'[10]

Gandhi's reply to Verrier's letter conveyed an unmistakable sense of being let down. He was not so much disappointed as saddened by their decision. He wrote: 'If you have humbly to acknowledge defeat [in leading the ascetic life] you should do so. Your defeat will be victory for the God of Truth. There is no waste in God's laboratory.'[11]

Gandhi's hand was strengthened when Ala Pocha, the young doctor in his ashram, told him, 'tears dropping from her eyes,' that some time ago Verrier had promised to marry *her*. 'How can I bear this?' wept Ala, 'It was agreed between us that we were both to remain single, or if we could not, we were to marry each other.' Gandhi asked Verrier to clarify what understanding there was between them. If 'your word was never given to Ala as she imagines it was, you and Mary have my blessings.' But 'if there is the slightest possibility of a breach (moral) of word given to Ala, you must both—you and Mary—be prepared to bear what will be the heaviest cross and sacrifice your cherished hope on the altar of Truth which is God. If there is a trace of suspicion of breach, you certainly and Mary and Ala—the latter two if they have the same living faith in Truth as I have credited you with—have to live single lives in spite of yourself.'[12]

Faced with Gandhi's disapproval, Verrier's intellectual conviction collapsed. He confessed to the previous romance with Ala but denied any promise of marriage. In Matheran, back in January 1931, they had 'made love for a few days . . . There was, of course, no carnal intercourse, but we embraced very affectionately. This was wholly wrong, but we were carried away. I have confessed it, and deeply repented. But at that very time it was made absolutely clear between us that there was never to be any thought of marriage, nor any tie or bond whatever between us.' He had seen Ala since, but their later friendship had been—at least on his side—wholly 'free of sex-attraction.' In any case, how could the Mahatma take seriously Ala's claim on him when 'twice in the last year it has been common talk that she herself was going to marry [someone else]?' Nonetheless Verrier expressed his 'sorrow and penitence for any wrong I have done. As you know, I think of my life here as nothing save an offering of penance, and I pray God to accept it.'

On Gandhi's advice this exchange was not shown to Mary. But the marriage itself was abandoned; it seemed the only way the disciple, called to account for a previous lapse, could make up with the master. They had a 'month of the purest happiness' in expectation of the union, wrote Verrier to Gandhi bitterly, but now realized 'to follow this course would be for us a descent from the highest ideal; it would make very difficult the practice of poverty; while it would undoubtedly mean better health for me, the coming of children might cut short our service in India; and it would tend to concentrate our love on one another instead of releasing it for the world. St Francis' message of poverty and your ideal of brahmacharya have made war on our dream of married life and conquered it.'[13]

Verrier consoled himself that he would now 'come closer to Bapu,' but this had been a rebellion thwarted only by the authority of a father figure. He had yielded, but not before a struggle, in the end preferring 'renunciation in all its bareness' to the 'sweetest dreams of marriage.'[14] Mary was not so easily reconciled. 'The pain in leaving the Christa Seva Sangh,' she wrote to a friend, 'has been nothing at all to this—and I have no doubt there are still more perilous mountains ahead.'[15] Gandhi for his part was mightily relieved. 'I was prepared to bless the marriage,' he told C. F. Andrews, 'but I cannot help saying that I blessed the change even more.'[16] In his eyes Verrier and Mary had now forsaken the transience of 'exclusive' marriage for the universal marriage with Truth. Gandhi sensed that Mary was less willing to accept the decision to call it all off. She must recognize, he wrote to Verrier, 'that before God there is no sex or we are all women—His brides married to him in an indissoluble tie. If she has realized the beauty of the immortal marriage, she must dance with joy that she is free from the bondage of the human marriage. The human marriage is good and necessary if the flesh is weak, but if the flesh is strong, it surely is a hindrance for the servant of humanity that Mary has become.'[17]

Verrier and Mary now reverted to living as brother and sister, but Gandhi, nervous that temptation would once again cross their path, advised them 'to separate for the time being and test yourself. [For] if you have shed exclusive love together you should feel happy as well in association as in separation.' He thought Mary should come to one of his ashrams to work among the untouchables, but she seems to have wished only to put distance between herself and the Mahatma. Asked to leave Verrier, she decided to go back to Europe, to visit the Eremo Franciscano in Umbria and then look for work in Austria, where she had friends.

In July, a brief six months after she had arrived (in her mind, at any rate, to stay forever), Mary left Karanjia. She proceeded with Shamrao to Bombay and her ship, having 'come down from the beloved mountains to very drab plains and a lonely road.'[18] Verrier meanwhile made his way to Poona to see Gandhi. The Mahatma had made the old Peshwa city his temporary headquarters; indeed, not long after settling Verrier's matrimonial affairs he began a fast against untouchability in the home of a prosperous Poona industrialist. The fast was over, but when Verrier saw its venue he was appalled. 'Gandhi fasting to death in a marble palace,' he told the Bombay journalist Frank Moraes, 'is like Jesus Christ going to crucifixion in a Rolls-Royce.'[19] As it happened he saw the palace only from the outside, for Gandhi's hostess, a Lady Thackersey, flatly refused to allow a Christian to stay in the house. Verrier made his way to the Servants of India Society, where untouchables like himself were always welcome. Here he ran into the poetess Sarojini Naidu. She told him that low-caste Hindus were not welcome in the marble palace either. 'Even for us,' said Mrs Naidu, 'the hostess is going to smash all the crockery we used and to have special ceremonies of purification after we have gone.'[20]

'I will remain loyal to Bapu to the end of my days,' remarked Verrier of this incident, 'but some of his followers make loyalty very difficult.' The protestation lacked conviction, and in fact Verrier found in Poona a more general disenchantment with Gandhi's leadership. When the new viceroy, Lord Willingdon, refused to meet him, Gandhi began preparations for another round of struggle. His colleagues looked upon the prospect of another term in jail with dread. They knew it to be a 'most stupid and futile business, a sheer waste of man power,' but were so dominated by the Mahatma that they could not but follow his lead. There was an air of sullen resentment all around, Verrier noting that 'the only really happy people were Devadas and his lovely bride Lakshmi, who were bubbling over with joy and quite determined not to go to prison.'[21]

Devadas was Gandhi's youngest son, whose recent marriage had not been subjected to brahmacharya. Verrier does not comment on the apparent hypocrisy—one rule for the adopted son, quite another for the real one—for it seems he had by now prepared himself to resume the ascetic life. From Poona he went to Bombay, said good-bye to Mary, and promptly fell ill with malaria. Then Gandhi sent a message asking him to come to his ashram; he wished to 'make up for the Poona episode.' Verrier dragged himself out of bed and took the night train to Ahmedabad with Shamrao. The Mahatma was 'wonderfully charming:' he had them stay in his cottage and gave them the bed next to his at night. But he took little interest in their ashram, making it clear that he would like Verrier to go back on his undertaking and return to England and promote the Congress cause there. Verrier was disappointed, but in this Gandhi was 'one with all the Congressmen I have met recently—they all think [my ashram] is a waste of time, and that it would be better for me to go about making speeches on their behalf.'[22]

From Ahmedabad Verrier returned to the K. E. M. hospital in Bombay. A relapse of malaria was followed by jaundice, on top of which he was visited daily by police officials checking on what he was reading, whom he was seeing. Weak and depressed, on a diet of milk, juice and glucose alongside two enemas and three doses of castor oil a day, he received a letter from his friends in Umbria asking whether they should admit Mary as a nun. Verrier's answer betrayed the terrific strain he had been under the past few months. Mary was 'too independent,' he wrote angrily,

> too much attached to 'causes' and 'movements,' to believe that the offering of the soul in its entirety to God is more important than anything else in the world.
>
> I think she should go back to her educational work, fight for the causes dear to her, and (I hope) get married. She should finally put out of her mind any idea that she has a vocation to a life in 'religion.' She has tested that vocation in three different places, and it is probable that she has not got it, although she loves Poverty and the poor. She loves Poverty but not obedience.[23]

In November 1933, his health restored, Verrier returned to Karanjia. There had been a slight emendation to their Rule, the addition of a clause enjoining members to 'curb animal passion,' to practice 'purity in personal life.'[24] Recent experience and the wishes of Gandhi thus taken into account, Verrier and Shamrao turned their attention to the programme of the Gond Seva Mandal.

The Ashram of St Francis now consisted of a chapel, a guest house, a dispensary, a retreat room for prayer, and a home for children. Shamrao and Verrier each had their little cell. The chapel, decorated with a painting by an Indian artist, had in front of it the saffron flag of renunciation and the sacred *tulsi* tree. Not that anyone except the founders prayed there, for the Gond Seva Mandal was resolutely opposed to proselytization. His refusal to take the Gospel to the Gonds brought Verrier a reprimand from C. F. Andrews. He should not idealize the tribals and their faiths, wrote Andrews on 12th November, 'as I tended to over-idealize Hinduism at one time.' 'Life in this primitive form,' he continued, 'often becomes a ghastly terror impossible to describe. It would be difficult to overestimate the freedom from these primitive terrors wherewith Christ has set us free . . . I am writing this because I myself have gone to the utmost limits of toleration, bordering on weakness, and I can see the same danger in your case.'[25]

The Bishop of Nagpur had chastised him likewise, but though Verrier vastly respected Andrews he would not budge. An essay published shortly afterwards confirmed that members of the Gond Seva Mandal would be encouraged, Gandhi-style, to deepen their faith by respecting the faith of others. 'In India today,' wrote Verrier, 'every religion can best express itself, not by a mad rush for converts or by erecting walls of self-defense against its rivals, but by the humble spirit of service . . . and through loving co-operation with others.'[26]

From Karanjia Verrier and Shamrao hoped to reach outwards, constructing a series of little branch ashrams in the Gond country. Verrier chose the sites for their beauty: the first at Bondar, on the banks of the river Kanwa, red cliffs on one side, on the other forest climbing up the hills; a second near the village of Harra Tola where the Narmada curved round, enclosing a hill in its embrace before descending to a waterfall; a third at Birbaspur, looking down on the fields of yellow mustard and an expanse of forest and meadow beyond.

The children in their schools were mostly Gond, the teachers moderately educated Hindus or Muslims. The curriculum was based on the Montessori method but flavoured with Indian nationalism. Students were taught the laws of health, simple science based on Jawaharlal Nehru's letters to his daughter from jail, and the teachings of Gandhi. Wearing clothes of khadi provided by the Mandal, the children sang songs composed by Rabindranath Tagore and the medieval Bhakti poets. No rewards or punishments were permitted, the 'ideal of all the teaching [being] the liberation of spirit through self-expression.'[27]

Medical relief, the other main plank of their work, was the province of Shamrao. To his dispensary in Karanjia flocked villagers from a thirty-mile radius, to be treated for gonorrhea, syphilis, leprosy, and an assortment of bites and bruises. A wonderful natural doctor, Shamrao quickly inspired trust among the tribals. When cholera broke out in the village the Gonds were convinced it was the work of witches. Shamrao went and got a stock of vaccines from Dindori town, inoculated the village, and the epidemic disappeared.

Shamrao also helped heal wounds other than the purely physical. In Karanjia he functioned as an unofficial arbiter of disputes, conflicts over land and over women. He sometimes had over fifty cases a month where his decisions, though unsupported by law, were respected. To Verrier, troubled by loneliness and ill health, Shamrao was 'the perfect friend in loyalty, steadfastness, and never failing humour and happiness.'[28]

But Verrier was the ideologue: his mission defined by one British newspaper as the wish 'to teach a primitive people the best things about our civilization,' by a second in the pithy headline, 'BISHOP'S SON ERECTS TEMPLE TO GANDHI IN HEART OF INDIA.'[29] Verrier might have put it less dramatically, but these assessments were on balance correct. A Puritan and Improver, at first he found little to commend in tribal values. The 'Gonds are so unenterprising,' he complained: 'They could easily better their condition by having gardens, but they don't bother.' The 'nomad habits of the aboriginal' made house planning very difficult. He hoped for the formation of a 'sort of Villagers' Association of all those who send their children to school, and are ready to pledge themselves to be temperate in drink, fervent for vaccination, zealous for manure-pits and sanitation, shunning the futility of "Expensive" weddings, jewellry and so on.'[30]

In November 1934 Verrier and Sham were visited by A. V. Thakkar, whose own work among the Bhils had been their early inspiration. Thakkar was shown around the schools and hospitals and later issued a sterling testimonial through the pages of Mahatma Gandhi's weekly, *Harijan*:

> Father Elwin, though a Christian in the truest sense of the term, is not out for proselytization. He does not convert Gonds, but merely serves them. He has no other aim than that of pure unadulterated service from a humanitarian point of view. For this type of service, he is neither thanked by Christians nor by Hindus. The former dislike him for the departure from the orthodox way of work, and the latter distrust him as they cannot imagine any Christian tabooing conversion . . .[31]

For this type of disinterested service Verrier was not thanked by the Christian and the Hindu; nor it seems by the Gond, to whom his Agenda of Improvement—abstinence, hard work, and so forth—did not appeal. When Verrier ordered a bundle of posters on the virtues of Thrift, Vaccination, Stud Bulls, etc., the Gonds could not be bothered to put them up. The chasm between the improving social worker and the conservative tribal was always conducive to disagreement. When the Mandal started sewing classes in their school, the girls were hurriedly withdrawn for their parents thought 'that by stitching they would sew up their wombs and have difficulty at their first deliveries.' A railway station-master, a fervent Hindu, toured the villages proclaiming that the Englishman was here 'not for their sake, but for his Empire.' When they planned to take the children to a picnic to the highest hill in the district, one landlord went round warning parents against this 'Christian innovation.' Their opponents derisively labelled Karanjia 'Isaitola,' the hamlet of Jesus.[32]

The police officials of the district were also most energetic in their opposition. Verrier and Sham were visited every other week by the sub-inspector, who would snoop around the house and demand they reveal their stock of revolutionary pamphlets. When none were forthcoming he would casually help himself, as Indian policemen are wont to do, to flowers and vegetables in the garden. Verrier irritatedly thought the police were working off their suppressed nationalist venom on him, a solitary and defenceless Englishman. More likely they knew of his pro-Congress sympathies and hoped that by harassing him they would please their superiors. On one occasion Shamrao was assaulted and beaten up by a policeman, unprovoked, in the bazaar. This incident at least rallied the Gonds around them for they had to be restrained from storming the police station.[33]

In *Leaves from the Jungle*—Verrier's record of life at Karanjia—irritation at Gond indifference to their work alternates with a more sympathetic understanding of the tribal way of life. Why would the Gond take to spinning, he asks, when no cotton is grown anywhere in his country? And why should the aboriginal practice temperance when his jungles were rich in *mahua*, the tree from which he distilled a most potent and liberating spirit? Asked his definition of Hell, one Gond replied; 'Miles and miles of forest without any mahua trees.' Another wished to be buried under the tree so that even in death he might 'suck some pleasure from its roots.' And why should Shamrao and he wear saffron and pray four times a day when the Gonds believed they were doing this only to bribe God into making them rich?

Handspinning, austerity and abstinence thus knocked out, that left only celibacy in the Gandhian credo. But this the Gonds didn't much prize either. Their view, as expressed time and again in their songs, was that 'You may eat, you may drink, but life without a wife is wasted.' Gond girls practised the art of coquetry to perfection; unlike the protected and prissy Hindu they openly encouraged their admirers in the field and forest. As for the men, nothing worried them more than impotence: they were dismayed when Sham's dispensary had no remedies for *that* ailment. Premarital liaisons were frequent, adultery even more so. Verrier counted nineteen elopements in one year in their village alone. Gond divorce was 'so wonderfully simple a ceremony' that it could with profit be adopted in Hollywood. The two parties appeared before their elders, broke a pot and then a piece of straw in half, and were freed of one another.[34]

Verrier had not come to Mandla to convert the tribes, but it was not long before they had converted him. Encouraged by the Gonds he began shedding his puritan persona piece by piece. In the monsoon of 1933, sick once again with malaria, he confessed to his diary a passion for beer which a 'possibly mistaken' adherence to Gandhian principles had prevented them from stocking. But it could not have been long before he was joining the Gonds in drinking, at marriages and festivals, their rather more intoxicating brews. When the villagers would not take to the spinning wheel Verrier stopped spinning too, though Gandhi wrote at regular intervals urging him to. The Mahatma reminded him that spinning was a form of *tapasya*, or asectic discipline: Verrier answered that it still wasn't the thing for the Gonds, but he and they could try a spell of rice-pounding instead. Then in September 1934 he went so far as to pull out his English clothes in preparation for a trip to Bombay. In Karanjia he wore the shirt and dhoti to be nearer the poor but saw little point in wearing a loincloth in the city. 'Ever since I saw the amazing company of crank disciples of the Mahatma gathered at Sabarmati last year with dhotis exposing more than they ought to and saris flopping about on white bodies I have been shy of wearing Indian dress.' In any case appearances were irrelevant, for 'it is the heart and not the clothes that Indians look at.'[35] He was also having second thoughts about celibacy, these sparked by a reading on the Calcutta Mail of *Virgin and the Gypsy*, D. H. Lawrence's suggestive tale of the seduction by a nomad of the daughter of a country vicar. Brahmacharya he now saw as the hypocritical and hopeless attempt to suppress human desires. When Winslow wrote telling him of a new order of celibates in the CSS, he commented sarcactically on

> The Degrees of Holy Chastity
> Loose Chastity
> Temporary Chastity
> The White Knight Chastity
> Virginal Chastity
>
> and so on. And of course Guided Chastity, which means being chaste till you're guided not to.[36]

Verrier was put off by Gandhism but found little solace in Christianity. The church continued to shun him, the Bishop of Nasik even forbidding his priests from visting the ashram. On a visit to Poona he sensed that members of the National Christian Council treated him 'like a Bishop's wife greeting a curate whom she suspects of having advanced views on Genesis'—which, in a kind of way, he had. After his mother complained that he was not seeing enough of his 'own people' he replied testily: 'I see as many as are willing to see me.' The Eremo Franciscano run by their friends in Umbria was, he remarked, the one little tributary of the great

Christian river from which Shamrao and he were allowed to drink. 'All other streams and rivers seem to have notices—verboten—written up above them.' Sham and he sometimes felt 'as if the whole world were against us.' In any case he found little to admire in a church that after all these years resolutely kept its distance from Indians, emerging from time to time from bungalows to initiate misdirected schemes of 'village uplift.' When his sister Eldyth contemplated coming out to a mission in the Nilgiris he told her to stay at home, for in India she 'would be forced to live the kind of existence against which my whole life is a protest.'[37]

The protest had already gone public in a review of a book by his schoolfellow Stephen Neill, now a rising missionary in southern India. This book, on the mission of the Indian church, was written 'in the awkward and borrowed phraseology of another age;' Neill was 'still preaching in a black gown.' Elwin singled out the phrases that most disturbed him, his italics marking the distance between him and even the most enlightened of Christian missions. 'We do not expect,' he remarked

> an ex-Fellow of Trinity, Cambridge, and a former leader of the Student Christian Movement, which is supposed to teach its members better things, to refer to the non-Christian in India as a *heathen*, or to fill his pages with such trite missionary cliches as 'work in *virgin soil* usually has to be carried on for a generation *without harvest*, 'On an average a convert is baptised *every five minutes throughout the year*, 'Every city staked out in the name of Christ, '*the front line of advance*,' 'Women have in the Civil Disobedience Movement undergone imprisonment *for what they believe to be the cause of their country*, 'The spread of the Good News.' While of village children he can write, 'These unkempt, shy creatures must be *caught* and *tamed*.'[38]

A 'Christian for the Congress' is how Verrier might have described himself when he first arrived in Karanjia. That label would not now stick on either side: indeed, Verrier was to report with malice and with glee a Gond boy's description of Gandhi (from a photograph) as a 'grumpy old bear with the ears of an elephant,' as well as an abusive exchange in the village in which, after cursing the opponent's mother and sister and casting doubts on his morals and intelligence, 'you cap it all by calling him a Christian.'[39]

In January 1936 Verrier penned a circular letter that captured his double disappointment in more serious terms. On a visit to Wardha the previous November he had found the Mahatma 'bored into a breakdown by his disciples. Some of the most tiresome of these are his Western followers, from whom he ought to be protected by law. Why one of the most acute minds in the country should be wasted settling the matrimonial difficulties of Western adventuresses is a mystery.'

The disgust here is with the mileu as much as the man; Verrier was not a 'crank disciple,' perhaps by now no kind of disciple at all. Gandhi would not be allowed any more to settle *his* matrimonial difficulties. The letter then turned to his troubled relations with the Church of England, of how and why he had at last been compelled 'by the irresistible logic of circumstances' to leave it altogether. He could not forget the 'extraordinary blessedness and happiness' of his early years as a priest, but now the distance between him and the church establishment was too great. One bishop (of Nagpur) said they were doing the work of the devil; a second bishop (of Bombay) called their outlook 'satanic' simply because he lived with poor Indians and had begun to see the world through their eyes. And Indians saw the Church, Protestant, Catholic or Orthodox, as being inescapably tied to racial domination: 'they look at us and remember King Leopold and the Congo, Mussolini in Abysinnia, General Dyer at Amritsar, the Allied Armies in China, the lynching of negroes in America:' acts and actors ignored or even supported by the Church. What right, asked this recreant priest, 'What right have we to preach to this profound, pacific India, while the guns thunder at our back and there lurk in the memory of our hearers a hundred cruelties and oppressions?' He thought the Church should dissociate itself from riches and power, and

> do penance for a hundred years. If we did, before two-thirds of that time were passed, India would be at the feet of Christ. If every Christian in India, led by the Bishops, were to throw off their privileges, forsake their wealth, give up chasing after the educated and well-to-do, in deep humility seek forgiveness and cleansing for themselves instead of preaching to others, and to go to the poorest of the poor, the most forsaken of the outcastes, to tend them and love them and protect them in the love of Christ, not trying to missionize them . . . but simply to wash their feet with the tears of their penitence and anoint them with the spikenard of their love, then they would have done, not any great thing, but their plain duty.

Verrier had come to India and in time to Karanjia to make reparation, but the thought animated few other priests. Unlicensed since 1932, he reckoned it would no longer be honest to remain within the Church at all. On 2nd November 1935 he wrote to the Metropolitan in Calcutta 'formally to announce to you my decision to be no longer a member of the Church of England either as a priest or as a communicant.'[40]

Verrier Elwin walked out of his church without much more than a backward glance, but without his knowing it his letter of resignation caused a great stir in England. High church figures, remembering the expectation with which they had dispatched Verrier and his colleagues back in 1927, wrote asking the Metropolitan to try and bring him back into the fold. One such was William Temple, Archbishop of York, who admired Verrier and had written forewords to his books. Bishop Wood of Nagpur, asked to reply to Temple, sent a long account of his relations with the dissident priest. While he was 'strongly attracted to Elwin and admired his splendid gifts, both literary and devotional,' it was clear that 'his attitude to the Faith was one with which I could not compromise.' The Metropolitan also heard from Bishop William Carey in Eastbourne, who had news that Verrier was very ill and might die soon. Carey was told by several of his friends, including W. E. S. Holland, that Elwin was the 'greatest saint' they had met. Before he died was it not possible 'that someone with love and authority should induce him to resume his priesthood?' He appealed to the Metropolitan in the name of Christ to approach Elwin, in his view fit to rank with the greatest of men thrown out by the Church. 'If he dies,' ended Carey poignantly, 'I shall feel almost an agony of shame that the C of E couldn't keep Wesley, Newman, Elwin.'[41]

Mrs Elwin knew her son would not die yet, but she was no less upset by his decision. With a mother's love and a believer's blindness, she too held the bishops responsible. 'Had my son compromised in the usual fashion of being all things to all men in this age of compromise,' she wrote angrily to the Metropolitan, 'he would now be a most popular preacher receiving a large salary and living in great comfort.' Instead he had followed Christ as he understood him, living in poverty 'among the neglected and suffering Gonds a life of complete devotion—ministering with his own hands to his leprous and repulsively sick folk such as possibly His Lordship of Bombay has never ever seen.' She appended, as a despairing postscript, a letter written her by an Indian which said 'it is men like your son, straight and sincere, the very embodiment of selfless love and truth that bring us to love and revere Jesus Christ . . . we feel more than ever religion has to be *lived* and not merely preached . . . etc. etc.' The letter was a sample of many but, asked this widow of a bishop, 'Is it such men for which the Diocese of Bombay have no use? Or Nagpur?'[42]

Mrs Elwin had got hold of the wrong end of the stick. She believed the Church had no use for Verrier. In fact it was Verrier who had no use for the Church.

Many years later Elwin claimed that the act of leaving the Church brought him 'a hitherto undreamt of intellectual freedom; it adjusted many complexes and inhibitions; it was a kind of conversion in reverse, integrating me and filling me with new life.'[43] The freedoms it brought him were as much sexual as intellectual. Verrier had once written of the celibate vocation that it was 'the offering to God of the most precious thing a man possesses for a special end. The celibate finds his sole joy in Christ: he is free from every tie in order that he might devote himself to the august and urgent needs of his Kingdom.'[44] For this Christian mystic Christ himself had been the lover: all his suppressed passion had been focused on him. In the past when temptation crossed his path—Mary, Ala, the unidentified woman-soul—he submerged himself anew in Christ. But when his faith finally collapsed, sex was the natural corollary.

Information on Verrier's sexual efflorescence, *c.* 1935–6, is meagre, and derives from notes made by an English friend and from the investigations of an Indian official who worked in Mandla in the nineteen sixties.[45] Both are agreed that it was as much an embracing of the tribal ethos as a rejection of Gandhi or St. Francis; a seduction of the virgin priest by Gond gypsies. The Indian investigator framed it in the apologetic if mildly censorious tones of the Hindu middle class. Verrier and Shamrao, he explained, 'did not create [in Mandla] any sort of a licentious society.' For 'a licentious society was already there and these gentlemen unable to raise an iron curtain around themselves were to some extent caught up in the same.'

Verrier put it differently. For the Gonds sex was a 'gesture between friends—neither was over-involved, neither completely in love.' It was most often a basis for liking rather than love. Relationships began in the most casual way. In one early encounter Shamrao met two Gond girls in the market who insisted on coming home with him. The tribal women came to Verrier and Sham not because of money, which they never took, but because they liked them. Monogamy, serial or otherwise, was not necessarily a virtue. Shamrao recalled this laconically: 'women used to change husbands as we change socks and forget about it.'

Verrier's first grand passion was Singharo, a Gond from the village of Sarwachappar. An English visitor described Singharo as having a 'long face, rather coarse features and a sweet expression.' She makes a fleeting appearance in *Leaves from the Jungle*, in a celebration of the Phag festival of May 1935, when she made a beeline for Verrier to douse him in coloured water.[46] Singharo soon went off to the Assam tea gardens, had affairs with the clerks there, and returned with syphilis. Verrier later regretted not marrying her but at the time he did not think himself prepared for it.

Verrier's sexual adventures were known and acknowledged by the Gonds, perhaps even encouraged by them. But they were kept hidden from the outside world: from his family in England, from the friends and patrons of the Gond Seva Mandal, and from Gandhi in his sexless ashram at Wardha. When Shamrao mischievously suggested that he should go to the Mahatma and make a confession in the interests of Truth, Verrier answered: 'How can I go and tell *him* about my girls?'

Some people might wish to change or uplift the tribals; the point, however, was to know them. Verrier's understanding was initiated by Panda Baba, a Gond magician who was both his native informant and his first truly tribal friend. He lived in Bondar, a village two miles from Karanjia, in a house adorned with the symbols of his calling: horse-hair and pointed rods, marigolds and peacock feathers. He was first recruited to teach Verrier and Sham the local dialect, Chattisgarhi. Soon they were accompanying him on his professional calls: to perform the *Bida* ceremony before sowing crops, to sacrifice a chicken and thus cast the evil spirit of disease out of the village. The magician had a phenomenal knowledge of Gond myths. On easy terms with the local ghosts, he alone among the villagers was not 'afraid of the demi-Atlas of our little world, the Sub-Inspector of Police.'[47]

In the first week of February 1934 Panda Baba took Verrier on a field trip to a remote part of the district, the forests of the Baiga tribe. They made their way leisurely, by bullock cart: day after day, wrote the traveller,

> we plunged deeper into the vast loneliness: at first we were in the living forest—there were birds, we could hear the chatter of a monkey teasing a tiger, we could meet people on the road. But later we reached the forests of Baiga Land where hardly a bird rustles the leaves in that uncanny silence and where you may go ten miles without meeting a soul. How thrilling the forest is, with its endless trees which now close in upon you and now open wide to a bare burnt glade, the trees sometimes tall as the mast of some high Ammiral, sometimes short with all their leaves withered by the frost.

The Baigas, when they got to them, were scarcely less thrilling. The men, covered in little less than a loincloth, were strikingly handsome, with slim, shapely bodies and magnificent wavy hair; the women stouter and less attractive, but with their hands and legs tattooed in intricate patterns. Encouraged by Panda Baba the Baiga put on a show of their dances and then, sitting around a fire under a cold moon, related a sad tale of decline in what was for them the darkest of ages, a Kaliyug. For the Baiga were once kings of the forest, free to hunt and fish, and to practice *bewar*, their characteristic form of swidden cultivation. But the forest department had confiscated their bows and arrows and forced them to take to settled agriculture. Their revered ancestor Nanga Baiga had instructed them never to lacerate the breasts of Mother Earth, but now because of hunger and the laws in Kaliyug, they had to dishonour her with the plough. In the old days their diet was rich in game, nuts and fruit, the bounty of the forest, but with the coming of the forest guards all they had, said the Baiga, was a 'little millet, disease and death.'[48]

Verrier was both enchanted by the Baiga and deeply moved by their predicament. Two years with the Gonds persuaded him that the tribals had to be protected from the corrosive influences of the outside world: from the 'exploitation of petty traders, the tyranny of petty officials and the enervating influence of the degenerate civilization of the small towns.' The Gonds were swiftly succumbing to these influences but the Baiga, more remote in their mountain fastness, might yet be saved.

Through letters and talks Verrier tried to interest his Congress friends, but to his dismay the politicians who were most vociferous in claiming swaraj would pay little attention to 'the necessities of the original inhabitants of their country.' 'No Congressman in our part of the country has ever lifted a finger to help us,' he wrote in April 1934, 'no member of the local Indian public has ever contributed a pie to our work.'[49] Ironically, the only outsider to show any interest at all was the odd ICS official. It was to one of these, the deputy commissioner of Mandla, that Verrier addressed the first of what were to be dozens of appeals on behalf of the Baiga. He urged the official to convince the forest department to restore the practice of bewar, for

> although it is obvious that the forest must be protected, I am afraid that the effect of depriving the Baigas of the right to bewar will be gradually to drive them into the Hindu fold. For bewar was the rallying point, the standard, the differentia of their tribe, from which most of what was distinctive about them derived. Now without bewar, without the right to hunt, they are becoming a little ordinary, and will be an easy prey to the Hindu propagandist.[50]

Verrier resolved to 'prepare a small monograph' on the Baiga, to document their customs and draw wider attention to the loss of their forests. He recruited two bright young tribals, Sunderlal and Gulabdas, to make regular forays to the Baiga and collect and transcribe their myths. The defender of the underdog had found a new subject, the most disadvantaged and least visible of India's poor—communities neglected even by a national movement that claimed to be wholly representative. Writing in the *Modern Review*, a Calcutta journal run for and by nationalists, Verrier complained that the hill and forest tribes were a 'despised and callously ignored' group. Their problem was as urgent as that of the untouchables: society had sinned against them as grievously, and yet

> the one has become a problem of all-India importance: the other remains buried in oblivion. Indian national workers and reformers—with the exception of the heroic little band associated with the Bhil Seva Mandal—have neglected the tribes shamefully. The Congress has neglected them. The Liberals have neglected them. The Khadi workers have neglected them.[51]

The colonial state and the nationalist intelligentsia both seemed to think of the 'forest people as mere cyphers in the population of India.' Determined to redress this, Verrier first sought to collect and publish the vivid folk-poetry of the Mandla tribals. Associated with the great Gond dances, the *karma* and the *dadaria*, were songs of romance which reminded the Oxford scholar of 'Elizabethan love-poetry, perhaps the finest and most direct love-poetry ever written.' Some of these were published by Sham and Verrier in *Songs of the Forest*, a book that brought together love poems with poems about work and nature. There were songs about grasping landlords and about unattainable women, on the poetry and the poverty of tribal life. Here are two examples, the first sung by Pardhan women, the second by Gond men:

> I am looking out of my house;
> The sun is but a bamboo's length above the hills.
> Where can you go now it is grown so late?
> Leaf of the Plantain, lover in whom my heart is bound,
> Like a dry leaf in the wind,
> You are ever blown to and fro away from me.
> Where can you go now it has grown so late?
>
> The palace is fashioned of chosen stone,
> The doors are also made of stone.
> In every corner burn the shining lights.
> But without a girl all is dark inside.
> On the new road the wheels run swiftly,
> So will I drag you to my heart.
> Inside, without a girl, the house is dark.[52]

Verrier hoped that when printed these songs would make city readers think of the tribals as 'real people, real as themselves,' as the subjects of fellow feeling rather than objects of condescension or pity. Writing was for him a more natural medium than giving injections or running schools. In addition to transcribing and translating the poems and stories of tribals he was working on a novel called 'No Mortal Business,' a detective story with a Christian gloss, a 'sort of combination' of C. F. Andrews and Edgar Wallace.[53]

The source for this teasingly brief description is one of Verrier's circular letters. The manuscript of the novel is lost or perhaps destroyed. The letters themselves were sent out to a range of people, 'from Evangelical pietists to Jewish psychoanalysts, from a German communist to Indian administrators, from a agnostic poet in Hongkong to an Anglo Catholic chaplain in the Leeward Islands, from an Archbishop to Ethel Manin.' One interested reader was the playwright Laurence Housman, whom Verrier befriended while campaigning for Indian independence in England in 1932. Sent the manuscript of 'No Mortal Business,' Housman thought it 'lacked technique as a novel, being far more a study of life and character in a series of incidents.' He asked Verrier to work instead on polishing his letters—that was his 'true literary line,' and from a publisher's point of view 'Letters from the Jungle' would have better prospects than a first novel.[54]

Leaves from the Jungle was published, with the help of a kindly shove from Housman, by John Murray in 1936. A preface sketches three tribal characters: Panda Baba, the repository of Gond myth and magic; Tutta, an epileptic and symbol of poverty who needs but a packet of cheroots, some cheap drink and a consort to be content; and Phulmat, a beauty with the grace and dignity of a princess, an accomplished dancer who represents the romance of the forest. The three faces of Gond life thus introduced, the book covers in diary form the first four years of their life in the village.

Leaves from the Jungle is author-centred but by no means self-absorbed. The Gond Seva Mandal is portrayed as a process of self-discovery, the narrator finding out more about himself as he finds out more about the Gonds. The book provides revelations, through flashes of irony and wit, of Elwin's growing rejection of Gandhi and Christ: as in a description of a khadi mosquito net which 'though utterly patriotic and highly mosquito proof, appears to admit no air whatsoever,' or a confession that he spent a day of rest reading Agatha Christie 'though aware it would be more suitable for me to employ my leisure reciting the Penitential Psalms.' The protective instincts of the anthropologist had replaced the improving agenda of the social worker. 'There are many elements in the Gond ethos which should be conserved,' writes Elwin, 'their simplicity and freedom, their love of children, the position of their women, their independence of spirit, . . . their freedom from many of the usual oriental inhibitions.' Indeed, the tribal 'has a real message for our sophisticated modern world which is threatened with disintegration as a result of its passion for possessions and its lack of love.'[55]

This comes from the only preachy passage in the book; otherwise, the defense of tribal life is conducted with an easy wit and lightness of touch. *Leaves from the Jungle* is the most readable of all Elwin's works, an illustration of 'rollicking anthropology' which celebrates the irreverent and irrepressible gaiety of the Gonds and their chronicler. It received a wonderful reception: the author, said the *Times Literary Supplement*, wrote with 'a Rabelaisian plainness of speech and a Pickwickian zest for the creature comforts of life, even though these pleasures are now enjoyable by him only in imagination;' the *Morning Post* called it a 'remarkable book,' written in a way that excited 'interest, sympathy and smiles;' the *New Statesman* remarked that through the diary 'we know the Gonds more intimately and more thoroughly than any primitive people that have been shown to us in books;' no European since R. L. Stevenson, commented *The Times*, 'has written so well of a life among browns and chocolates.'[56]

The success of *Leaves from the Jungle* confirmed a shift in vocation that was already well under way. Providing education and medical relief were not his line—these were best left to Shamrao. But Verrier could write on the tribals; indeed, he could help the tribals by writing about them. By the time *Leaves* was published the Gond Seva Mandal had shifted its headquarters from Karanjia to the village of Sarwachappar, twenty miles further inland. Their landlord had been giving trouble—he thought the Mandal would make his tenants too independent—and in any case Verrier wanted to move closer to the edge of the great forest and the Baigas. Their new centre had a leper home, a dispensary and a school, but no chapel.

In his first letter from Sarwachappar, written in June 1936, Verrier announced that he had converted to a new creed. 'For however dark and obscure may be my ecclestiastical position,' he remarked, 'in ethnography I am a quite definite and almost bigoted adherent of the Functional School of which [Bronislaw] Malinowski is the proponent.' But this follower of the great Polish anthropologist had more than a strictly scientific interest in the subject, for he believed that

> ethnography is itself a powerful instrument for the succour of the tribesmen. The more you can make people known, the more you will make them loved. If we can inspire officials, traders, contractors with a genuine interest in the life and culture of the villagers with whom they have to deal, they will treat them far better and try to further their interests.[57]

An early visitor to their new home was the sculptress Marguerite Milward, in the middle of a tour of India in search of exotic and interesting subjects. She arrived in Sarwachappar to a grand reception: fifty Gonds threw garlands of marigolds around her neck, until she felt like a temple goddess. The next day she commenced her search for models. The Gond men she found undistinguished but she was enchanted with the women. With Verrier's help she found two 'Gondins,' attractive, much-married, each in the throes of a divorce, and, unlike the Hindu women she knew, confident and eager to pose for the chisel.

Miss Milward was also taken by her hosts to the land of the Baiga. The Gond Seva Mandal had acquired a motor car, gifted by Oliver Fielding-Clarke, formerly of the Christa Seva Sangh. Loaded with people and provisions, the car made slow progress through the jungle, on dirt tracks badly damaged by the rains. The vehicle was abandoned at the foot of the Baiga uplands, whereupon Miss Milward was put onto a *dandi*, a stretcher carried by two Gond bearers.

The Baiga, forewarned and primed by the anthropologist, put up a great show for the visitor. Four villages came together for a gala dance that went on late into the night. Liquor was passed around in tiny leaf cups, and Sham and Verrier danced to merriment and wide approval. The Baiga reminded the sculptress of Italian wandering minstrels—feathers in their hair, colourful beads around their necks and rings in their ears. All in all, the 'fun waxed fast and furious;' everyone was a little drunk and very happy.

But tribal life was not all song and dance, and Miss Milward was also exposed to its other side, poverty and disease. She spent time in Sham's Leper Home, moved by the sight of men and women who accepted 'their awful fate with patience and seemed happy and content.' One night the dancing was stopped when they learnt of the death of a young Gond girl, fifteen and newly married, struck by a disease no one could fathom. Verrier and Sham led a sad little procession to the middle of the forest where a grave was dug with a crow-bar, the evil spirits wished away, and the little corpse lowered to the ground.[58]

Miss Milward left Sarwachappar with a vivid memory of the home of her hosts: 'a typical Gond hut backed up against the wild jungle and facing the sunset and distant plain; a wide verandah, a long room with all the front open to the elements, and in the centre a great desk covered with the Baiga manuscript piled high' (to this had the 'small monograph' grown). When in the village Verrier worked inside the hut, Shamrao for the most part outside it. The sculptress found that the two friends of the Gonds were known as Badabhai and Chhotabhai, little brother and big brother. This nicely expressed their physical contrast—Verrier, tall, fair and broad-shouldered, Sham short, sturdy and dark—as well as their respective vocations. Sham was the little brother in the tribal family, always in close attendance, ready to run errands or provide assistance; Verrier the big brother, affectionate but a little distant, whose help the tribal sought to keep off their backs the unlovely trinity of landlord, moneylender and grasping official.

CHAPTER SIX

Defending the Aboriginal

The noble savage of North America is a very different character from the poor squalid Gond of central India: and not even the genius of a Longfellow or a Fenimore Cooper could throw a halo of sentiment over the latter and his surroundings.

James Forsyth, *The Highlands of Central India* (1871)

The pen is the chief weapon with which I fight for my poor.

Verrier Elwin, in a letter of July 1938

In October 1936 Verrier Elwin went to England for a two-month vacation. The bank balance of the Gond Seva Mandal was running low, down to twenty pounds by the time he bought his ticket. When their patrons frowned on this act of apparent frivolity, he answered that missionaries had their furlough once every few years and he didn't see why, just because he was now freelance, he should be denied privileges granted to the 'regular troops.'

While in England Verrier collected money for the Mandal, spent time with his mother, and made three trips that he had planned. The first was to the Albermarle Street office of John Murray, publishers of the recently printed and hugely acclaimed *Leaves from the Jungle.* He went back several times, to feel himself part of literary history in front of the fireplace where Byron's letters were burnt, to meet and mingle with other Murray authors, and to further a growing friendship and discuss future books with the youngest member of the firm, John Gray Murray.

A second pilgrimage, looked forward to as eagerly, was to the famous

Thursday seminar run by Bronislaw Malinowski at the London School of Economics. Verrier first wrote to the anthropologist asking for a date when he could come. 'You have been a guide and inspiration to me for a long while,' he told him, adding, 'One day a pet monkey ate my copy of your *Sex and Repression in Savage Society*, and although apparently sweet to the taste it was bitter in the belly and it attacked me with great violence. The story has no moral, but I feel it gives me a link with you.'

The great man thought otherwise. When Verrier attended the Thursday seminar, he went up afterwards and repeated the tale of Malinowski's book and his monkey. It was quite the wrong thing to do, for the Pole, working overtime to establish his discipline on a solid scientific footing, had little time for levity. His story told, Verrier looked around hopefully at the master and his disciples, but there was no reaction—all he saw was 'a ring of solemn sociological faces' and he made a quick getaway.[1]

The third visit, even more difficult, was to the office of the secretary of state for India. Verrier had decided it was time to mend fences with the Raj. Most officials of the Central Provinces, high and (especially) low, still treated him as an undesirable alien; they thought he was on the side of Congress, knowing little of his break with Gandhi and the Gandhi-men. The local landlords, meanwhile, continued their propaganda against this 'Christian' social worker, not knowing he no longer considered himself one. Isolated and abandoned, without the anchorage once provided by the Christian faith and the Gandhian church, Verrier wished only to be allowed to continue writing, and for Shamrao to run their hospital and schools without interference.

Seeking a rapprochement with the rulers of India, Verrier once again sought the help of the missionary William Paton.[2] At Paton's request he put down on paper a withdrawal of his philo-Congress views, explaining how he had come to differ with a movement he had once uncritically and completely championed. Since he had begun working with the Gonds, he noted,

> it has been evident that sooner or later I should find myself in opposition to the Indian nationalists, and in the last three years there has been a steadily increasing difference between me and the Congress Party, for which at one time I had considerable sympathy.

> For example, it seems to be the aim of the Congress politicians to bring the aboriginals within the Hindu fold and then to treat them as though they had no special claims; they resent the establishment of Excluded and Partially Excluded Areas [established by the British government to protect the aboriginals]; they dread the claims of Anthropology to guide these areas. This company of vegetarians and tetotallers would like to force their own bourgeois and Puritan doctrines on the free wild people of the forests.
>
> On the other hand I myself consider the aboriginals to be pre-Hindu and that the adoption of Hinduism will be a major disaster for them; I welcome the Excluded Areas, and only wish that there were very many more of them; I consider that scientific anthropology should guide and regulate the administration of all primitive peoples and that they should not be handed over to elected politicians who have no knowledge of their special problems; and I think that the social and moral outlook of the Congress would cut the tap-root of vitality of aboriginal India. . . .
>
> I want therefore to make it clear that although I have still a few personal friends within its ranks, I am no longer a supporter of the Indian National Congress, and I want rather to carry on my work for the aboriginals in the closest co-operation with the local officers of the British Government . . .
>
> In view of all this, I think it would be a good thing if my position could be cleared. I do not see any reason why I should now be regarded as a politically suspicious character: on the contrary, I think that there is every reason why my humanitarian and ethnographical work should be supported. Certainly, some steps should, I think, be taken to ensure that I am not needlessly humiliated and that my work is no more wantonly obstructed by local officials . . .
>
> It has not been easy to write this, for it is never very pleasant to admit that one has been wrong. But for the sake of my villagers, for whom I would do anything in the world, it is essential that I should make my peace with Government.

This was an extraordinary recantation, more so for being voluntary, unlike the undertaking to stay away from politics that the government had extracted in 1932. Forwarding the statement to the India Office, William Paton described Elwin as 'a man whose spiritual sensitiveness has led him astray, [but] he is wholly unselfish, and is, I think, now concerned wholly with the well-being of these Gond people.' It was 'difficult sometimes to realize how great is the change that has been wrought in him by some years of continuous labour in the jungle, but I have no doubt of the fact.' 'I can assure you,' wrote Paton, that 'Elwin is one of the most interesting and attractive people anywhere to be found: a first-class mind, a real scholar, and altogether a rather outstanding person. He will, I think, kill himself in India with overwork, and I wish I could find some way whereby he could be more effectively guided and helped.' The India Office was persuaded this was a genuine change of heart, that Elwin was now 'purely a philanthropologist, who was most anxious to make his position right with the authorities.' But they wondered how minor officials could be stopped from harassing him, 'short of furnishing a placard to put on his back labelled, "This man is now *persona grata* with Government!" '

Elwin knew a better way. On the 25th of November he met R. T. Peel of the India Office and told him his difficulties would at once be solved if he was appointed to an official position and made an honorary magistrate. This would keep the police at bay and might also be a real help to the tribesmen, at present forced to place their cases in the hands of lawyers and their touts in distant Mandla.

'This is as complete a retraction of his former views as one could wish for' gloated Peel, and his colleagues by and large agreed. R. A. Butler, an ambitious M.P. marking time in the India Office, summed up the case in magisterial fashion: 'Father Elwin was a nuisance in my father's day but the report of Mr Peel is conclusive. Father Elwin will always be better at humanitarian work than politics. His note in the volume presented to Paret on the aborigines was interesting rather than practical.'

The man Butler called Paret was actually the Oxford anthropologist R. R. Marett—a volume was indeed presented to him in 1936 but Butler, a future Master of Trinity, had not read it, for Elwin was not among its contributors. Butler's note did not of course reach Verrier, but he was able to check another of its errors. As in 1932, he would correct the India Office on a technical theological point. 'I am "Father" Elwin no longer,' he told them, 'as I am no longer in the Church. Perhaps that is symbolical. Father Elwin is dead in more ways than one.'

When the file reached India the governor of the Central Provinces initiated steps to appoint Elwin honorary magistrate, with powers to hear and dispose of tribal litigation. His office did not 'bear any grudge for his previous errors;' this 'repentant sinner' was now doing 'really good and self-sacrificing work.' Less impressed was R. M. Maxwell, home secretary to the Government of India who, between 1930 and 1932, had been assigned by the Bombay government to monitor Elwin's work for the Congress. This was 'not a very well-balanced person,' warned Maxwell: 'I should not be surprised to see him carried away by his sympathies if Government once more came into conflict with his former friends.'

Just before he left England Verrier was interviewed by *The Observer* on his work among the Gonds. 'The aboriginal tribes are now in a minority,' he told the paper, 'and they have neither writers or politicians of their own. I am trying to establish myself as an authority, to get myself into a position where I can fight for their interests, otherwise they will be swamped by a very corrupt form of civilisation, not the finer side of Hinduism and Islam, but the exploiting greed which comes from the towns.' He hoped to see the Gonds 'develop a new kind of tribal life based on the old, but free from some of its inhibitions such as witchcraft and magic—a revivified tribal life.'[3]

The interview set out Verrier's new mission for the Gonds; to renew from within rather than civilize from without. But when he returned to Sarwachappar in the last fortnight of 1936, he found that their landlord had evicted them from one of their buildings. The grouse was apparently that the Gond Seva Mandal was making trouble by teaching tribal tenants to read and write and keep accounts.[4] It was not a happy omen. Soon, Sarwachappar and its surroundings were engulfed by a movement to bring tribals into the Hindu fold. Local reformers wanted the Gond to wear the sacred thread, abstain from liquor, give up music and dance, not keep pigs and chicken, not plough their land with cows, and put their women in purdah. And so

> Song and dance, the only distinctive elements of Gond culture, have been driven from our district. Chickens and pigs are the only tax-free animals. The Gonds have been compelled in the name of religion and government to kill them off—a very serious economic loss.
>
> The poor Gond has often to yoke his cows (who are past giving milk) to the plough. Now he is not allowed to do so . . .
>
> Liquor is the only tonic available to the malaria-ridden Gond. It is the

> one warming and cheering thing in his nakedness. Now this is taken from him and nothing put in its place.
>
> One of the most attractive features of the Gond was the decent way he treated his women, and his refusal to regard any human being as untouchable. He has now been forced to adopt the Hindu attitude in these matters.[5]

Verrier found the Gonds had gone flat, like stale beer; there was no more kick in them. He warned his tribal friends that if 'they went in for this sort of thing, the anger of heaven would be upon them, taxation would increase and rain would fall all through the hot weather.' Shamrao, more to the point, told the men that since eating eggs was vital to good sexual performance, killing chickens would bring on an epidemic of impotence. Defying the refomers, the Gond Seva Mandal organized a series of dance competitions, each with a first prize of fifty rupees. In the first of these, in February 1937, only five villages participated; two months later, when the frenzy had subsided, as many as fifty came forward to dance.

The 'Raj Gond' movement, as it was called, coincided with the coming to power of Congress in the elections of 1937. In Verrier's mind the two were not unconnected. In August he visited Gandhi at his new ashram at Wardha to acquaint him of the aboriginals' plight. But he found that for 'all his desire for Home Rule Mahatma Gandhi did not appear to think that the original inhabitants of India deserved any special consideration.' The Congress, he concluded cynically, wished on the one hand to use the tribals as cannon-fodder in their political campaigns and on the other to convert them all to vegetarianism, abstinence and settled cultivation—the plough was 'everywhere the symbol of the Congress-Hindu culture that is sweeping tribal areas.'[6] He now had a personal grouse to add, for one of the first acts of the Congress ministry had been to abolish all honorary magistrateships, his included, this when 'there were other reforms of greater urgency to which they might have turned their attention.' Verrier was so fed up with their 'caste and humbug and prohibition' that at times he felt like fleeing India for 'one of the Buddhist countries like Burma or Ceylon.'[7] There was the odd politician he still liked—such as Jawaharlal Nehru, liberal and cosmopolitan, 'all breed and backbone.' After having lunch with Nehru in Bombay in September, Verrier wrote to his mother: 'What a prince he is! Such a gentleman. And so utterly civilized.'[8] But Congressmen in general were a 'lot of Puritanical Nosey-Parkers.' Verrier reported a conversation on religion between two ministers, one a typical 'Evangelical Hindu,' the other a rare Modernist. The Evangelical remarked solemnly that he could never begin his day without spending an hour in prayer and meditation. The Modernist replied: 'It would be much better if you spent it attending to your files.'[9]

In his Poona days Verrier had seen Congress as little less than the liberator of all Indians, especially the poor: but now, in Mandla, he set against its indifference the 'kindness and sympathy which I have found from the higher officials of the Central Provinces Government, and the keen interest and concern with which they view the primitive areas.'[10] The governor of the Central Provinces, Sir Francis Wylie, lent a sympathetic ear to Verrier's diagnosis of the tribal problem—so much so that this former enemy of the British empire found himself a frequent visitor to, and the occasional guest of, Government House, Nagpur. Verrier wrote to his friend Sarat Chandra Roy, the Ranchi lawyer and doyen of Indian anthropology, that Wylie was 'keenly interested in the things that interest us,' that is, the condition of the aboriginals. The governor was even to visit their village in due course.[11]

In 1938 the Gond Seva Mandal changed its name to the Bhumijan Seva Mandal, to acknowledge its work for other tribes and castes ('Bhumijan' simply means 'people of the soil'). That, at any rate, was the official explanation, although irritation at the Raj Gond movement might have had something to do with it. The reformers had also forced Verrier and Sham to change their headquarters. In June they moved from Sarwachappar to Patangarh, a village nine miles to the north, situated on a promontory just off the Amarkantak–Dindori road. On the edge of the hill stands a shrine to Thakur Deo, a stone idol resting under a pipal tree. Village folklore has it that Verrier and Sham first wished to build their home around the shrine. While work was in progress Verrier had a dream in which the deity conveyed his anger at their trespass. Fence and walls were dismantled forthwith and a new building begun on a spot a hundred yards further east.[12]

The new ashram consisted of low thatched mud buildings around a courtyard gay with flowers, a neem tree with a monkey in the middle. There were two old pipal trees in their property: a platform was constructed around one as a meeting-place, the second served as graceful backdrop to Sham's informal court. From Patan there were magnificent views in all directions, views of the shining waters of the Narmada half-a-mile away, and of the great hills of the Maikal Range 'piled up on one another.' A visitor found 'the colours in the ever-changing landscape a perpetual delight.'[13] The villagers were warm, amusing, friendly; there was a fair sprinkling of Pardhans, the rather improper and fun-loving tribe of minstrels who lived with the Gonds and gave life to them. 'The Gond Puritan movement has made no headway *here*,' crowed Verrier. Coming to Patangarh from Sarwachappar was like abandoning a conventicle of the Plymouth Brethren for a cocktail party.[14]

In the last weeks of 1938 Eldyth Elwin came out for a three-month visit.[15] She found her brother looking 'very sweet—pink and blue-eyed,' spending his days writing, directing the garden, playing with children, the 'little girls and boys clasping him as he anthropologizes.' He worked most mornings in the library, its bookshelfs built into the wall. In the middle of the room lay a vast table made of planks supported on mud legs, covered over with books and notes. On the floor below lay copies of the *TLS*, the *New Statesman*, *Time and Tide*, and *Punch*. While Verrier read or wrote Eldyth helped Sham with the injections and tried to teach English in the school. Both the friends were much loved: 'If they are not vocal about religion at the moment,' wrote Eldyth to Mrs Elwin consolingly, 'they certainly live it in that respect.'

To impress his sister Verrier took her to Nagpur. They stayed at Government House, meeting and mingling with the chief justice, the home member, and sundry secretaries and brigadiers. Eldyth accompanied Sir Francis Wylie to a cricket match: 'sentries, flags flying on car, greetings by Vice-Chancellor, special seats, all just like Royalty.' Sir Francis rather preferred his outings with her brother, the long walks in which they got 'such visible pleasure from talking to each other. Verrier being an unofficial intellectual H. E. can let go on him.'

For all the pomp, Eldyth was decidedly ambivalent about the official British in India. In her breathless letters from Government House, full of parties and bigwigs, she paused to remark: 'Sometimes I like it, at others I don't at all!' Her brother's feelings were more mixed still, for he had to keep both the governor and the government (a Congress one) in good humour. Eldyth was also taken by him to a nationalist *tamasha*, the annual session of the Congress held that year outside Jabalpur. To this show the

Gond Seva Mandal brought a troupe of tribal boys who put on a great display of their dances to a crowd of five thousand. Verrier and Sham hoped that this would lead to a warmer appreciation of tribal culture, perhaps even an incorporation of Gond dances in the curriculum of all schools within the province.

The tribal dance was very much a sideshow to the main business of Congress, which that year was a famous fight for control of the organization between Mahatma Gandhi and the young tiger from Bengal, Subhas Chandra Bose. Eldyth found 'great speculation as to whether Gandhi or Bose will die first.' But a large fat woman doctor, a member of the reception committee, would talk only of Verrier, for she was 'steeped in his works.' In the Central Provinces of 1938 British imperialist would not speak to Indian nationalist, but for the sake of his tribals Verrier Elwin would speak to and write for both.

While still in Sarwachappar, battling the Puritans, Verrier found time to finish two novels. The first, *Phulmat of the Hills*, published by John Murray in 1937, tells the story of a Pardhan girl of extraordinary sweetness, a gifted dancer much admired in her village. Struck by leprosy, Phulmat is abandoned by her lover. In grief she takes to the road, and after a long, difficult journey opens a shop in a distant village where her antecedents are not known. Here she lives out her days, selling cigarettes and betel nut and thinking of her lost lover.

The narrative of *Phulmat* is replete with poems, riddles and stories put in the mouths of its characters, interspersed with straight dialogue. The tribals set great store by the artful telling of stories, good music and fine dancing, all activities at which the tragic Phulmat excels. Yet if Elwin's aboriginals are not savage, they are not always noble either, being subject to the everyday human emotions of greed and envy: thus the possessiveness of lovers, the jealousy of those spurned in love, the casting of spells upon enemies. Panda Baba, the Gond *gunia* of *Leaves from the Jungle*, makes a cameo appearance in the novel, aroused by a Baiga magician who steals his clients.[16]

Phulmat is a tale of some ethnographic interest, held together by the focus on the fate of its central character. One reviewer, H. E. Bates, thought the book 'a piece of the best kind of romance, rich in emotion but unsentimental, rich in colour but firmly rooted in fact, . . . realistic and as frank, in its portrayal of love, as Maupassant.'

A Cloud That's Dragonish, published by Murray in the following year, has a less convincing plot. *Cloud* is a tribal whodunnit about witchcraft, each of its chapters carrying an epigram on the persecution of witches in medieval Europe to remind its readers that their superstitions were once just as absurd. The book describes a mysterious series of deaths in the village of Sitalpani, deaths of livestock, pets and human beings. The villagers believe this to be the handiwork of a witch and suspicion shifts from one woman to another. They are finally convinced that the culprit is Motiari, a beautiful Gond girl. But the Gond *gunia* Panda Baba magically appears from his own village fifty miles away and through a series of deductive inferences uncovers the real murderer. This is a Pardhan youth, Lamu. Lamu's mother had been persecuted as a witch and killed in another village by Motiari's father. Vowing revenge, when he grows up Lamu kills the murderer and is determined to kill the daughter as well. On being exposed by Panda Baba he commits suicide.[17]

In a circular letter announcing the publication of *Phulmat*, Verrier warned his friends they might find the book 'coarse and realistic. So it is. But it is no good trying to describe a primitive village as though it were a Brompton drawing room.' The Gonds and the Baigas, he said, 'are more or less absorbed in two things—food and sex—and their conversation is like the prose parts of Shakespeare. So I want you to believe that "Phulmat of the Hills" is not pornographic, but simply photographic.'[18]

Although the tribals in these novels change partners as they would socks, the author's treatment of sex is in fact highly coded and discreet. Love-making is mentioned but never described, the beauty of the female form alluded to but never anatomized. Far more explicit in both respects was his long-awaited ethnography of the Baiga. In late 1937 he posted the manuscript to the publisher. John Murray were worried by its frank discussion of sex: marking out in an early draft the passages and sections deemed 'unsuitable for the feminine lay-reader.' This kind of stuff, they said, was foreign to their tradition. Elwin revised the manuscript, '"restrained" and "censored" to the utmost limit that I find compatible with the demands of science.' If Murray still found the discussion troublesome, he advised them to hire someone who would 'turn all the dubious stuff into Latin.'[19] The compromise finally agreed was to place the main chapter on sex in the middle of the book, with the author stating most clearly in the preface that he did not hold up the Baiga's 'sexual philosophy or practice to imitation.'

Richly suggestive, massively documented, written with verve and passion, *The Baiga* ran to 550 closely printed pages, the most complete account of an Indian tribe yet published. In the tradition of functionalist anthropology, the book presented a full account of tribal social organization, treating in some detail the rules of marriage, the rituals of birth and death, the production and consumption of food, the principles of jurispudence, the forms of magic and dance. In all this pride of place was given to two elements of Baiga life: the practice of sex and the history of *bewar* (shifting cultivation).

When Elwin came to publish his ethnography of the Baiga, he had before him the example of Malinowski, the author of *Sex and Repression in Savage Society* (1927) and *The Sexual Life of Savages* (1929). Where Malinowski's work had given Elwin scientific sanction and a honourable precedent, the Pole was a dry-as-dust technician analysing the sexual consciousness in terms of incest taboos and mother-right, the totemic organization of clans and the economy of wife-exchange. In his books the discussion of sex is generalized rather than particular, with individuals subsumed for the most part in the grid of social structure. In contrast Elwin's account is animated and vigorous, illuminating through character and example what was for the tribe, as for him, 'the most important and enthralling thing in life.'

An early chapter presents life histories of fifteen typical Baigas. This is a rich portrait gallery where individual memories cluster around common themes—wives and lovers, disease and death, official penetration and official exploitation. Making sense of these lives, the anthropologist contrasts the apparent poverty of material circumstance with the richness of remembered sexual experience. Lahakat, an elderly man wrapped in a torn blanket, has conquered fifty girls before turning twenty-five; Baihar, a haggard old woman, was once a famous beauty, wept over by many men, successively and successfully seduced by a forest guard, a magician, and her own brother; Rawan, a celebrated hunter, would track down girls to the river, break their water pots with a well-directed arrow, and make love to them on the spot. And there is Yogi Dewar, a sprightly centenarian who remembers the 1857 Mutiny in astonishing detail and who has twenty-five children by six wives, the last of whom is his granddaughter.

Ancient India was 'rich in sexological literature,' remarks Elwin, but recent writers 'have generally been too much under the influence of the prevailing Puritan conventions to treat the subject freely.' Science called him to break the taboo, for the Baiga he found were ruled not so much by the forest guard and the police constable as by the raging fires of sexual desire. In their lives 'celibacy is unheard of, continence is never practised.' Their children were apparently born with a 'complete equipment of phallic knowledge.' Baiga knowledge of each other's bodies was extraordinarily attentive to detail: the men, for instance, could distinguish between twelve kinds of breasts, ranking them in almost precise order of attractiveness. Even Baiga *gali* (abuse) was rich in sexual suggestiveness.[20]

Baiga sex was free, warm and spontaneous, a necessary background to the material concerns of the tribe. These centred around bewar, the system of axe-cultivation to which they were passionately attached. God himself had established the Baiga in the practise of bewar, with the admonition: 'You must not tear down the breasts of your Mother Earth with the plough like the Gond or Hindu.' These sentiments were given short shrift by the British who, from the beginnings of their rule, tried systematically to destroy bewar. Colonial objections to *bewar* were rooted in an ideology of Improvement (settled cultivation would 'civilize' the tribes by curing them of their wayward habits) as well as driven by commercial forestry and its need to exclude the Baiga from areas where timber was being felled. Bewar was quickly banned in almost all districts of the Central Provinces, being confined ultimately to a small patch of forest, about 24,000 acres in all, in the Ramgarh *tehsil* of Mandla district. This was known as the Baiga Chak (reserve).

When the Chak was formed, the government received a good many petitions from Baiga who lived outside the reserve. Dholi Baiga of Udhor, writing in 1892, said that after bewar was stopped,

> We daily starve, having had no food grain in our possession. The only wealth we possess is our axe. We have no clothes to cover our bodies with, but we pass cold nights by the fireside. We are now dying for want of food. We cannot go elsewhere, as the British government is everywhere. What fault have we done that the government does not take care of us? Prisoners are supplied with ample food in jail. A cultivator of [the soil] is not deprived of his holding, but the Government does not give us our right who have lived here for generations past.

Forty years later, when Elwin first arrived in the Baiga country, he found the aboriginals still not fully reconciled to the ban on bewar. 'Every Baiga who has yielded to the plough,' he remarked, 'knows himself to be standing on *papi-dharti*, sinful earth.' 'When the bewar was stopped and we first touched the plough,' remembered one Baiga, 'a man died in every house.' Another claimed that before the forest department made them ordinary serfs, the penis of the Baiga had been five times as large as anybody else's. Elwin was convinced that restrictions on bewar, coupled with the ban on hunting in the forest, had crippled the tribe. By depriving them of their livelihood, by tearing a page out of their mythology, by bulldozing them into a way of life foreign to their tradition and inclinations, the state had done colossal harm to their spirit.[21]

What could be done? The Baiga dreamt of a new Baiga Raj, with a king of their own, the restoration of bewar, and unlimited opportunities to hunt and fish. 'The English are giving everyone swaraj,' said one, 'why can't they give us *bewar-swaraj*?' Elwin thought the solution lay in the formation of a national park covering the wilder and inaccessible part of Mandla, where the Baiga would be sovereign. Non-aboriginals would be excluded, as would missionaries of all stripes, Christian as well as Hindu. The Indian Penal Code would be withdrawn and the Baiga governed by their own laws. Above all, they would be given the freedom of the forest so that their 'once proud-quivered loins' need not tremble any more 'at the lash of every little whipper-snapper of a forest guard.' Thus might the Baiga be saved from the fate 'which an over-hasty and unregulated process of "uplift" and "civilization" has brought upon aboriginal peoples in other parts of India.'[22]

The Baiga was the work of a novelist who had strayed into anthropology. In the prefaces to their books, professional anthropologists like to thank Professor X and Dr Y, the director of this archive and the keeper of that museum. But Elwin gave pride of place to

> my Baiga friends [to whom] I owe the real making of this book and, in passing, some of the happiest hours of my life spent in their company. I cannot name them all, but at least I must not forget my *mahaprasad* Mahatu (my 'family magician,' a great adept, though his love-charms are faulty) and his sons, Mithu and Jantri; Jethu, the lame gunia of Bohi, and those entrancing boys Panku and Charka; Hothu, who was my generous host in Taliyapani, and Bahadur who entertained me at Hirapur; Dhan Singh and Thaggur who have often brought the mysterious benefits of their magic to my own village; Pachlu, the 'professional savage' of Jholar; Rawan, the great hunter of Bilaspur; Lahakat, the Don Juan of Amadob; Daseru, dreamer of strange dreams; the mild and gentle Ketu; Yogi Dewar, the Mutiny veteran, whom I have not seen sober; the many-husbanded Mahi, a perfect 'Cockney' type, coarse and irresistible; the old and knowledgeable Baisakin and her co-wife Malho, just a little jealous; and the children, Phagni and Gondin, Mangli and Bhairi, Goru and Jhingra.[23]

It was the novelist J. C. Squire who first drew attention, delightedly, to this decidedly unscientific preface.[24] The book's uncertain location between literature and science was also pinpointed by the philosopher Alan Watts. In a report to the publisher Watts called it

> a curious mixture—on the one hand a piece of very valuable, thorough and apparently reliable research, and on the other a collection of weird, amusing and bawdy stories. The author frequently changes his style to suit the subject; at one time he writes in the cold and technical jargon of science, and at another in plain (and almost cheerful English), and in the latter instance the book is always entertaining, though often unsavoury, reading.

Presented as an anthropological monograph, 'this was beneath the surface . . . [a] most human and delightful book. The author does not regard the Baiga tribes as laboratory specimens; it is quite evident that he loves and respects them, and often succeeds in making the reader share his feelings.' Thus the work's 'scientific thoroughness is enhanced, as it were, mellowed by a thoroughly human and sympathetic approach to the subject.'[25]

Early reviews of *The Baiga* were heartening. The author, remarked the *TLS*, was an 'anthropologist by grace' rather than by profession, 'doing his best to think as black as his firsts in the Oxford schools will let him.'[26]

J. H. Hutton, Professor of Social Anthropology at Cambridge, thought the book 'the greatest thing of its kind that has been done,' showing 'Elwin's complete entry into the primitive point of view.' Beryl de Zoete spoke in the *New Statesman* of 'a vast and entirely fascinating encyclopaedia' deserving of 'extraordinary praise.' W. V. Grigson of the Indian Civil Service commended the book's ethnographic merits and its practical value in 'pointing out to the Hindu majority the conditions of their less advanced fellow-countrymen and, of even greater importance, those elements of tribal culture which are of permanent survival value: they are many.'[27]

The views of the Hindu majority are unrecorded, as are those of the Gandhians, although what they might have thought of the book had they cared to read it can be inferred from the remarks of a Christian in the *International Review of Missions.* The sections on sex, wrote this angry reviewer, 'are characterized by a gusto strangely out of place in a professedly scientific treatise.' This critic closed the book with an uneasy conscience, for 'in the name of science the ragged "purdah" of the Baiga has been violated and the world at large invited to take a good look. In circuses and zoos the cages of anthropoid apes are screened from curious eyes, at certain intimate moments of their occupants' lives. Mr Elwin's humble friends and confidantes have been less fortunate in this respect than captive chimpanzees.'[28]

The Baiga was published in September 1939, days before the outbreak of war in Europe. 'Poor book!' remarked Verrier when the first copy arrived in Patangarh: 'Who is going to buy it in war-time?' There were other reasons why his support for the European 'struggle of democracy over totalitarianism' was less than enthusiastic. When his mother wrote of the difficulties of life in war-torn England, Verrier seized on the note of patriotic hysteria that her letters seemed to betray. 'We are amused at you calling this a safe and peaceful place!' he wrote in early November; 'I suppose there is not one of our people who could not with advantage change places with a Tommy in the trenches. The expectation of life here is lower than in the Maginot Line, and leprosy, malaria, syphilis and other diseases are more frequent and more deadly than bombs.' Three weeks later, having submitted an essay on aboriginal policy for the Wellcome Medal of the Royal Anthropological Institute, he noted: 'I don't see why, when everyone is getting medals for killing people, I shouldn't try to get one for suggesting methods of keeping them alive.'[29]

The exchanges with his mother, of which only his side has survived, lay behind a combative circular letter that he sent out in January 1940. England's war aims, he insisted, 'must include a square deal for the aboriginals as well as for India. And the "war aims" of the Indian Nationalist should equally include normal human rights for the original inhabitants of India.' Appealing to subscribers not to abandon the Gond Seva Mandal, Verrier said the tribals of Mandla were not really 'out of the war,' for they lived

> permanently under war conditions. There is a black-out in the village every night. Every evening, far more deadly than the Messerschmidt, comes a flight of mosquitoes with a load of parasites that kill three million annually. We always have a rationing system, for the villagers never have enough to eat. For four months in the year the rains set up a great blockade of mud between these villages and the outside world. The Gond is just as down-trodden and oppressed as the Pole or the German Jew. Many years ago, his kingdoms and great estates were taken from him by conquest or deceit. The Baigas, lords of the jungle, have been robbed of their ancestral home, deprived of their human rights, taxed and suppressed and regimented into decay by the very people who now profess to stand up for the integrity of small nations. Nearly every wrong that the Nazi has inflicted on the Czech and Pole has been suffered by our aboriginals. [30]

The war lost the Gond Seva Mandal some old supporters, but *The Baiga* had meanwhile enlisted some new ones. One of these was W. G. (Bill) Archer, an unorthodox and most untypical member of the ICS based in Bihar. A historian of sparkling intelligence from Cambridge, Archer and his Oxonian wife Mildred had opted out of the stuffy social circle of the civilian elite. They made friends easily with Indians and especially with tribals. Posted in Ranchi, at the edge of the forest, Archer began collecting the tribal folk songs of Chotanagpur. *The Baiga* appeared as he was finishing a book of his own, on the folk poetry of the Uraon. He at once wrote Verrier a fan-letter inviting him to Bihar.

The Archers had 'long known Verrier by reputation, admired his writings and been attracted by his unconventional way of life.' When he arrived at their doorstep in January 1940 they were not disappointed. He was a world removed from the company of the PWD engineer and the superintendent of police, the dreary circuit of district town and hill station that comprised much of their life. When they took him to Patna, the seat of government, Verrier insisted on going around to Government House to sign the book, dressed in shorts, sandals and a bright blue shirt. The ADC on duty fidgeted nervously but his hosts were delighted. The attraction was mutual, for the Archers were in their own way as unconventional as he—Bill a poet and aesthete, at odds with the stiff and arrogant image of the ICS man, Mildred a writer and left-leaning Labourite, no memsahib at all.[31]

The two Englishmen paid a courtesy call on S. C. Roy, the lawyer-ethnographer who lived in Ranchi. Verrier was tremendously impressed by Roy who, as a native, had a clear advantage over white men when it came to doing field-work with the tribes. 'I do wish we were both small and black,' joked Verrier, 'and could go and live in a [village] without attracting any notice. That is my one constant prayer that in my next incarnation I may be small and black and very very clever, so that I can do something worthwhile.'[32]

Verrier returned from Ranchi to find a vast pile of letters waiting at Patangarh. One was from Mahadev Desai, a second from Sir Francis Wylie—both wanted to visit. What if they arrived at the same time? That would be a 'real Trimmer's cross-roads,' he thought. In the event neither came, so he was able to get back to work. The tour with the Archers inspired him to return to a subject he had temporarily set aside. While living in Karanjia he had woken each morning to the sound of bellows from a furnace run by the Agaria tribe of iron-smelters. In Bihar he had been taken to the territory of the Asur, metal workers who lived high up on the Chotanagpur plateau and who were distantly connected to the Agaria of Mandla. Verrier now went back to his notes on the tribe. His book on them was completed in April 1940 but published, when Hitler's war allowed it, only two years later.

The Agaria tells a melancholy tale of the decline of an ancient craft at the hands of state hostility and market competition. Each furnace was taxed at eight rupees a year, more than a quarter of an Agaria's total earnings, which were a measly thirty rupees. The new forest laws forbade the collection of wood and its conversion to charcoal. The Agaria went into the state forests anyway, by stealth, but with a guilty conscience—many of their dreams were about being surprised by forest guards. That other great innovation of British rule, the railway, had flooded the market with factory-made iron. Breaking forest laws, migrating to districts where taxes were lower, persuading peasants that their softer ores made better ploughshares, the Agaria survived with a 'heroic persistence.' All the same, the number of operating furnaces fell from 510 to 336 between 1909 and 1938. The decline of material culture everywhere brought 'idleness, dulness, immorality and hunger.' Where the furnaces had closed down, 'all the romance, mythology and religion that centred around Lohasur,' the god of iron, had disappeared too.[33]

The Agaria was the first of Elwin's books to be published by the Indian branch of Oxford University Press. John Murray were not willing to take it on in wartime; the OUP were, but even they wanted a subsidy. This was procured from the great steel-making firm of the Tatas, whose head, J. R. D. Tata, had a well-deserved reputation as a patron of science and scholarship. I doubt that he or anyone else in the firm really read the book—its defense of an indigenous craft was at the same time an indictment of their factory-made product. The method and subject were of course more to the liking of Gandhians—as close to their professed interests, we might say, as the author's previous book, *The Baiga*, was distant. It is a mark of the absoluteness of Verrier's transition from the attractions of monastic asceticism to those of tribal hedonism that he asked OUP to approach potential Gandhian customers on their own. 'How far would any of the Gandhi-people be inclined to buy the book,' wrote the author to his editor: 'It is after all an account of an indigenous village industry with whose preservation the Congress is supposed to be vitally concerned. I am so out of touch that I do not know who are the proper people to approach in this matter, but I expect you could find out.'[34]

A most revealing review of *The Agaria* was published in the *American Anthropologist* by the French-Hungarian scholar George Devereux. He allowed that the data was 'rich, detailed, authoritative;' what was lacking was systematic conceptual analysis. With Elwin flitting back and forth between 'the card-index pattern, Frazerian comparisons, functionalism [and] psychiatry,' the book had 'neither internal or external order.' But behind these symptoms lay a deeper cause: quite evidently Elwin had spent 'too much time in the field.' What he needed 'most at this juncture is a refresher, a plunge in the Pieran spring of the London School of Economics, or one of the progressive departments of anthropology in the United States.' Devereux hoped that 'in the interests of science some foundation [would] stake this most distinguished field-worker and scholar to such a venture.'[35]

This last comment recalls M. N. Srinivas' later formulation of the three births of an anthropologist. For Srinivas, an anthropologist is 'once-born' when he goes to the field for the first time, thrust abruptly into an unfamiliar world. He is 'twice-born' when, after living for some time among the community, he is able to see things from their perspective: a second birth akin to a Buddhist surge of consciousness for which years of study or mere linguistic facility do not prepare you. An anthropologist is truly 'thrice-born' only when he moves back to the university, his field-work completed. Here he reflects on his material and situates it in a theoretical context, while being alerted to competing subjectivities by colleagues returning from their field-sites and communities. The anthropologist's special allegiance to his own tribe can never be entirely abandoned, but his third incarnation allows him the hope of achieving at least a partial objectivity, which is the mark of a scholar as distinct from a propagandist.[36]

In his own way Elwin anticipated this formulation, for in one of his books he beautifully describes the anthropologist's second birth. 'In every investigation of a civilization not one's own,' he writes, 'there comes—usually only after months or years of routine investigation, tedious checking and the patient accumulation of facts—a moment of sudden glory when one sees everything fall into place, when the colours of the pattern are revealed, and one finds oneself no longer an alien and an outsider, but within.'[37]

The charge that he was not anthropologist or scientist enough was one with which Elwin was to become tiresomely familiar. To the professional who prides himself on his detachment Elwin would remain forever in the stage of twice-bornness, always and invariably seeing things from the perspective of the community he studied and identified with. A third birth required a move to the academic founts of the LSE, and this was not a move he was willing to make. It was not so much that no foundation was willing to fund this venture, but rather that, unlike the university anthropologist, he had come to the field with no intention of going back to the Senior Common Room.

But on the other hand being in the field for so long gave Elwin an insider's view of the kind denied to scientific anthropologists, for whom the tribe or village is rather frequently a fact to be placed in a theory or, if one were inclined to be cynical, simply the vehicle for professional advancement. Elwin placed no such burdens on his field-site—actually his home—which is why *The Agaria* and *The Baiga* are marked by this unusual ability to see tribal life from within. These are studies in salvage ethnography, sympathetic portrayals of ways of life before the drowning wave of progress finally rolled them over. Writing in the middle of the most savage war in history, Elwin contrasted the 'millions of tonnes of death-dealing steel employed in modern battle' to the 'few thousand tonnes smelted annually in the clay furnaces of central India,' these being used for making the ploughs and harrows that raised rich crops in the Maikal Hills. 'This aboriginal iron has brought the law of plenty to the jungle,' he remarked, while 'that civilized iron is bringing the law of the jungle to the lands of plenty.'[38] The fate of the Agaria was thus a 'implicit condemnation of industrialism,' the plight of the Baiga an indictment of the 'scientific' and narrowly commercial forestry that had displaced them.

The Baiga, remarked Elwin in his great book on that tribe, 'know little of civilization and think little of it.' He himself knew a great deal about civilization and yet thought little of it. In this sense he might be said to exemplify the ideology of 'cultural primitivism,' defined by A. O. Lovejoy and George Boas as the 'discontent of the civilized with civilization, or with some conspicuous and characteristic feature of it.'[39] Primitivism has of course been one of the most enduring strands in European thought; in the words of a more recent commentator, Tzvetan Todorov, it is 'less the description of a reality than the formulation of an ideal.'[40]

Elwin's own espousal of cultural primitivism was not wholly an invention. For one thing the Gond, the Baiga and the Agaria all believed that the past had been better than the present, that there had truly once been a Golden Age when their kings ruled, when their powers of magic and healing were unimpaired, when their beloved bewar and iron-smelting were freely pursued. Elwin's attack on civilization was also splendidly timed, for, with the long shadow of Nazism cast across the warring nations of Europe, the primitivist could effectively challenge a view of human progress in which savages of the forest were placed at the bottom of the hierarchy and modern European society at its apex.

Most of all Verrier Elwin must be distinguished from other primitivists in that he actually lived with the communities whose culture he so vigorously celebrated. The narrator of primitivist reveries has the choice, which he generally exercises, 'to return, at the end of his sojourn, to the highly civilized countries he came from.' From Vespucci to Chateaubriand down to the anthropologists of the twentieth century, the European traveller in search of the exotic invariably goes back to where he came from.[41] In an unpublished fragment of autobiography, Elwin wrote of what marked him out from others who extolled the primitive life: 'Not many of those who wrote so eloquently of the return to nature,' he remarked, 'were prepared, however, to take the journey themselves, *at least not without a return ticket.*'[42]

Verrier Elwin lived with the primitive, he loved with them, he defended them. There is a poignant and heroic logic to this which distinguishes Elwin's brand of activist anthropology from academic anthropology. The Baiga, he wrote, 'have for the last seventy years consistently and bitterly criticized the inequity in their treatment. But they have no champion to fight for them, no spokesman to voice their grievances.' Likewise, iron-smelting was one of a score of village industries being destroyed by the Industrial Revolution, but thus far 'no mahatma has arisen to revive it.' Champion, spokesman, even mahatma perhaps, that is how Verrier Elwin saw himself. By trumping Gandhi with sex and the bishops with anthropology, this Christian for the Congress had now become a defender of the aboriginal.

CHAPTER SEVEN

Going Gond

I am rather anxious about his future, which seems to me to be very obscure and uncertain. He is a man of very great possibilities, but I begin to doubt somewhat gravely whether they will be realized.

William Paton on Verrier Elwin, September 1933

Mr Verrier Elwin
Deserves and may well win
Renown in the world of letters
For recording the life of our
moral betters.

Bombay journalist, *c.* 1940

Elwin—you mean the anthropologist who married his fieldwork?

Professor of Sociology, Delhi University, *c.* 1990

The villages of the upper Narmada valley were remote and inaccessible when Verrier Elwin lived there, and so they are today. When I visited them with a friend in the first weeks of 1998, we began our journey by boarding the Utkal Express at New Delhi. This is a sad and grimy train, twenty-two coaches pulled along by the sheer will power of a dying diesel engine. Its condition suggests the countryside it shall pass through: eastern Uttar Pradesh, Rajasthan, Madhya Pradesh, Bihar and Orissa, the poorest parts of India, millions of acres of farmland occasionally fertilized by rain and worked tirelessly by underfed and unschooled peasants.

A long day and a night later we get off at Anuppur, in the Shahdol district of Madhya Pradesh on the edge of the Maikal Hills. We take a jeep to Amarkantak, a two-hour ride up the ghat. We climb through open canopy forests, native sal trees interspersed with exotic pine and eucalyptus. We pass a truck parked astride the road, in front of it a group of Gond girls, dancing. They are dressed in vivid polyester sarees and are demanding *chanda* (tribute) from the driver, for it is the day of Makar Sankranti, the harvest festival. We are now in recognizably tribal country, the forests thicker and with the sal having successfully stood its ground against interlopers. At Kirar Ghat the driver halts to allow us a view of the Sone valley below.

We stop again at Amarkantak, briefly, to confirm our reservations at the Kabir Chabutra rest-house. This lies a further six miles into the forest, in a lovely isolated spot overlooking a deep gorge. The bungalow was built by the Public Works Department in 1913; twenty-five years later it was where the governor of the Central Provinces stayed when he came to visit Elwin. My companion is himself a high official of the Government of India, here travelling more-or-less incognito. He is, I tell him, the most distinguished civil servant to stay at Kabir Chabutra since Sir Francis Wylie.

Kabir Chabutra is within striking distance of the villages once patronized by the Gond Seva Mandal. Wylie must have walked down to see Elwin—or was carried there by *dandy*—but we can go more conveniently, by jeep. The road winds through old-growth forest well stocked with Hanuman langur, black-faced creatures who go swinging on trees or sit by the road-side watching trucks go by. The forest has other residents too, as some posters by the side of the road inform us. One, a spectacular sketch of a forest fire with tigers and elephants fleeing, soberly tells the reader that it is his duty to protect the woods from burning (*vano ko aag se bachaiye/ vano ki suraksha aapka daayitva hai*). The illustrators and copywriters of the Madhya Pradesh government have chosen the eight miles from Kabir Chabutra to Karanjia as a prime target for their art. The posters are plentiful and varied, seeking to bond the tribals to a government they might not so willingly heed. *Kisano ki sarkar, aapki sarkar*, your government is of and by the peasants, says one signboard, and then on the reverse, *savdhaan!*—be cautious. This is addressed to the rash driver but could perhaps be read as a warning to the Gond not to take the first slogan too seriously. One poster seems calculated to displease the feminist: *Chauka, baasan aur putai, phir bhi mahila kare padhai:* The woman may cook, wash and clean, yet in school she must still be seen. Another would have offended Elwin: a moralistic Gandhian attack on drink, the tribal's sustenance, it read: *Nasha nischit maut hai, aaj svayam ki, kal parivar ki, parso rashtra ki* (Drunkenness is certain death, yours today, the family's tomorrow, the nation's day-after.)

Karanjia is a large, sprawling village spread across both sides of the road. It boasts a quiet police *thana* and a busy high school, with portraits of Bose, Gandhi and other nationalists on the walls and lots of chattering children within. There is also a timber yard, filled with logs of sal trees once attacked by the borer beetle and since cheerfully felled by contractors. It is, as in Elwin's day, a mixed village, dominated by Gonds but with more than a handful of Pankas, Baigas, Banias and Ahirs. His name is known by all but his face is remembered only by two ancient Gonds of the Baghel clan who studied in one of his schools. But it is an Ahir cowherd who takes us to where *Badabhai* and *Chhotabhai* lived, on the hill above Tikeri Tola. Elwin had an eye for views and the ashram of St Francis would have looked out across fields to the Amarkantak hills beyond. The sight is glorious, and Mary Gillet's words ring in my ears: 'Hills and valleys and blue skies and peasants singing.' Sadly, of the buildings where she briefly lived there is not a sign. The walls of the ashram have returned to mud, washed away in the many monsoons that have hit the hill since Verrier and Shamrao moved down the valley to Sarwachappar. There is a nice pipal tree, planted by them apparently, and a sturdy stone well at the foot of the hill built for their convenience. That is all.

In the oral history of Karanjia, we discover, Elwin is mentioned only in dispatches. Next on our tourist route is the village of Ryatwar, three miles away, where we have reason to believe his memory is rather more enduring. The road to Ryatwar is a dirt track, mustard fields on both sides, the terrain gently sloping down to the Narmada beyond. We ford a little stream flowing into the great river and approach the hamlet. The jeep stops next to a group of Gond men, squatting and smoking under a *harra* tree. Heart in mouth I approach them and ask: '*Aap batayinge Elwin ka makaan kahan hain.*' Could you tell me where the house of the Elwins is? They direct me back a hundred yards, to a pink washed school building.

Adjacent to this is a low Gond house with mud walls plastered white and a tiled roof, its small garden ringed, English style, by a thorned hedge. In the courtyard stands an old lady wearing a white sari with a discreet striped border, her head covered. It is late afternoon, the most written-about hour of the Indian day, the time the cows come home and the sun starts to set. '*Aap Kosi behn hain*,' we ask. '*Ji haan*,' she answers, '*wo hi hoon*:' Yes, I am Kosi. The moment will not return, so I ask her at once whether I can take a picture. She nods in assent, adjusts her sari, smoothens her hair, and pulls her *palloo* more closely around her head. The ease and grace, the sheer naturalness with which she composes herself, takes my breath away, for she has not, I think, stood before a camera in half a century.

But there was a time when plenty of people took plenty of pictures of her. For this was, indeed is, Kosi Elwin, once the wife of Verrier Elwin.

The lady in the courtyard that magical afternoon in Ryatwar was born Kosi Armu but took the name Elwin before a magistrate in Jabalpur almost sixty years earlier. Verrier and Kosi were married on 4th April 1940: a decade later the union ended in divorce. The memory was so wounding that Elwin could not bring himself to write about his first wife in his autobiography, where Kosi and the years of their marriage are disposed off in two paragraphs. 'I cannot even now look back on this period of my life without a deep sense of pain and failure,' he remarks—'indeed I can hardly bear to write about it.'[1]

Written in the nineteen-sixties seemingly for an audience of home-loving, petty-bourgeois Indians, *The Tribal World of Verrier Elwin* is not an autobiography in the confessional mode. Kosi gets two paras, while other, more fleeting loves—Mary Gillet, Ala Pocha, Singharo—go unmentioned. Elwin's reticence is an open invitation to the biographer. But the keepers of his flame have kept the tracks well covered. His literary executor denied me access to Elwin's diaries for the period because of what they contained about Kosi. Elwin's English family, in making their generous donation of his letters to the India Office Library in London, took care to efface traces of the marriage. Verrier's weekly letters home, from his arrival in India in September 1927 to his death thirty-six years later, can all be consulted except those letters in which he might have talked of Kosi. No evidence can be found here of where he met his first wife, or of when and how he told his family of his wish to marry her. About the only letter on the subject is one to Mrs M. O. Elwin from Sir Francis Wylie, governor of the Central Provinces, conveying his failure in persuading her son to call off the marriage. The fact that Wylie's letter is preserved is symbolic, perhaps; the warning of a Big Man ignored at one's peril.

The story of Kosi Elwin has been subject to a mildly Stalinist obliteration in which Verrier, his family and his executors all seem to have collaborated. The biographer has to make do with letters written to friends who preserved them, and whose families had no reason not to place them in the public domain. We are lucky, too, that by 1940 Verrier was something of a public figure, his marriage to a tribal girl attracting the attention of journals and journalists. The evidence from both private letters and public prints suggests that at the time of their marriage, and for several years after, Verrier was deeply in love with Kosi. Their relationship seems also to have placed a part, perhaps even a central part, in the making of some of his best (and best-known) books. Love and work, the personal and the public, were joined in Verrier Elwin's evocative portrayals of tribal culture in works like *The Aboriginals* (1943) and *The Muria and their Ghotul* (1946).

The influence of Kosi on Verrier's subsequent career can more easily be understood by asking the kind of question the professional historian is taught to scorn. *What if* Verrier had defied Mahatma Gandhi and married Mary Gillet in 1933? The union would have confirmed them in a life of social work, working for but not with the Gonds. Their children, like the children of other expatriates, would have been sent to school in England. More than a lone Englishman, a white couple would have stood apart from the Gonds—racially, culturally and imaginatively. Married to Mary Gillet, Verrier would have doubtless led a life of service and sacrifice but not, one thinks, of colour and controversy.

'I do wish Verrier would get married,' wrote Shamrao Hivale to Mrs Elwin in August, 1939, adding, 'If we go to Bombay in November he might find a good girl there.' His mother was being gently set up, for Verrier was in search rather of a woman to take with him to the city, not a 'city wife.' He now wanted a permanent relationship but, as he told Bill Archer, at the same time 'shrank from holing with a mistress.' That was 'too surreptitious' and would 'complicate ordinary social relations' (outside the village, that is). He had his eye on Kosi, one of the more attractive and certainly the most intelligent of the girls around Patangarh. They must have first met when Verrier was still in Karanjia, for Kosi remembers briefly attending the Gond Seva Mandal school. This would have been in 1934 or 1935. A little later, the girl having become a woman, the acquaintance was renewed and deepened. At this distance in time Kosi's powers of recall are understandably attenuated; nor would she easily talk of her former husband. But she did remember, quite clearly, Eldyth Elwin's visit of 1938–9. This means Kosi would already have been a habitué of Patangarh, the village a good four-hour walk from her native Ryatwar. She and Verrier were very likely lovers living under the same roof when Elydth was around, although whether the sister approved one can't tell. At any rate, Verrier seems to have waited a year or so before deciding to take the next step. Shamrao's letter of August 1939 was an early testing of the waters. Once mother had assented in principle to Verrier marrying, they would ease her by stages into the real situation. A hint was dropped that the daughter-in-law would be Indian, though of the less unpalatable, i.e. city-dwelling and English-speaking, kind. The revelation that she was a tribal would come after the deed was done.

Mrs Minnie Elwin would certainly have regarded her daughter-in-law as a savage. But Kosi would tell you herself that she was a *Raj* Gond, a member of the tribal aristocracy who claimed kinship with the Gond monarchs of medieval Chattisgarh. Kosi's family were poor, but 'devilish dignified' in view of their lineage—in Verrier's description much like 'decayed baronets in a P. G. Wodehouse story.' They would not approve of their daughter marrying out of caste, so Verrier resorted to what he termed 'Love-Marriage-by-Capture.' He took Kosi off to Jabalpur, where they were married under the Special Marriages Act, designed for such inter-religious and inter-racial unions. The deed done, the bride's family were brought round by a feast and a promise that the legal bond would be confirmed by a ceremony according to Gond rites.[2]

The tribal wedding was carried over four full days, as described by the groom in his scholarly essay 'I Married a Gond.' The first day was taken up with the construction of a wedding booth made of wood and bamboo, and with the customary preparation of Verrier and Kosi. On the second morning the bride and the groom were separately anointed, with oil and turmeric, then bathed and dressed—in his case in a yellow *dhoti*, a long cassock-like upper garment, and a crown of coloured paper. The two then watched as their respective parties fought a mock battle with sticks and spears. The battle's result was foretold in favour of the groom who 'at a Gond wedding is a hero not subject to casualties.' Finally, in the evening Verrier and Kosi were taken three times around the wedding pole in the ceremony that confirmed their union.

On the third day Verrier carried Kosi off in triumph to his home village. This, as both lived in Patangarh, was deemed to be Sarwachappar, the hamlet ten miles distant where the Bhumijan Seva Mandal still maintained a home for lepers. At Sarwachappar they went thrice more around a pole and then settled down to hear the marriage sermon. The Gond *pujari* tailored his talk to the extraordinary circumstance of a tribal girl marrying an Englishman. As bullocks are yoked to a plough, began the priest,

> so too have you been yoked together today. Listen, brother, when she is foolish, do not despise her thinking her a mere daughter of the forest. Never find fault with her, or grumble at her. And you girl, never say he is bad, he forgets me, he does not love me, and so leave him. He is English. He has come from another land to love us. From how great a distance have you and he come together, over land and sea, over mountain and forest, drawn together by fate. To you he is *Raja;* to him you are *Rani*, and because of you two we are all of royal blood. And listen again, brother! Today you eat her tender flesh; tomorrow do not despise her bones. Never leave this girl, nor leave this country, for she is yours and this land is yours. All things taste sweeter as they ripen, but with a woman it is not so. But you must consider her always, and in your mouth she must taste sweet even in her old age. And brother, for love of this girl do not forget us. For love of woman makes a man forget all things and turns his mind aside.
>
> And now take this girl. We are giving you a winnowing-fan full of gold. Use it well. Eat and live in joy. Live for age after age. Of one may there be twenty-one by the grace of God.

Verrier's account of the marriage pays close attention to the rituals and to the eating, dancing and singing that accompanied them. Scientific accuracy is leavened with irony and self-mockery, and the essay drops its veil of objectivity altogether when it comes to the ceremony's concluding ritual. This was the shooting, early on the fourth day, by the groom of a model of a deer made of leaves. Performed in front of a large crowd, the act was redolent with sexual symbolism and Verrier was to describe it privately as a 'frightful ordeal.' For if he had missed altogether he would have been thought to be impotent and Kosi was not the 'sort of girl with whom that affliction could be regarded as a matter of indifference.'[3] There are echoes here of George Orwell's essay 'Shooting an Elephant,' with marksmanship in this case proof of marital fitness rather than the authority to rule. Verrier failed to knock down the deer in six tries but on the seventh attempt sent 'a perfect shot right through the deer where its heart would have been, and the [tribal] boys with shouts of triumph picked it up and carried it home. . . . It was a great relief—*Oxford* was not decadent after all.'[4]

Verrier's rich and extended description of his marriage gave a novel twist to the anthropologist's credo of 'participant' observation. Some thought then and later that he had married Kosi in the spirit of science. Eldyth and her mother consoled themselves that it was all a 'whisky-inspired whim,' although an elderly uncle, pious and suspicious, declared Verrier married Kosi because 'he had to.'[5] In any case the first reaction of both family and friends was chilly disapproval. The couple received only three wedding presents from outside (one came from Bill and Mildred Archer), while a number of donors, among them the American Women's Club of Bombay, withdrew support to their Leper Home and schools on account of Verrier having married a 'savage.'[6]

At the time of the marriage Verrier was thirty-seven and had been twelve years in India. He lived and ate much like the Gonds he had come to serve, yet his education and orientation radically marked him out from his milieu. He spoke Chattisgarhi, the local dialect, but knew no other Indian language, and was always most comfortable speaking English. In some ways indeed he still thought of himself as an Oxford man. By 1940 his inclinations were increasingly towards literary and scientific rather than humanitarian work. This was nicely captured by a Bombay journalist who, on meeting Verrier a year before his marriage, described him thus : 'He drifted in looking very healthy, blue-eyed and happy, with that scholarly stoop of his, a roll of proofs in his hand and a cheery smile that, I thought, must light up the forest glades wonderfully.'[7]

Verrier was tall and fair, his bride dark and diminutive. A contemporary photograph shows a very pretty young woman, perhaps twenty to her husband's thirty-seven, with an alert and amused expression, beautiful even teeth and hair worn short, Western-style. There is no trace of selfconsciousness. Kosi's poise was in contrast to the diffidence, even fear, which her husband reported other tribals showing when confronted by his camera—they feared his box was 'a sort of anthropometric instrument by which I could measure the stature of likely recruits for the Army.'[8] Born and raised in a village near Patangarh, Kosi did not know a word of English ('except "Get Out" which she could hardly fail to pick up'), had never been in a train or seen a film or listened to the wireless. Effervescent, a gifted singer and dancer, 'a mine of poetry and ideas,' Kosi was, to quote Bill Archer, 'a raging, roaring girl' not in the least in awe of her husband.[9]

His friends' reservations appear on the face of it to be not without foundation. His family too had made it plain that they'd much rather he'd married someone of his class and colour. These criticisms wounded Verrier and seem to have penetrated deep into the subconscious: a diary entry reports a dream where he'd 'bigamously married Margaret Moore [an English acquaintance] and spent many distracted hours wondering how on earth to get out of it.' The announcement of the marriage was Verrier's first *public* avowal of his flight from celibacy, and he now had a good deal to explain and answer for. Characteristically, he answered his critics with defiance. To those who supposed that Shamrao and he had taken a lifelong vow of brahmacharya, he replied that the Gonds themselves viewed the unmarried life as 'something abnormal, almost as a perversion.' In their folktales the celibate Hindu sadhus were represented as greedy and lustful villains. But where village life made it impossible for Verrier to marry an Englishwoman, it seemed both 'logical and intelligible to take a tribal wife.' His marriage to a talented and witty Gond girl would in fact anchor him to the people he worked with and identify him more fully with their cause.[10] Indeed, in Kosi Verrier loved 'not only a beautiful and accomplished individual but a whole tribe.'[11] Some of his friends might disapprove because they looked down on aboriginals but, as Verrier wryly noted, 'Kosi's family, though very nice about it, consider that she has married very much beneath her.' A circular letter written on Christmas Eve took on the opposition. 'My wife's people,' wrote Verrier, '*my people*, have more of the secret of living—love, truth and non-attachment—which is the secret of Christmas than the warring nations of Europe.'[12]

Verrier was to take heart in the reception that Bombay, itself a city of mixed marriages, accorded Kosi. When he took Kosi there in the last week of July they spent a marvellous fortnight being feted everywhere. 'All the gloomy prophecies that my marriage would mean social death were falsified,' wrote Verrier to Bill Archer: 'Kosi was absolutely lionised: reporters hovering around, the guest of honour at the Taj Hotel, a reception for us at the smart Willingdon Club, dinner with the Tatas, the iron king of India, the Wadias, the Khataus.'[13] At the Willingdon Club Kosi sat next to Krishna Hutheesingh, Jawaharlal Nehru's younger sister. Kosi was dressed in a cotton sari patterned with flowers, 'with picturesque silver *dhars* ornamenting her ears, silver amulets on her arms and a belt hanging loosely from her slim waist.' She attracted 'some curious looks cast in her direction now and then'—when spoken to she 'replied with a charming smile which changed her whole expression.'[14] Verrier was giving one of his fund-raising talks at the Willingdon, but Kosi had her chance to peform too. When her husband spoke over All India Radio on 'The Folk Poetry of the Maikal Hills' the lecture was illustrated by snatches of Gond forest songs, *dadarias*, rendered by Kosi in 'a clear, natural voice that was very charming.' The programme, said one reviewer, was 'easily the most attractive feature of the week.'[15]

Kosi's own impressions of Bombay are not entirely unrecorded. She visited the cinema several times; what amused her most was a movie with the title 'Too Many Husbands.'[16] Interviewed by a reporter of the *Illustrated Weekly of India*, Kosi described the city in vivid metaphors. The long line of cars on the Marine Drive 'raised in her mind a picture of lines and lines of crows in a vast forest expanse,' the roar of the sea 'reminded her of the shrill winds whistling through their forest trees on a dark night.' The journalist marvelled at the 'calm dignity with which Kosibai, whose life hitherto had been spent in a tiny mud hut in a remote village, rose to her new experiences' in the city, showing 'no signs of embarrassment before the complicated etiquette' of the banquets in their honour. Kosi told the reporter of the 'very privileged position' enjoyed by women among the Gonds and Baigas, for which feminists might well envy them. Women had the right of revenge, most spectacularly in the festival known as 'Stiria Raj,' when wives cast spells and intimidated their husbands, singing, 'We have now taken control of the kingdom.' Tribal women, remarked this Gond wife of an Oxford man, 'have a very happy family life, there being a tolerant understanding between the sexes which is lacking in other "civilized parts of the country." '[17]

These words might have come out of one of Verrier's essays. I suspect they were his, made up as he translated his wife's Chattisgarhi into the reporter's English. But Kosi Elwin was very much her own woman: independent, intelligent and self-willed, and in some matters vastly more experienced than her husband. Her view was that sex was her right: she'd 'shout and rage, get tight, brag of her lovers, scorn V's skill and then expect a night of passionate love.' Verrier found her elusive and fascinating. To Bill Archer, who was married to a proper Englishwoman, he bragged often of Kosi's skills. 'I very much wonder if your Uraons do not sing to each other in bed,' he wrote: 'It is such a delightful and—for them—natural way of love-making. Kosi is very good at it.'[18]

This was a tease, for Archer, despite writing a book on the Uraons, never got close enough to study them in bed. Through Kosi Verrier could triumphantly underline a greater intimacy with *his* tribe. In October 1941 Kosi gave birth to a son whom they named Jawahar, both for the Gond Raja of Sarangarh, a friend of Verrier, and for Jawaharlal Nehru (but the boy was usually called Kumar). Fatherhood appears only to have confirmed Verrier's love for his tribal wife. He was delighted when a friend said the boy bore something of a resemblance to the British prime minister. How perfect, he answered, that a Jawaharlal should look like a Churchill.[19] When Kumar turned one, his father hailed him as a 'great character and brilliantly clear;' like Jeeves, 'his head sticks out at the back and his head sparkles with the purest intelligence.'[20]

Now that Verrier was married, his friend had to follow suit. 'I am anxious for Shamrao to get married as soon as possible,' wrote Verrier to Bill Archer, 'for—of course—as my younger brother he is a menace' (as a potential lover of Kosi).[21] Sham was at first interested in a Pardhan girl but unlike Verrier he preferred to wed a virgin. These were not easy to locate in Patangarh. The problem was alleviated by the fact that his family's wishes on the matter were paramount. In early 1941 he married their choice, Kusum, an Indian Christian from Poona. In Patangarh the two couples lived under one roof, the wives being socially guided by the husbands. Kusum and Kosi took English lessons together so as to partake of the dinner conversation.

The great ecologist G. Evelyn Hutchinson, himself thrice married, believed that sex is 'a part of living behaviour which at least in man, and no doubt in some other vertebrates, is largely on the side of love.'[22] This sentiment Verrier would have endorsed, although in his years as a follower of St Francis and Mahatma Gandhi he had tried hard to believe otherwise. His marriage to Kosi was a final repudiation of both those traditions and for the rest of his life he joyfully celebrated sex, identifying it largely with love. With the Gond and the Baiga he had come to believe that 'the physical must express and interpret the desires of the mind and the heart.'[23]

But as it turned out, Kosi also helped the anthropologist win wider acceptance amongst the communities he was studying. Verrier's old Warden at Merton College once claimed that the marriage to Kosi 'was made in the interests of science. It was the only way in which he could get initiated into the mysteries of her people.' This claim was made when the Warden's successor, alarmed at the prospect of having to entertain Elwin and his aboriginal wife at High Table, wished to terminate Merton's research grant to the anthropologist.[24] Verrier's marriage to Kosi had some beneficial consequences for science which were not anticipated. He married Kosi because he loved her.

Kosi's contributions to Elwin's scientific research were made in Bastar, a large and isolated chiefdom adjoining the Central Provinces which had an overwhelmingly tribal population. Densely forested, Bastar was rich in timber and minerals, coveted by British merchants and entrepeneurs. In 1910 a major rebellion broke out against the state's attempts to curb tribal rights in forests in favour of timber companies. A British battalion was called in to quell the uprising. Thereafter the administration were more circumspect. A key figure in the new policy of letting the tribals be was W. V. Grigson of the Indian Civil Service, who was Diwan (Administrator) of Bastar in the 1920s and 1930s.[25]

Grigson was an officer of exceptional intelligence and foresight with a deep commitment to the tribals. His book *The Maria Gonds of Bastar*, published in 1938, first alerted Verrier to the rich possibilities of ethnographic research in the state. Restless, in search of new tribes to write about, Bastar seemed to him the perfect escape from the 'foul and rotten company of lawyers and landlords' in the over-administered and over-civilized district of Mandla. Grigson put Verrier in touch with his successor as Diwan, E. S. Hyde, who helped make the arrangements for his research. He was appointed Honorary Ethnographer and Census Officer of Bastar State, which gave him the freedom to move around in the territory. The Maharani of Bastar further smoothed his path by providing an elephant, the only effective all-year means of transport in the forest.[26]

In the autumn of 1940 Verrier and Kosi moved to their new home in Bastar, in a village close to the capital Jagdalpur, within easy range of the hills. For the sum of three hundred rupees Verrier built a house with high walls and long low windows looking out to the best of Bastar's many splendid views, the Chitrakot falls on the Indravati river. This began what Shamrao Hivale called 'probably the happiest years in Verrier's life.'[27] One reason for the happiness was the love and companionship of Kosi, and in time of Kumar; another, the dignity and freedom of the state's aboriginals. The chiefdom, Verrier told his mother, was 'unbelievably peaceful;' its people 'gentle, friendly, with no desire for property or power.' He contrasted Bastar's tribals to warring Europeans. The tribals were a 'great lesson to the world at this time. So long as men cling to the desire of empire and wealth such catastrophes as the present one are certain to occur.'[28]

Bastar also appealed to Elwin on account of its apparent success, under Grigson and subsequent diwans, in guaranteeing tribal autonomy and independence. The tribals appeared happy and content. Their religious and cultural institutions were thriving, their indigenous industry had not been destroyed, their sense of beauty remained keen, their standard of human enjoyment was exceptionally high. They were in sum a 'dignified and noble people,' supported by a sympathetic administration whose 'prophylactic and remedial measures' had done much to protect aboriginal rights in land and preserve village institutions. Bastar was unquestionably 'the brightest spot in the aboriginal situation,' an example worthy of study by both the 'Congress people and the Administration of British India,'[29] especially the former, who were waiting in the wings to take power once the war got over. Verrier knew from experience that Congressmen were likely to be indifferent to the tribes. 'My only hope,' he remarked, 'is the little group of intellectuals round Jawaharlal Nehru: his National Planning Committee is prepared to consider the anthropological point of view with regard to the aboriginals.'[30]

In private letters and published essays Elwin drew a pointed comparison between the aboriginal situation in his own Central Provinces and in Bastar. In the C. P., he noted, 'hunting has been forbidden for decades, adventure has been wiped out by Law and Order, achievement has been dented by disease and hunger.' There the tribesmen were oppressed by landlords and moneylenders, and subject to extortion by state officials. But the Bastar aboriginal retained control over his lands and forests, while an administration specially adapted to his needs had protected him from scheming politicians and corrupt officials. The 'vigorous and healthy' life of tribal society in Bastar contrasted with the 'decay and inertia' elsewhere in aboriginal India. He found it 'most refreshing to go to Bastar from the reform-stricken and barren districts of the Central Provinces.' Every time he entered the state from British territory he seemed to hear the whole countryside bursting into song around him.[31]

While touring in Bastar Verrier heard of the death of his old headmaster Dr Flecker, the man who 'caused me a great deal of trouble when I was a child.' Christianity in all its forms he had long since rejected, but he now found to his surprise that he had to revise his opinion on another of the great faiths. Since he came to Mandla he had developed a strong dislike of Hinduism, for it was Hindus who—as moneylenders, landlords and officials—were the chief tormentors of his Baiga and Gonds. But in Bastar he discovered that Hinduism as a theological system was not that far removed from aboriginal thought. For the social life of the chiefdom revolved around the Dassera festival, when thousands of tribals from the hills descended on Jagdalpur to pay tribute to their king, whom they worshipped as the messenger on earth of Durga.[32] The anthropologist concluded that the faith of the Bastar tribal 'was really closely related to Shaivite Hinduism. It is true that the feeling-tones are different but so are those of Protestantism and Catholicism. Yet we call both those totally different faiths Christianity.' Like Buddhism and Jainism, tribal religions were part of the Hindu family, although 'the members of the family are undoubtedly more attractive than the parent.' Despite its undeniable connection to the greater Hindu tradition there was a freedom and flexibility to tribal faith—in Bastar 'religion is always on the move. Even the legends change from village to village.' And, what mattered most to this former priest, there was 'no sacred book, no canon, no deposit of faith committed to a central authorized guardian, no regular liturgy.'[33]

Verrier Elwin's research in Bastar at first focused on one tribe and one institution—the *ghotul* of the Muria. The ghotul, a dormitory for initiating the young into the mysteries and wonders of sex, fascinated the anthropologist, himself finding his own way, rather late in life, through these wonders and mysteries. Within a few months of moving to Bastar he resolved to write 'a fairly long book on the subject, which might well be a best seller.'[34]

He spent over a hundred nights in different ghotuls while a battery of research assistants gathered information on other dormitories. His field research was enormously helped by the presence of his wife who, as a member of the greater Gond family, could claim kinship with the Muria. Her beauty attracted young men who clustered around her in village after village. This irritated Verrier who for more reasons than one wished her to be with the women. A stenographer accompanying the couple recalled that Kosi was 'instrumental in winning over the Muria women-folk,' allowing Elwin a glimpse of aspects of their lives which were otherwise a closely guarded secret.[35] Among the tasks assigned to Kosi were the playing of a gramophone to break the ice in a new field site, and the learning and performing of their dances with Muria girls. The dreams of these girls and women were also recorded by her. The anthropologist taught Kosi the use of a camera, which she then used to furtively photograph distinctive features of Muria apparel—such as the *mudang* or decorated waist-band—which no one except other women and husbands were allowed to see. It helped that Kosi was a common name among the Muria and Elwin happily expended film shooting his Kosi with one of theirs. The ethnographer's acceptance was further aided by their child, a great draw passed adoringly from hand to hand by the Bastar villagers.[36]

The ghotul is described by the anthropologist as something of a night club coming to life at dusk, after the day's work in the fields. It was an arena of encounter and friendship, of play, music and dance where *chelik* (boy) and *motiari* (girl) formed deep and loving relationships. But life in the dormitory was also regulated. Chelik and motiari were expected to come every day, to keep the dormitory clean, to share in the common labour, and to not quarrel or fight. Sexual transgression—sleeping with someone else's chosen partner, for instance—was also punished. Discipline was maintained by senior boys and girls and, as the Muria said, 'We obey our ghotul laws more faithfully than the laws of government, for we ourselves made [them].' The anthropologist noted with interest that though dormitories had doors, these could not be shut from the outside: 'The ghotul is never locked up. It is a shrine and no one would steal from it.'

Training the young in the arts of sex and the conventions of social life, the ghotul was also a stimulus to artistic expression. Its walls were painted with models of motiaris and tigers, its pillars carved with animals fighting or tribals dancing. Within, girls decorated themselves with colourful head-bands and a profusion of necklaces and bead-collars, all hand-crafted. The art of combing and comb-making was highly developed. Combs came in many shapes and sizes, carved by the chelik for his motiari. They were used for the hair and to titillate the skin on arms and back. If a girl possessed a large number of combs it implied that 'she has a very devoted lover.'

Elwin's research bore fruit in a detailed, candid, evocative account of pre-marital sex, of the role of touch and smell in arousing a partner, the use of love-charms in winning a reluctant lover. Sex was fun: the 'best of *ghotul* games . . . the dance of the genitals . . . an ecstatic swinging in the arms of the beloved.' But it was not, at least among the Muria, disfigured by lust or degraded by possessiveness or defiled by jealousy. Nor was it a bed of primitive promiscuity. Indeed, in the classical, *jotidar* type of ghotul, individual chelik and motiari paired off in a relationship that might last as long as five or six years, till both left the dormitory. In a diary entry of 12th December 1941, quite early in his fieldwork, Elwin noted: 'It is amazing how little jealousy and permissiveness there seems to be generally in these ghotuls.'

In defending the ghotul from the obvious criticisms of the civilized world, Elwin pointed out that that there were virtually no cases of venereal disease among the Muria. Prostitution, rape and child marriage, so visibly present in more 'advanced' societies, were all too absent here. More strikingly, the sexual freedom of the ghotul was followed by a stable, secure, serenely happy married life. In the process of growing up the 'life of prenuptial freedom' ended in a 'longing [for] security and permanence.' In any married couple, neither was virgin absolutely: but *both were virgins to each other.* Husband and wife had each been carefully trained in the arts of sex. Statistics provided proof of the strength of the Muria marriage bond. By Elwin's calculations, among the Muria of Bastar the divorce rate was less than three per cent, whereas among the Gonds of the Patangarh area the percentage was in excess of forty. Before and after marriage, he concluded, 'Muria domestic life might well be a model and example for the whole world.'[37]

The Muria and their Ghotul was described by its author as a 'pocket battleship' of a book. It ran to seven hundred and thirty printed pages, almost two hundred more than *The Baiga*, featuring one hundred and fifty photographs and almost as many line drawings. But beyond its rich description of a tribe at work and at play the book can be read as a statement of Elwin's own attitudes to love, sex and marriage. He reports, for instance, the tribal view of celibacy that men and women who practise it are restless and frustrated, and, after they die, a perpetual nuisance to those left behind on earth—on whom they cast spells. 'The state of *sannyas* (renunciation),' remarks Elwin, is 'everywhere associated in the aboriginals' mind with idleness and beggary rather than with chastity.' Against that Hindu and Gandhian ideal, the Muria and Elwin insisted 'sex is a good thing, healthy, beautiful, interesting, the crown and climax of love.'[38]

In the last pages of his book Elwin bravely connects the Muria ghotul to a pre-Puritan India, to a time when Hindus had cultivated and lovingly memorialized the pleasures of the body. The message of the ghotul, he claims,

> that youth must be served, that freedom and happiness are more to be treasured than any material gain, that friendliness and sympathy, hospitality and unity are of the first importance, and above all that human love—and its physical expression—is beautiful, clean and precious, is typically Indian. The ghotul is no Austro-asiatic alien in the Indian scene. Here is the atmosphere of the best old India; here is something of the life (though on a humble scale) portrayed [in the paintings] at Ajanta; here is something (though now altogether human) of the Krishna legend and its ultimate significance.

In reaching out to a hostile public Elwin hoped to enlist the aid of Jawaharlal Nehru, the modern Hindu most likely to sympathize with the culture of the Murias. Preparing his book for the press, he wrote to his editor wishing he'd get Nehru to write a Foreword 'intelligently from the point of view of education,' and adding, 'I doubt if it were possible.'[39] The doubt concerned not Nehru's intelligence but his availability. Locked up in Ahmednagar jail at the time, Nehru could not be reached by author or publisher and the book finally went out into the world without his stamp.

The Muria and their Ghotul was completed in 1943 but only published four years later, its production held up by wartime shortages of paper and film. It took a grant of two hundred pounds from Merton and eight thousand rupees raised by Verrier's Bombay friends—the Parsi industrialists J. R. D. Tata and Jehangir Patel—before Oxford University Press felt able to send the manuscript to a printer. Well before its publication the book's contents were a source of much speculation. One interested party was Henry Luce's *Life* magazine which, in June 1944, bid for exclusive excerpt and photo rights to go with an interview with the author. The story was to be written by Bill Fisher, a *Life* contributor who had visited Elwin in the field.

The attentions of a popular illustrated magazine are not to be scorned, but Elwin's authorial vanity was tempered by more practical considerations: to wit, the likely fall-out among nationalist and puritan circles in India. As it was, a series of illustrated essays he was publishing on the Bastar tribes and which were appearing in the *Illustrated Weekly of India* had attracted a torrent of letters from readers worried that portraits of half-naked and bejewelled tribals would 'degrade India in the eyes of the foreigner.'[40] Now it was being proposed that more revealing pictures be published under his name, and this in an American magazine. 'I think it would be most unwise,' wrote Elwin to his publisher, R. E. Hawkins of OUP,

> to hang a *Life* story about me on a lot of stuff about girls and boys poking each other. The reaction in India might be most unfortunate. It is one thing to write a large, heavy and complete work on pre-nuptial freedom in the ghotul. It is quite another to have bits of it splashed in a popular magazine as a means of introducing me to the American public. You might increase sales in America, but it will not increase sales in India if I begin to be regarded as a second Miss Mayo.
>
> I also think that the photographs used must be chosen with discretion. There must be no busts or bosoms, which Bill Fisher was anxious to have. We mustn't give 'savage' pictures . . . This is an excellent chance for advertisement, but I feel very strongly that we must not do anything in America that will have bad reactions in India.[41]

'No busts or bosoms' was not a condition *Life* were prepared to meet. They did not run the story, but the Muria ghotul eventually found its way into American consciousness through the Kinsey report, where Elwin is cited more often than the great Sanskrit treatise on love-making, the Kama Sutra.[42] *The Muria and their Ghotul* is not, I think, Elwin's best work of anthropology, but it is indisputably the best-known. It has been translated into several languages and appeared in an abridged edition with an alluring title, *The Kingdom of the Young*. The ghotul itself has been restudied by several later anthropologists,[43] and the BBC even made a film on it.

The Muria and their Ghotul, wrote W. G. Archer in *The Listener*, was an encyclopaedic work written 'with incisiveness and charm,' an 'unforgettable picture of an Indian tribe at work and in love.' A more dispassionate reviewer in a more weighty journal, *Man*, was Edmund Leach, one of the rising stars of British social anthropology. Leach thought likewise that 'this lavishly produced work worthily upholds its author's reputation both as a conscientious ethnographer and as a writer of exceptional aesthetic sensibility.' True, the professional would complain that 'on the theoretical side generally, the analysis is crude and old-fashioned,' yet it remained 'Elwin's remarkable achievement to describe [ghotul] behaviour with sympathy, intimacy and detachment. If this part of the book were to appear as a supplementary volume to Havelock Ellis's *Studies in the Psychology of Sex* it would be in proper company. In its own way it is masterly.'[44]

By the early forties sexual behaviour was well established as one of Elwin's chief scholarly interests. The author, a decade earlier, of tracts on *The Supremacy of the Spiritual* and *Mahatma Gandhi's Philosophy of Truth* was now publishing essays in learned journals on 'The Theory and Practice of Sexual Intercourse among the Aboriginals of the Maikal Hills' and 'The Attitude of Indian Aboriginals Towards Sexual Impotence.' *The Muria and their Ghotul* deepened and consolidated this interest, prompting a Bombay friend, Evelyn Wood (in whose house the final draft was composed), to write a 'Triolet on the Union of Anthropology with Psychotherapy:'

> Ellis to Elwin! Shades of Sex:
> Waves in one human spectogram
> In whose green heart may love annex
> Ellis to Elwin.
>   Shades of sex,
> Long may your bonds and lusts perplex
> Those who hate fact—love holy sham
> Waves in one human spectogram.[45]

The Muria and their Ghotul might be viewed as the last act in a long-drawn-out Oedipal conflict with 'Bapu,' Gandhi the father. Oddly enough, while he was working on the book he had been asked to contribute to a *festschrift* for the Mahatma's seventy-fifth birthday. He could scarcely draw upon his latest researches but was not up to writing on Gandhi either. He finally settled on a tribute to his friend Mahadev Desai who had just died in jail. The Mahatma's secretary was one of the few 'Gandhi-people' with whom he had remained in touch. In the preface to his new translation of *The Story of my Experiments with Truth* (1940), Mahadev wrote that 'from the point of view of language [the translation] has had the benefit of careful revision by a revered friend, who, among many other things, has the reputation of being an eminent English scholar. Before undertaking this task, he made it a condition that his name should on no account be given out. I accept the condition. It is needless to say that it heightens my sense of gratitude to him.'[46]

The abbreviated c.v. provided by Mahadev Desai points to Verrier and no one else. But why would he not want his name 'given out?' Because he thought it would violate the terms of the October 1932 agreement between him and the India Office, clause (iii) of which specified that he would 'refrain, as far as possible, from associating with any persons engaged in political agitation'—and Gandhi was then planning a fresh satyagraha? Or because he did not want to sail under false colours and be seen as the servant and intimate of the Mahatma when he no longer was?

The essay on Mahadev is a minor gem, a homage to the human being and the *litterateur.* Mahadev was a man of wide culture with a catholic taste in art and literature. He was 'too big to be mean.' Verrier asks us to see Mahadev as Gandhi's Boswell, perhaps also as Plato to his Socrates, the interpreter who most conscientiously and definitively put his message out to the world.[47]

The intention might have been to take the Mahatma down a peg or two, for the other contributors to the book, who included Nehru and Albert Einstein, wrote on Gandhi himself. Yet even the tolerant Mahadev is unlikely to have approved of Verrier's book on the ghotul. When that work was in press the author recieved a letter from the Archers, who were reading with interest Ethel Manin's book *Privileged Spectator* (1936) in which the British writer and traveller had written of Verrier as 'a remarkable follower of Mahatma Gandhi.' Verrier, in reply, imagined Bill and Mildred 'reading those bloody paragraphs [on Gandhi and himself] shitting with laughter and making dirty cracks between each one. The only thing that gives me satisfaction is the thought of the intense annoyance those pages must have given the divine Mahatma if ever he saw them and found himself bracketed with a drunken ping-pong and you know what, like me.'[48]

Neither *Privileged Spectator* nor *The Muria and their Ghotul* were likely to be high on Gandhi's reading list. But some of his followers had read about Verrier and his book and formed their own opinions. One who was part of the Mahatma's circle at this time, when asked about Elwin, angrily replied—'That man a follower of Mahatma Gandhi! He was, waist-downwards, totally immoral!'[49]

The attention surrounding *The Muria and their Ghotul* has obscured a second book that Elwin wrote in Bastar. This was a study of murder and suicide among the 'Bison-Horn' Maria who were, on the face of it, a particularly violent tribe. Their annual incidence of homicide well exceeded the average for Bastar as a whole and they were also more prone to taking their own life.

In his book Elwin sought to understand the origins of violence and set it in context. He worked with a sample of one hundred murders and fifty suicides, in each case using the court record of the crime as a basis for further, first-hand investigation in the village where it had occurred.

The anthropologist found that murders among the Maria were not, as commonly supposed, strongly linked to the consumption of alcohol. Crimes were rarely committed during festivals or marriages, when drink was most freely consumed. Nor were murders committed for gain. One cause of Maria crime was witchcraft, the tribals believing it right and proper to kill a witch or sorcerer who through magic and spells disturbed the social order. But in killing witches the Maria were a victim of 'intellectual error' rather than of 'murderous passion.' As Elwin pointed out, two hundred years earlier the 'best brains' in Europe believed and acted likewise.

Adultery was also a common motive for murder. Maria men were 'suspicious and exacting' husbands, 'jealous and possessive' by temperament. Some men considered themselves quite justified in killing a disloyal wife. This contrasted with the extraordinary lack of sexual possessiveness among the Muria. There the ghotul—absent here—alerted the young early to the 'impropriety of jealousy.'

In this slim and concisely argued book Elwin sought to explain tribal crime, perhaps even explain it away. Despite the record of the Maria,

Indian aboriginals had on the whole 'a high reputation for their pacific and kindly character.' In any case, compared to the 'dark and complicated wickedness of so many European murders,' Maria crime was most often committed in a fit of passion or rage: rarely premeditated, it was borne out of an 'astonishing innocence.' These tribesmen, wrote Elwin,

> do not cheat and exploit the poor and the weak. They are mostly ignorant of caste and race prejudice. They do not prostitute their women or degrade them by foolish laws and customs. They do not form themselves into armies and destroy one another by foul chemical means. They do not tell pompous lies over the radio. Many of their darkest sins are simply the result of ignorance. A few of them are cruel and savage, but the majority are kind and loving, admirable in their home, steadfast in their tribal loyalties, manly, independent, honourable.

Elwin hoped that magistrates who read *Maria Murder and Suicide* would show more understanding in their judgements. The book ends with an account of the sufferings of Maria prisoners, their loneliness and deprivation in Jagdalpur jail. The anthropologist urged that murderers condemned to death be allowed, on the eve of their execution, to visit the temple of Danteshwari, the tutelary goddess of Bastar. More daringly, he hoped for the creation of a special prison for aboriginals where jail life might be enlivened by dance and song, and where the prisoners would be taught crafts useful to them after their release. This would be a camp rather than a jail, where the aboriginal spirit would be 're-created, not broken.'[50]

'I don't think we will do any "social" work, except perhaps a little medicine to help the people.' Thus wrote Elwin to the administrator of Bastar while planning his move to the state.[51] By the end of his stint, three years later, the one-time social worker's preferred self-description was 'anthropologist.' Elwin had by this time consolidated his professional status by taking over, with his friend Bill Archer, the running of the quarterly journal *Man in India*. This periodical was started in 1921 by Sarat Chandra Roy, the Ranchi lawyer commonly acknowledged as the founder of Indian anthropology. Elwin himself had great affection for Roy, a 'kindly amiable spirit' without whose efforts he believed 'Indian anthropology might never have come to birth at all . . .' When Roy died in 1941 Archer and he moved quickly to take over the journal from the family, the coup helped both by Verrier's friendship with the old man and Bill's status as a high official in the Government of Bihar. [52]

Elwin's area of research had now shifted to the eastern province of Orissa, a shift well marked by the essays he was to publish in *Man in India*. With its numerous tribes 'unknown' to science, Orissa was territory even more virgin than Bastar. Verrier first visited the province towards the end of 1942 on an assignment arranged by Norval Mitchell, a former administrator of Bastar who had taken over as political agent to the princely states of Orissa. Almost the first group he met in the uplands of the Keonjhar district were the swidden-cultivating, leaf-clad Juang, 'quite the wildest and strangest' of all the tribes he had encountered anywhere. The Juang were shy, reclusive and distinctly unhelpful. Verrier complained that they 'do not want visitors and they do not mind saying so. They refuse to show the traveller the right road or point out to him a wrong one. They give fantastically incorrect directions to prevent him from proceeding on his tour . . . The distances are great and the paths difficult even with elephants. There is no tradition, as in Bastar, of village hospitality.'

The Juang's suspicion of outsiders went back to an incident in 1871, when a fanatic English official began a campaign to rid them of their leaf-dress, well suited to the climate and terrain, in exchange for more civilized attire. This campaign culminated in a public meeting in which two thousand pieces of cloth were handed out to the women, after which the leaves that had previously clad them were silently burnt.

Elwin found that the Juang looked back to that episode much as a conquered nation recalls the day of defeat in battle. Although some interior villages clung defiantly to the leaf-dress, the tribe as a whole had 'suffered a psychological and spiritual shock from which it has never recovered.' 'Civilization,' he commented bitterly, 'which in the course of a hundred years has done nothing whatever for the Juang, which has given them no hospitals or schools, which has taught them neither agriculture nor any industry, has paid its debt to the tribe by a forcible attempt to stop the leaf-attire.'[53]

As with the Baiga, Elwin was both enchanted by the tribe and depressed by their fate. 'A really beautiful girl in leaves is a sight for the gods,' he wrote to Archer, 'and I have recklessly expended colour-film.' The Juang were now threatened with the expansion of the forest department, but the anthropologist hoped 'a book might save them. I am now mewing my far-from-mighty middle-age for a great battle with the Forest Adviser.'[54]

The debate with the forest department was carried out in two reports the government had asked him to write. One report pertained to three small chiefdoms, the other to areas administered directly by the British. Elwin's brief in both cases was to recommend ways of containing shifting cultivation without causing popular discontent. This was a theme close to his heart and here he carried forward the arguments presented with such eloquence in *The Baiga*.

The Government of Orissa, persuaded by its forestry officials that swidden was a pernicious practice that destroyed the forest and caused floods, assigned Elwin the limited task of showing how the aboriginal could be 'led away from shifting-cultivation into the settled life of the permanent cultivator . . .' His own reports subtly but persistently undermined the premise that swidden should be done away with altogether. He demonstrated that axe-cultivation proper, following long rotations and where the earth was broken up only with a stick, allowed for vigorous regrowth of forests on fallow fields. Only in areas where the plough had been introduced were erosion and deforestation serious problems. And like the Baiga, the Orissa tribes were unwilling to abandon a form of livelihood that had sustained them for centuries, and which no previous ruler sought to contain.

Just as he distinguished between kinds of swidden, Elwin distinguished between different tribes practising it. Some communities were in close contact with the wider economy and society, and thus more likely to adapt to change. Here settled cultivation could well be encouraged, taking care that the aboriginals were properly protected from moneylenders and landlords and provided schools and hospitals to help them hold their own in the modern world. Rather different were the 'real primitives' living in isolated valleys, who had a strong mystical attachment to the territory inhabited by them and a clear sense of collective ownership over hill and

1. Baby Verrier with Bishop and Mrs Elwin (OUP)

2. Verrier, aged five (British Library)

3. Dean Close's prize student, 1919 (OUP)

4. A gent with a dog collar—the Vice Principal of Wycliffe Hall seminary, Oxford, 1926 (Wycliffe Hall)

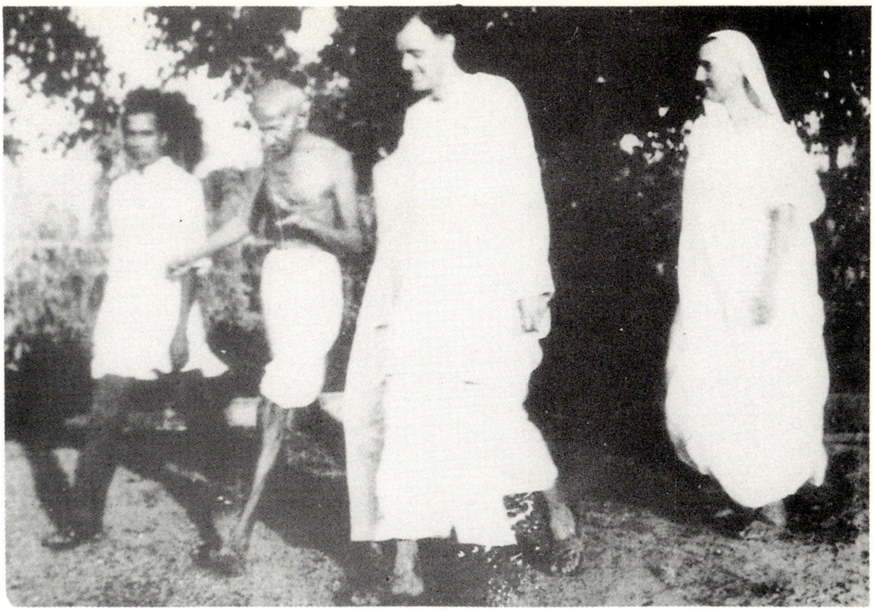

5. Elwin with Gandhi, Sabarmati Ashram, 1931, the dutiful Miraben following (OUP)

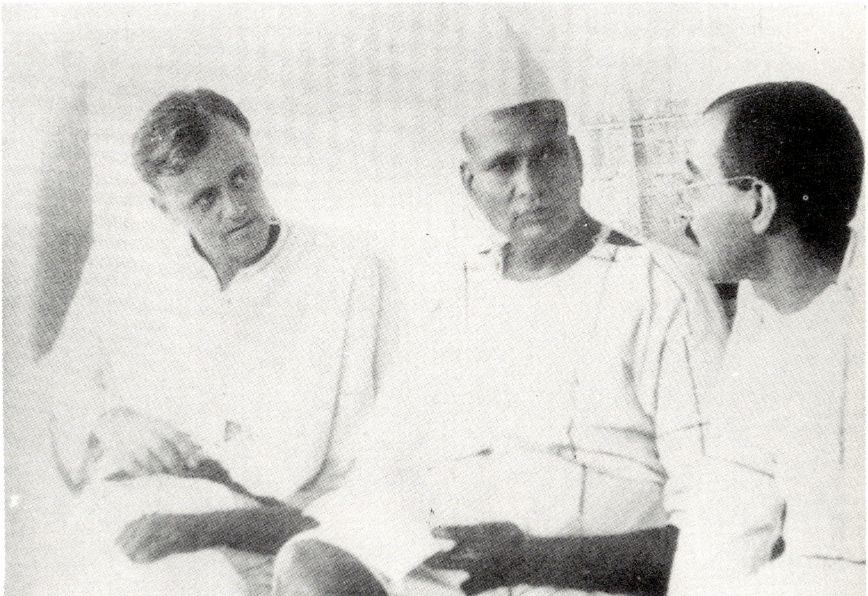

6. Elwin with his fellow followers Jamnalal Bajaj and Pyarelal (in spectacles), Dhulia Jail, 1932 (OUP)

7. Mary Gillet, in the courtyard of the Gond Seva Ashram, Tikeri Tola, 1933 (Verrier Elwin/British Library)

8. Shamrao Hivale, sometime in the mid 1930s (Verrier Elwin/ British Library)

9. Kosi Elwin, c. 1940 (Verrier Elwin/British Library)

10. A Baiga veteran (Verrier Elwin/OUP)

11. Muria chelik and motiari outside the ghotul (Sunil Janah/OUP)

forest. It was here that the prohibition of swidden was 'likely to cause psychological damage and thus in the long-run deep-rooted hostility to Government.' Alert as ever to the telling parallel, Elwin wrote that at a time when the conscience of the world was 'vigorously condemning the Nazis for depriving the minorities of Europe of their freedom and their lands,' the expropriation of aboriginal lands and forests would not be judged kindly by history.[55] He thought the Government of Orissa should restore to these communities the rights over the forest, himself marking out three potential sanctuaries where tribals could cut swidden freely, each family being allotted the exclusive use of twenty acres of forest. All outsiders—landlords, moneylenders, and missionaries—ought to be removed from these reserves.[56]

Wherever he roamed in Bastar, the Central Provinces or Orissa, Verrier Elwin discovered deep differences between tribal communities relatively untouched by the outside world and those that had been radically affected by it. In the Orissa districts of Ganjam and Koraput he found one class of aboriginals who were 'poor, miserable and diseased . . . They have lost their standards; they no longer have the beauty and dignity of an ordered coherent culture to support them; they are adrift in a modern world that so far has done little to afford them anchorage.' But travelling in the interior hills he found 'a very different picture. Here we find living in almost unfettered freedom and in the enjoyment of ancient and characteristic institutions some of the most ancient people of India . . . These people have maintained their morale and their will to happiness. Geographical factors have protected them and still contribute much to their well-being.'[57]

The tribal protected in his mountain fastness was distinguished for his love of nature, his community spirit, his open and unrepressed attitude towards sex, and not least the position of his women. The Baiga woman 'generally chooses her husband and changes him at will; she may dance in public; she may take her wares to the bazaar and open her own shop there . . .; she may drink and smoke in her husband's presence'—freedoms all denied to the caste-Hindu woman.[58] The Baiga were no exception, for in most tribal societies

> the woman holds a high and honourable place. She goes proudly free about the countryside. In field and forest she labours in happy companionship with her husband. She is not subjected to early child-bearing; she is married when she is mature, and if her marriage is a failure (which it seldom is) she has the right of divorce. The lamentable restrictions of widowhood do not await her: should her husband die, she is allowed, even enjoined, to remarry: and in many tribes she may inherit property. Her free and open life fills her mind with poetry and sharpens her tongue with wit. As a companion she is humorous and interesting; as a wife devoted; as a mother, heroic in the service of her children.[59]

But it was only the tribal isolated in the highlands who really *lived*; his religion characteristic and alive, his social organization unimpaired, his traditions of art and dance unbroken, his mythology still vital. 'It has been said,' wrote Elwin in his 1943 pamphlet *The Aboriginals*, 'that the hoot of the motor-horn would sound the knell of the aboriginal tribes as such; but now petrol rationing has stepped in to delay the funeral.' In the 'old days when there were neither roads nor motor-cars,' he was told by a Bastar tribal, 'the Muria were honest, truthful and virtuous.'[60]

Even where their souls were not soiled with the grime of passing motor-buses, the aboriginals were assaulted by civilization in numerous ways. British economic policies, favouring individual titles to property and creating a market for land, dispossessed thousands of tribal families and placed many others in a position of bondage to moneylenders. Forest and game laws reduced the access of aboriginal to the fruits of nature, and in some instances, as for example where shifting cultivation was banned, deprived them of their livelihood altogether. The suppression of the home distillery, forcing the tribal to buy liquor only from outlets licensed by the state, had brought him into contact with a most 'degraded type of alien,' the liquor contractor. The Indian Penal Code and the Indian Forest Act formed two pillars of a massive, alien system of jurispudence which ran counter to tribal custom, subjecting them to endless harassment at the hands of lawyers, lawyer's touts, and ill-informed judges.[61]

Colonial policies worked to impoverish the aboriginals but Hindu society, where it did penetrate tribal areas, attacked their culture with equal ruthlessness. Extended contact with Hindus crushed the aboriginals' love of art, music and dance; taught them to worship alien gods and develop a contempt for their own; introduced child-marriage; constricted their 'generous hearts' with the practice of untouchability; and encouraged them to put their free and happy women in purdah.[62]

This collective deprivation had resulted in a psychological trauma, a 'loss of nerve.' Facing economic decline and the hostility of the state, the Agaria dreamt that when he dug for iron he came up with stones. The Baiga attributed the decline of his powers of magic to the plough. Most cynical of all, the Mandla Gond believed that when the railway came 'Annadeo, the God of food, ran away from the jungle. He sat in the train and went to Bombay, and there he makes the [city] people fat.' It was a world in which the livelihood of aboriginals had been taken away, their culture crushed, a world where even the gods had turned against them. *Abika raj kalau, larka larki malau* (The world today is black, our boys and girls are like monkeys, degraded) remarked a Muria of Narayanpur, a comment that sums up Elwin's own view of the clash of cultures in aboriginal India.

Starting out in one village in Mandla, Verrier Elwin had become by the early forties a spokesman for all twenty million tribals in India. 'The pen is the chief weapon with which I fight for my poor,' he had written to an Italian friend in July 1938 while completing *The Baiga.*[63] That book was the first in a series of rich ethnographies and essays through which Elwin fought for his poor, the voiceless aboriginal. His mission is best explained in the preface to *The Muria and their Ghotul.* It was A. E. Housman's ambition, wrote Elwin

> that one day a copy of *The Shropshire Lad* taken into battle should stop a bullet aimed at a soldier's heart. I have a similar desire for this, as for all my other books, that in the battle for existence which the Indian aboriginal now has to wage, it may protect him from some of the deadly shafts of exploitation, interference and repression that civilization so constantly launches at his heart. If this book does anything to help the Muria to continue as they are today, free and innocent, I shall be content.[64]

CHAPTER EIGHT

Anthropologist at Large

FOR VERRIER ELWIN

Beyond the white fantastic mountains
The war is fracturing the foreign cities
The Western style makes toys of the dead
And in the little brittle churches
The girls are praying with long hair
For the hours of the future and the sexless houses.

Among your burning hills, the lonely jungle
Roars in the summer. The sterile land
Rests; and news comes up like clouds
While you are active in the needs of peace
Saving the gestures of the happy lovers
The poems vivid as the tiger
Faced with destruction from the septic plains
And with your love and art delay
The crawling agony and the death of the tribes.

W. G. Archer

The only fear that haunts me day and night is, 'Will they separate Verrier and me?' No, they won't, for I shall go wherever Verrier goes.

Shamrao Hivale, on hearing the news of the fall of Burma

For Verrier Elwin the 1940s were a time of intense activity, at home and in the world, yet he was to draw a veil over them in his memoirs. His reticence with regard to Kosi has been noted; likewise, the attention generated by his work for and with the tribes is summed up in this solitary sentence: 'A lot of people were down on me in those days and, for an ordinary person, I had a rather disproportionate volume of notice in the press, some of it extravagantly kind, some bitterly hostile.'[1]

Of course Elwin was not an ordinary person at all. 'Verrier Elwin and Tribal India,' recalled one senior Indian scholar, 'were terms of instantaneous association: one could not be thought of without the other.'[2] He was especially well regarded in Bombay, a city with a dense concentration of intellectuals and policymakers which was at this time the commercial and in many respects political capital of India. His circle of admirers included Parsi millionaires who financed his research and his books, expatriate Englishmen who published them, Hindu and Muslim writers who looked to him for guidance and inspiration.

Elwin basked happily in the adoration. He loved the company, the food, the attention, the luxuries of Bombay. He would return to the forest from the 'contagion of the troublous city' knowing always that he would be back next year. When he visited Bombay in the monsoon, newspapers gave handsome coverage to his talks and lectures to the Rotary Club, the Asiatic Society, the Progressive Group, on subjects as varied as 'The Poetry of T. S. Eliot' and 'Aboriginals and the Census.' As an admiring journalist said in 1941, Elwin had been adopted by Bombay society as its 'pet anthropologist.'[3]

The journalist was D. F. Karaka, biographer of Gandhi and Nehru. With the exception only of his fellow Oxonian Frank Moraes, Karaka was the most eminent newspaperman of his generation. In his columns in the *Bombay Chronicle*, as well as in his books, he captured the influence and singular appeal of the Merton scholar who had made his home with the tribes. 'Brilliant in conversation, cultured and polished in speech, a man of letters whose prose was of the best of our generation,' he wrote, 'Elwin's work in anthropology ranks among the great modern contributions on the subject of Man.' There are other people who have attested to the quality of Elwin's prose and scholarship, but for the power of his presence and speech we are obliged to a transcript kept by Karaka. 'We are so used to poverty in India,' Elwin told the Rotary Club, that

> we forget what it is. I remember one day a family coming to us in tears, for their hut and all they possessed had been destroyed by fire. When I asked how much they wanted to put them on their feet again they said, 'Four rupees'—the price of a single copy of *Brave New World*.

> That is poverty.
>
> In Bastar State once, a Maria was condemned to death and on the eve of execution they asked him if there was any luxury he would like. He asked for some chapatti and fish curry, made after the city style. They gave it to him and he ate half of it with great enjoyment, then wrapped the remainder up in the leafplate and gave it to the jailor, telling him that his little son was waiting outside the prison door. The boy had never tasted such a delicacy, but he should have it now.
>
> That is poverty.
>
> Poverty is to see little children taken from you at the height of their beauty. It is to see your wife age quickly and your mother's back bend below the load of life. It is to be defenceless against the arrogant official, to stand unarmed before the exploiters and the cheats.
>
> Poverty is to stand for hours before the gate of the court of justice and to be refused admission. It is to find officialdom deaf and the great and wealthy blind.
>
> I have seen children fighting over a scanty meal of roasted rat. I have seen old women pounding wearily at the pith of the sago palm to make a kind of flour. I have watched men climb trees to get red ants to serve instead of chillies.
>
> Poverty is hunger, frustration, bereavement, futility. There is nothing beautiful about it.[4]

Elwin's speech, wrote Karaka, was the finest he had heard since 'the day George Lansbury [the Labour politician] spoke at the Oxford Union.' The anthropologist was himself

> of the Oxford that has done and will do something in the world as distinct from the Oxford of the layman's conception—the Oxford that produced two Masters of the Fox Hounds, one drunk and one platonically patriotic. Elwin is the genuine article. I can almost see him walking out of the Gothic entrance of Merton, across the cobbled street, his shoulder raised in his characteristic style, hands in his pockets, books under his arms. Is it Schopenhauer or Huxley or the symphony of Beethoven he is thinking about?[5]

The journalist marvelled, as Indians will, at the element of heroic self-sacrifice, at the distance between the Gonds of Mandla and the dons of Merton. Like Karaka, thousands of urban Indians were first told the meaning of poverty by an Englishman whom tradition and history should have marked for an Oxford college or Anglican cathedral. Consider now the testimony of Krishna Hutheesingh, a member of political India's first family. Hearing Elwin speak at Bombay's smartest and most select club, she

> went absolutely numb as he unfolded tale after tale of poverty and woe . . . I looked around at all the wealth, beauty and power present in that room, and I wondered how this story of a forgotten people was affecting them. Some faces looked quite unconcerned, others seemed to be smiling. Was it such an incredible story, I wondered, that they could not really believe it and hence the slightly sarcastic smile? Perhaps they thought that even if it were true, was it not after all ordained by the Almighty that some people should be poor and others rich?
>
> But there were other faces, too, listening to every word Elwin uttered . . . I chanced to glance down and my eyes fell on my hands and clothes—hands that had known no hard work and clothes that might easily have cost enough to feed ten Gonds or even more! Clothes on which I had spent time and money with never a thought what that money could be used for. I felt terribly ashamed of myself and felt I could not in my fine clothes face Verrier after his talk. I wanted to hide somewhere away from prying eyes, so upset did I feel.[6]

There was notice that was 'extravagantly kind' and notice which was 'bitterly hostile.' Elwin's diagnosis of the tribal predicament was always contentious. Congress-minded Hindus like his old friend A. V. Thakkar complained he was an 'isolationist' who wished to keep the aboriginals away from the national movement and all it offered. Elwin replied that he was a 'protectionist' who wished to protect the aboriginal from aggressive and insensitive outsiders. But the charge stuck. An associate of Thakkar then wrote that he was 'more than a descriptive anthropologist; he is a politician with a policy to propound and propagate.' He accused Elwin of wishing, like the Muslim League, to divide Mother India on communal lines, their 'Pakistan' to be matched by his 'Aboriginalisthan,' a special protectorate to be ruled by ethnographers like himself.[7]

Elwin's antagonists seized on a proposal made in the closing pages of *The Baiga* where he argued for the creation of a National Park. Here the tribe would have freedom to hunt, fish and practice bewar and non-aboriginals would be prohibited entry. The term 'national park' was unfortunate for it led critics to immediately accuse him of wanting to put the tribe into a zoo wherein the anthropologist, alone among outsiders, would have privileged access. As this criticism has dogged appreciation of Elwin's work down to the present,[8] his own answer is worth recalling. 'One of the more foolish things that has been said about us recently,' wrote Elwin in March 1942 on behalf of the Bhumijan Seva Mandal,

> is that we want to keep the aboriginal in a zoo. This is particularly ungenerous in our case. For what is the meaning of putting an animal in the Zoo? You take it away from its home, you deprive it of its freedom, and you rob it of its natural diet and normal existence. But my whole life has been devoted to fighting for the freedom of the aboriginals, to restore to them their ancestral jungle and mountain country which is their home and to enable them to live their own lives, to have their own diet, and to refresh themselves with their traditional recreations.[9]

This lover of the aboriginal had his own ideas of what was bizarre and what normal. 'If I wanted to have an Anthropological Zoo'

> I would not fill it with Marias and Baigas; I would have a very different company. I would put in one enclosure the whole of the Sevagram Ashram; in a pleasantly-furnished cage within speaking distance of the Mahatma I would confine the President of the Muslim League. Some way off the office-bearers of the Bombay Purity League would draw crowds of sight-seers eager to watch them sip their lemonade. Elsewhere, carefully segregated, I would include a selection of Hindu Sanatanists as well as a sprinkling of the more diehard officials of the Indian Civil Service. Such types, which will soon be as extinct as the dodo, are of the highest sociological interest and certainly ought to be preserved. The mentality of [the viceroy] Lord Linlithgow will surely be a matter of far greater interest and astonishment to the scientists of another age than that of some poor Santal. I would like to put [the secretary of state for India] Mr Amery too in my collection, but such specimens are expensive and the cost of transporting him from England in war-time would be too great.[10]

This spendidly witty spoof on the fanatical and feuding factions that were messing up Indian politics was simultaneously and implicitly a clarification of his own position on the absurdity of an aboriginal zoo. Yet the charge that Elwin wished to put away aboriginals into a reserve and thus keep them away from the mainstream of Indian life would not go away. It was made most effectively perhaps by G. S. Ghurye, professor of sociology at the University of Bombay. In character and style of scholarship Ghurye was worlds removed from Elwin. He was a careful textual scholar who never left his desk, a library worm who had all of three days' field research to his credit. He was also a Brahmin steeped in Sanskrit and a puritan who did not allow his wife to put spices into their food or his college-going daughter watch movies. Conventional and fastidious in matters of dress, clothing and deportment, Ghurye demanded and received deference from students, colleagues and family alike.[11]

In September 1943 Ghurye published *The Aborigines—So Called—and their Future.* Elwin is the often named and sometimes unnamed antagonist of this book. Basing himself in the main on *The Baiga*, Ghurye attacked Elwin as a 'no-changer' and 'revivalist,' as one who wished to see 'the aborigines reinstated in their old tribal ways, irrespective of any other consideration.' While 'everything savouring of the Hindu upsets Mr Elwin,' the Bombay professor demonstrated through a wealth of examples the parallels between tribal and Hindu beliefs. Tribals, he pointed out, had long been involved in Hindu religious movements and structures of authority. The 'only proper description of these people,' argued Ghurye, was that they are 'the imperfectly integrated classes of Hindu society.' Anthropological accuracy demanded that they be called 'backward Hindus' rather than 'aborigines.'

Ghurye accepted that tribal encounters with Hindus sometimes led to distress but disputed the claim that economic loss was followed by psychic despair, the alleged 'loss of nerve.' Indeed contact with Hindus might benefit the tribals—by exposing them to better methods of cultivation or curing them of drunkenness. Nor would he agree that assimilation would make tribals serfs and destroy their culture and suppress their women. He saw in nationalist India a mood of equality: popular movements among Hindus themselves against untouchability and for the emancipation of women would countenance neither tribal entry at the bottom of the caste hierarchy nor the exploitation of their women. Likewise, the growing interest in folk culture and folk dance would work to protect some aspects of tribal song and dance; these would form part of 'the total complex which is arising called Indian culture.' And where Elwin detested the practice of child marriage Ghurye thought its introduction would temper tribal sexual license, check the spread of venereal disease, and contribute to marital stability.

In Ghurye's eyes British imperial rule was the larger cause of tribal discontent. It was the inroads of the British system of law and revenue that had in the first place created conditions for the erosion of tribal solidarity. The establishment of individual property rights in land, the creation of a land market, stringent forest laws, and an exploitative excise policy had all worked to impoverish tribals, pushing them into the clutches of landlords, moneylenders, and liquor contractors. As the economist D. R. Gadgil noted in a perceptive foreword to the book, Hindu exploitation of tribals was a secondary phenomenon enabled precisely by the primary phenomenon of British dominion. It was the establishment and consolidation of British rule that had 'brought about a revolution in the nature and extent of the contact with the aborigine.' The problem of tribal poverty was thus inseparable from the history of colonial exploitation, a connection which had escaped isolationists like Elwin.[12]

The professor's own values emerge at various points in his book. He had a strong aversion to drink, which he saw as a curse on tribal life—leading to unsteadiness, dissipation of energy, and indolence—as well as a distaste for pre-marital sex. Ghurye was both a Puritan and an Improver whose interpretation of tribe-Hindu relations flowed logically into an enthusiasm for reform.

While *The Aborigines—So-Called—and their Future* was in press the OUP put out Elwin's *The Aboriginals*, which presented to a wider public the policy of the protectionist. This appeared as number 14 in a prestigious and widely circulating series called 'Oxford Pamphlets on Indian Affairs.' Other contributors included leading economists and future ministers writing on finance, land, language, the position of women, and other subjects facing the Congress government-in-waiting. The pamphlets were much read and much discussed, Elwin's more than most others. Professor Ghurye was furious: *The Aboriginals* had appeared too late for him to take account of it in his book. The job of demolishing this latest heresy was assigned to his most able student M. N. Srinivas. Reviewing the pamphlet in the *Journal of the University of Bombay*, this young scholar dismissed Elwin's invocation of 'loss of nerve' as a 'conveniently vague expression,' a misleading application in the Indian context of the idea of a loss of interest in life which the anthropologist W. H. R. Rivers had developed in Melanesia and where it had a solid and verifiable basis in depopulation, disease and starvation. Srinivas also challenged the claim that the policy of protection was based on the authority of science. To the argument that an importation of plough-cultivation would prove fatal to the bewar-loving Baiga, Srinivas responded:

> Mr Elwin here forgets a fact which every tyro in Anthropology knows: cultures are never static, but dynamic. Old traits are thrown off or modified and new ones adopted. And that is life. Of course a certain immigrant trait may be disastrous to the group. But that has to be proved in every case. There is nothing to prove that the Baigas are incapable of taking to [plough] agriculture. We may have to do it with special caution and slowness, but that is quite different from maintaining that it can't be done at all.[13]

In an interview with me, M. N. Srinivas recalled that he was specifically asked by his teacher to take on *The Aboriginals*. There is little question that Ghurye had a deep animus against Elwin. He was jealous of Elwin's popularity and disapproved of his personal life (or what he imagined it to be). Ghurye never forgave one of his students, Durga Bhagwat, for taking Elwin's advice before doing fieldwork with the Gonds. When he found himself in the same room as Elwin in a seminar at the Asiatic Society of Bombay, he turned to a friend and whispered: 'Do you see his face? He has the mouth of a sexual pervert.'[14]

As it was, Elwin most keenly felt the force of Ghurye's attack. Two comments in Shamrao Hivale's book *Scholar Gypsy* are revealing. One refers to a 'very unfair book' by a 'Bombay scholar:' the other, identifying the scholar by name, talks of Elwin's admiration for Ghurye's intellect and power of stimulating research in his pupils, but continues: 'unhappily he lacks the social gifts.'[15] As ever, it was in a letter to Bill Archer that Elwin most fully revealed his feelings. Ghurye's book, he told his friend, was an 'odious book written by [an] anthropological Quisling . . . [which] may do incalculable harm to the aboriginals and to our whole cause, if it is not well and thoroughly refuted. I do beg you to take this very seriously indeed. The fact that Ghurye has chosen me for his chief attack is quite unimportant. My reputation will not suffer because of the criticism of

Ghurye, but I am deeply concerned about the effect that such a book by a Hindu may have on the minds of politicians and administrators dealing with the aboriginals.'

I believe Elwin protested too much, that he knew Ghurye's book might harm his reputation as well as the tribal cause. He now wanted to set aside an issue of *Man in India* to 'putting Ghurye in his place,' with reviews of the *The Aborigines—So Called—and their Future* commissioned from W. V. Grigson of the ICS, the Austrian expert on Indian tribes C. von Fürer Haimendorf, and the Indian anthropologist B.S. Guha—all men likely to come down on Elwin's side. On Archer's advice, though, *Man in India* took the more prudent and politic course of ignoring the book.[16]

Ghurye's book was to deeply scar Elwin, its influence manifest in what he was to write and do in the months and years that followed. In January 1944 he delivered the presidential address to the anthropology section of the Indian Science Congress, speaking on 'Truth in Anthropology.' The subject was inspired, he said, by Mahatma Gandhi, who 'has set us all thinking again in terms of Truth.' His talk was for the most part an exercise in self-justification. He separated himself from the anthropologists (unnamed, but obviously British) who 'interested themselves in the complicated business of deciding the exact way in which aboriginal religion should be distinguished from the Hindu religion.' He also drew the line at 'Indian writers, whom I will not name, [who] have produced articles and monographs after a week or a fortnight's stay in tribal villages. My own book on the Baiga was published seven years after I had settled down in the Baiga country . . .' He complained of the poor quality of illustrations and book production in Indian anthropology, saying that 'art and poetry are the sisters of science in the great family of Truth.' He ended his address on a mystical note, offering science as his secular path to salvation:

> And the scholar's quest is one that cannot fail. Truth is the one thing that cannot be sought in vain. He may not find the truth he expects, or even the truth he wants, but he will one day, if he has been loyal to the spirit that drives him onwards, see the veils of ignorance and delusion torn away and the

> shadows of partial understanding banished by the pure radiance of Eternal Truth in its beauty. Then the scholar will himself be transformed into Truth, and one with Truth that is eternal, he will find his immortality, perhaps the only immortality there is.[17]

In May of that year Elwin was awarded a Doctor of Science degree from Oxford University. He had submitted *The Baiga* and a few essays in lieu of a dissertation, asking Merton to forward and follow up the case. It was an award he energetically lobbied for, with a sharp awareness of the legitimacy it would confer on his work. 'This will do us a lot of good in India,' he told his mother—she received the degree on his behalf—'because my critics had always been saying, "Why, if he poses as a scholar, isn't he a doctor?" '[18]

In the late summer of 1944 Oxford University Press issued two books by Verrier Elwin, each identifying the author on the title page as 'D.Sc. (OXON).' In theme and substance the works nicely complemented one another. *Folk-Tales of Mahakoshal* presented 150 folk tales collected from all over the Central Provinces, stories laboriously transcribed in those pre-tape recorder days by Verrier, Shamrao, and especially their two assistants Gulabdas and Sunderlal. These were wonderfully complicated stories of love and adventure, the chase for a beloved conducted on earth and through the underworld, the man in pursuit of his princess thwarted by ogres and demons but aided by kindly animals. Other stories spoke of sibling rivalry, the jealousy of older brothers against a cossetted younger one, or of the rivalry between the several queens of a single raja—again with the youngest the object of envy and hatred by the older occupants of the king's bed. The tales showed a 'strong sympathy for the underdog,' for the little brother and the newest queen generally triumphed over the hurdles placed before them.

The quarrels in the royal harem pointed to the 'dangers and distresses of polygamy:' otherwise, as the collector happily noted, the tales had no 'moral.' Some of the best ones were collected from his two villages, Patangarh and Karanjia. All were tribal in origin but their structure and idiom borrowed heavily from the epics. As Elwin delicately put it, 'even the remotest and shyest aboriginals have been affected by the wide diffusion during the centuries of the chief motifs of Hindu fiction.'[19]

Folk-Songs of the Maikal Hills drew even more directly on Elwin's home turf, presenting in verse form the poetry of the Gond and his neighbours. He was helped once more by local assistants, while 'to Kosi Elwin a special debt is due for the singing of many beautiful songs.' The book was co-authored with Shamrao Hivale and was in essence a careful elaboration of their modest early effort of a decade before, *Songs of the Forest.* Many of the songs were meant to accompany Gond dances—the karma, the saila, and the dadaria. The book helpfully provided musical notations as well as discussed the techniques of the dances.

A large chunk of the 600 songs in *Folk-Songs of the Maikal Hills* dealt with romance, often with the parrot as a go-between and carrier of messages between lovers. There were songs of the seasons and poems about the tortured relationship of mother-in-law to daughter-in-law. Other songs were less traditional, being commentaries on the artefacts of modernity entering tribal life. One poem poignantly captured the oppressions of civilization:

In this kingdom of the English how hard it is to live
To pay the cattle-tax we have to sell a cow
To pay the forest-tax we have to sell a bullock
To pay the land-tax we have to sell a buffalo
How are we to get our food?
In this kingdom of the English how hard it is to live
In the village sits the Landlord
In the gate sits the Kotwar
In the garden sits the Patwari
In the field sits the Government
In the kingdom of the English how hard it is to live.

The Gond was thwarted at every turn. But, as a poem placed by the translator on the facing page explained, there was at least one remaining source of solace:

Liquor, you turn us into kings
What matter if the world ignores us?
The Brahmin lives by his books
The Panka boys run off with Panka girls
The Dhulia is happy with his basket
The Ahir with his cows
But one bottle makes a Gond a Governor
What matter if the Congress ignores us?[20]

Also finished in the summer of 1944, but its printing held up by a publisher anxious to stagger the productions of his most prolific author, was a collection of the folk-poetry of Chattisgarh. This took as its theatre the territory to the south and east of Mandla, the districts of Durg, Raipur and Bilaspur, where tribals lived cheek-by-jowl with Hindu artisans and peasants. The presentation of verses was linked through a narrative commentary which drew parallels between Chattisgarhi images and English ones. Some motifs reminded Elwin of a poem by an English modern—Huxley, Dylan Thomas or Lawrence; an image here and there reminded him of a great romantic—Wordsworth or Blake; and the odd idea recalled even older works by Chaucer or Shakespeare. For good measure comparisons with the Spanish of Garcia Lorca and the Chinese-to-English renditions of Arthur Waley were thrown in. Some of this was pure showing-off but it was also, I think, an attempt to elevate the 'primitive' to the level of European poetry, to show him as part of some Jungian collective subconscious or of the greater human family, using similar symbols and images for the same basic feelings and emotions.

As for the songs themselves, they dealt with love and marriage in the main, or with the financial privations of village life. Elwin liked these short, sharp disquisitions on impotence, a subject 'discreetly veiled in sophisticated society' but 'discussed with the utmost frankness in the Indian village:'

There is a lock
On the new door
My key is broken
What shall I do?

There is a charred shaft
For the new axe
I was not thinking
That is how I spoilt it.

The golden ring
Looks lovely in your ears
Your husband is impotent
So you take delight with others.

My own favourite is a satirical poem about 'The Soldier on Leave' which reveals the continuing innovation in folk poetry:

This year he is enjoying his Holi
A topi on his head, a pair of boots, gaiters
Coat, waist-coat, pantaloons
A five-coloured muffler around his neck
Cigarettes in a packet and a box of matches
He cleans himself with a brush
He has done his hair 'English style'
No oil for him—he puts attar
He looks like a Bengali
His dhoti goes down to his ankles
At home he talks English, the house-folk do not understand
He calls for 'Water' and when they bring bread
He abuses them for their ignorance
'Commere, commere' he says to his friend, 'let's go to the istation'
Babu has shown 'Singal down,' the train will soon be coming
He talks English *gitpit gitpit* and no one understands
No more 'Salaam' or 'Ram-ram' for him, he bids you 'Guda moraning.'[21]

Elwin's collections of folk poetry and myth did for the tribes what his Oxford mentors Garrod and Nicol Smith had done for English poetry: that is, produce consolidated, critical editions of the classic literature of a place and a people. But as ever, there was a polemical purpose. The publication of the poems and tales would he hoped help banish the 'dark and gloomy shadow over a great part of aboriginal India of the Puritan "reformer" and the missionary of whatever faith,' and challenge the leaders of the 'abominable movement' to stop tribal recreations on the grounds that they were 'indecent.' To 'steal a song,' wrote Elwin, 'is far worse than to steal gold.' The American Baptists in Assam and the Gandhian nationalists in Orissa were both working overtime to abolish the village dormitory and the great feasts, and to introduce prohibition among the tribes. But as Elwin pointed out, 'the romance and gaiety of tribal life is necessary for its preservation.' The new taboos would destroy the dancing and religious life of the tribals and fall most heavily on one section among them. For 'so long as song and dance is free, village women get a square deal. With the coming of a taboo on their dancing, comes also a restriction of their freedom, the decay of their morals, the loss of rights.' He quoted, strategically, the Indian poet and collector Devendra Satyarthi: 'India's national movement does not seem to have recognized the importance of folk-songs as yet. A nation reborn must be inspired by its folk-songs . . . [by] the colour, fire and sparkle of the peasants' poetry . . .'[22]

No sooner had he sent off his collections to the printer than Elwin commenced a battle against the puritans. While he had been away in Bastar Catholics missionaries were making steady progress among the Gonds of Mandla. By the middle of 1944 there were thirty-five Dutch priests in the district, working with a large body of clerks and teachers brought from Ranchi in Bihar, an old centre of missionary work among tribals. Their activities expanded enormously in the war years, helped by massive covert government funding. To his horror Elwin counted more than a hundred schools run by the Catholics, schools that bore 'little resemblance to educational institutions' but were 'simply centres of proselytization.'[23]

In a polemic circulated for support in June 1944 Elwin criticized missionary work as an anachronism: no one believed any longer that salvation was to be found in the Catholic church, an institution that had fathered the Inquisition and had a long history of supporting dictators. Free countries did not permit their populations to be proselytized and India, on the verge of its own independence, was not a 'savage' or 'heathen' country but had religious traditions far older than Catholic Europe. The aboriginals of India themselves had 'their own life, their own art and culture [and] their own religion, to which they are deeply attached and which is by no means to be despised.' All over the world the conversion of tribals by missionaries had undermined traditional political institutions, intensified personal rivalries, and implanted a false sense of prudery and sin. The change of religion, in India as in Africa or Melanesia, 'destroys tribal unity, strips the people of age-old moral sanctions, separates them from the mass of their fellow-countrymen and in many cases leads to a decadence that is as pathetic as it is deplorable.'[24]

Elwin was also appalled by the Dutchmen's attack on Gond culture. The priests wanted the government to pass a law providing 'quick punishment of the man a married woman runs away to.' They claimed the love of the Gond for the karma dance was instrumental in the break-up of tribal marriages: the 'first reason' why women deserted their husbands was 'the excessive sexual excitement caused by frequent singing and dancing of karma with its obscene songs and drink throughout the night.'[25] Married to an accomplished Gond dancer himself, Elwin reacted sharply to these judgements. Forbidding the dance might lead to more adultery than less for it would make life intolerably dull for the woman. Karma was 'the sole surviving instrument of Gond culture; it is a symbol of the freedom and independence of the Gond woman; it is a source of a living art and poetry, in Mandla especially its tunes and rhythms are some of the most beautiful in India.'[26]

Elwin's most effective attack on the Catholics was an essay which appeared in *The Hindustan Times* on 14th June 1944. Both the timing—just months after Ghurye had mauled him—and the place of publication—the foremost nationalist newspaper—are significant. So too is the imagery, an unmistakably Hindu one. The priests in Mandla, claimed Elwin

> are the Chindits of the Christian Army. Compared to them, most other missionaries get to work like Italian infantrymen. These Fathers are from Holland. Fortified by the philosophia perennis, inspired not only by a divine love of souls but by the remarkable Dutch instinct for colonial expansion, they are busy turning Mandla into a Dutch colony . . . Within ten years Mandla—the ancient home of the Rishis, former kingdom of the Gonds, whose fields are blessed by the sacred Narmada—will be virtually a Dutch colony with a hundred thousand Catholic converts.[27]

Three weeks later Elwin sent in an update on the situation in 'the occupied territory of Mandla,' with more evidence of conversion through coercion and bribery. His comparisons were characteristically focused and most carefully chosen. The priests, he reported, had given the tribals medals to kiss morning and evening. On one side of each medal was embossed the image of the Queen of Heaven, on the other 'the unprepossessing features of the Italian potentate who blessed Badoglio's armies on their way to the rape of Abysinnia. It was not indeed, a bad symbol for the conquest of Mandla—for the aboriginals and Hindus of the district are as simple and as defenceless against foreign aggression as were the ill-armed Abysinnians.'[28]

Elwin's attack brought forth a wide-ranging response from his adversaries. In three separate replies in the *Hindustan Times* the priests acknowledged their intention of making converts, but denied coercion.[29]

A well-attended meeting held at the Catholic Institute in Nagpur recorded the protest of the Christians of the Central Provinces at Elwin's challenge to 'the inherent and fundamental Christian right of absolute freedom to propagate the Gospel of Christ in any part of India.' One speaker warned 'Hindu friends that any move to restrict freedom to propagate religion would come back on them like a boomerang.'[30]

Echoes of the debate reached distant Ranchi where an Oraon convert published a pamphlet in defense of missions and missionaries. Unlike Elwin and like Ghurye, this tribal thought his people needed more, not less, civilization. 'Mr Elwin may deride our schools, but we prefer ignorance to knowledge,' wrote Simon Bara. Let 'the death of ancient dialects and the disappearance of venerable customs be a loss to science; we are the gainers by becoming partners in the common cultural heritage of mankind.' Christian priests, he claimed, had saved the Bihar tribals from 'degrading superstition and excessive indulgence in drink . . . out of dying and dwindling tribes' they had 'made virile and vigorous races which face the future full of hope and courage.'[31]

The Dutch Catholics even made contact with Leo Amery, secretary of state for India, a devout Christian and fanatic imperialist. The attitude of British officials towards Elwin had swung from open antagonism (*c.* 1929–32) to cautious suspicion (after 1933). Practising Christians all, they could not abide this latest manifestation. 'Father [*sic*] Elwin is not a highly responsible individual,' said one London bureaucrat. 'As regards Verrier Elwin,' remarked the Governor of the Central Provinces, 'for an objective account of his career please see "Who's Who." Elwin is in short an eccentric who has gone "all tribal," especially since he married a tribal.' The government's policy, said this official, should be 'to let Elwin butt his head against the stone wall of the Christian missionary spirit throughout the world.' The under-secretary of state for India saw 'nothing but disaster from excluding Christian missionaries from work among primitive people. The anthropologists would seem to me far more guilty of exploiting people unable to look after themselves if they were to succeed in getting them pickled as an exhibit instead of being helped to develop to the full stature of the human race [as Christians, that is].'[32] Amery himself wrote scornfully of the 'gospel preached by Verrier Elwin, which is, I gather, that the backward tribes should be isolated in reservations, shut off by ring fences, from the rest of India. [This] is already becoming impracticable and may prove dangerous: to say nothing of the political morality of maintaining those people as "museum pieces." ' Amery's own hope was that the tribal areas in India would be constituted as a Crown Colony, directly ruled from London, 'until such time as His Majesty's Government, after the inhabitants have been consulted, feel justified in transferring them to an Indian Government . . . [These areas] might remain under the Crown Representative for a generation or more.'[33]

Some MPs in Britain even asked the secretary of state to deport Elwin from India. Amery wrote hopefully to Lord Wavell, the viceroy, but Wavell, a sensible and fair-minded man, answered that to interfere in the 'unedifying dispute' between Elwin and the priests would only 'arouse suspicion both between the various communities and against the British.'[34] But Elwin had also been seeking help, writing to the industrialist Purshottamdas Thakurdas, the veteran Congress leader Bhulabhai Desai, and his old mentor and more recently adversary A. V. Thakkar. After visiting Mandla Thakkar deputed his associate P. G. Vannikar to organize a Gond Sevak Mandal in cooperation with Shamrao. They were soon joined by a Hindu service organization, the Arya Dharma Seva Sangh. In a short while the three groups were able to close down twenty five mission schools. By the end of 1946 Elwin could report with satisfaction that the stone wall of the missionary spirit was in fact made of sand, that the advance of the Dutch priests 'had been halted and their work greatly constricted.'[35]

The struggle with the missionaries allowed Elwin to reaffirm his Indian identity, to make a tenuous peace with nationalist social workers and sociologists. Elwin was in principle opposed to both Christian priests and 'Congress minded Hindus,' but, asked (or forced) to choose, there was little doubt which side he would come down on. For one thing he saw the Congress as a less intrusive force: he acknowledged aboriginal religion had some affinity with Hinduism, none at all with Christianity. For another, he was keenly aware of Congress's rising influence with the coming of Indian independence.

Elwin's moves were tactical and opportunistic, but not in a narrowly personal sense. By allying with the nationalists he thought he might more effectively protect his tribals. 'The aim of the movement against the missionaries,' he wrote, 'is to awaken the Hindu community to its duty towards the aboriginal.' We would 'ensure greater permanent good for these people by frankly admitting that they are members of the Hindu family and by saying to the Hindu, "This is essentially your job; get on with it." '[36] He urged 'all Hindu organizations interested in this problem to pass resolutions accepting the major aboriginal communities as Kshatriyas which is what they are and what they claim to be, to stop talking of them as "backward" and "depressed" [and] to drop the horrible word "uplift" from their vocabulary.'[37]

Elwin had a great liking for debate and polemic—'How I do love controversy,' he once remarked, 'it is one of the keenest choices of the mind and I can well understand the feelings of Poets like Milton and A. E. Housman in their love of fighting German scholars.'[38] But he also understood the value and purpose of the strategic retreat. In an India on the verge of independence, with Hindu politicians and modernizing technologists set to assume power, he knew how and when to moderate his criticisms of civilization. The first (July 1943) edition of his pamphlet *The Aboriginals* had seen Elwin at his most combative:

> Let us finally face an unpleasant fact. There is no possibility in India and the world as things are today of substituting civilisation for primitiveness: the only alternative to primitiveness is decadence.
>
> Until modern life is itself reformed, until civilization is itself civilized, until war is banished from Europe and untouchability from India, there is no point in trying to change the aboriginals.
>
> Far better let them be for the time being—not for ever, of course; that would be absurd. Perhaps in twenty, fifty, or a hundred years a race of men may arise who are qualified to assimilate these fine people into their society without doing them harm. Such men do not exist today.
>
> I advocate, therefore, for the aboriginals a policy of temporary isolation and protection, and for their civilized neighbours a policy of immediate reform.
>
> If you want to help the aboriginal, do not try to reform him: reform the lawyer, the doctor, the schoolmaster, the official, the merchant, with whom he has to deal. Until that is done, it is far better to leave the aboriginal alone . . .[39]

These paragraphs were all dropped from the revised edition of the pamphlet printed in November 1944. In the meantime Elwin had been attacked by Ghurye and others and done some rethinking of his own. The corresponding section on policy now more clearly distinguished between two classes of aboriginals: the twenty million who already had some contact with civilization and the five million 'real primitives' who had thus far stayed away from it. The first class would have 'to take their chance with the rest of the population;' their problem was that of poor peasants everywhere. It would be 'deplorable if yet another minority community, which would clamour for special representation, weightage and a percentage of Government jobs, were to be created. The twenty million aboriginals need what all village India needs—freedom, prosperity, peace, good education, medicine, a new system of agriculture and a fair deal under industrialization'—to be achieved by plans and schemes devised by 'wiser heads than mine.'

It was the remaining five million tribals who 'should be left alone and should be given the strictest protection that our Governments can afford.' Elwin admitted that this was 'a desperate measure and one that is easily misunderstood and still more easily misrepresented.' It was 'based on no philosophic principle. Least of all does it suggest that the aboriginals are to be kept for ever primitive. I only urge that unless we can civilise them properly it is better not to interefere with the small minority of the most primitive hillmen at all. Casual benefits only destroy and degrade; it needs a lifetime of love and toil to achieve permanent advance.' 'I do not suggest,' wrote Elwin, 'that the primitive hillman is better than the finest flower of modern culture, but my experience, which is now extensive, is that these tribes in the freedom and glory of their mountains are infinitely better and better off than the semi-civilised and decadent clerks and coolies which is all that we seem to produce by our present methods of uplift and reform.'[40]

Verrier's one-time guru Mahatma Gandhi liked to speak of the 'beauty of compromise.' In tone and content the revised edition of *The Aboriginals* makes many concessions to the dominant mood. But, again like Gandhi Elwin would not bargain on the essentials. Reform the reformers, respect the tribes: such was the message conveyed by the stirring paragraphs that ended both editions of the controversial pamphlet:

> We may fight for three freedoms—freedom from fear, freedom from want, freedom from interference. We may see that the aboriginals get a square deal economically. We may see that they are freed from cheats and impostors, from oppressive landlords and moneylenders, from corrupt and rapacious

officials. We may see that they get medicinal aid from doctors with some sense of professional integrity. If there must be schools, we may see that these teach useful crafts like carpentry and agriculture, and not a useless literacy. We may work to raise the prestige and the honour of the aboriginals in the eyes of their neighbours. We may guard them against adventurers who would rob them of their songs, their dances, their festivals, their laughter.

The essential thing is not to 'uplift' them into a social and economic sphere to which they cannot adapt themselves, but to restore to them the liberties of their own countryside.

And finally, the pointed reminder to 'freedom-fighters' who spoke self-righteously of themselves as Indian and others as foreign:

But whatever is done, and I would be the last to lay down a general programme, it must be done with caution and above all with love and reverence. The aboriginals are the real swadeshi products of India, in whose presence everything is foreign. These are the ancient people with moral claims and rights thousands of years old. They were here first: they should come first in our regard.

While writing ferociously for the popular and not-so-popular press, Elwin also found time for extended spells of fieldwork. At the urging of Sir Francis Wylie (by now political adviser to the viceroy), he had been appointed honorary ethnographer to the Government of Orissa. In wartime, when transport and supplies were difficult to come by, official status made fieldwork that much easier. Between 1943 and 1946 he toured Orissa each year, renewing contacts with known tribes and meeting, for the first time, unknown ones.

In the winter of 1943–4 Elwin travelled among the Kuttia Kondhs of the Baliguda hills. The country was wild but not especially beautiful: occasionally one got fine views but otherwise 'a sense of extraordinary isolation.' The girls were attractive, their hair most appealingly fluffed out to the sides. 'Boys and girls rampage up and down in each other's arms,' he noted in his diary: 'best girl dancers wriggle bodies in singularly seductive manner.' But the anthropologist was also drawn willy-nilly into the tormented past of the Kondhs. The catalysmic event in their recent history had been suppression, in the late nineteenth century, of the practice of human sacrifice. Elwin sympathized rather more with this manifestation of the civilizing mission, yet drew attention to some of the consequences. Although the Kondhs explained away the origins of human sacrifice in terms of divine intervention, he thought their stories about the suppression distinctly regretful. Their priests still possessed the old instruments of sacrifice—the knifes, chains and bowls to catch the blood of the victim. These were now used to sacrifice buffaloes but the priests said that on full moon nights they sometimes heard these tools weep for the human blood now denied them. As a Kondh song went, 'Long ago there came sahibs and we gave them elephants and horses / And all they did was destroy our customs.' The sahibs of the nineteen forties would not leave them alone either. The forest department had started a campaign to enclose forests, stop swidden, and bring Kondhs down to the plains and make honest rice-cultivators of them. 'We took a goat to a Sahib,' recounted one tribal, 'and told him our woes, saying we must cut swidden in the forest reserve, or we'll die. He said don't cut or the conservator will tie you up and take you to jail. We said that will be better than this jail.' 'Who made the forest?' asked the Kondh: 'For whom did He make them? For the Government or for the people?'[41]

A tribe that Elwin came to know well were the Bondo, who lived on a remote and elevated plateau in the district of Koraput, 'their life characterized by great independence, liberty and equality—and the highest homicide rate in India.' On his first two visits, in December 1943 and March 1945, the villagers were most unhelpful—the men would come round begging for tobacco but would not, in return, sell food or help them shift camp. When he tried to take photographs the Bondos stopped him; they thought the camera would extract a vital essence from their bodies. Rumours were abroad that the sahib had come to take recruits for the army, or send all the children to America to become Christians, or worst of all to introduce prohibition. But by the time of his third trip, in January 1946, Elwin found that suspicion had eased: 'no depredations from tigers had followed my earlier visits, there had been no fresh taxation, no policy of prohibition had been introduced, no girls had been carried off to the war, we had begun to fit into the picture'—to the extent that some of his best friends were convicted murderers.[42]

On this last trip Verrier was accompanied by two English friends, a timber contractor H. V. Blackburn, and an aircraftsman Harry Milham. Milham has left an account of the field methods of an anthropologist who could not stay sober. Their visit was timed to coincide with the 'pao parab,' the Bondo's annual festival of the full moon which had never been described before. From the rail-head at Raipur the three Englishmen drove eight hours to Jeypore in the heart of the Koraput hills and the seat of its ruling prince. Over a bottle of rum in a dak bungalow Elwin told his colleagues about the tribe they were soon to stay with. The 'temper of the people,' he said, ' was quite unpredictable and it was quite possible they would "bump us off." '

The trio set off next morning for the Bondo country. They were preceded by Elwin's faithful research assistant Sunderlal Narmada, who prepared the ground for their arrival. From the road-head it was a steep climb to the Bondo villages. En route Elwin badly bruised his toe. He was climbing barefoot as was his custom, and had what 'appeared to be his usual argument with a projecting rock.' They finally reached the village of Bodopalle where the first person they met was Muliya, a double murderer released from prison after a life sentence and apparently a 'great pal' of Elwin.

After pitching camp the anthropologist played his gramophone and handed out cigarettes. Even the womenfolk came out to listen to the music, but then, to his fury, Elwin heard that the villagers had postponed the festival. The 'official' explanation was that the first crop of millet had not yet been gathered, but the visitors had an uncomfortable suspicion that the real reason was their own presence as outsiders. When 'all the blandishments and bribery' they could muster 'were met with smiles and inaction,' Elwin tried to stir things up with a bow-and-arrow competition. He put up a cigarette packet at a distance of fifty feet and invited shots. Two men hit the target three times in succession. Then the timber contractor, Blackburn, took out his .22 rifle and gave an exhibition of marksmanship. He shot a dove and a jungle fowl, retrieved by a 'retinue of delighted boys.'

The Bondos still wouldn't put on their show, so the party moved on to the next village, Bodopada. The setting was gorgeous: 'the green of the trees among the thatched roofs, the plaster and bamboo walls of the huts, the dark green of tobacco plots, all against a background of gently sloping hills with their patches of cultivation and the light green of sago palms and shrubbery.' Here too the English trio played the gramophone, then chased and fought each other to amuse the villagers. Elwin showed photographs taken on his last visit and the Bondos excitedly identified themselves. Milham had by now downed his inhibitions in plenty of Gordon's Dry and was taking a long look at the women:

> Their dress is very little, a bark fibre strip about 9 inches in depth and held around the waist by a string. The cloth, which has regular vertical patterns of colour, drops alarmingly at the back, leaving most of the behind bare. The left thigh is completely bare and the cloth looks very insecure but it normally does the job for which it was intended . . .
>
> The upper body is bare except for a most amazing collection of beads which give quite a well clothed appearance from a distance. Their arms carry many metal bracelets. Their shaven heads with their bands of yellow bamboo strips, make them appear ugly at first sight but one realises that some of them are very beautiful and all have really lovely eyes . . .

Elwin, who had seen all this before, remained depressed. He thought the village was deliberately holding up the moon festival. They had not yet made the special food known as Kirimtor, a kind of vegetarian sausage made of rice flour and boiled pulses. Then at nightfall came the welcome news that the Bondo were at last making Kirimtor. The festival itself commenced the next morning, around noon. A space was cleared out in the middle of the village ground and the drummers assembled. To their music two boys of eight started fighting with sticks. The drumming got faster and the hitting fiercer, till the headman judged the contestants had had enough. The boys hugged one another and then went over to the priest to accept their leaf plate of Kirimtor, which they passed on to their proud parents.

The battles continued with other boys, successively older and more violent in their hitting. The spectators meanwhile were steadily drinking mahua. The anthropologist made up a theory on the spot: 'The origin of the ceremony,' he claimed, 'lay in the attempt to prove that hitting a man can result in a friendly solution rather than a murder.' By now it was dark, and although it was a full moon night a fire was lit to illuminate the arena. Village girls sang to the music while men danced in bamboo head-dresses with peacock feathers popping out. Elwin was dragged into the ring and swung around in a tight circle, straining to keep time. He danced till midnight, drinking very quickly between dances. Sunderlal, who had seen all *this* before, did his best to get him to go to bed. But he wouldn't listen and as soon as the music started would stagger up to join the dance.

Milham and Blackburn were watching from the sidelines. There came a time when their friend disappeared from view. Sunderlal was alerted and he walked into the crowd to find Elwin lying in the middle, flat on his back and dead to the world. He was carried to his tent and dumped into bed, fully dressed. But he woke up later, said 'Good Heavens,' got up and rejoined the dance. He got a great ovation, as it was now 4 a.m.

The next day the party started back for Jeypore. On the climb down Elwin cut his toe again. To the pain in the foot was added a pain in the head. He was in no mood for conversation, remembered Milham, and 'as he sat down on a rock, holding the top of his head with both hands, he would have made a perfect subject for one of the teetotal pictures of the 1890s. The evil effects of Demon drink were shown in every line of his drooping body.'[43]

Another tribe that charmed the anthropologist were the Saoras, who were less prone to violence but equally wary of the outsider. They worshipped a god called Sahibosum who helped keep away touring officials. Located strategically, at the boundary of the village, Sahibosum was made of wood in the image of a sahib, complete with trousers and sola topee. If the sahib came anyway, the Saoras would mark his departure with a purificatory sacrifice. For this they had a standard tariff: a goat for a forest guard, a fowl for a constable, a big black pig for the anthropologist.

The Saora villages were situated on stone terraces built up one above the other. The fields were walled in and well cared for, irrigated with skill and producing rice of high quality. Their theology was as advanced as their agriculture. It centred on sacrifice and was run by shamans. The Saora were adept artists, their paintings crowded over with whimsical deities and dangerous animals and officials. The pictographs were made by the householders, under the close direction of the shaman, who identified the gods to be portrayed or appeased.[44] Collecting material on Saora religion, Elwin wrote to Archer that it was 'so restful to work on something which has nothing to do with sex.'[45] The novelty of the subject was also communicated to his old publishers. He had not published with John Murray for some time. The war had something to do with this, but perhaps also the nature of the books he offered them. He now wrote to Murray asking whether they would consider publishing a book on Saora religion, a book with 'not a word about sex from cover to cover.'[46]

Elwin was now planning a series on Orissa tribes, each book focusing on a different theme: 'Bondo—megalithic culture, crime and character; Saora—religion; Gadaba—weaving; Kond—agriculture; Juang—functional character of myth.'[47] The writer and polemicist had completely supplanted the social worker. Patangarh was for him merely home base, the place he returned to from his travels to unpack and transcribe his notes, thus to better write his books. When he returned from one of his trips and began immediately to draft a new chapter, Kosi commented that 'I married a man not a typewriter.' Anxious to get on with his work Verrier then ran away to Sarwachappar, saying he could not write his book with everyone screaming at the top of their voices. This was an act of self-centredness that even Shamrao would not condone. He hoped that Kumar 'does not become like Verrier who seems to do nothing in life but work.' Kosi was more scathing. She took to calling his books his *chutki*, or younger wife, implying Verrier was more in love with his books than with her.[48]

Verrier once confessed to Bill Archer that both he and Kosi were polygamous by nature. 'Each infidelity made her more fascinating—without it he might have tired of her after two or three years—with this common background casual encounters with other girls were both necessary and possible. [He] would take it whenever he could;' once with a Panka ayah in Patangarh, at another time with a beautiful Jewish girl in Bombay. Kosi also would take it whenever she could. Verrier told Archer, not without pride, of her seduction by an English friend in Bombay. After Kosi had retired to her room the men talked and drank and Verrier, true to form, seems to have passed out first. To get to the lavatory the other fellow had to go through Kosi's room. He went 'four times in one hour and first time smiled, the second touched her hair—the third stroked her—the fourth time took her.'[49]

By 1944 Verrier was utterly absorbed in his books and the marriage came under some strain. To his mother he presented an encouraging picture of Kosi as a bourgeois wife: 'she is doing very good knitting; she is making woollen scarves for the lepers.'[50] One doesn't know about the lepers, but Kosi was not pleased with her work-obsessed husband. While he was away in Orissa she began an affair that was anything but casual. Late in 1945 she became pregnant; we cannot be certain by whom, although we know it was not by Verrier (it was probably a Muslim shopkeeper named Sahid). After the excitement of Kumar's arrival he was most laconic about the appearance of this child. He was touring in Orissa when Kosi went off to Bombay to 'produce her second edition.' From Gunupur in the uplands of Koraput he wrote to Archer: 'I must go and see Kosi and the baby on 20 May: *I can't put it off any longer.*'[51]

In July 1946 a conclave was held in Bombay. Jehangir Patel, the textile magnate who was now the Bhumijan Seva Mandal's most reliable patron, thought Verrier should file for divorce. Even Shamrao, the arch reconciler, insisted that Kosi could not be forgiven. He took her and the baby off to Patan while Verrier talked with a firm of solicitors. But after he returned to the village Verrier decided he would give his wife another chance. He had just been offered a job in the Anthropological Survey of India; the Survey was based in Banaras but was soon to move to Calcutta. Might he and Kosi not forget the mess in Patan and move to the city? 'I am going to start what I hope will be a new life with Kosi,' he wrote to Patel. To his solicitor he sent a remarkable letter explaining why he did not wish to proceed with the divorce. He listed the reasons for his change of mind:

1. My affection for my wife has remained unaltered by anything that has happened. She has done her best to kill that love, but since it has proved tough enough to survive even this, there must be something in it.
2. From the very beginning I have told my friends that I regarded the blame

for the crisis that arose to be as much mine as Kosi's. The few faults in my wife's life are more than matched by far graver faults in mine . . .

3. There is another reason why I cannot bring myself to blame Kosi. She is a victim of what we anthropologists call acculturation. That is to say she is an aboriginal, whom I took out of her moral surroundings and religo-cultural sanctions and taboos. It is generally found that when this happens, the aboriginal suffers an extreme disturbance and often behaves in a way that we would not call normal. It may be that I too am a victim of acculturation—for I have suffered almost as complete a transplantation from the life of the ordinary barra sahib as she has from the life of her village.
4. There is to me something almost intolerable in saying things even privately, still more in open court, against the woman who has honoured me by becoming my wife. I wanted to arrange matters so that she should divorce me, not the other way, but I feared that such a course might injure my scientific work . . .
5. I am now probably going to live in Calcutta and I want to make one last attempt to turn my married life from failure to success. Kosi may be happier there; she will have the children with her, and we have many friends in the city. For the first time I will be in a position to give her the comfort she deserves. We will, on both sides, forgive and forget. If this new attempt is a failure, we will then have to revise the situation.[52]

Kosi for her part had agreed to tell her 'Mussalman shopkeeper off.'[53] Both Jehangir Patel and J. R. D. Tata, Verrier's friends and sponsors, were not happy with the reconciliation. 'I don't know whether to be sorry or glad about his decision,' wrote Tata to Patel, 'but I suppose it is up to him in the end and to shape his own life and his friends can only advise'[54]—as well as keep the secret, he might have added, for these two Parsi captains and the Parsi solicitor were apparently the only people outside Patan who knew of the affair.

Verrier had to suppress the infidelity and illegitimacy for various reasons—mother, their patrons, and not least the puritan nationalists who were at once the main audience for his work and the likely future rulers of the tribes. Kosi's second son he named Vijay after the cricketer Vijay Merchant, then playing with great success on the All India Tour of England, but referred to him in private as his 'interim baby.' Reading between the lines of a letter to his mother, it is possible to distinguish his feelings for one Elwin boy from the other: 'Kumar and Vijay are well. Kumar in particular is a supreme darling, the dearest, tenderest little boy you ever saw, most understanding and intelligent, though at present backward academically.'[55]

Through the nineteen forties, while Verrier was travelling on government commission and in search of new tribes to study or protect, Shamrao Hivale was rooted in Mandla, carrying on the work of the Bhumijan Seva Mandal. Under his friend's influence, and with his assistance, Shamrao also completed a study of the Pardhans, the community of ministrels who lived alongside the Gonds.[56]

Shamrao was an unlikely and even unwilling author, yet the year 1946 saw two works published in his name: *The Pardhans of the Upper Narmada Valley* and *Scholar Gypsy: A Study of Verrier Elwin. Scholar Gypsy* reproduces massive chunks of Verrier's circular letters, reviews of his books, and admiring comments from Indian and European visitors, linked by the odd paragraph of connecting commentary written by Shamrao himself. It is a very scarce book, almost impossible to find even in the best Indian libraries. Nor was it much noticed when it appeared. The idea behind it seems to have been to provide Verrier a reliable curriculum vitae to live and work in independent India. Not unexpectedly, the book highlights the years of service to the Congress and the bitter battles with the Church. The controversies with sociologists are mentioned obliquely, but the reservations with regard to the Mahatma not at all. To the charge that Verrier was obsessed with sex Sham offered a statistical refutation: only 280 out of 2750 pages of his major monographs dealt with the subject, which 'hardly suggests that he is absorbed in sex.' Other criticisms, such as that the anthropologist wished to pickle tribals as museum-pieces, are answered with words—Verrier's words.

Scholar Gypsy is very much a commissioned work, with Sham the scribe, narrator and propagandist for Verrier's achievements. I suspect the subject chose the illustrations as well. There are several of him in his Gandhian years, with Mirabehn, with J. B. Kripalani, and by the Mahatma's bedside when the old man was ill. There are two photographs of

Kumar—here called Jawaharlal—but none of Vijay. The rare comments that Sham allows himself are in character. On Verrier's personality: 'I have watched him in various capacities—as a most loving, loyal and gentle friend and husband and father. But I have also seen him as a hard and determined enemy of those who have tried to meddle or interfere wantonly in the lives of his people.' On his faith, or rather lack of it: 'The greatest change has been in Verrier's attitude to religion. When I first knew him he was almost a religious maniac. Today he has no religion at all, believing neither in a Supreme Being nor in the future life. But his scientific interest in religion remains, and he is at present engaged on what may be the most important of his books, a study of primitive religion among the Lanjhia Saoras.' And most evocatively, on what he threw away:

> There can be no doubt that if he had continued as he began, he would today have been a Prince of the Church, living in his Palace at Durham or Winchester, in dignity and honour. And now when I look at him, sitting at his desk, bare-foot, in patched and tattered clothes, perhaps struggling against the onset of malaria, I wonder if his sacrifice was worthwhile or whether, when he turned his back on Oxford, he did not make a terrible mistake.[57]

For Shamrao the production of books was merely a diversion. While Verrier was on the move he worked devotedly among the poor and diseased. He supervised ten primary schools, ran the dispensary, and paid a weekly visit to the lepers in their home in Sarwachappar; an eight-mile walk each way from their village of Patangarh: in the rains, 'a most exhausting tramp through mud.' A government official visiting the Leper Home said of it that 'whatever can be done by human love has been done.'[58] In 1943 Shamrao was at last appointed an honorary magistrate in belated recognition of a dozen years of service among the Gonds. This appointment saved villagers the long journey to the court in Dindori town, where they had previously to contend with sharp lawyers and canny officials. Shamrao had more cases in a month than Verrier had in the year (1937–8) he was a magistrate; almost all disputes he handled were settled by mutual agreement.[59]

Verrier once wrote that Shamrao was his 'constant companion, supporter and consoler.'[60] It seemed sometimes that all of Patangarh regarded him in this light. Perhaps the strangest of all his cases was the affair between a fifty-year-old Pardhan woman, married with three children, and a Gond boy of seventeen working as her field servant. When the news reached their house Verrier took out his copy of Freud, for this was 'a clear case of mother-substitute fixation.' But Shamrao at once summoned the concerned parties and commenced to reconcile them. The woman declared her passion for her lover in a loud voice: it was reciprocated. The husband sat in a corner, abashed, while the crowd of assembled villagers could not contain their mirth. The counsellor persuaded the woman to return to her family and sent the Gond boy off to work in one of their hostels in Sunpur, a better job and in a different village. He succeeded in doing for free 'what a Harley Street psychologist would probably have charged a heavy fee for.'[61]

Shamrao and his mate were to be separated when Verrier moved to Banaras to join the Anthropological Survey of India as deputy to the director, B. S. Guha. A Harvard-trained scientist with a fascination for blood groups, Guha visited Verrier in the field in Bastar and endeared himself as a 'caustic and entertaining old thing, with the lowest possible opinion of all anthropologists except himself and me.' The Survey was a new department of the Government of India, charged with studying and prescribing policies for rural communities. Verrier was attracted to the job partly for economic reasons: he had a growing family to support, while donations to the Bhumijan Seva Mandal had dried up during the war. Moreover, with an interim Nationalist Government headed by Jawaharlal Nehru in office, this was a chance to influence aboriginal policy in free India. When Elwin joined the Survey, Nehru had just made an 'admirable statement on aboriginal policy:' the task was to convince 'his less intelligent colleagues that the primitive presents any problem at all to the modern world and that to open cheap little primary schools and make people teetotal does not necessarily cure all their ills.' Elwin now saw a 'great and urgent danger that Nationalist India, which is naturally anxious to get on after a century of stagnation, will be in too great a hurry to reform and change her aboriginals and, by forcing the pace, will bring social and cultural disintegration upon them.'[62]

The Survey seems to have had its genesis in a note Elwin wrote to Francis Wylie in November 1944, suggesting that a full-time adviser be appointed to advise the Government of India on aboriginal problems. 'The appointment of an Indian scientist of distinction,' he wrote, 'would convince people that Government means business. It would be a token (long overdue) that we did not believe that the only people capable of handling aboriginals were foreigners. It would, I think, inspire Indians themselves to work for the aboriginals and to take them seriously.' Wylie passed on the note to the viceroy, and in time the Anthropological Survey was formed with Guha as director.[63] In September 1946 Verrier left Patangarh to take up the first job he'd had in twenty years (since Wycliffe Hall). 'I am now the hell of a chap,' he wrote to Bill Archer: 'Deputy Director of the Anthropological Survey of India.' At last he had 'emulated his revered male parent' by becoming a 'D.D.'[64]

Bill Archer himself was at the time deputy commissioner for the Naga Hills. In May–June 1947 the DD went to see the DC, taking the uninitialled Shamrao with him. For the past few months Verrier had been sitting on a mountain of files, and he looked forward to getting out of his office. Archer took them to the *morungs* or dormitories of the Konyaks, with the decorated boys dancing, 'delicious creatures,' to the girls singing in their deep voices. They were less impressed by the Naga religion, the fervent Christianity of the new convert carried out in 'hideous tin Baptist chapels.' But Verrier was charmed by the capital of Assam, Shillong, a town set among hill and pine. 'What a lovely place, what superb people!' he wrote to his mother, ' I feel we have wasted twenty years messing about in central India instead of coming here.' Both he and Sham felt depressed when they got into the Assam Mail and crossed the Brahmaputra back into the plains.[65]

The DD now had the funds and status to explore new tribes and new areas. His larger hope for the Anthropological Survey was that it would play its part in integrating the elements of a culturally diverse nation. For the acquistion of knowledge was 'not only of scientific importance, but of the utmost practical value in administration, as well as for ensuring fellowship and understanding among the population.'[66] His own experiences tended to confirm the practical value of anthropological research. His book on the Baiga helped free the tribe from forced labour, diluted the state's drive to abolish shifting cultivation, and induced a sympathetic attitude among officials. As a result of his Agaria study the tax on their furnaces was reduced by half. He was greatly encouraged by the interest taken in his work by administrators in Bastar and Orissa, a concern he thought likely to translate into steps for the alleviation of aboriginal discontent.[67]

In Elwin's view the craft of anthropology aided cultural understanding and provided a scientific basis to policies aimed at the poor and vulnerable. As for the anthropologists themselves, they were natural allies of the oppressed. As he put it in a broadcast over All India Radio in 1947,

> The fact today that the world has a conscience about its primitive populations is to no little extent due to the anthropologists and the new attitude on which they have insisted. I do not know of any body of men . . . who are more devoted to the poor than these scientists. The anthropologist is the true Dinabandhu [friend of the poor] for he lives among the poor; he learns to love them as people, he does not think of them as 'masses' to be uplifted with a vague and too-often sterile enthusiasm.

'All over the world,' he continued,

> the anthropologists have fought for the rights of primitive folk; they have transformed the situation in parts of Central Africa; they have tempered the destructive impact of civilization in Indonesia and Australia; the great American and Russian Bureaus of Ethnology have not only helped to weld those vast continents into unity but they have gained for their ancient populations a square deal.[68]

What Elwin did not, could not, add was that he had done as much as anyone else to awaken the conscience of society to the plight of 'primitive' peoples, to temper the often destructive impact of civilization and to try and gain for the aboriginals a square deal in a country on the verge of political independence.

CHAPTER NINE

Staying On

God has already heavily punished any Englishman who tries to bring East and West together, instead of throwing in his lot entirely with either belligerent. His life is one long penance: he gets the stones from both parties—the Indian regards him as a lukewarm, if not false, friend, the British Imperialist says 'he is the most dangerous man of all, for he sometimes seems to talk sense'—that is, of course, sense from a British point of view. At the Last Day both Indian Nationalist and British Imperialist will find at least one point of agreement—in voting that such men be sent to Jehannum, Narak, Hell.

E. J. Thompson[1]

On 15th August 1947 India became independent. In New Delhi Jawaharlal Nehru delivered a famous speech on his country's 'tryst with destiny,' while at a more modest ceremony in Banaras the deputy director of the Anthropological Survey helped hoist the national tricolour. Reporting the latter event Shamrao Hivale recalled a day, nearly twenty years earlier, when his friend had unfurled the Indian flag above the ashram of the Christa Seva Sangh, an act as 'dangerous then as it is now respectable.' Verrier's dearest ambition, commented Shamrao, was 'to take the nationality of our free India so that he may be able to do legally what he has always done in fact, belong to our nation.'[2]

Some other Indians were not so sure about Verrier Elwin's *bona fides.* Two days before Independence he found himself testifying before a subcommittee of the Constitutent Assembly of India. One of its members sharply asked Elwin about his 'policy of isolation.' Now a government servant, Elwin explained his position (as he was to tell Bill Archer) in phrases 'nicely trimmed to the spirit of the age.' Isolation, he told the committee, had once been advocated by him as a strictly temporary measure to protect the weaker tribes from the economic exploitation and psychic degradation that might result from uncontrolled contact. He had not recommended it for the vast majority of tribals whom he called, in a very heavily trimmed phrase indeed, 'Hindus in the kindergarten class.' These had to be 'educated, developed and brought into the mainstream of modern Indian life as soon as possible.' Moreover, with a national and socialist government in place Elwin saw that there was no place any more for isolation or exclusion. This government would protect the aboriginal by eliminating landlords, checking moneylenders, and keeping out missionaries: all of which the colonial rulers had conspicuously failed to do. True, carefully trained officials were needed for the 'wilder and weaker tribes,' to monitor and guide their welfare, to make sure they received the best and not the worst that civilization had to offer. However, a policy of isolation *qua* isolation had no place when 'the imperative need of the country is for unity. We do not want any new minorities. We want one people, advancing together towards a common goal. Separate areas will promote the habit of disunity. Separate electorates, separate representation, separate areas should all disappear with the passing of the old regime.'

The India of 1947–8 was a country determined to make the most of an overdue independence, to put behind it the divisive conflicts of class and community that had so painfully marked the last phase of the struggle for freedom. The Pakistan movement had been successful, taking with it a huge chunk of the territory of Mother India: in what remained, the talk was only of 'national unity' and 'solidarity,' or, in the economic sphere, of 'building socialism,' inclusive, catch-all categories that pre-empted critics of the mainstream advocating their own distinctive and partial interests. Like representatives of the Muslims and the Untouchables, this defender of tribals had to adopt the language and phrases of the nationalist, to swallow hard and swallow them. But even at his most conciliatory Elwin would enter a note of defiance. When other people discuss the aboriginals, he remarked, they almost always

> stress the bad things in their habits and customs. I do not know that their society is disfigured by worse evils than those that affect general civilization, whether Asiatic or European. But may I remind you that they have many beautiful and noble qualities also—their manly virtue, their freedom and

> independence, the very high place they generally give to their women, their truthfulness, their freedom from mean and petty vices, their capacity for artistic creation, their instinct for recreation expressed in dance and song, their capacity for laughter, their simple natural attitude to life and its pleasures, the courage with which they overcome poverty and disease. These are precious things. In Britain we are proud of our hillmen, the highlanders of Scotland. We too should not be ashamed of our aboriginals, we should be proud of them and look forward to the fine things they will give us. And so, in pleading for caution and care in dealing with them, I plead also for sincere reverence for them; they must not be despised as savages; they have gifts we need and they will in time contribute to the national life.[3]

Ask not what civilization can give the aboriginal, remember only what he can give it.

In this testimony of 13th August 1947 Elwin uses 'we,' in relation to *both* Britain and India. This unselfconscious invocation might be proof only of his identification with both cultures; or, despite what Shamrao Hivale had to say, of his unwillingness, at the moment of the transfer of power, to completely abandon one national allegiance for the other.

The patriotic fervour released at Indian independence made Verrier's position a uniquely vulnerable one. Forgotten by now was his work for Gandhi and civil disobedience in the early thirties. Fresh in nationalist memory was his more recent defence of the tribes. To the unthinking patriot this seemed another ploy to 'divide' India. His unhappiness and insecurity find poignant expression in a letter mourning the departure for England of Bill Archer, who was returning home with other members of the ICS. Archer was himself very depressed. He had wanted to stay on in the Naga Hills, where he was, in December 1947, serving as deputy commissioner. But that post was not meant for an Englishman in free India. Abruptly transferred and offered a choice between a posting in the plains and early retirement, he chose to go home. 'You may console yourself,' Verrier told him, 'that I am if anything being tortured more; for I have hell within as well as without. We poets in our youth begin in gladness but thereof in the end comes despondency and madness.' He continued:

Your friendship has been precious to me beyond words, and I dread your going from India. Soon there will be nothing to drink, no one to talk to, and no one to copulate—and I shall sink down to being a poor white, brooding over unpublishable manuscripts and thinking up unprintable jokes.'[4]

The Anthropological Survey was then based in Banaras. Verrier thought the city 'intolerably dull' and looked forward to the Survey's impending move to Calcutta. Meanwhile at home trouble was brewing again. A series of one-line entries in his diary says it all: 'Frightful quarrel between Sham and Kosi (who had taken bhang) [10th July 1947].' 'Kosi fights all day on the best whisky and vermouth [25th July].' 'Kosi tight and quarrelling for the first time in a month [20th November].' 'K. broke Sham's box and got tight again [21st November].' 'K. again tight. I felt very exhausted' (25th November). In between bouts Kosi still had the capacity to charm. An entry of 4th August reveals some of what had first attracted the scholar to the Gond: 'Kosi says, "How I love the wind and the smell of the green green grasses," and one day, speaking of dead leaves whirled about by the wind, "The leaves are flying like butterflies." '

On 31st December 1947 Verrier marked in his diary books sent to press and in progress, adding: 'This was the first year I've had money of my own and travelled everywhere first class. But this was more than offset by the annoyance of being a subordinate.' In the last week of the first month of the next year Mahatma Gandhi was assassinated. How did the disciple-turned-rebel take this? His letters do not speak of the happening. His diary is only marginally more revealing. On the day of the shooting, 30th January, he wrote: 'News of Bapu's assassination in evening about 10 minutes after event. Listened to radio all evening.' And the next day: 'All day preoccupied with Bapu's funeral. Listened to broadcast, off and on, from 11 am to 5 pm.'[5]

Verrier had not spoken to Gandhi after 1940 or 1941, and there is no record of his reactions to the events of the last years of the Mahatma's life—the Quit India movement, the fasts and walks for communal harmony, the Partition of India. Emotions now swirled around in his mind, some negative, others more positive. It is striking that he calls Gandhi 'Bapu,' Father, for it had been a long time since he had thought or spoken of him as such. Were his feelings akin then to those of the Delhi newspaper which the day after the event substituted sombre commentary with the eloquently simple banner headline, 'FATHER, FORGIVE US'?

In early February the Survey finally moved its office and officers to Calcutta. Boarding the train at Mughalsarai on the 5th, Verrier dared to 'hope, but probably fruitlessly, never to see this damned Ganges again.' His companions on the journey were a Sikh CID man and two Bihari merchants. They 'discussed, at the top of their voices, Gandhiji's assassination, but I did not think that their hearts really bled for him.'[6] There is strength of feeling here, the quasi-proprietorial claim of the disciple who had worshipped Gandhi in the flesh, as against the fainter bleeding hearts of those who knew the saint only through story and picture.

Calcutta meant friends, interesting ones, but the atmosphere in the Survey was the same, 'phoney and futile.' The work in the office bored Verrier; he was drafting reports rather than writing books. He decided to resign with effect from the 1st of February 1948, and go back to Patangarh. 'I am planning to sit on my arse and write,' he informed Archer, 'so long as I don't develop boils. I have my "Saora Religion" and "Orissa Legends" to finish, which will keep me busy and happy for a long time. It is a big jump back in the dark, and into a dark rather darker than before, but I expect we will be all right.' Within a month he had been made to change his mind: 'Tremendous pressure has been put on me from everybody, especially Sham and the family, to stay on and so I am staying on, for a little longer. I doubt it will be much longer.'[7]

He stayed on in the Survey, only to find relations with his boss steadily deteriorating. Guha was resentful of his greater renown and cussedly interfered with his research. The director warned him not to be in contact with Grigson, Archer and other 'imperialists.' Those associations, he said, would bring the Survey into 'disrepute.' Verrier took a 'certain cynical amusement in reflecting that it was not so long ago that the Government of India made me give an undertaking not to associate with any of my Congress friends.' Then he was denied permission, due solely to the colour of his skin, to do research in the border regions of Assam. 'We are surrounded by treachery,' he wrote bitterly to Archer, 'it is hard to say who is one's friend.' Guha, his boss, claimed the ban came from the Governor of Assam, Sir Akbar Hydari, but Hydari told Verrier 'it was "your pal" Guha who had warned him against me.'[8]

Verrier sought solace outside work. His flat on Pollock Street was the centre of a circle of highly talented friends, their company in the evening compensating for the dullness of the job during the day. They included the painter Jamini Roy, the poet Sudhin Datta, the editor Lindsay Emmerson, the dancer Ragini Devi, the photographer Sunil Janah, the geologist John Auden (brother of the poet), and the communist P. C. Joshi. There were lots of parties in their houses and his, and hangovers every other morning.

At these parties Kosi drank, but who could she talk to? Sunil Janah recalls her at a gathering of poets and intellectuals, painfully shy and totally out of place.[9] Her husband's diary entries tell of heroic but ultimately vain attempts to keep the marriage going. 'Took Kosi to a bad dinner at Firpos [10th May 1948].' 'Went with Kosi to Peiping Restaurant and then to "The White Unicorn," which we much enjoyed.' This seems to have been the last of the happy days. The entries turn progressively more serious. 'All the morning Kosi still tight and nearly drove me crazy, specially as I was trying to read Hill's excellent "My own Murderer" [6th July].' 'Still fighting against ill-health. Anderson put me on a curious diet of enormous meals. These were days of great strain, for we were working up to the parting with Kosi [1st to 8th August].'

The 'we' refers pre-eminently to Shamrao, who had come from Patan to preside over the ruins of a marriage that could no longer be saved. A young man from Patangarh, recruited by Verrier for the Anthropological Survey, remembers how ferociously Mrs Elwin attacked the bottle in Banaras and Calcutta: '*din raat tun thi*,' he said, she was smashed day and night.[10] Kosi's second son seems also to have been a complicating factor. Verrier maintained that he was prepared to love Vijay as a creation of Kosi's. It was 'not the illegitimacy he minded,' he said, 'it was K's bragging attitude.'[11] Sham took Kosi back to Patangarh, where she moved in with her old lover Sahid. Although he found it 'unpleasant and hypocritical,' Verrier had to start divorce proceedings in the Calcutta High Court to obtain custody of his son, Kumar. The case was handled by the firm of Fowler and Sons with Sahid named as co-respondent.[12]

When I met Kosi, forty-some years later, it was remarkable how little bitterness there was, overtly, towards Verrier. True, she referred to him only as 'Elwin,' the impersonal form perhaps denoting that from this distance in time he could be viewed as part of the history of her self and her tribe. Our conversations were slow-moving, in deference to her age and our strangeness, stretches of silence interspersed with the odd question from me and the odd, mostly single-sentence, comment from her. Two of these reflected sharply on Sham. '*Saas ne mujhe England bulaya*,' she said sudddenly, Mother-in-law asked Verrier to bring me to see her in England, and then: '*lekhin Shamrao bola ki main bhi teri seva karta hoon, aur agar Kosi jayegi to Kusum ko bhi jaana hai.*' Sham apparently insisted that if Kosi went Kusum must go as well, and of course there wasn't enough money for both. Kosi even claimed that Mahatma Gandhi called them to Wardha, but again the cussed Sham said Verrier could not take her unless Kusum and he accompanied them.[13]

Kosi also spoke of a visit successfully made to the bungalow of J. R. D. Tata high on Altamount Road in Bombay. In her eyes it was Shamrao who came in the way of her more fully participating in the spacious social world of her husband. '*Koi bade ghar jaana ho to Sham bol padta tha, ham ko bhi aana hai*,' she said: if we were invited to a big man's house, Shamrao would say they had to come too. Sham was possessive about his friend, certainly—'*main bhi teri seva karta hoon*,'—the remark he is supposed to have made to Verrier, would translate literally as 'I also serve you.' He saw himself as having prior claim on Verrier, as one who had shared his life long before this Gond girl came into it. But in Kosi's recollections there seems also to be some kind of displacement, a retrospective refusal to recognize the serious incompatibility between wife and husband, the all-too-natural and characteristically Indian tendency to blame it on someone else.

In March 1949 Verrier was granted a Decree Nisi granting the divorce and custody of the elder child, with the Decree Absolute due in another six months.[14] All that now kept him in the Anthropological Survey was the money, and in the end it was not enough. He left the Survey in April, concluding what he called the 'most wasted and uncreative' period of his life.[15] Back in Patangarh, without job or wife, Verrier was now 'rather oppressed by many anxieties.' If he had the money, he told Archer, he would go 'to live in Micronesia or Tahiti or somewhere.' In another letter he listed the places he wished to visit or stay in—'Paris, the South Seas and Oubangui-Chari, in that order.' After twenty years in the hamlets and forests of India Verrier was, with reason, tired of it, fantasizing of a move to a glamorous, disease-free environment.[16]

His reservations about life in India were as much political as personal. The Congress, having moved from being a party of protest to the party in power, was now enforcing its command on a not entirely willing populace. Verrier dared not openly criticize the new rulers of free India; but more discreet methods were available. From this period date two murder mysteries that he wrote under the pseudonym of Adrian Brent. In plot and portrayal of character these novels are undistinguished and were not to find a publisher. Each makes playful reference to the 'anthropologist Verrier Elwin', author of *The Muria and their Ghotul*, 'a book which discusses primitive sex in an amiable and reticent manner' and which had attracted German anthropologists to the study of Indian tribes. However, the novelist's comments on the state of Indian politics are penetrating and deadly serious. The first novel is set in Bombay, a colourful, cosmopolitan city, much loved by the author, but at this time ruled over by a pious and interfering Congress. The provincial government is headed by Morarji Desai, the most ascetic and humourless of Gandhians. This government 'with Puritan enthusiasm was banning more and more of the legitimate human pleasures [drink and sex], with the natural result that people turned to those that were not so legitimate.' One of its ministers, in a cameo appearance, is caught 'hurrying from a meeting of the Anti-Vivisection Society, where he had had tea, to preside at a conference of the Bombay Anti-Contraceptive League, where he would be given lemonade.' The cloth of these politicians, the handspun khadi, once the 'symbol of insurgence against British rule,' is now 'an almost official uniform, the sign of authority and power.'[17]

The second novel, set in Calcutta, more directly addresses the status of Europeans who stayed on. Here an unidentified white woman carries out a series of murders. After this story breaks in *The Statesman*, the newspaper's sales that day 'broke all records. Marwaris, who had never read anything but the financial news, Congressmen whose literature was confined to the *Harijan* and the *Amrita Bazaar Patrika*, sent their servants to Chowringhee Square to obtain copies.' But by the morrow, titilation gives way to xenophobia. In the afternoon

> a public meeting was held on the Maidan to demand a round up of all the white women between the ages of 18 and 35 in India . . . Students of the Intermediate Classes in the Calcutta University, prompted thereto by agitated paterfamiliases, took out a procession protesting against this latest attempt by the white races to dominate India. An officer of the Tourism Promotion Department flew from New Delhi to remonstrate; such agitation would ruin the tourist trade, already badly hit by Prohibition.[18]

This white man had committed no murders himself, but his past had been contentious and controversial, and he felt deeply vulnerable in the India of 1948 and 1949. For the first time since landing on the Malabar coast twenty-two years earlier, Verrier seriously contemplated leaving India. In the summer of 1949, more or less immediately after quitting the Anthropological Survey, he visited England for the first time in a decade. This was a trip he much looked forward to, not least to visit his beloved Oxford, where he was to talk at the Institute of Social Anthropology. He hoped also to persuade Merton to renew their research grant to him, which the College had let lapse at the end of the war.

Verrier expected Oxford to mean friends and allies. But it had been a long time since he was last there; few remembered him, fewer still wanted him. Meyer Fortes, a coming name in British anthropology, was warm and helpful, but the doyen of the Oxford school, Edward Evans-Pritchard, was cold and distant. So too was Evans-Pritchard's (and formerly G. S. Ghurye's) acolyte, 'the unpleasant little [M. N.] Srinivas.'[19] All in all the visit was a crushing disappointment personally, and what hurt Verrier more, intellectually. He had chosen to screen and explain a film he had shot on the Muria ghotul. It was a choice of subject inappropriate to the place and audience, and was frostily received by the Oxford anthropologists.[20] Evans-Pritchard was particularly scandalized and wont in later years to refer to Verrier as 'that sex maniac.'[21] A more material blow was Merton's refusal to revive their grant. His old Warden, Sir John Miles, had retired, and his successor disapproved strongly of the anthropologist's 'strange conjugal relationships.' It did little good when Verrier told him they had ended; the difficulty was that they were contracted in the first place. If he wanted money, he should look for it in India or America. In any case, the college felt he should have left India when others of his class and colour did. 'The time was ripe,' remarked the Warden, 'for you to leave your work in the field for a time and put in for a chair in England.'[22]

Verrier was also put out by the outlook of the British upper classes, struggling to come to terms with the loss of empire. The mother of the anthropologist and ex-ICS man J. P. Mills remembered how 'it was so nice in Simla in '15 and '16. The babus were not allowed on the Mall. I hear it is different now.' His own mother complained bitterly about the Labour government; she resented the working classes getting medical relief and living for the first time in halfway decent houses. She even told Verrier he should not share things with Shamrao. Other friends avoided talking about India 'as a man avoids talking about his wife whom he loved but had to divorce.'[23]

This last comment was made without any self-consciousness. We are left to supply the gloss: the British elite would forget India as he was forgetting Kosi. The British upper classes had been served up a socialist government instead; Verrier's own substitute was altogether more palatable. Before his trip to England he had begun an affair with Kachari, a Pardhan girl of Patangarh. Kachari was staggeringly beautiful. A photograph of the time shows her sitting on a stone bench beneath a ficus tree, a white sari setting off her dark and glowing skin, her long hair beguilingly left untied, a radiant smile on her face, altogether uncommonly appealing.

Kachari moved in with Verrier sometime in late 1949. He was enchanted with her, giving her the name 'Lila,' which may be *very* crudely translated as play or playful love. His inspiration was the most sensually evocative of Indian love stories, the Krishna Lila. This Lila was no Kosi. She did not drink and was a fine home-maker and cook, her Pardhan repertoire generously accommodating the humdrum English preparation of liver-and-onions which was a particular favourite with her lover. For all her beauty and competence Verrier was most reluctant to formalize the relationship. City friends who had predicted the failure of his first marriage were still at hand. One of them told him that if he loved another tribal, better to keep her as a mistress than a wife. True, Verrier would write in his diary of his 'Pardhan in-laws,' and in the code of the village they were probably treated as such. But there was no thought in his mind of a legal marriage, even though Lila was soon expecting a child by him.

The child, a boy named Wasant, was born in October 1950, when the father was not in Patangarh but in Colombo, where he had gone at the invitation of his old Oxford friend Bernard Aluwihare. While in Ceylon Verrier showed his photographs and spoke out on the condition of the island's aboriginals, the Veddas. The countryside was beautiful beyond words: 'the flowering trees along the roads, the fine rest-houses, the rivers, the mountains, the handsome youths, the lovely girls . . .' 'How charming it is,' he wrote to his mother, 'one long enchantment.' The Singhalese he found 'so sensible—the people of the Middle Way. What India might be like without the Congress . . . Everything I do goes into the papers—shopkeepers ask for my autograph! I shall be thoroughly spoiled for dear old India with its mess and dust and muddle.' But with independence had also come race-feeling. Some Sinhalese he spoke to were clear that the planters and other whites would have to go. In any case, he concluded, 'India is *deep*—Ceylon perhaps a little superficial.'[24]

Verrier returned to Patangarh and left almost immediately for a field trip to the Saoras. He spent seven weeks on tour, in villages so remote that not even a constable had visited them. He went seven weeks without a drop of either fresh milk or alcohol. He had put himself on this wagon despite the knowledge 'that aboriginals like their anthropologists a bit high.' It was a time of linguistic temperance as well—not a word of English, which was 'quite a record even for me.' On this trip he had one of the most moving encounters in all his years with the tribes. In the hamlet of Serango a little boy who was dying of malnutrition attached himself to the anthropologist. Raisinda would climb on Verrier's lap, put his head on his shoulder and try to sleep. He couldn't lie down for he choked terribly when he did. Sitting on Verrier's lap he exclaimed, 'Mother!' Sunderlal, Verrier's assistant and Man Friday, gently corrected him: 'That is Bodo babu (big brother).' 'No,' replied the boy, 'he is my mother.' Verrier dreamt at night that he was in a great cave in utter darkness and the Jamuasum (the Saora god of death) was coming for the boy in the form of a vast shape rolling irresistibly across the ground. I tried desperately to strike a match to bring some light, but every match failed and I woke sweating with horror, but the words on my lips—'Love is the true weapon; love is the dress; love is my gold.'

> Love the true weapon, because just before going to bed I got the news of the UNO defeat in Korea; love the dress, because I had realized that bitterly cold night that I was warmer because I had less bedding, some of it having gone to Raisinda; love is my gold had reference to our financial situation which is very serious.

One day Verrier found Raisinda 'fumbling with one of my pockets. I wondered what he was looking for—but he was putting a half smoked very precious cheroot into my pocket for safe keeping.' Soon afterwards he died. Verrier's attentions and medicines came too late to save the boy, who 'epitomized all the hunger and loneliness of the world in his frail body.'[25]

Raisinda died in late December; on the last day of the month, and year. Verrier summed up the situation in his diary:

> 1950. Not really a successful year. Applications for grants and fellowships all failed, except for the Leverhulme Grant—which was really a damned insult. My attempt to be a detective novelist, on which I wasted a great deal of time (though I enjoyed it), was also a failure. The implications of life in free India slowly become more and more depressingly apparent. It also gradually becomes evident that TWARU was not likely to function as a effective unit. The year was overshadowed by constant quarrels and tensions—most of them emanating from one source—most of which were quite unnecessary. I myself was too often worried by financial and other worries. Kumar can hardly be said to have made progress.
>
> On the other hand, my own visits to Bombay in February and to Ceylon in October were successful, and my Saora tour in November-December was one of the best I have had. In the field of research, most of my work was tedious but very necessary . . .
>
> Financially, the year has ended with us in a worse position than we have been for many years.
>
> In health, I had one bad attack of dysentery and three sharp attacks of malaria in the last three months. I felt a good deal older, less resilient and it is increasingly hard to endure hardship.
>
> My attempts to give up alcohol have been to some extent frustrated by the efforts of friends, but I managed it for considerable periods, especially during the last four months—Ceylon was almost, and the Saora trip entirely

> dry. It has not had a good effect, but I do not see that, financially, there is any alternative.
>
> Above all, the present has been continually shadowed by the future. How long can this go on? Shall I be forced to adopt some new profession? Is it going to be possible even to do research, let alone do anything to help the aboriginals, in India today?[26]

Elwin intended his diaries to be seen by a future biographer, but in those left behind there remain huge gaps: months and years at a stretch. It is not clear who did the weeding—the writer, his executor, his family, or unaffiliated termites. In what remains there are also silences and references left unexplained, for an Englishman will have his reticences, even with his diary. Who, for instance, was the 'one source' of the year's quarrels? Various candidates present themselves. Was it mother, asking him to return home for good? Or the puritan-Gandhian capitalist Jehangir Patel asking for accounts of money spent and work accomplished? Or Shamrao's wife Kusum, known to be frustrated in the village, with little money and four or five children to rear and educate? Or the gentle Lila, hoping he would formalize the relationship by way of marriage?

The speculations will stay. We must move back to empirically firmer ground,. Over the last weeks of fieldwork in Orissa during January 1951, Verrier was joined by Shamrao and their friend Victor Sassoon, a photographer from a prosperous Calcutta family. Victor quickly substituted Bill Archer in Verrier's affections: it helped that he was a good ten years younger, an admiring younger colleague rather than an equal and contemporary. Victor was rich and daring, a man who would fund Verrier's research and go into the forest with him. The Orissa trip was the first of several they made together. From the Saora hills they came down to the holiday resort of Gopalpur-on-Sea. Their hotel was full of Jesuits who glared at Verrier, and he back at them. After two months of rice and *dal*, he was pigging it: 'for breakfast, porridge, whiting, eggs and bacon, and all the bread, butter and marmalade you can put away; for lunch—oyster, soup, mackeral, meat curry and rice, an excellent pudding, fruit and cheese.'

But he still didn't know what to do with his life. Victor offered to take him to Africa.[27]

On his way back from England in 1949 Verrier had spent a couple of weeks in West Africa, travelling through the Ivory Coast and Nigeria. For some reason he stayed clear of Freetown, his father's old bishopric. The 1951 trip with Sassoon was to the other side of the continent, the British-ruled territories of Kenya and Tanganyika. Its highlight was a meeting with Louis Leakey, a self-confessed 'White African' whose career in so many ways paralleled his. Leakey showed him around his museum and his Maasai. Verrier was impressed by the legend, 'a real charmer and quite brilliant,' but less so by his second wife, the paleontologist Mary, whom he found 'very learned but rather dreary.'[28]

About Africa Elwin had mixed feelings. Both Sasoon and Bill Archer, knowing his depressed state of mind, urged him to move there. 'We would plead with you,' wrote Archer, 'to consider the world of African poetry which is still almost completely unexplored and to which you could make a uniquely exciting contribution. But I expect you will prefer to go your own rather wilful way—only don't kill yourself, just yet!' Although Verrier had enjoyed his visits to the continent and even contemplated writing a narrative of his travels, any thoughts of permanent residence were dispelled by the mounting antagonism he noticed between whites and blacks. 'There is something so fundamentally wrong,' he wrote to his mother, 'in the white settlers grabbing all the best land from the Africans [and] in the real hatred of the English for the Indians here.' In this atmosphere of hatred the figure of the Botswana chief Seretse Khama stood out. He had married an Englishwoman, for which he was hated by the whites and thrown out by his own clan. The marriage, and the social location betwixt and betweeen, reminded Verrier of his own. He wrote a sonnet on Khama and for a while even thought of writing a biography.[29]

Almost the first news Verrier got on his return to India in June was a report of a speech by Jawaharlal Nehru in Bangalore. The prime minister had expressed the view that prohibition should not be introduced in tribal areas, saying, 'you will break up their lives if you suddenly introduce it.' Verrier was temporarily pleased. Of course the killjoys had not been vanquished by Nehru's words: when he read of Nehru' speech he was in fact staying with one, Jehangir Patel. The magnate would wake him up at six a.m. and make him do yoga. One evening, when Verrier wasted his food at dinner, Patel coolly reminded him of the history of famine in India. 'What humiliation and misery it is,' thought Verrier, 'to be poor and so dependent on such creatures.'[30]

Verrier returned to Patangarh, where a letter from Mother awaited him. 'You can't go on as a cave man,' she had written, 'when God has given you brains and powers for larger use. My darling boy, I am sure you should be finished with Patan and such life.' He was not finished with Patan yet, nor was Sham, but Kusum Hivale was. She moved to Jabalpur with her kids and Kumar, who all went to school there. Back in the village Sham began an affair with a Gond called Bilsi, somewhat disturbing the domestic arrangements. Lila did not like the new entrant, which meant that Verrier had occasionally to cook for the love birds and take the food to their nest, that being Sham's room, now usually bolted from the inside. He worked when he could on his Saora book. The house was ideal for writing, he wrote to Victor Sassoon, but one grew old too quickly in Patangarh:

> The days are not full enough
> And the nights are not full enough
> And life slips by like a field mouse
> Not shaking the grass.[31]

Restless, uncertain, confused, Veririer took up an old invitation to visit Thailand. He went there in December 1951, accompanied by Sham, their host an old Oxford mate, the poet and professor A. C. Braine-Hartnell. A week in Bangkok was all they could take. But then another Englishman, Gerald Sparrow, offered to take them north. A former president of the Cambridge Union, now a flamboyant Bangkok lawyer, race-horse owner and night-club proprietor, Sparrow had left his English wife for a Siamese sweetheart. He booked four seats on the plane that linked the Thai capital with the northern temple city of Chiengmai. When they reached their destination Chaluey, Sparrow's companion, thought it a shame that Verrier had no girl with him. The 'iced-up' English gentleman, she said, needed someone presentable to make him come out. So they were joined by Rada, a lively and well-travelled dancer. Shamrao either did not want a partner or did not get one. Anyway, the party then spent a glorious week eating, drinking and visiting the old Buddhist temples all around. On their last night they dined on roast suckling-pig washed down by Black Label whisky and Thai beer. Afterwards Rada was persuaded to dance. She started with a spoof on the American idiom, 'the primitive and idiotic characteristics of the dance exaggerated and guyed,' followed appropriately by a classical Siamese dance, with its 'measured dignified rhythms, her face retaining the mask-like passivity that the performance demanded.' When Chaluey followed with a plaintive Malay love song Shamrao was heard to mutter, 'If only India was like this!'

Next morning they had to take the plane back to Bangkok. Reluctantly, most reluctantly, they 'waved farewell to our lovely and gifted Rada. As we became air-borne, we saw her waving a little lace handkerchief until we were out of sight.'[32]

When Sparrow published his account of the visit some years later, Verrier denied the existence of the enchanting Rada. His friend had made her up, he said, to make him more interesting.[33] It is possible that Sparrow embroidered more than the handkerchief, but by the time the tale appeared in print Verrier had good reason to deny any liaison in Chiengmai. It remains Sparrow's word against Elwin's. The definitive evidence may lie in the guest book of the Doi Sutep temple, which the lawyer claimed was signed by 'Verrier Elwin, Shamrao, Rada, Chaluey, Gerald Sparrow.'

A pleasing consequence of the Thailand trip was a series of poems written about Verrier. Shaun Mandy of the *Illustrated Weekly of India* thought he had first claim on anything that came out of his friend's travels, but this time Lindsay Emmerson of *The Statesman* had obtained a commission beforehand. When Mandy heard that he was not going to get an account of Thailand he wrote

A PLEA FOR DR ELWIN

I'm most terribly afraid
You've already been waylaid
By that genius of The Statesman, Lindsay E
Who'll purloin your Thailand pix
With his lucre and his trix
Till there's nothing left at all for me to see.

If it isn't too late
You could lurk around and wait
Till Lindsay E's absorbed in prolix edits.
And snatch some prints away
For The Weekly to display
With the loveliest banner lines for you as credits.

Please, Dr Elwin, don't let Lindsay E
Run wild about the garden and
Eat every gooseberry
Don't let him rape the trees, until there's nothing left
And the garden's all bereft.
Please, Dr Elwin, keep a bush for me.

Lindsay Emmerson offered, in response, this untitled poem on

An Editor in Bombay
Once wrote to Calcutta to say—
    Though with compliments kind—
    A piece of his mind
About luring V. Elwin away.

The recipient has, in Calcutta,
An unlimited stomach for butter;
    Yet discovers in it,
    And its flashes of wit,
The mild reprobatory matter.

The learned man living in Patan,
In conditions remarkably Spartan,
    Is well known to be,
    For photography,
What the Weekly has got a good start on.

Yet when he returned from Bangkok—
Not to give other journals a knock,
    But because he is Verrier,
    And the more of him the merrier—
We naturally collared his stock.

Then from camp Ukai on the Tapi River in Gujarat came this learnedly allusive commentary from the geologist John Auden, a man with poetry in his blood:

What strange flirtation can this be,
Two begging for what but one did see,
And having seen, did then imprison
Without any aberration
In a box where light
Defeats the darkest night?

No vision here of Aunt Emily,
Eldest sister of unwedded three,

Archly smiling as the man did bid,
Corsetted of all that must be hid;
Unlovely bosom;
Too sterile womb.

Nor is there exposed our uncle when,
Mayor of Margate, he had risen
To the summit of his smug cancer,
Chain on navel, verbal diarrhoea;
Striped were the pants
of his sycophants:
Bad too the breath
Of coming death.

No, our Guru from the Patan heights
Had other things in mind, quite other flights
Of mental fancy, as on air he ran
To the loveliness of Siam.
Unbroken hearts
Where no fear starts.

Uncolonised, no dignity to span,
No color bar across the face of man,
No sooty fumes from dismal terraces;
Ecology of those old heresies
Which bred in Marx
His parallax.

Pantheistic and free to be
One with the apple on its tree,
All nature there in paradise,
Not heeding overmuch advice,
Nor what Newton saw
In universal law.

Could it be that Emmerson,
And his friendly rival Sean,
Could exahaust the great Guru's stock
Before it blossoms in a book?
Not yet indeed,
Even in their need.

Lava quod est Emmerson
Riga quod est Shawn-Sean.

And now, briefest and best, Mandy's final reply:

> Did you hear anything? Hark, listen, hist!
> Why, that's the MUSE of a geologist.
> The Muse, you say, she surely shows a bit.
> —The Saucy, florit chit!
> But just the type, perhaps, that neatly vamps,
> Geologists when lonely in their jungle camps.[34]

Not to forget editors in their dark cubicles. These pedestrian verses are of interest principally to the biographer. As illustration of how Englishmen in exile, drunk and bored, amused themselves, they are fairly typical and regrettably undistinguished.

Once more, Verrier's return to India is marked in his diary by a reference to Nehru. In England, on his first official trip there, Nehru had spoken in the House of Commons for a 'new type of association with a touch of healing' between the United Kingdom and India. Verrier commented, justly, that these words 'in their context are a miracle.'[35]

Nehru's words were also eminently Gandhian, as Verrier well knew. He was now deep into a reappraisal of Gandhi and thus of the land from whence he came. In his memoirs Verrier was to write of what made him move away from the Mahatma: his 'emphatic views on Prohibition (which I considered damaging to the tribes), his philosophy of sex-relations (which I considered damaging to everybody), and what seemed to be a certain distortion of values—the excessive emphasis on diet, for example, . . . separated me from him.' Then he added: 'Today I feel very sorry about this, for it was in his last years that Gandhi reached his highest stature and I deprived myself of the warmth of his affection and the strength he would have given me during a difficult period. But it was a feeling of Truth that kept me away from going to see him and from this point of view my instinct was right.'[36]

As we have seen, Gandhi's assassination provoked a fresh assessment, a striving towards balance in Verrier's feelings for the man. Travelling in

Africa in 1949 he had been disturbed by the rise of a 'national movement without a Gandhi:' that is, without goodwill towards its opponents. The next year he helped Valji Govind Desai, an old friend from the Sabarmati days, with his translation of Gandhi's *Satyagraha in South Africa.* In contrast with his coyness when Mahadev Desai wanted to thank him with regard to the *Autobiography,* this time he allowed his assistance to be placed on record.[37] There is also a telling exchange in one of his unpublished novels. When an Eurasian says that all Indian policemen and officials are corrupt and can be bribed, it is significantly a Muslim named Masood who replies: 'Well yes, Mr Gore, most of them are. But you must not forget Mahatma Gandhi. He was a very great man. I don't think that you European gentlemen have ever quite understood his influence. Some of his followers can never be bribed, not by anything. They will give up their lives to defeat us.'[38]

This partial, posthumous reconciliation with Gandhi was contemporaneous with and possibly a source of influence on Verrier's reconciliation with India. Various alternatives had been tried and found wanting. Ceylon and Thailand were superficial, England inhospitable, Paris and the South Seas unreachable. Africa seemed the most likely but he had not the willingness, approaching fifty, to begin life afresh in a continent seething with racial tension. When Sassoon wrote saying he and Archer were working on a Colonial Office fellowship for him to do research in Africa, Verrier asked them to stop proceedings. 'I wouldn't take a job from the Colonial Office,' he wrote, 'I have spent my life in opposition to them and all they stand for, and it is too late to change now.'[39]

Reading these pages, with their tough account of a tormented decision, at least two kinds of critics shall sharpen their knives: the hidebound patriot who doubted Elwin's commitment to India in the first place, and the theorist of multiculturalism, always ready to judge and criticize. To the former I would say that this Englishman did more than anyone to make visible the plight of a deeply disadvantaged and numerically substantial section of the Indian nation. As for the second kind of critic, who speaks of the happy mixing of cultures through processes of 'hybridity' and 'translation,' this sort has almost without exception made the voyage *in,* from the colonized culture to the colonizer. They have moved from East to West, from disease-ridden and poor countries to aseptic and rich ones. Since the transition has been easy for them, they will see in Elwin's hesitation and uncertainty a negative attitude to the culture in which he had made his home.

The patriots and the multiculturalists both need to be reminded of a remark of the Cambridge historian F. W. Maitland: 'That which is now in the past was once in the future.' A passport is now almost a matter of convenience; in Elwin's time a change of nationality was a real struggle. And how can one forget that he had moved the other and indisputably more difficult way, from the life of the privileged among the privileged to a life among the Gonds? After twenty-five years of this, if he occasionally tired of the illness and poverty, are we in any position to cast stones?

Once Verrier decided to stay on in India, Shamrao and he reverted to their familiar division of labour: social work for the one, writing and advocacy for the other. The Bhumijan Seva Mandal changed its name twice after independence. In 1949 it became the Tribal Art and Research Unit (TARU) and then, a year later, the Tribal Welfare, Art and Research Unit (TWARU)—this to recall its original aims and also to acknowledge Shamrao's continuing welfare work. By any name, the organization was starved of money. After independence some businessmen who had supported their work withdrew in the belief that the national government would now take care of tribal welfare. They came to depend more and more on the largesse of Jehangir Patel. Verrier also suspected that Congress propaganda against him had contributed to their financial crisis. His letters of the time speak repeatedly of TWARU being 'right out of funds.' Their difficulties were compounded when in May 1951 a typhoon destroyed their home in Patangarh. It was of course uninsured and had to be rebuilt from scratch.[40]

Shamrao carried on regardless: healing physical wounds in the dispensary and leper home, healing emotional wounds everywhere else. Verrier thus described a typical day in his friend's life, the variety of people and problems he attended to:

> someone's precious buffalo is sick; there is trouble over land; a wife has run away and must be reconciled to her husband; an old woman has no food in the house; a simple Gond has got entangled in the law-courts; a barren woman is accused of being a witch; there is a scare that kidnappers have come

> for children (on behalf of the Public Works Department!) to sacrifice in the foundation of shaky bridges and the people have to be reassured; a dying child calls for comfort.[41]

Verrier liked to compare his comrade to a Hindu widow, old style, at everybody's beck and call, but Shamrao more wryly believed the social worker's lot to be like that of a peon (*chaprasi*) in a government office, for 'he never knows what he will have to do next.' Hindu widow or chaprasi, he was deeply devoted to his wards. Here is Shamrao's description of their home for lepers:

> It is a very beautiful home, built in the simple style they appreciate, with a large garden that in the rains at least is quite lovely, and views of mountains in all directions. The home is indeed the creation of a poet. Verrier once said that when he felt really depressed he went to the lepers to get cheered up! Often when I have been by myself at Patangarh and feeling lonely I go and sit among these brave and simple people and look at their flowers and the surrounding hills which make one forget the ugliness and the wounds; their great disaster puts one's little troubles in their right proportion. It is astonishing how humorous and witty the lepers are and how interested in the outside world; they always ask first about Verrier and the children, and then about the war, the Congress and India's freedom.[42]

If the lepers asked about Verrier it was because he was not much in Patangarh: his province was the entire tribal population of the peninsula, his task bringing their situation to wider notice. His own work with the pen was justified, as he saw it, by the fact that the

> real protector of the aboriginals is knowledge. Only Knowledge can give the general public the right angle on these people. Only Knowledge can convince administrator and reformer alike that they are not mere savages to be uplifted, but human beings like themselves with a logical and often admirable way of life well adapted to the physical and economic conditions under which they live. Only Knowledge can escort them safely through the perilous passage of acculturation. Only Knowledge which goes on to Love, can inspire men and women with the desire to go and serve them in lonely and malaria-ridden places.[43]

It was typical of Verrier that he would think of aboriginals and their predicament in the plural. It was left to Shamrao, silently but no less effectively, to express *his* love in a more intimate, immediate, personal sense, to one-tribal-at-a-time.

CHAPTER TEN

An Englishman in India

ADIBASI 1952

by Verrier Elwin

How tired they are, and what a sombre grace
Time has drawn on the wise old faces, grey
With the death of children, and no release
From want that rules day after anxious day.

There was life there once, and joy in recreation,
Dancing and laughter, love among the trees,
But little now save sullen speculation
Of what the future has and where it leads.

Old rules are broken, boys go to the town;
Children are married in a loveless tie;
The ancient forest is no more their own;
The women lose their treasured liberty.

New customs which are little understood
Drive out the old, leave nothing in their place.
The old men suck their wooden pipes and brood,
And tremble for the future of their race.

'Verrier Elwin is only really happy when he can think of himself as a misunderstood and persecuted man.' So said the Bishop of Bombay back in 1936.[1] In some senses Elwin was really happy only as a *writer*, for the break with the Church and Gandhi had then released a surge of creativity. Now here he was, in the nineteen fifties, once again a misunderstood and persecuted man, confused about his nationality, without a job, his marriage in tatters, a son to look after and educate. Characteristically, he found happiness anew in his work and a stream of books and articles poured forth from his pen.

Of these the longest in preparation was a personal record of tribal art. A draft was assembled as early as August 1947, with Verrier keen to have it published soon, to pre-empt his friend and fellow collector. 'Archer is straining every nerve to forestall me,' he wrote to R. E. Hawkins, 'and we should get out our book before he gets out his, if for no other reason.'[2] The OUP wanted a subsidy to pay for the 230 illustrations. The book was finally published in 1951 with the aid of ten thousand rupees provided by Jehangir Patel, the Bombay cotton magnate who had long and generously supported their work. When the book appeared Verrier wrote in triumph to his mother: 'Bill Archer is very jealous of it; he wanted his name to be on the title-page, but when I refused he began saying it was no good, poor fish.'[3]

Elwin remarked to an Indian friend that the book wished to show in 'the most emphatic way the cultural and aesthetic traditions of the *adibasis*.'[4] With rich detail, but a minimum of interpretation, he documented the varied forms of decoration in tribal life—of the body, of houses, of objects of worship—as well as the materials from which these were made. But the book is also pervaded by a sense of wistfulness, a note of loss almost; for the opening up of tribal areas had taken a huge toll of their creativity. In matters of art the 'great days of the Indian tribesman are gone; all we can do now is search in the debris for traces of inspiration and scraps of beauty.'[5]

While they collected money to print *The Tribal Art of Middle India* the OUP put out *Myths of Middle India*, the fourth volume in his series on the contributions of Indian tribals to the literature of the world. The collection, said Elwin modestly, 'attempts nothing more than to present samples and specimens of an oral literature whose variety and extent is still largely unsuspected by scholars.' An American reviewer more accurately termed the book 'a landmark in the exploration of the intellectual history of mankind.'[6] It was an aboriginal Purana, a compendium of tribal stories about natural and human creation, rich in expressive imagery, with stars flashing and gods appearing and disappearing, tales of magic and wonder impossible to summarize or condense.

Let me try, nevertheless, with a Baiga tale about the origin of drink. Bhimsen, the Pandava of legendary appetite, asked Bhagavan for food—having demolished twenty-five sacks of rice and twelve of *daal*, he then asked for a drink. God had none, so Bhim went into the forest and searched. After a long time he came to a mahua tree, with birds of all kinds pecking into its hollow and nodding their heads. The mighty Pandava leaned into the hollow, had a gulp, and decided he must introduce Bhagavan to the holy spirit. The subsequent developments underlined a basic truth of tribal, indeed human, life—that some can take it and some can't. 'Then Bhimsen filled twelve gourds full of the mahua liquor and brought it back for Bhagavan to drink. They sat down, Bhagavan and the wind and the crow, and they drank the liquor out of leaf-cups. Then when their heads were nodding, Bhimsen got up and walked round the earth.'[7]

In 1950 appeared Elwin's study of the Bondo, the tiny tribe living in the uplands of the Koraput district in Orissa. *Bondo Highlander* is in some respects the most disappointing of all his books. It is a conventional, gazetteer-like ethnography, a synoptic survey of the chief elements in Bondo social organization: the rules of marriage, individual affiliation by clan and moiety, the tribal pantheon and the rituals for cementing village solidarity, the role of weaving in the life of their women. Absent from this book is the polemical edge of his other studies, for it is not about a great tribal institution (bewar, the ghotul, whatever) under threat. There is a weariness to the narrative, perhaps because the anthropologist himself was not much attracted to the tribe. One reason was that Bondo dancing was 'wretched stuff,' with 'little rhythm, no variety, no dignity.' But there are withal some characteristic touches, as for instance a swipe at the 'puerile reformist evangelism of self-conscious Hindu propagandists,' and a singling out, among the Bondo of the Jeypore chiefdom, of the 'absence of obsequiousness and the sense of being in a historic tradition [that] is one of the most pleasing characteristics of state subjects everywhere in India.'[8]

Elwin predicted that *Bondo Highlander*, being a comparatively light book, was 'not likely to please the anthropological pundits, but it might go all the better with the public for that very reason.'[9] A particularly vicious piece of punditry was a review by D. N. Majumdar, Professor of Anthropology at Lucknow University. Majumdar had reason to dislike Elwin. He had studied tribals, even tribals in Bastar, long before the Englishman. But Elwin's reputation quickly eclipsed his; worse, he thought Elwin's barbs at anthropologists who hurried in and out of the field were aimed especially at him. When S. C. Dube published his first book, on the Kamar, Elwin gave it a generous review in the *Illustrated Weekly of India* but wondered why the bright young scholar was keeping such dubious company. The reference was to the Ethnographic and Folk Culture Society of Lucknow, a society floated by none other than D. N. Majumdar, which had published Dube's book.[10] Now, as he prepared to review *Bondo Highlander*, Majumdar's attention was drawn to one of Elwin's recent articles which said emphatically that 'there has been more shoddy and second-rate work done in this subject here in India than in any other country in the world. "Tip and run" anthropologists visit an area for two or three weeks, take hundreds of hurried and inaccurate measurements, ask a lot of leading questions, and retire to their Universities to write pompous articles about what they have failed to observe.'[11]

Majumdar's review, when it appeared, answered all the slights accumulated over the years. It started by referring to 'Verrier Elwin, formerly Rev. Father Elwin.' Anthropology, said the Professor, 'is Elwin's latest hobby,' which he was helped to indulge in by wealthy friends and patrons:

> The Tatas and Sarabhais find money for his books, his researches are paid for by the Warden and Fellows of Merton College, Oxford, by the Government of India, for the five [*sic*] years he was working as the Deputy Director of Anthropology Department, and by the various State Governments who subsidise his work or his welfare activities. He has created a class of readers who eagerly await his book, and they sell. All handicaps that stifle anthropological research and create frustration among anthropologists are inoperative in his case.

Elwin was was thus blessed, and according to Majumdar dishonest too. It was Christoph von Fürer-Haimendorf who had 'opened up the Bondos' and written a number of papers on them, preparatory to the production of an authoritative monograph: 'professional etiquette should have restrained Elwin' from writing a book on a subject which the Austrian had clearly marked out as his own. The book itself was what one could expect of an ethnographer who 'does not even require to know the language or the dialect of the tribe.' There was also Elwin's sentimentalism, which 'appears to have compromised with science, and the reader is often left to guess how far his vivid pictures of tribal life are real and how far they are tinged by his imagination and flair for description.' Of course the book would find its buyers for, said Majumdar in conclusion, 'the nude pictures make the book eminently saleable.'[12]

Majumdar's review suggests malice tinged with envy rather than scholarly disagreement, but the truth is that Elwin himself ranked the book very low in his list of creations. It was priced at thirty rupees, or one pound and two shillings, which, as Verrier admitted, was 'too much, even in these inflated days, for there is not really very much in the book.'[13] *Bondo Highlander* is the work of a man tired with his craft. In the years since he began, the craft of anthropology had become a science, moving away from its origins in folklore and literature towards the structural analysis of kinship, power, agrarian relations and other impersonal phenomena. The professionals had little time any more for the gifted amateur, but nor had he for them. Professionalization had brought with it a soulless dissecting precision far removed from the literary liveliness he so valued in anthropological writing. It bored and exasperated him. While finishing his book on the Bondo Verrier wrote with disgust of the scientific ethnographies reaching him from England which, like the works of Tommy Tupper, were 'distinguished mainly for their rectitude, exactitude and appalling dullness.' The days when an anthropologist such as James Frazer could inspire a poem like *The Waste Land* were far behind them. For 'the thrill of Tylor, Frazer and Jane Harrison has departed: there was life there, poetry, drama, loveliness, turns of phrase like a flashing of a sword, chapters with stars at elbow and foot.' The field had now passed into the hands of the 'serologist, genealogist, the utterly dreary folk,' men (and one woman) for whom Elwin proposed this anthropo-Dunciad, naming the most famous British anthropologists of his generation:

Where Evans-Pritchard, Fortes and the rest
Suck social facts from Audrey Richards' breast,
And should you ever see me really bored
I'm trying to read a book by Daryll Forde
Though, I confess, of thousands who get me down,
There's no one to compare with Radcliffe-Brown,

There's only one good thing to say for Marret
And that is, he's as dead as Browning (Barrett)
If from pre-history you'd me deter
Just show me moribund Professor Fleure.[14]

Bondo Highlander was supposed to be the first in a series of books on the Orissa tribes, but Verrier had energy and time for only two more. The first was a collection of tribal myths in the province. The stories were presented with little comment or analysis; the author, it seems, was written out, for he referred the reader to the critical essays in his *Myths of Middle India.* The topics covered were much the same: the origin of the world, of different plants and animals, of man and his institutions. A nice tale featuring Bhim illustrated the absorbing interest of tribals in the forest. When Mahaprabhu made a Raja for men and appointed chiefs and headmen too, the trees complained that he had not made a government for them. So God sent Bhim to the forest, where the Pandava engaged in friendly combat with a specimen of every species. The tamarind resisted most strongly, so Mahaprabhu, on Bhim's advice, appointed it king of the trees. But he also chose the *banyan* as the *mantri*, or minister, and the *pipal* as the watchman, saying to the latter: ' "Whenever any wind comes, warn the other trees." That is why the pipal shakes its leaves to let the other trees know when even a little wind is in the air.'[15]

Unquestionably Elwin's best book on Orissa was his ethnography of the Saora, finished in 1952 and published three years later. Elwin first visited the Saora in 1943, and over the years went back to them whenever he could. He enjoyed working with the tribe, not least because the Saora countryside was 'so beautiful that it takes one's breath away.' Through the hills and valleys of the Ganjam district he tramped barefoot, a ragged shirt on his back, a hat of leaves on his head—and while he rested a chair under his bottom and a pen in his hand. The Saora themselves were spendidly truculent, refusing to allow schools be opened in their villages and resisting puritan pressures to give up tobacco and drink.[16]

The anthropologist chose to focus on religion, a theme which took him back to his days at Oxford, when faith had absorbed him just as much as it absorbed the Saora now. As the book was about rather an Oxford subject, he joked to his publisher that it should be subsidized by the vast resources of the University Chest.[17] The intensity of spiritual experience among the tribe also recalled the high drama of the Catholic faith to which he had once been so powerfully drawn. To get from the Saora villages to the neighbouring Gadaba country, he remarked, was 'like passing from Catholic Spain to Protestant England. To the Saora, religion is art, drama, life itself; to the Gadabas it is "something for Sunday morning," something for the main crises of life, like birth or death but not for every day.'[18]

Elwin's study of the Saora has been called 'the most detailed account of an Indian tribal religion that ever flowed from an anthropologist's pen.'[19] It covers an impressive range of topics: the apparatus and techniques of ritual, the causes and cure of disease, the rites of fertility and the rites for the dead, the varied forms of invocation and prayer. The book also pays careful attention to the artefacts of Saora religion: the different types of altar, the instruments and objects of sacrifice, the ikons or pictographs through which religious sensibilities found artistic expression.

The centrepiece of *The Religion of an Indian Tribe* is its account of Saora shamanism. Shamans, who could be both men and women (for the latter Elwin coined the term 'shamanins') led a peculiar kind of double life. Each shaman had a tutelary, a spiritual spouse so to speak, who lived in the Underworld. Union with a tutelary did not rule out marriage in Saora society, so that the shaman had two spouses and sometimes two sets of children as well. It was the tutelary who, by possessing the shaman, acted as an intermediary between the village and the nether world.

The divine world of this Orissa tribe was a malevolent one. Both gods and ancestors brought danger to the Saora: by breaking up marriages, attacking crops, or bearing disease. Here the shaman came into play, to cajole, flatter and placate ancestors, to keep them away from mischief in the living world.

The book is on a scrupulously non-political subject. But submerged in the dense thicket of ethnographic reportage and theological discussion are occasional flashes of Elwin the Protectionist, the defender of the integrity of tribal culture. There are cracks against the tyranny of caste and the 'visiting Congress busybody,' against the rigorous puritan ethic 'of self denial and ascetic renunciation, the dismal code of condemnation of free happiness'—a code thankfully alien to the Saora. And there is a celebration of the 'united and democratic character' of the tribe, their loyalty to one another, and the high and honoured place of their women.

Saora women, indeed, had 'an important role alike in festivity and funeral;' their 'voice is not unheard in tribal affairs: they can more than hold their own with their men.' To 'this happy state of affairs the institution of the shamanin had made its contribution. For here is a body of women dedicated to the public service and fulfilling that dedication with grace and energy. Here are women, believed to be vitally in touch with supernatural affairs, on whom one can rely, women who respond to the sick and anxious with professional thoroughness and affectionate concern.' The tribal woman had already won the status the city-based feminist was fighting for.[20]

When the Saora book went to press Elwin was just short of his fiftieth birthday. He saw it at the time as his last major work for his health was indifferent and he was not in the mood for fresh fieldwork. He told Archer he found it 'difficult to start again the whole weary business of writing another monograph.' 'The poetry field is very fully exploited,' he added, 'and I am dubious now how far any more treasures are to be found. Tribal art is virtually dead.'[21] 'Now that I have finished off my big books,' he wrote to his mother, 'I am writing articles mostly . . . It is odd how much more fame and how much more money one can get from an article in a newspaper, which may take two hours to write, than from a book which may take five years.'[22]

The comment recalls Arthur Koestler's remark that he would gladly exchange a hundred readers of his work today for ten readers ten years later, or for a single reader a hundred years later. The fame of a newspaper or magazine article is fleeting, forgotten tomorrow or in a week. Only books, good books, endure. Elwin's 'big books' are still read and admired and reprinted. His articles, virtually unknown, lie buried in old, yellowing periodicals in decaying Indian libraries.

Out of work, and with research money drying up, Elwin found that book reviews and newspaper articles were a quick and painless way of sustaining his and Shamrao's families. His output in these years was prodigious. Between 1949 and 1953 he wrote hundreds of reviews for the

Times of India of Bombay and *The Statesman* of Calcutta, all of which were, in the custom of the day, unsigned. The books piled up in Patangarh while he was on tour: he attacked them ferociously on his return, sometimes writing as many as five reviews a day.[23]

One must suppose Elwin took more care of his signed articles, of which too there were not a few. A stray page in his papers, undated but probably from the early fifties, contains these jottings of articles to write and journals to place them in:[24]

Possible Articles:

Tribal Poetry for 'The March of India'
Twenty Years [in Tribal India] for Christmas Statesman
The Weapon of Poetry for Christmas Statesman
East Africa, for Thought
Ideas of Beauty, for Statesman

Humour:

Thurber	Saki
Crispin	Wilde
P. G. Wodehouse	Dickens

Biography of the Gods:

Nanga Banga
Lingo
Kittung
Kariya Kuar
Nirantali
Hirakhan Kshattri

Tribal Folklore:

Rainbow
Bees
Death
The Land of Women
Eclipses
Birds
Trees

Picture Features:

General of Tribal India for National Geographic
Page for Statesman
Africa dance
Fishing
Gopalpur
Priestesses
Sahebosum

This listing draws upon forty years of wide reading and twenty of deep research, but its diversity and range of themes is astonishing all the same—from English literature through African poety and Indian folklore to autobiography. Some of these essays were obviously written for fun, others for effect, and all for money. There was one set of essays not mentioned in this list that he was deadly serious about. These were published between 1950 and 1955 in the *Illustrated Weekly of India*, the magazine edited from Bombay by Shaun Mandy, and most popular among the Indian intelligentsia.

Elwin's essays in the *Illustrated Weekly* aimed above all at alerting the Indian elite to the rich culture and present dilemmas of tribals. The Bombay magazine was then patronized by the educated upper class, from whose ranks were drawn the businessmen, bureaucrats and journalists who constituted the core of India's ruling class. This was a class separated by a huge cultural gulf from tribals, yet possessed substantial power to influence their lives.

Some of Elwin's essays introduce individual communities to his readers; others highlight the forms of recreation in tribal India; yet others focus on material culture, for instance on weaving and carving. The depiction of tribal life is introduced and sustained by a rhetorical strategy which helps ease the reader into an unfamiliar world. A fine example is an essay on the scroll paintings of the Jadupatua, a sister community of the great Santhal tribe of eastern India. These paintings are compared by Elwin to the comic strips of the modern world: they comprise stories with a strongly moral tone, where justice and truth always triumph in the end, though not without a struggle. Through their renditions of folk legends the Jadupatua scrolls purveyed 'some kind of elementary moral teaching, that pride and meanness and theft, and refusal to fulfil one's moral duty, are bad things.'[25]

The celebration of tribal life and values is inevitably a key motif in these essays. A series on forest tribes singled out the Baiga for 'their wit and poetry and character;' the Sacra for their industry, manifest in their carefully terraced fields, 'rightly praised as works of great engineering skill;' the Gadabas for their 'happiness . . . [their] jolly, carefree children' and the dignity, charm and independence of their women.[26] And with regard to the Muria love for dance, Elwin notes that the tribe 'can put on an evening's programme which is perhaps more varied and expert than anywhere else in India.'[27]

This celebration is as ever interwoven with a critique of civilized society. Sometimes the tribal ethos is claimed to be years ahead of the civilized: 'tribal women are as free today as all India's women were yesterday and will be tomorrow . . . There is no purdah, no ban on widow-remarriage; men and women work together as comrades in field and forest.' Much 'of what the women's reform leaders demand so sonorously from public platforms has been the Gadaba woman's right for generations.'[28] Or else, the presence of virtues in one society is highlighted to pinpoint their absence in another. A beautiful essay on games played by children of the forest ends with these words:

> . . . nearly all the games are just—games. There is singularly little competition. Even when villages dance against each other, or children go in for guessing games or Hunt the Slipper, there is no prize—or rather, as in "Alice," everybody wins and all have prizes. If a visitor offers a prize for any games the winning child immediately divides it with everybody else.
>
> . . . The tribal games do not divide people, do not excite jealousy or make a weak child despondent. The ugly, the poor, even the deformed have their full share in the fun, and no one is left out, no one loses, no one is ever a failure.
>
> There is much wisdom in these things.[29]

Cumulatively, Elwin's essays in the *Illustrated Weekly of India* hoped to persuade the Indian elite of the beauty, dignity and variety of tribal life. Tribals were not just an 'interesting and picturesque "extra," ' but worthy and hardworking citizens with much to contribute to national life. He asked his readers 'to use their influence wherever possible' in protecting tribal art and culture from the forces that threatened to destroy it.[30] As always, he hoped to foster an attitude of love and understanding towards the tribes. At the heart of all work for aboriginal India, he wrote, is

> the need for a change of attitude. Modern man must treat these people with respect. Words like 'backward,' 'uplift,' and all that savours of scorn or patronage must go from our vocabulary. Knowledge must come first and then the love that is the only thing strong and untainted enough to make work lasting. We have tried to work for this new attitude. By books, articles, films, pictures, lectures—extending now over a long period—we have tried to show the beauty and dignity of tribal life, that it is not something 'savage' of which we are to be ashamed and which we must eliminate, but that it is something with fine and durable values to give to modern India and the world.[31]

The modern man whose attention Elwin most eagerly sought was the Indian prime minister, Jawaharlal Nehru. The run-of-the-mill Congressman he despised, but Nehru was a different matter: fun-loving rather than puritanical, catholic rather than insular, liberal, humane, a writer and scholar, out of Harrow and Cambridge, in his own words the 'last Englishman to rule India.' Elwin's *Weekly* essays were meant for the intellectuals and civil servants who, at one or more remove, clustered around Nehru. Elwin must have hoped that they would be read by the prime minister too. On one occasion he was able to address the great man himself. Asked to write for a volume marking Nehru's sixtieth birthday, he commented on the 'strange link, which has often been noticed by travellers and scientists, between the most highly cultured and the most primitive of mankind.' Elwin had 'no doubt whatever that this instinctive rapport and sense of kinship is invariably felt by Jawaharlal Nehru whenever he meets an aboriginal.' The thirty million tribals of India, he went on, 'have cause to rejoice that in this time of rapid culture-change there is at the head of affairs a man who combines a scientific intelligence with a broad humanity.'[32]

In public Elwin urged a fair deal for the tribals. In private he continued to be deeply pessimistic about their future. Six months after independence he saw only 'one Protector of Aborigines in India, and that is the mosquito. May it infest every pietist and reformer with cerebral malaria.' There was no hope even for his beloved Bastar, which had been merged with the Central Provinces, 'and that means the end of the ghotul and the bison-horn dance within five (three, two?) years.' All that one could do, he remarked, 'was to assist at the funeral of delight and laughter in the tribal hills.'[33] Two years later, in July 1950, he had added one more Protector of the Aborigines, which were now 'the Mosquito and Corruption.' Where the mosquito might deter outsiders (unlike the tribals, not genetically protected against malaria), corruption made sure that 'the attempts to open up tribal territory by road fail because the Public Works Department officers pinch the money. Schools don't do much harm because the Inspector and teachers pinch the money. Even the reformers have caught the prevailing urge.'[34]

This was a depression reinforced by his circumstance: the loss of the Anthropological Survey job and Kosi, TWARU in constant need of his efforts to raise money, and not least a child to care for. Since Shamrao had several, the friends had invested in a house in Jabalpur. Kusum Hivale lived in the town with the children, who went erratically to school. Sham's wife wanted him with them, but he preferred to commute between Patangarh and Jabalpur. Sham was torn between family and friend: he was, as he wrote to Mrs Minnie Elwin, sometimes 'in a pathetic state, for I daren't leave Verrier alone in Patangarh during the rains [when he came down unfailingly with malaria], and at the same time I have frantic letters from Kusum and Suresh begging me to come to Jubbulpore. I am going tomorrow for a few days, but I have made all arrangements and I am sending [Verrier] plenty of vegetables, fruit, bread and even sardines from there.'[35]

Kumar lived with Shamrao's family, going to school with his mate Suresh Hivale and coming over to Patangarh during holidays. At this time (1951–2) he was, with Verrier's encouragement, playing with Meccano sets and collecting stamps, very English pastimes for a tropical boy with a tribal parent. The father thought the boy 'a beautiful and affectionate child:' to Verrier's delight he revealed a distinct talent for painting and drawing. Might he not, when he grew up, go to Tagore's school at Santiniketan? But the Gond in him would also come out, for there was little he liked better than climbing trees and imitating bird-calls. He was once thrown out of class for mewing like a cat, and a minor scandal erupted when he sold a New Testament (a present from his English grandmother) to a Parsi boy, buying himself sweets with the proceeds. The principal summoned the father, who was secretly pleased. His son, he thought, 'might do worse than become an anti-clerical gourmet.'[36]

The real trouble was that Kumar was hopelessly laggard at his studies. His father, alas, had little time to take care of *that.* At last, and reluctantly, Verrier decided to put Kumar in boarding school, choosing St Mary's, Bombay, where his progress would be watched over by priests and the family of the journalist Frank Moraes, whose son, the boy-poet Dom, was two classes ahead of him.[37]

Verrier went to Bombay when he could, taking his son to the beach and the zoo. In between visits he would be sent reports by Dom Moraes. 'Kumar is thriving, or so I think,' wrote the precocious guardian, 'but I don't think his exam results were very good. Does it matter?'[38] With the reports would be enclosed Dom's latest poems. The failed old poet and the aspiring younger one forged a deep friendship, helped no doubt by the absence of Dom's father—a famous and continually travelling editor—and the lack of learning of Verrier's son. The man criticized the boy's verses and introduced him to his own favourite poets: Dylan Thomas, Sidney Keyes and Wordsworth. From the jungle Verrier's 'long badly-typed letters crossed the thousands of miles to Bombay. They spoke of arduous trips and of fever, but only briefly: otherwise, as though he was writing them from rooms in All Souls, they discussed poetry, and on occasion, life.' Years later Moraes remembered the man himself as 'very tall, with a scholarly stoop. He had vividly blue eyes set in a kestrel face and longish, white raggedly out hair. He smoked terrible black cigars and chuckled constantly to himself . . . He loved poetry and in a way lived it.'[39]

Kumar had been placed, he hoped, in safe hands, but how to spend the rest of his own life remained a problem. The present headman of Patangarh, then a boy, remembers the daily routine, *c.* 1951–2, of the village's most distinguished resident. First, in the morning, Verrier would have his bed-tea (*palang chai*), at least three kettles of it, followed by a bath and breakfast. He would then retreat to his room, saying no one should disturb him, and work non-stop till lunch. A siesta, more work, a walk though the village, and it was time for dinner and bed. The little Pardhan boys would say of Verrier banging away on the typewriter: '*bade bhaiyya notaa chaap rahe hain*' (our older brother is printing [currency] notes).[40]

What he was doing was writing the essays that would bring him and Sham a few of those notes. But life in Patangarh was dreary, lacking variety and challenge, and newspaper articles bored him. Putting the last touches to *The Religion of an Indian Tribe,* Verrier felt 'so homesick for the Saora country I could almost cry, and I kick myself daily for not going and settling there while there was still time.' His 'real trouble,' he confessed to Bill Archer, was that he had

> an insatiable desire to experience and create—and neither seems within the bounds of possibility. Sex doesn't bother me very much now, at least not the sex that demands satisfaction. But I do want sexual stimulus. That is to say, whatever new research I do must be among a sexually attractive people—nudes or half-nudes. I don't want to have them, but I do like having them about.[41]

The tragedy was that the tribes of middle India, even the most isolated ones, were clothing themselves in the soiled garb of civilization. In January 1952 Verrier was on a field trip in South Bihar, scouting around without much enthusiasm for fresh tribes and fresh themes. He had with him a cook, a driver, and the indispensable Sunderlal but felt lonely, 'with no one to talk to in English. Shamrao, like an owl, is sitting in Jubbulpore.' Verrier wrote to Sham that either he must tour with him, or that he must himself marry Lila, or marry someone else, or get a 'new beautiful and intelligent male disciple. But there is no fun in touring by oneself like this.'[42]

He called on Bill Archer's old tribe, the Uraons, to find they had 'sadly deteriorated in the ten years since I was here last.' Fearful of puritans, they now referred to their dormitory, the *dhumkuria*, as the 'meeting-place.' The way Uraon women covered their heads at his approach made him feel as if he had entered a ladies' lavatory by mistake.[43] Sitting in a dreary rest house in the town of Hazaribagh he wrote to Archer:

> At fifty a man's chief temptation is to ask whether Pound the poet or the pound sterling is more important. I haven't any real doubts, but occasionally, especially when sitting on my arse all by myself in this conspicuously depressing dak bungalow, I wonder if I had . . . or if I had . . .
>
> What I really want, my Bill, is a woman and an assignment. How happy I was in Bastar with something to *do*, that called out something in me, and

> when I could afford to do it. How happy too in Orissa. But now I have no more excuse to travel still that loved hillside . . .
>
> When I say a woman, I mean a legal woman, a registered woman, a woman I can tell the world of, in brief a wife.[44]

The break-up with Kosi behind him, Verrier looked eagerly for a 'stable, happy marriage.' He was now willing to renounce the casual encounter for the right wife. Some clues to the kind of woman he was in search of might be found in his book on the Bondo, which was sent to press soon after his divorce. Among the Orissa tribe sexual practices were discreet, controlled and carefully guided; both boys and girls appeared to be 'remarkably abstinent during the pre-bethrotal, if not the pre-marital period.' The Bondo were unique among the tribes he knew in their attitude to sex and marriage, seeking permanence and attachment rather than passion. In this respect at least the anthropologist had once more found a tribe to match his predilection and circumstance. In the nineteen thirties, when Elwin was unmarried and in the process of freeing himself from an ascetic past, he had gloried in the Baiga's open and joyful delight in sex. A little later, working with the Muria of Bastar while his own marriage was doing supremely well, he contrasted the tribe's premarital freedom with their post-marriage fidelity. Now with the Bondo, a failed marriage behind him, he marvelled at their steadiness and steadfastness, their search for a legal, lifelong, yet romantic attachment with a partner of their choosing.[45]

Despite his love for Lila, Verrier was worried that a second marriage to a tribal might end as badly as the first. Sometimes he felt that the right wife this time could only be an educated Indian. To Bill Archer he specified an awesome list of features. She must not be too soft, but something hard to strike on; musn't be too acquiescent or yielding; must have a mind and personality of her own like the poetess Sarojini Naidu but with sexual charm. Another model he had in mind was Shiela Auden, a great beauty from the Bengali aristocracy, herself a painter, married to John Auden of the Geological Survey of India.[46]

By the middle of 1952 Lila and he had been living together for almost three years. Some friends knew of her but the time had not come to make their relationship public or formal. She was pregnant once more, but this made him even more hesitant to make her his wife. It was decided now that India would be his country, but his partner and profession were yet unclear. In May he received a letter from Jehangir Patel asking him to look for a job, the implication being that the patronage was finite. Verrier wrote a pathetic letter to Victor expressing his mixed-up feelings for J. P.—

> So easy it is for a little Bombay cotton broker to write off the work and ideals of over twenty years. I have replied that I propose to carry on and do what I can. As a matter of fact, I wish I could get JP out of my hair; I think many people, with whom he is most unpopular, might give us more assistance and he is becoming more and more of an irritant rather than a help. But of course, I am very fond of him in one way and he has been a great help to us in the past.[47]

In the last week of May Lila gave birth to their second son, Nakul. The birth is merely noted, not commented upon, more space being given in his diary to a letter from the editor of the *Illustrated Weekly of India*, Shaun Mandy, passing on a communication he had received from Harold Acton. At Oxford the two had inhabited very different worlds, but Acton had now written to Mandy of his admiration for Elwin's writings and 'envy [of] his achievements, which makes me seem a sad materialist by contrast.' More cheering still was the news of an address delivered by Nehru to a conference of social workers in New Delhi. The prime minister had condemned those who wished to make tribals 'second-rate copies of ourselves.' Nehru said the civilized had much to learn from the tribals, for 'they are an extremely disciplined people, often a great deal more democratic than most others in India. Above all they are a people who sing and dance and try to enjoy life, not people who sit in stock exchanges, shout at one another and think themselves civilised.'[48] Verrier was buoyed by the report of a speech which was 'the Elwin message almost word for word on those illustrious lips. It must have driven the reformers to fury.' Although he acknowledged that Nehru's talk was 'as far from reality as I am,' he was now a 'little more hopeful about the future of the tribes.'[49]

In August 1952 Verrier was due for his customary visit to Bombay. This time the trip was a special one, to commemorate his fiftieth birthday and the completion of twenty years with the tribes. To get to Bombay from Patangarh was quite a task for two travellers who had neither the official support commanded by sahibs nor the comforts and conveniences of modern travel. Verrier and Sham, two middle-aged men, first walked five miles in the monsoon mud to the main road, then hitched a ride on a lorry to the nearest dak bungalow. Up early the next morning they took another lorry to Dindori town, then a bus to Jabalpur (this a seven-and-a-half hour ride, and bumpy), where they caught the train to Bombay.

Having got to the city, Verrier was a good deal more hopeful about his own future. Ebrahim Alkazi and Alyque Padamsee, young lions of the Bombay stage, had put up a production of Ibsen's *Ghosts* sponsored by the 'Verrier Elwin Committee.' The industrialist Sir Homi Mody presided over a Neptune Ball in aid of 'Verrier Elwin's Tribal Welfare and Art Research Unit.' Jehangir Patel, knowing little of his protege's mixed feelings, invited a hundred guests to the Taj Hotel for a lobster lunch in his honour, followed by a champagne dinner. This was the first of a round of parties in tribute:

> a great reception at the Rotary, flowers and flags, a dinner presided over by the Chief Justice who called me a 'great scholar and a great gentleman;' a grand other dinner by the Chairman of Indian Airways to which the American Consul and British High Commissioner and a score of others were called to meet me; and a tea party with the Indian Chancellor of the Exchequer; and drinks with India's most famous novelist [Mulk Raj Anand], and a gathering yesterday of an Art Society which made a chocolate cake in the shape and titling of *The Tribal Art of Middle India.*[50]

This account was penned for his mother, the bishop's wife, who was always impressed by big names. But Verrier was terrifically proud too. The affection and enthusiasm with which Shamrao and he were met and the coverage in the press (which had been particulary tickled by his remark that 'in the matter of puritanism, the people of Bombay and the aboriginals seem to be in the same boat') confirmed for him that their cause was prospering once more. From Bombay they proceeded to Delhi, where Verrier's talk at the Rotary Club was chaired by Jaipal Singh, also an Oxford man and a rising tribal politician from Bihar. When Verrier finished Jaipal offered a splendid vote of thanks in which 'he was so rude to the Hindus that my delicately put cracks were quite forgotten!' 'Our ceaseless propaganda is having a little effect,' wrote Verrier to his sister, 'even these wretched Congressmen are coming round a bit.' He was now feeling more secure: when Eldyth reported that a friend had told her 'India had finished with Verrier,' he replied angrily, ' I fear not.'[51]

In Delhi Verrier had hoped to meet Nehru, but the great man was on tour. He left a letter for him nonetheless: 'Dear Jawaharlalji,' he began,

> it is a long time since the days when I used to have the happiness of meeting you when I was working with Gandhiji, but I venture to write to you now. Partly I want to thank you for the magnificent speech you made on the tribal problem last June, which so exactly expressed my own feelings and which gave me personally enormous encouragement and support. It is now just 21 years since I first went to live among the tribal people, but nothing has cheered me so much and promised greater happiness for the people whose own I have become.

He told Nehru of his wish to study the beautiful objects of Assam in order to write a sequel to his *Tribal Art of Middle India.* He did not need the state's support—the money was being raised, as ever, from the Bombay millionaires—but sought its seal of approval. 'It would help me greatly,' he wrote, 'if I knew I had your approval of this and perhaps commendation from you to the Assam Government.'[52]

Nehru then wrote, in the manner of one wretched Congressman to another, to the governor of Assam, Jairamdas Daulatram. The governor was a practical fellow, a no-nonsense Gandhian: why should he allow the anthropologist to collect art when he could be of much better use to him and his government? Daulatram invited Elwin to Assam for three months. He could do his research on the side, but he might also write a report on the prospects for the region's tribes who were untouched by Hindu influence and prone to rebellion against the state.

To Verrier, looking for a way out of the mess in Mandla, this was an offer he could scarcely refuse. The Assam trip was pregnant with promise but also fraught with danger. Indications that Verrier thought it might be another turning point in his life, the last perhaps, lie in a will he drafted the week before he was due to go. This left five thousand rupees, the bulk of his savings, to Lila, the rest to Sham. He was not leaving any money separately to his son, he said, for Kumar already had shares and certificates in his name and would inherit money from his aunt Eldyth. However, Verrier directed 'Mr and Mrs Hivale to care for him as if he was their own child.' As for his other possessions, the library went to Shamrao, 'except that I direct that my copy of Temple's "Legends of the Punjab" which is one of the few perfect copies in existence, shall be presented to the National

Library, Calcutta, and that my copy of Dalton's "Descriptive Ethnology of Bengal" shall be presented to Mr J. P. Patel.' Finally, his 'collection of ethnographic negatives should be presented by Mr Hivale to any person or institution which in his opinion is likely to make good use of it. The five reels of cine-film now with my sister Eldyth should be presented to the Royal Anthropological Institute.'[53]

Verrier set out with Shamrao for Assam on 15th November, driving from Patangarh across the breadth of the subcontinent. Calling at Jabalpur, Maihar, Banaras and Gaya, they arrived after a week at a dak bungalow on the banks of the Brahmaputra, their first stop in Assam. They had driven through shifting landscapes—flat plains, sal forests, tea gardens—and their accommodation had been as varied—'one night in a comfortable hotel, one night in a Punjabi hotel crawling with bugs, sometimes on the ground, sometimes in the car.' And now at last they were in Assam; looking out across the water to the Himalaya the state presented 'a lovely first view to the visitor.'

On 3rd December Verrier met the governor in Shillong. From 'this enchanting place, with its pines, lakes and perfect scenery and friendly people, both great and small,' he moved on to an extended tour of the Nagas of Manipur. He was fifty and overweight and the marches were hard—rough paths straight over the crest of eight-thousand-foot mountains—but the Nagas hospitable and the views magnificent. Verrier revelled in 'the natural scenery and the charm of the people,' gathering for his collection specimens of cloth and ornaments. In a village high up in the Thangkhul Naga hills, with an Assamese deputy commissioner who also adored P. G. Wodehouse, he felt 'on top of the world.'[54] They had climbed all day, arriving at their destination to find before them a

> scene of fantastic and unearthly beauty. In a great grove of orange trees some thirty splendid youths, their limbs glowing golden in the setting sun, clad in rich red cloth and having on their heads great white crowns like wings, were marching up and down with spears, and chanting ancient melodies that recalled a long-forgotten world. It was a death chant, and it was one that I should be proud to have sung over my own body when it goes to the dust.[55]

Here were people who really lived: their control over land and forest complete, their traditions of weaving and dance splendidly intact. Singing, dancing, eating in common out of a great big wooden platter, these were tribes that had not decayed. Verrier later recalled feeling 'violently excited' by the tribes he saw on this trip.[56] He was now convinced that his future, or what was left of it, lay in the north-east. Stopping at enchanting Shillong on his way home he submitted his report to the governor with a personal note asking him to 'look on me as someone who would count it a great happiness to be at any time of service to you in the Adibasi cause.'[57]

On his way back from Assam Verrier tarried awhile in Calcutta. Walking down Chowringhee one day he was stopped by two American girls. 'Was he Dr Elwin,' they asked. They had seen a photograph of him in *The Statesman*—then, as now, with his trademark cigar. The girls, or ladies rather, were Jean Merrill and Ronnie Silbert, Fulbright scholars in their late twenties, one studying folk-tales, the other folk-lore. They were pleased to meet the established scholar and he was delighted with Jean in particular. She was pretty and witty, a former journalist who was 'very sound on Ezra Pound.' For two weeks they saw Calcutta through his eyes and then Verrier invited them to Patangarh. His friend John Auden believed the American girls were lovers but Verrier thought (or hoped) not. Sham and he had convinced themselves that in Jean lay the 'perfect solution to our problems.' After the girls came to Patan Verrier took Jean for a walk up the hill and proposed to her. Alas, she turned him down like a 'bloody bedspread,' although she was very sweet about it.

Verrier was disconsolate—'I have given civilisation its last chance and it doesn't want me,' he wrote to Victor. His feelings were expressed in language that came out of Jane Austen via P. G. Wodehouse:

> If the Creator had sat down to think out how to make a perfect wife for that poor fish Verrier, and had made her to my ideal specifications, with a few improvements of his own, he would have produced something like Jean, not quite so good perhaps but near it. We had built up a whole world of dreams; we had made our arrangements with Lila; I had a bottle of champagne ready, and now . . .[58]

One doesn't know how seriously to take all this. I suspect Verrier fell in love with the idea of Jean, the idea of a girl who was well read, urbane, civilized, up on poetry and literature and the cinema, in sum everything a tribal girl was not. There was the feeling in him that if at fifty he let go of this apparition of beauty and beatitude, nothing like it would come his way again. He also seems to have mistaken the typical American openness and frankness for amorous interest, even love. In relation to Lila, even if he had made no commitment of formal matrimony, his behaviour seems less easy to excuse: she was already the mother of his children. On Jean's part one supposes she was not uninterested in a fling with a widely travelled and experienced Englishman—though it appears the affair was not consummated—but marriage was a different kettle of fish altogether. Why would a Fulbright scholar chuck up country, career, prospects, for an isolated life in village India of the fifties?

In his diary Verrier marked the last day of February with a line by Sidney Keyes: 'There was a month and two people walked in it'—and continued:

> What a month! I shall never write the word 'February' without a slight tremor. It has been dominated by the Impossible She, who should have been the ideal, the perfect solution. It has been a month of paralysis, of bitter-sweet lessons learnt about myself, of great goodness and unselfishness on the part of Sham [who was prepared both to accept Jean and to supervise an amicable parting with Lila], of love from Wasant, of passionate affection from Lila, of divided aims, of conflicting duties. I thought I might grow young again, that life would become a new thing. But evidently it was not to be that way, so we must find another way. The essential thing is that failure in one thing should never mean failure in everything. The essential thing is that we should not let disappointment make me old. The greatest problem of all is to remain young. Our real enemy is not scandal, nor poverty, nor hardship, nor even our vices—but Time. Jean would have halted Time—she would have, as Rabelais might have said, touched its arse with a thistle.[59]

That Verrier was more in love with the idea than the person is made to seem more likely by the verve with which he bounced back. For close at hand was the Other Way, the Possible She. She would keep him young, was in fact keeping him young. Soon after Jean left Patan he decided he would make a honest man of himself by marrying Lila. He introduced his future wife to his mother in the most roundabout way. 'I forgot if I told you,' he wrote, 'I had adopted a lovely little Pardhan boy called Wasant, who is now about two-and-a-half years old and is completely fascinating.' It took another three months for Wasant to be identified as Lila's child. On 19th June Verrier wrote home of his decision to marry again:

> Dr Johnson said of a friend who married a second time that it was the 'triumph of hope over experience,' and let us hope that Hope, that blessed thing, will be rewarded this time. I did not write about it before because I was not quite certain, and I never like to start a hare until it is necessary!
>
> Her name is Lila, and she is a Pardhan, a member of the tribe about whom Shamrao has written. The Pardhans are the witty, charming, music-and-poetry-loving tribe who live with the Gonds and give life to them. Lila is 30 years old and has two exquisite little boys, from a previous husband whom she has divorced. One of them is Wasant, whom I have already adopted, and who is the joy of my life, the most perfect child I have ever seen. I will send you photos of them by the next mail. She is a very sweet girl, beautiful to look at, good-tempered, doesn't drink, and will be a great help to us in our work, for she is extremely competent. When our grass was burnt this year, she immediately set to (when Sham and I were away) and got 20,000 bundles of new grass—had she not done so we would never have been able to build the house. She is very tender-hearted towards the poor . . . She can read and write in Hindi, and I am teaching her English. I think she will be a very good wife, especially as she is very fond of me.[60]

The fib about the children from a previous husband was necessary under the circumstances. Otherwise, Verrier was stressing what made Lila different from Kosi—the domesticity, the stability, the abstinence—but his mother and Eldyth were 'terribly disturbed' by the news. Mrs Elwin wrote to Kusum Hivale of her wish that Verrier could marry again,

> *suitably*, but to again marry a girl from a tribe, however dear and fine she may be, involves too many risks—too much of what she may inherit and pass on to his children, if he has any more. He is now a man of position and influence and as such should travel widely and have contact with many men and women. I pray much about it and for my darling first born—but I dare not interfere and in any case, he takes his own way—and his poor old mother hasn't much influence.[61]

The devoted Shamrao, pressed by Verrier to comfort Mother, insisted that 'there was no fear of it turning out the way his first marriage did.' Lila 'understands Verrier and his ways almost as well as I do;' she would make a great difference to the eleven months of the year that her son spent in village India.[62]

Mrs Elwin remained unconvinced, as did Verrier's friends. Bill Archer, who had welcomed Kosi straightaway, this time warned that 'trouble' would start if Lila accompanied her husband to Bombay or Calcutta, for she might have 'her head turned by her status.'[63] Jehangir Patel assured Verrier of his 'full co-operation if you do marry Lila,' but felt nevertheless that the advantages

> are more than counter-balanced to my way of thinking (and I may be wrong) by the blunt fact that Lila will not be able to become your companion as far as your 'head' is concerned. A wife should be a pal for 'the head and the heart' and now around the age of 50 the 'head' is more than the heart to be reckoned with. If you are not able to satisfy Lila the same thing will happen as with Kosi. Of one thing I am quite sure and confident and that is on no account should you have any more children. It's selfish and most unfair to the child. Perhaps and naturally Lila will want a child. The fact that she has already experienced motherhood—as you informed me—is also against your union being happy.[64]

The words of caution were well meant, but Verrier had made up his mind to trust in Hope over Experience. Within all this dilly-dallying over Lila, it seems always implicit that Lila herself would want nothing other than marriage to Elwin; which, given the times and the context in which she was placed, was almost certainly true. Elwin asked the registrar of marriages in Jabalpur for a date but was told they would have to wait two months. In anticipation he set about remodelling their house. The best Gond artists were called in to decorate the living room: one wall painted over with animals, tiger, crabs and cows, the other with warriors fighting and magicians 'divining all sorts of things.' The bathroom had a scene of Gond girls at a well, trees growing exuberantly above. The carpenters meanwhile had put his books in a glass-fronted case, his radio-set in a recess tastefully tucked away in the wall.

The house having now become a home, Lila and he were married before a magistrate in Jabalpur on 20th September 1953. That morning he felt a last twinge of panic, but with an effort of will it disappeared: 'Felt apprehensive at dawn that this was perhaps the most foolish thing I had ever done. Social death, the end of my career, a finis to sexual adventure, a lifetime of low-voltage contentment—are these ahead of me now? Later, cheered up a bit. This is a good thing to do. I have loved Lila for a long time and still love her and she loves me. The way of attainment is through endless pity, forgiveness, love—and I need these things fully as much as she does.'[65]

His town friends threw a party after the registration, the scene finely described by the bridegroom-novelist-anthropologist: 'The Nags provided Indian sweets and the traditional sprinkling with rose-water. Ishwar Singh, the old fat ex-Director of Public Instruction; the Deputy Inspector-General of Police; Romesh Misra, the family doctor; Narad, the chief journalist in his Gandhi cap; the Director of Railway Traffic and his pretty wife; the Conservator of Forests and some others.'[66] In the last category fell an old student of Deccan College in Poona, who in the thirties had been lectured to by the *upacharya* of the Christa Seva Sangh. 'To hear Father Elwin read Shakespeare was an unforgettable experience,' as indeed twenty years later was the first sight of his second wife. Lila on the day of the wedding, wrote this former student, was 'young, dark and healthy in appearance, her masses of hair extravagantly oiled falling about her shoulders, like a mantle.'[67]

Unlike the first time, registration at Jabalpur was not followed by a formal village wedding (and the groom prudently refrained from writing an essay titled 'I Married a Pardhan'), but the celebrations in Patangarh were anything but muted. A huge feast was thrown on the 30th for 312 invited guests and a number of gatecrashers. The party began with drums and music at eight in the morning. The goats were killed at ten and drinks served at noon. By early afternoon the crowd had begun to warm up, and Lila and Verrier were whirled round an improvised marriage pole. The company only sat down for lunch at six-thirty and stragglers were still being served food at midnight.

Verrier had his wife. All that remained now was the assignment. In May the education minister of the Government of India had written offering him the directorship of the Anthropological Survey, in succession to B. S. Guha, but the pay was not enough to 'reconcile one to living in a city like

Calcutta.' He also had word that he might be asked to advise the governor of Assam, a job he 'would like to do even if they paid nothing.'[68] He suspected that Guha, his friend turned rival, had suggested Verrier's name for this, if only to clear the decks for his getting another term at the survey.

Anyway, once the balloon was floated it was kept aloft by some officials at the ministry of external affairs who admired Elwin, and by their boss who admired him too. Nehru had recommended Elwin to the governor of Assam in November 1952; later, when sent his tour report, he forwarded it to all chief ministers of states with tribal populations, asking them to take heed of its warning that if 'we try to impose our ways on [tribals], imagining that we are doing them good . . . , we merely alienate them and, at the same time, probably injure them in many ways. They lose their artistic way of life and become drab imitations of something else.'[69] Now, as minister for external affairs (a portfolio he held all through his prime ministership), he quickly acquiesced to the suggestion that the anthropologist be drafted into the administration. With his approval Verrier was appointed, in November 1953, as Tribal Adviser to the administration of the North East Frontier Agency (NEFA), based in Shillong. The appointment took effect from the 1st of January 1954, in the first instance for a period of three years.[70]

In the second week of December Verrier visited Delhi to be briefed. Lila came with him and acquitted herself splendidly in their meetings with ministers, members of parliament, writers and journalists. His wife, he told his mother, met 'all these VIP's with such poise and charm—a week turned her into a new girl.' In Delhi he 'fell in love with her all over again.' She even accompanied him to Teen Murti House, where they had breakfast with its occupant. Lila's impressions of the prime minister are not known but her husband was carried away: 'What a charmer he is! And what style he keeps!' They saw his Giant Panda, and when the two men went for a walk in the garden, Nehru told Elwin he hoped he would advise them not only on the frontier but 'on the whole tribal problem in India.'[71]

Lesser Indians whom Verrier met in Delhi included the health minister Rajkumari Amrit Kaur (another ex-inmate of Sabarmati), the writer Khushwant Singh and assorted MPs from the north-east. He also met Gandhi's son Devadas (now the editor of the *Hindustan Times*), who asked after mother and Eldyth, and the Mahatma's secretary, 'dear old Pyarelal, now married to a sweet ugly little woman, who also enquired tenderly for you both.'[72] Calling on Gandhians, being briefed by Congress ministers, Verrier had made an honourable peace with Indian nationalism.

The Elwins returned to Patangarh only to pack and leave in a hurry. Verrier knew already that this was a job with real possibilities: for in isolated NEFA, tucked away in a corner of the Himalaya between India, Burma and Tibet, there was still hope the 'tribesmen would escape the cultural and moral degradation that is rapidly overtaking their fellows in some other parts of India.'[73] He was much pleased by a letter from J. R. D. Tata who was 'happy that the Government of India have at last awakened to your existence and immense value to the country, in your life-time.'[74] Tata wrote this as one whose own value to India was never really recognized by the powerful, within whose blinkered socialism even the most patriotic and productive industrialists were suspected of avarice.

Verrier felt like someone who 'asked for a sandwich and has been handed a eight-course banquet.' His contract was for three years but the ministry told him they would like him to go on till he was dead. 'This is a stupendous business,' he told his friend and editor R. E. Hawkins, 'and I don't know how far I will be able to fulfil it. But the field is so exciting and so virginal that I will do my best to penetrate it.' Sham would stay on in Mandla for the time being, but if 'all goes well we might hand over the Patan show to another organization and shift everything to Assam for a final effort before departing this life.'[75]

Verrier confided to his diary that his emotions on leaving Patangarh were 'less acute than I feared. I hate leaving the house, every corner of which was built with such loving care; but the garden is rather a flop and the people whom we have loved for so long, have become rather boozed and dreary. I have a feeling that we have done our stuff here and perhaps the new Assam assignment will prove a much bigger and more exciting thing, a door to a new life, to being useful for once.'[76]

To his new boss, the governor of Assam, Verrier wrote of his wish to start, on the side, an independent research institute with 'associated welfare activities' to be run by his companion of the past quarter-century. He hoped thus to 'gradually close down our work in Mandla and bring everything over here. Shamrao Hivale, who has been with me for 27 years and from I do not like to be separated, might well be used by us . . .' While Sham awaited the call, Verrier would move to Shillong, a change of residence that also involved a final and irrevocable change in nationality. He had already asked for the forms through which to apply for Indian citizenship, writing to the governor that he was now 'spending his last few days on earth as a formal Englishman.'[77]

CHAPTER ELEVEN

A Sahib (Sometimes) in the Secretariat

Grigson has pulled over his creative activity the very efficient condom of official promotion.

Verrier Elwin to W. G. Archer, August 1942

I don't think we can live without each other—at least I can't. You have your work and books, but I seem to have nothing. But I do have you that I know.

Shamrao Hivale to Verrier Elwin, November 1953

In December 1953 Verrier Elwin flew from Calcutta to Guwahati and took a taxi to Shillong. Following him forty-four years later I found the road out of the airport lined with policemen, a man with a rifle at every fifty yards. The driver explained that the prime minister had been in Guwahati the previous day, inaugurating his party's campaign for the forthcoming general election. Such politicians, coming and going, were now potential targets for the insurgents of the United Liberation Front of Assam.

Just before the bridge over the Brahmaputra river we turned right, by-passing Guwahati town. We crossed the border into the state of Meghalaya, carved out of Assam in 1972. Flatlands gave way very quickly to hills and the policemen disappeared. I tried to match the landscape to others I knew. The shape and height of the hills were reminscent of my native Garhwal, but the hills themselves were greener and not disfigured by limestone mines or steeply cut terraces or eucalyptus plantations. Bananas like Bengal, areca nut palms like the Western Ghats of Karnataka, sal trees like Madhya Pradesh—out here *everything* seems to grow. The predatory capitalism of the rich and the over-population of the poor have not reached this part of the world.

We climbed higher, along a surprisingly gentle gradient. The hills were still richly covered with trees, plants, creepers, bushes; now and then an odd pine, and a lovely tree with lilac blossoms. Also a sign, every two hundred yards, asking us to KEEP MEGHALAYA GREEN—which it is. We rounded a bend and saw water. It was a lake, getting bigger and bigger, curving round two hills, enveloping them. Some foreigners were nearby filming the water. I asked the Bengali driver what the lake was called. 'Barapani,' he replied, 'Big Water.' So it appears to the plainsman, but the local Khasi, as I was to discover, call it 'Umiam,' or tear-drop.

After Barapani the pines dominate: pines, peasants, lakes, hills. They had once beckoned the Wordsworth-worshipping Elwin. Even the village houses were pretty, built on stilts and with quaint little windows.

We approached the city on the hill. On its outskirts is a settlement called Mawlai, peopled by Khasis originally converted by Welsh Presbyterians. In three minutes, and looking all to one side of the road, a church advertised 'Bible Study Classes,' a house was called Amazing Grace; there was a theological college, a graveyard, a Mary Magdalene Convent. It seemed an old settlement. Elwin would have passed it on his way up. But was Shillong so expressively Christian then? Perhaps not. In 1954 this was not the state of Meghalaya, but the state of Assam, whose capital city was run by Hindus. Only after they departed down to Guwahati did the Khasis come into their own.

By the time I reached my lodgings it was five o'clock, too late and dark to visit the Elwins. I walked down to the bazaar and bought the day's newspapers. Two reports dominated the front page: Prime Minister Inder Kumar Gujral's speech in Guwahati and a series of bomb blasts on certain trains. The previous day, I suddenly realized, had been 6th December, the fifth anniversary of the demolition by a Hindu mob of the Babri Masjid in Ayodhya. Gujral marked the occasion with a homily on the traditions of Indian secularism, on the need to make minorities safe and secure in the land. The bombs were the handiwork of Muslim extremists, an act of vengeance for the work, five years earlier, of their Hindu counterparts.

I. K. Gujral was the poor man's Jawaharlal Nehru, a politician schooled in the old school of Indian nationalism. He lacked Nehru's charm, charisma, intellect, and moral authority, but stood nonetheless for the same idea of India: an India that is inclusive, tolerant, accommodating different faiths and traditions: the idea of India that Elwin came to Shillong to help Nehru build, the India now threatened by corrosive corruption from within and religious fundamentalism from without. As I walked down to dinner I recalled, with a chill not owing to the winter wind, a remark by Elwin: 'If, after the passing of the present leadership in India, there was a strong reaction towards a more orthodox Hinduism, as many leading Christians and Muslims, rightly or wrongly, fear, then the Christian tribals would be likely to react against India.'[1]

Verrier Elwin approached his new job with much excitement and just a little trepidation. 'If I am to succeed in this Frontier assignment,' he noted in his diary,

> certain things will be vitally necessary:
> 1. Physical fitness, for which
> I must be careful not to exceed in food or drinks
> I must not over-tire myself unnecessarily
> I must have a better and fuller sex-life with Lila
>
> 2. Mental fitness, involving
> elimination of irritated thoughts
> elimination of petty grievances
> elimination of worry about small things
> elimination of jealousy
>
> 3. Financial stability, for which
> I must save all I can
> Avoid expenditure on alcohol
> I must spend more on essentials.

This was written on Christmas Eve 1953, in Patangarh. The next week Verrier set off for Calcutta, where he picked up his friend Victor Sassoon.

They flew to Guwahati on New Year's Eve and drove on to Shillong. Victor helped find a decent house, a lovely isolated bungalow on a hill, shaded by pines and with a garden full of marigolds. Restoring the water supply, which had been cut off by the neighbour after a fight with the previous occupant, was Verrier's first priority; the purchase of a second-hand car, which was also chosen by Victor, was the next. There was no telephone, but 'after twenty years of Mandla anything seems comfortable.' Shillong itself, with its bracing climate and pine forests, reminded him of the Alps. 'I wished we had always lived here,' he wrote to his mother; 'the air is delicious, like Swiss air, and it will probably add ten years to my life.' Lila and the boys had also arrived. He was pleased, she much more so, telling him: 'How happy I am when I am with you.'[2]

Elwin's appointment was for three years in the first instance, at a salary of Rs 1500 per month, the rent paid for. But as he told the governor, 'I now want to settle down in Assam for good, whether or not my official services are required later.' There was here a 'whole new world of exploration and research;' with luck he might independently open a small institute for research and welfare. If that took off they would close down their work in Mandla and Shamrao would come and join him. His old mate, Elwin told the governor, was 'uniquely gifted in dealing with tribal people. I hope that in the end he will come here and work with me, either officially or unofficially.'[3]

In his first fortnight at Shillong Verrier bumped into Devadas Gandhi. Devadas was in town, showing a film of the Old Man. To Elwin, his half-brother in a manner of speaking, he was 'most friendly.' The meeting with the younger Gandhi was symbolic, for Verrier was an employee of the Government of India, hoping also to become a citizen of India. In his citizenship application he provided a crisp summary of all that he had done in and for his adopted land: his association with Gandhi during the Civil Disobedience movement, his reports on behalf of the Congress in Gujarat and the North-West Frontier, his twenty years' work for the tribals of central India. 'I mention these things,' he told the official processing his request, 'to show that my desire for Indian citizenship is not a new or merely sentimental thing, but has been tested by circumstances over a long period. And further India is my home and my love; I am deeply attached to her thought, her culture and her people; half my life has been spent within her borders; and I have the happiness to be married to an Indian lady.'[4]

In an appendix to his application Elwin listed the places where he had been resident since September 1927: as a Christian for the Congress with the Christa Seva Sangh in Poona; as a social worker with Shamrao and the Gond Seva Mandal in Mandla; as a roving ethnographer on his own in Bastar and Orissa; as a research administrator with the Anthropological Survey in Banaras and Calcutta; as an adviser to government in Shillong. Many different homes and assignments: but there was one entry I have left out. Against the years 1929–30 was inserted: 'Sabarmati Ashram, Ahmedabad, Bombay Presidency.'

While a frequent visitor to Sabarmati, Elwin was never strictly speaking resident there. To call Gandhi's ashram one of his Indian homes was not of course a patent untruth, more an embellishment. But that he sought to place it alongside his more authentic homes reveals the continuing insecurity of an Englishman in hyper-nationalist India. For if any claim could certify his patriotism, it was this.

The North East Frontier Agency (NEFA) is now Arunachal Pradesh, a full-fledged state of the Indian Republic, with its own legislature and council of ministers. In January 1954, however, it was directly under the Foreign ministry at New Delhi. The governor of Assam, based in Shillong, was in effect the Government of India's man on the spot, with additional charge of NEFA. A key figure was the adviser to the governor, in Verrier Elwin's time usually a member of the Indian Civil Service. Elwin's own designation was 'Adviser on Tribal Affairs.'

Placed where the Himalaya move into monsoon South East Asia, Arunachal Pradesh is a land of extraordinary beauty, dominated by steep mountains, thick forests and fast-flowing rivers. The hills climb up to Tibet on one side, Bhutan on another, Burma on a third. More than half the size of England, the territory was in 1954 home to a mere half million people, most of them swidden cultivators. The pastoralists of the high valleys near Tibet practised Buddhism; otherwise the tribes were marked by a heterogeneity of belief and custom, worrisome to the administrator but, one supposes, attractive to the anthropologist.

British rule had exercised a shadowy suzerainty over NEFA. Three political officers had controlled the territory, their main job being to prevent tribals raiding the Assam tea estates. About once a year they undertook a long march through their domain, accompanied by a couple of hundred coolies and bodyguards carrying salt and tea and tobacco for the chiefs. The main nationalist party, the Congress, had no presence here. In parts of Nagaland, which bordered NEFA to the south-east and where American missionaries were active, there had arisen a separatist movement led by A. Z. Phizo.

The Government of India, coming in when the British left, knew it must move slowly among a potentially hostile populace divided into numerous tribes, previously unknown to science and to Hindu civilization. An elected assembly on the principle of universal adult franchise was deemed premature; advocated instead were village and district councils through which the 'most educated and progressive' tribals might be associated with the administration. To make them and their fellows feel 'one with India,' officers were chosen and trained with care. As a foreign ministry official wrote in 1953, NEFA required 'special types of officials and workers who will go and mix with [the tribals] socially, live and eat with them and endear themselves to them by serving their real interests.'[5]

The new Adviser on Tribal Affairs had much practice in living and eating with the tribes. Now there were new ones to know and the family had barely settled in when Verrier was off on his first tour. He chose for this the Tuensang Frontier Division bordering the Naga Hills, the scene of a bloody encounter with the army just the previous October. The governor offered him an escort; this he refused, saying that as a disciple of Gandhi he would go to the Nagas non-violently.

Verrier deposited his citizenship forms on 27th February; the next morning he left on a two-month-long trip. From Shillong he went by car to Jorhat, the Assam town surrounded by tea plantations; from there by jeep to Mokokchung, a distance of forty-seven miles which he had walked in 1947 to visit Bill Archer. The next morning the jeep took him to Tuensang town, where the road ended.

Over the next seven weeks Verrier walked more than two hundred miles amidst superb scenery, fine weather and new tribes. These last he knew would fall on his route, and so he took along only one book, Boswell's *Life of Johnson.*

The first tribe he met depressed him. They were the Tagins of the Sipi valley, horribly affected by dermatitis, their white skin peeling off in flakes. The Tagins 'make one want to weep, poor creatures; they are half-starved, have no dances, no arts (except cane-work) and not even any stories.' He moved on to the Konyaks, a tribe more to his liking. They had wonderful glowing bodies and fine skills in woodcraft, brassware and weaving; indeed the boys and girls were 'in the ornamentation of their own persona, themselves works of art.' Verrier stayed in a *morung*, the village dormitory or guard-house, with its lavatory above a pig-sty outside. The idea was to squat and shit from a raised platform while the animals below cleaned up the bounties they received from above. The arrangements appealed to Verrier; he felt so fit all week that on only one occasion 'did the pigs turn away from their breakfast, rightly revolted.'[6]

Two poems written in quick succession nicely capture Verrier's conflicting emotions, the romance of being with new tribes tempered with the responsibility towards what he had waiting for him in Shillong. The first one is

ON A KONYAK GIRL SEEN AT NIGHT

Delicate light of a torch
On bare delicate limbs
In a dark street.

Golden-brown the porch
Of the house of desire.
Swift were her feet.

Where were you going? To steal
The heart of a lover waiting
Behind the door?

At least he could touch you, feel
And enter the luminous house.
I only saw.

This reads like one of his better, more heartfelt efforts, yet it made him feel guilty, for on the next page of his diary we find a tribute

TO LILA, ON BEING BORED AT MON

Great hills lie lonely broadening down
To desolate valleys cut by angry streams
And the shadows of the clouds pass over them,
But there is no one, no one but in my dreams.

No one at all to whom I can open my heart.
Yet there is everyone, a world of beauty around
Beauty delicate, stirring, abiding yet quickly passing,
As lovely, as elusive as I have ever found.

The laughter, excitement, wonder passes me by,
For without you to share it, what is the gain?
The lonely heart turns only in on itself,
And joy in solitude is three parts pain.

When will you come to me, breaking out of my dream?
Tangibly come with your quiet and tender heart?
Or, must I hasten to you, forgetting adventure,
Crossing the cruel hills, all that hold us apart?

The Konyaks and their neighbours, the Phoms, had been headhunters, and headhunting had been recently forbidden by the Government of India. As the first outsider to move in these villages without an escort, Elwin found the people friendly but not pleased with the ban. 'If you talk to a Phom or Konyak on such tedious topics as theology, economics or social organization he quickly slips away to have a refreshing drink of rice-beer. Open the question of head-hunting and his eyes light up, his whole body comes to life and a torrent of exciting and highly improper information pours from his lips.'[7]

In the village of Shiangha Chingnyu, where 400 skulls were displayed in the morung, the headman told Verrier their one desire was to go to war again. 'Our young men have become women,' he said, 'our soil is no longer fertile.' Across the valley was Chokayu village which had lost 700 heads on a tragic morning in 1947: *they* were quite happy with the ban. Elwin allowed that the stop to head-hunting without a shot being fired had been a 'marvellous achievement.' But as it happened the dance among the Konyak had since become 'deplorably dull,' and the once splendid morungs had fallen into disrepair. A real need was 'to find a moral substitute for head-hunting'—dance, art, weaving, games—'something that will preserve the qualities of courage and daring, of discipline and organization, of artistic effort and colour that characterise head-hunting and war.'

An alternative moral code of a kind had begun seeping into Tuensang. This was the Baptist faith, brought in by Ao pastors from Nagaland. Verrier found fifty schools in the division run via 'remote control' by American priests themselves forbidden to enter NEFA. But the native evangelists trained by them were, alas, 'more fanatical, more irresponsible, and more effective than any foreigners could be,' teaching 'undiluted communalism' in the form of religion, promoting a 'scurrilous villification' of Hinduism, promising material advance through conversion, sowing the seeds of separatism. The teaching of the pastors, he thought, led 'straight to a xenophobic and separatist mentality in which there can be no love for "heathen" India.' But his worries were as much aesthetic as political. The Baptists he termed, in an inspired comparison, 'the R.S.S. of Christianity,' like that Hindu sect reducing a great religion to a set of narrow-minded prejudices. It would rob the tribesmen of their art, their dance, their colour, and give nothing in return. He quoted R. S. Thomas on the work of the Baptists in the Welsh valleys:

> The adroit castrator
> Of art: the bitter negation
> of song and dance and the heart's innocent joy.
> You have botched our flesh and left us only the soul's
> Terrible impotence in a warm world.

Wandering in Tuensang, among naked or near-naked people—'the more naked a tribe is the more fuss it makes about its clothes, when it wears them'—caught up in the excitement of the chase, identifying and parrying the shafts of civilization, Verrier was defending aboriginals once more, and with an official mandate to boot. His Tuensang report—thirty closely typed foolscap pages—was a harbinger of dozens to come that likewise mixed reportage with poetry, philosophy and practical action. The principle he held out to the locust-army of officials coming into NEFA was that 'it is better to let change come from within rather than be imposed from outside.' He was especially angered by the mockery of tribal customs. One schoolmaster instructed Phom women not to shave their heads; an official dressed the boys in hideous and ill-fitting black suits; another warned that the government would be displeased if they did not abandon the custom of placing their dead in the high branches of banyan trees. This last interference brought forth a passage of vintage Elwinism:

> Now although in the cosmopolitan city of Bombay, one of India's most advanced communities [the Parsis] expose their dead to the beaks and claws of vultures, although in Benares the corpses of those [Hindus] dying of cholera are flung upon the bosom of Mother Ganges and allowed to drift down the stream, I agree that it would be a good thing if the Phoms and Konyaks buried, or better still, cremated their dead. On the other hand, the evils of their usual custom have been exaggerated. I went very carefully into this, visiting the disposal-places in every village, and I found that generally the dead were treated with reverence and dignity. The bodies were wrapped in cloth and leaves, often placed in wooden coffins, and with very few exceptions, placed well outside the village. Great care is taken to decorate the tomb, grave-effigies are carved, and some of the Konyaks make remarkable stone amphoras in which the skulls are ultimately interred.
>
> Now we have already disturbed tribal sentiment to the depths by stopping head-hunting. The people are saying that their crops are less fertile, their young men less virile. This is inevitable. But I wonder if it is wise to inflict a still further blow to tribal sentiment by interfering with their death-customs. Anyone who has read Frazer's 'The Fear of the Dead in Primitive Religion' will know how extraordinarily sensitive tribal people are to everything connected with the disposal of a corpse. Should there now be an epidemic, or a crop-failure, it might well be attributed to the fact that corpses are being buried instead of being disposed of in the classic manner. . . . A Gaonbura who was showing me the new graves said rather bitterly, 'You see we are all Christians now.'

In mid-April Verrier returned to Shillong, establishing a pattern followed unvaryingly for the next few years: summers in the secretariat, winters on tour. Shillong itself was a charming little town, a smaller, less stuffy version of the great imperial summer capital, Simla. And Verrier was now a sahib. This casual attire of shirt and shorts or kurta pyjama, which had carried him through twenty years in central India, had been exchanged for a suit and tie—in office, at any rate. At home he liked to wear an Adi coat over his shirt. He had also become a member of the Shillong Club, an institution he simply had to join even though he was often bored by its members. At home he entertained his colleagues and their wives, for which purpose he sometimes borrowed the cook of his neighbour, the Maharaja of Mayurbhanj. Verrier's collection of tribal artefacts quickly became one of the sights of Shillong, a port of call for all visiting dignitaries, whether 'Income Tax people, Admirals, hotelliers, club secretaries, tea-planters [or] All India Radio Types.'[8] Lila, meanwhile, had become a memsahib, a hostess uncannily matching drinks with social types—there she was 'swimming among all the guests like a queen, so self-possessed and gracious, now pressing a large whisky on a Brigadier, now handing a tomato juice to a Hindu financier.'[9] Dressed in vivid colours, her glorious head of hair left untied, she attracted the admiration of the men and of a good many women too. He was of middling rank, she of lowly origin, but the Elwins were nonetheless the first family of Shillong, an invitation to their home more prized than an entreé to Government House.[10] K. L. Mehta, as Adviser to the Governor who was technically Elwin's boss, told him that 'your house is like a eighteenth-century salon where everyone comes to get inspiration and ideas.'[11]

But let me dispel the note of cynicism that has crept in here. The NEFA job was for Elwin a 'sort of crown to all those years of struggle' in which he had tried desperately but with little success to protect communities in Bastar, Balaghat, Mandla, Koraput, Ganjam and god-knows-where. Now, in these disease-free highlands, backed by the Indian state and its benign head, he thought he and his tribals had something more of a chance. Certainly he worked ferociously hard, recruiting officials, training them, sending a steady stream of cautionary notes to his superiors. He liked putting a 'Secret' stamp on his letters. It made him feel like a character in a thriller. But the recipients were not always pleased with the contents. Their complaints reached the governor, who suggested that if Elwin 'wished to be rude the telephone did not commit one so finally.'[12]

A final printed commitment of sorts was called for when Elwin was asked in May 1954 to write a book introducing Gandhi to the north-east. It was a short study, fifty pages in all, yet he found it 'extremely difficult' to write.[13] He had now to settle accounts with a man to whom he had successively been student, interpreter, disciple, son, rebel and stranger. He offered a chastened version of his old Second Coming interpretation of

Gandhi the Mahatma. The carrier of a new civilization had become the sympathetic outsider with a message for the tribes. For the adivasis, wrote Elwin, Gandhi's

> life and teaching has vitally important lessons. There is first the lesson of peace. Disputes between villages and individuals can never be really solved by violence . . . Love is the only way of progress, forgiveness is the true discipline and bond of social life.
>
> Then there is the lesson of self-reliance. We are to be ourselves, not imitations of other people. We are not to be ashamed of our own culture, our own religion, our art, our dress; however simple it may be, it is ours and we may be proud of it. That is the meaning of *swadeshi* . . .
>
> And then there is the lesson of tolerance, which is also the lesson of unity. Bapu loved India as a whole. He saw it, in all its diversity of hills and plains, as a single unity. He saw its people, with their different languages, their varied dress, their distinct religions, blended into one great nation, a family united in the love of Truth and Peace, moving forward to a time when all men could live together in friendliness and equality.[14]

In September, as Verrier was finishing the book on Gandhi, he was visited by Shamrao, who could not but compare his friend's circumstances with his own. Sham stayed two weeks and then returned most reluctantly to Patangarh. Writing to Eldyth about her brother's happy new life, he wished he 'could say the same about my life—but I cannot be happy unless I am with him [while] he can be [happy without me] because he *has* his *work* and now even Kumar' (who had moved from his boarding school in Bombay to St Edmund's in Shillong). 'I wish I could fly back to Shillong right now,' remarked Shamrao, but in his loneliness he was also dreaming of more distant and pleasurable locations. 'England will always live in my memory as the dream-land,' he said, 'and if a rich friend gave me a few thousand pounds, I would leave Mother India for England, as if a man-eater was chasing me! If only one of my children could go to Oxford. But I am afraid none of them are clever enough to get a chance of that kind.' Life would not be the same for Shamrao after his companion left Mandla, but even in his grief this saint would think of others. It was only now, he told Eldyth, that he understood how she and her mother felt, separated from Verrier for so long.[15]

The separation from Shamrao was not to Verrier's liking either. Otherwise life was much less of a struggle than it ever had been: a happy home, a steady job, support for his work from high quarters, indeed from the highest quarters. 'I am very well,' he wrote to Archer in the last week of September 1954,

> and happier than I have been at any time for the past 20 years, happier, I think, than when I first went to Karanjia. But of course painfully respectable now, a fact which, say what you will, takes a little of the adventure out of life. Yet there is nothing like being legally married to a girl you are in love with, and I am extremely happy with Lila and grow fonder of her every day. Kumar is growing up as a very good sweet boy, with no academic interests at all, but a passion for painting and a certain instinct for art . . .
>
> It is refreshing to work with people one can respect, and most of our men are really first-class and I am extremely fond of some of them. The Governor is a pet, though naturally difficult at times . . . But what is satisfying is that I do have a chance to influence things in the right direction—all the training of officers has been put into my hands, for example.
>
> But of course, however sound the P.M. may be on the tribal problem (and he is very sound, as is the Governor), and however carefully we may brief our officers, the mere contact with this miserable outside world is going to destroy a great deal. The thing is to do as little harm as possible and as slowly as possible![16]

A month later his adored wife gave birth to a boy, her third, his fourth. Verrier at first wanted to call him Shamrao Victor but finally decided on Ashok, after the great Mauryan emperor. Ashok's arrival delayed the winter tour, but for only a few weeks. In late November Verrier was with the Wanchos of Tirap, 'many of them stark naked, many girls attired with flowers and ornaments.' The tribe put on a war-dance for the visitor. A party of painted warriors pretended to invade the village and cut off heads, celebrating the triumph with deep-throated singing. The views were spectacular. From the top of one village he looked down upon the rolling plains of the Brahmaputra on one side and up to the snow peaks of Tibet on the other.

On tour in Tirap, Verrier wrote in his diary that he had 'much better control than before and tend to brood less over things. But I must conquer my resentment at not being treated as a person of importance. This is a great defect. And when I get back, I must do more for and with Lila: it is essential to hold and deepen her love by expressing my own deep love for her. I must get more lust into me: I am growing tame.' The introspection is less intense, less anguished than before, and indeed the routine end-of-year retrospect, entered the next day, simply read: 'So ends a great and happy year.'[17]

From Tirap Verrier moved up the Siang river towards Tibet and the homeland of the Abor tribe. The terrain was the most difficult he'd encountered in twenty-five years of touring, but the people were welcoming and friendly. Outside each village they were met by gaily-clad girls bearing gifts of rice-beer and sugarcane. The girls escorted them to the village boundary where Abor men pelted them with bananas, this a 'prophylactic measure designed to drive away any infectious disease you may be bringing with you from civilization.' The women were always at their looms, their weaving almost as fine as the Nagas. Verrier collected twenty different patterns to go with as many folk tales.[18] Only in one 'sleepy dull village' was the reception less than enthusiastic; after the highs of the past few weeks Verrier felt as 'flat as a Congress Minister without a crowd.'[19]

At fifty-two, every tour seemed the most arduous ever, but the compensations were enormous. In March Elwin 'did' four valleys in four weeks: the Sipi, the Simmi, the lower Kamla and the Pein, each with different and distinctive tribes. To meet these he 'walked or rather waddled, scrambled, tumbled and slithered for 150 miles.' In April he visited the Sherdupkens of the Kameng Frontier Division. The Buddhist herders were gentle and warm, their land 'a mixture of Scotland and Austria.' As ever, it was only the sign of civilization that displeased. The Sherdupken chief, Dorje Thong-Dok, an 'exceptionally intelligent and charming' man, looked 'like the prince he claimed to be when he is wearing his national dress, but in a homburg hat and an English suit he looks rather like a tout on a race-course.' The nobility had set the tone for Elwin also saw one commoner clad in blue trousers, green shirt and velvet sweater, a second in shorts, khaki coat and chauffeur's cap. 'Compared to the splendid tokens of prestige which tradition has sanctioned,' he remarked ruefully, 'these sartorial infelicities look clownish and pathetic.'[20]

Back in Shillong Verrier worked away at his files and gave evidence before the States Reorganization Commission. At a party for the commission one of its members, the historian and diplomat K. M. Panikkar, announced in a loud voice that the great translator of Japanese and Chinese poetry Arthur Waley had told him that if he wished to understand the poetry of India he should read Verrier Elwin. This 'naturally inflated me greatly,' wrote the man so honoured, 'because Waley had said so, partly because Panikkar remembered it, and naturally above all because he said me and not Bill Archer.'[21]

Shamrao came calling in May, this time with Kusum and the kids. There were ten children in the house: the host found it 'a distraction, a very happy one, but still a distraction.' An eleventh arrived in June when Kusum gave birth to her seventh child. The work and bills mounted, Verrier giving expression to an early intimation of mortality: 'Expenses here are terrible,' he wrote to mother, 'and I am using up a lot of such savings as I had; I shall have very little to leave Lila and the children when I am gone.' Sham was most keen to move to Assam but it appears that Lila did not think it a good idea. While they lived in Patan they could share and share alike, but in Shillong there were fearful costs associated with a sahib's life: guests to be entertained, clubs to be seen in, wife and children to be clothed up to a certain fashion. Lila knew, and her husband knew too, that if the Hivales came one family would pay most of the bills.

The Hivales left in August, flying out in two batches from Guwahati to Calcutta. Verrier noticed a 'curious difference betwen east and west; he [Shamrao] must go in two planes, so that if one crashes some members of the family will survive. While I—and Lila too—feel that if we are to be killed we would prefer to die together!' Verrier accompanied them to Jabalpur to sort out the TWARU accounts and draft a report that would reasonably satisfy Jehangir Patel to keep his grant going. He then proceeded to Ahmedabad by way of Bombay. The administration had asked him to inspect the Calico Textile Museum as a possible model for one in NEFA. Verrier took an afternoon out to visit the Sabarmati Ashram, to see after a very long time the place where he and Gandhi had once prayed.[22]

For almost a decade, from 1928 to 1936, Gandhi had been the determining influence on Elwin's life. The break with the Mahatma was all the more bitter for the closeness of the bond. Now, as the breach healed within Verrier, he was coming closer to the other great Indian, Jawaharlal Nehru. If Gandhi is acknowledged as Bapu, the Father of the Nation, Nehru was often called 'Chacha,' the father's younger brother. The terms precisely capture what both meant for Elwin: the one an inspiring but occasionally overbearing father-figure, the other a benevolent and helpfully encouraging uncle.

In late August Nehru was in Shillong on work. He insisted on a tour of Elwin's museum despite the open jealousy of the governor—Jairamdas Daulatram had been replaced by an army general obsessed with hierarchy. The visit and its aftermath are described in a letter to Eldyth that can only be set down in full:

30.8.55

My darling Eldyth,

Let me set down some of the highlights of these two remarkable days.

About a month ago I wrote to T. N. Kaul, Joint Secretary in the Ministry of External Affairs and suggested that the Prime Minister might care to come and see my small collection of art specimens and photos; I also wrote a personal letter to the P.M. himself. To my great surprise I got a reply saying that the P.M. had written to the Governor suggesting that this visit might be included in the programme.

Intense passions were immediately aroused. But I must say that the Adviser, Ken Mehta, was most generous about it. He himself suggested it and while ordinarily, if the P.M. had gone anywhere, he should have gone to him, he backed up the proposal for him to come to me. After all, it was the devil of an honour. The Governor, however, who is a small mean man, did all he could to prevent it and after it was arranged had the press informed that the P.M. was not coming to our house but to the NEFA office. I forestalled him, however, for I have many friends among pressmen, though even so a number of papers reported the story as a visit to the NEFA office. The old bastard grudged me even my small hour of glory.

The P.M. arrived in Shillong on the 27th. That day we were visited by the D.C. and the S.P. and a body of C.I.D. men, who inspected everything. The police thought the visit was a bad show; far too many trees and bushes about—how are we to protect him? They went through the house, peered under beds, peeped under bushes, and departed muttering.

On the 28th I had to go off to Raj Bhavan at 9.0. I arrived a quarter of an hour too soon, sweating a bit, and was ushered in into what I thought was a rather inferior room (for a P.M.) at 9.35. [The P.M.] was completely charming, chatted away as if we were a pair of old buddies, and kept me for 40 minutes, though he had a long list of interviews. At the conclusion he asked me to stay on in NEFA after my three year contract was over.

Then I went out, and the Adviser and the Development Commissioner had interviews. At 11.0. we all trooped into a Conference Room—Ken Mehta, Raschid Yusuf Ali, Rathee (Financial Adviser with a heart of gold), the formidable and arrogant L. and the Governor himself, who sat throughout in an obsequious attitude which gave us all pleasure. The P.M. then spoke for little over an hour, one of the most superb impromptu speeches I have ever heard, and all the more gratifying in that he emphasised all the things that I have been advocating since I came here. Dress, customs, excess of staff, attitude to the tribes—it was a great triumph. The Governor sat with a face of doom, as he heard one after another of his plans crumbling into dust. L., who had made a very mean crack at me, got it in the neck, and cut a very sorry figure. I sat between dear Khemlal Rathee and Raschid and it was all we could do to avoid cheering as point after point came out on our side in exquisite language.

But cornered rats can bite and we must be humble.

The party broke up and I hustled into a staff car and we went as fast as we could towards our house. The Governor (who insisted on coming to ensure that we didn't get up to any mischief) and P.M. with his private escort, a charming creature called Handu, followed in another car. The roads were lined with people and they waved to us under the impression that we were persons of importance.

All this time, Lila was in the house, which was surrounded by C.I.D. and security police. She gave tea and sweets etc. to no fewer than 35 of them! Four ladies were invited—Mrs Rathee and her lovely five children, Mrs Mehta, Amina Yusuf Ali and Mrs Luthra. They supported Lila during the long period of waiting, but on such occasions Lila is really wonderful, completely self-possessed and much less nervous than me.

We arrived and the children gathered on the front steps, while photographers and police clustered round, and there was a bit of a wait. Then the pilot car with the D.C. and the S.P. drove up, and then the P.M. and Governor, followed by a number of jeeps containing the usual escort. The P.M. got out and Kumar and Dharamvir Ratthee garlanded the visitors with Tibetan scarves which I had brought back from Kameng. The P.M. selected a spray of orchids from the flowers in the car and gave it to Lila (we are presssing it under the mattress of the big bed).

Introductions were made and the great man closely accompanied by the little man went round the house. He saw the show-cases, then went round the picture-room of NEFA, then into the picture-room of Orissa and Bastar, and finally into the Santal Room. I offered him a cup of coffee or, I said in my agitation, would you prefer a cup of sherry. As the Governor was present, he said, 'No, I would much prefer coffee,' which I don't believe. After this I showed him the old pictures, 100 years old, by Dalton and some of the 1847 Butler paintings. It went well, but I was paralysed, as always by the presence of the Glaxo Baby (as he used to be known in Congress circles) and was curiously nervous. But the P.M. is so incalculable that you never know what he will do. He asked me about polygamy; he saw a photo of a girl with her breasts covered with a bit of cloth and observed, 'I suppose the dirty-minded photographer made her cover them up;' he asked me what a 'falsie' was. I said it was something to make you bulge a bit and he said he didn't suppose most tribal girls needed that. But though I think I did pretty well during my private interview, I am afraid I was a bit of a flop during the inspection.

But at least he showed no signs of desiring to return to the conventional boredom of Raj Bhavan, and sat down and spread out his legs, though it was now 1.10 and lunch was scheduled for 1.15, at least a quarter of an hour away. He talked about a Dance Academy and a general Museum for Assam, while flash bulbs flashed and people peered through the windows trying to get a peep. At last they decided they must have lunch and said good-bye.

Directly they had gone we got out the rejected sherry—it was the most expensive Shillong could provide and we had borrowed some glasses suitable for such eminent lips—and had quick ones, then we ourselves got into the staff car again and went back to Raj Bhavan for lunch.

Here, as usual, the food was bad, and the conversation uneven. With all the recourses of modern cookery, why should one give the greatest man in the world, who has banqueted from China to Peru, brain cutlets and an unappetising curry-rice followed by an ice-cream which the P.M. tasted and laid aside. He made up, however, on fresh fruit. For the first ten minutes he sat with his head on his chest, brooding, and didn't say a word. Naturally no one else said a word either. I was sitting, for some curious reason on the Governor's right (a good place, however, for all the best tit-bits are set round that august presence), and he did make one or two whispered remarks to me. Then suddenly the P.M. woke up and talked brilliantly . . . He wanted to see Indian music paganised—for how can you sing with your eyes shut and your head sunk in reverence on your chest. The Russian singing was far better, and he described how he had heard 500 Russian girls singing the Indian national anthem magnificently and far better than it was ever done in pious India.

Even the weariest river winds somehow safe to the dessert and in the end we got up and he bade us farewell. By now I was pretty well pooped, but I felt I must talk over things with Khemlal, so I dragged him home with me and we discussed the events of the morning over a cup of tea.

The day was not yet over, however. There was the dinner to attend. I got into my tuxedo and went along. There were all the Ministers and one or two Deputy Ministers, and a few Assam high officials. Never have I seen such a gang of morons. Two of them sat in corners of the room reading magazines. Others sat round in apprehensive silence. I found myself on a sofa with the Minister for This and That (for the life of me, I can't remember either his name or function). I would make a remark, he would reply and then stare straight in front of him again. After a bit I gave up and stared straight in front of me myself. For 20 minutes we didn't even get a tomato juice, and all the world a solemn silence held. Then in came the Governor and [the P.M.], and we at least got the tomato juice and I was able to break away from my Minister and had an entertaining conversation with Handu (I always get along well with high-placed policemen) about Science Fiction; I bet he was the only man in the room, beside the P.M. who had read Forster's *The Machine Stops.*

But all too soon, the dread words 'Dinner is Ready' were uttered and we trooped reluctantly into the palace of gastronomic irrelevancies. I have eaten the same dinner so often that I know it by heart, the off-colour canape, the soup, the made-up fish (this was the best dish and I wish I had the courage to take two portions), the shocking curry-rice, and the cake pudding, dry and tasteless.

Raj Bhavan dinners do have at least a valuable ethical effect, for they are carefully calculated to show you just where you stand in the scheme of things. I of course was at the bottom of the table and my only consolation was to see that Ken Mehta, whose income is exactly double mine, was in a corresponding place, though on the right and not the left, to mine at the other end of the table. I watched the Ministers pretty closely. Sushir Datta, the Chief Secretary, a brilliant Cambridge man and an enthusiastic drinker, was between the Minister for Excise and the Deputy Minister of Cow-Protection (or something of the sort). They didn't speak to him and he . . . didn't speak to them. Five of the Ministers, to my certain knowledge, didn't open their mouths throughout the meal, except of course to eat, which they did heartily and with apparent pleasure. The Governor, our host, sat in embattled silence from soup to nuts. Poor [P.M.] did his best, but he had enough of solo lecturing and after a time he wearied and for minutes at a time, this glittering company sat silent except for the clicking of dentures and the smooth susurration of ingesting vitamins. There was one old Minister near me in a beard and a dhoti tucking in as if he had not had a square meal for weeks.

When at last we got away and returned to the drawing-room; the Governor had given orders that cigars were to be brought for Dr Elwin, but when it was discovered that you had to buy 50 at a time, it was supposed that there might be audit objections, so the project was dropped; and we sat round in embarrassed silence. [The P.M.] lay back in a chair; the Governor and Chief Minister sat near twiddling their fingers but not saying a single word; after 15 minutes of this entertainment the P.M. evidently thought he would be more comfortable in bed and got up and went away.

Even now the day was not over, for on reaching home I found Lila in tears, and Nakula very bad with his whooping-cough. So I sent the car for Dr Dilip Guha and he came and spent about an hour making his examinations, and we eventually got to bed very late and worried about the child . . .

The next day I felt rotten but had to struggle through a heavy day's work. Whooping cough is a distressing disease to watch.

With very much love
Verrier[23]

On Nehru's return to Delhi he sent the NEFA administration a note urging them to go slow and not uproot tribals 'from their way of life with its standards and discipline and give them nothing in its place.' He asked them to listen carefully to their Adviser on Tribal Affairs, for 'Verrier Elwin is a recognized authority on the Indian tribes [who] brings to his task an understanding and sympathy which is unusual and most helpful. His advice is therefore of great value.'[24]

The certificate was pocketed with pleasure. Indeed, in his day-to-day work in NEFA Elwin shrewdly and effectively used the prime minister's name and prestige to advance his own agenda. Writing to his superiors on shops, or architecture, or dancing, he would cite Nehru prefatory to his own suggestions. 'The Prime Minister has spoken so emphatically on the matter . . .;' 'It is, as the Prime Minister has said, grossly presumptous for us to tell [the tribals] what to do and what not to do . . .;' 'I have simply been trying to implement the very emphatic and explicit notes of the Prime Minister . . .'—phrases such as these are strewn through his notes and memoranda of the time.[25]

The prime minister's appeal for Elwin is easy to understand. As long as he lived, writers, thinkers and scientists flocked to Nehru, the world's philosopher-king in a democratic age. Nehru's absence of racial feeling, his complete lack of bitterness towards the men who had once ruled India, was very apparent and endearing. In 1955 Nehru met Churchill in London, a meeting of two prime ministers but also a meeting between the most fanatical opponent of the Indian freedom movement and the man who had spent fourteen years in British jails. A newspaper reported Nehru greeting his fellow Harrovian with the remark, 'And how are you, sir?' Elwin was moved to circulate the report within the NEFA administration, with the comment: 'What in slavery would be obsequious, in freedom is an act of courtesy.'[26]

Equally, Nehru was much attracted to Elwin: to the brilliant Oxford scholar (Nehru himself had an indifferent Second from Cambridge); to the lover of good books and the writer of several; to the gypsy who in the thirties and forties had roamed the wilds while he had been in prison. Soon after Elwin had joined the government, Nehru told Jehangir Patel that 'I hear such mixed reports about Verrier. He womanizes, etc.' Patel replied, 'What does it matter to you?' The prime minister, roaring with laughter agreed: 'Yes, it is quite true. What does it matter?' Patel then launched an eloquent defense: 'Why do you measure Verrier with the yardstick that you would use for Bapu and the other saints? I will trust Verrier all my life. Nobody knows his job as he does. Look at the great books he has written. You have written books yourself and you know how much it takes. He couldn't have written them without great work, could he? We have had great quarrels but I never had a chance to quarrel about his work.'[27]

Nehru had reason to admire Elwin's work and, surrounded by files and file-pushers, relish his company too. When the anthropologist visited Delhi in October 1955 he called on the prime minister, who gave him nearly an hour of his busy morning. Nehru was 'most affable and delightful,' but Elwin was too awed to speak. As he put it: 'afterwards I thought of so many things I might have said and got across that I felt as depressed as I used to preach and felt that the Spirit had not been on me.' However, it seemed to have gone all right for in the afternoon he received a cheque from the prime minister's special fund, to be spent at his discretion 'on art and dancing in NEFA and other places.'[28] Soon afterwards Nehru wrote of being 'overwhelmed by bankers and financiers' whose company he must have disliked as much as he enjoyed Elwin's. On a later visit to the capital Elwin went round to the prime minister's house to discuss NEFA affairs, but Nehru seized on the opportunity to talk instead of Vladimir Nabokov's *Lolita*.[29]

An early victory of the Adviser on Tribal Affairs was to retain the term 'political officer.' When word reached him that the governor wished to replace it with the more orthodox 'deputy commissioner' he was outraged. The term 'P.O.,' he noted, 'does give a certain sense of romance and adventure to what is an extremely difficult task; it also stresses the unique character of the work; and is in many ways appropriate to an enterprise which is both political and humane.' To call POs DCs would 'conventionalize' NEFA, bring it closer to the districts of the plains, 'subject to the same corruptions, the same lawyers and merchants and the same unwieldy apparatus of a Deputy Commissioner's office.'[30]

Every winter on tour Elwin experienced afresh the unconventionality of NEFA, the absence of lawyers, merchants and other corruptions of civilization. In November 1955 he set out for the Mishmi Hills, taking Lila. This was her first journey outside Shillong since she had arrived there almost two years previously. The Mishmis lived in long low houses, each branch of the family making itself a new set of rooms off the main corridor. They were not head-hunters but hair-and-thumb hunters, traditionally marking their conquests with tufts of hair hung up in their house, burying the thumbs of their victims with the skulls of wild animals taken in the chase. The Idi Mishmis reminded him of the Baigas, 'very wild and shaggy, real jungle folk,' with their poisoned arrows and bows fired like a gun. Halfway through the tour he suffered a 'real disaster' when Sunderlal—whom he had come to depend upon so heavily for twenty years—fell ill and had to return.[31] Lila returned too, while Verrier struck deeper into the interior. From an Idu village in Dibang he wrote to an English friend on 'a table the size of a postage stamp.' The Mishmis were completely enchanting, he said: once he had done with them he would move on to the Wanchos in Tirap before proceeding to Delhi for a round of selection interviews. He hoped then to return for a long trip to the Tibetan border in northern Siang, to conclude the winter's touring with a visit to the Kalyo-Keagnyus in Tuensang. Counting the tribes and the valleys on his list he remarked: 'When I put this all down I wish I was twenty years younger!'[32] Otherwise he was content enough, his year-end summary speaking of good tours and reports, happy relations with Lila and the children, and new friendships. The only black spot was an increased worry about Shamrao. He listed thirteen new year resolutions for 1956: to be a better father, husband, to drink less, etc., the most elaborate being to 'follow Truth fearlessly, to speak my mind without fear of consequences, to fight harder for the tribes and their real benefit and happiness—but to be tactful about it if possible.'[33]

On some of the more difficult tours Verrier was accompanied by his eldest son Kumar. In the last week of 1955 they reached Nisa, a village in Tirap last visited by a white man sixty years earlier. Their entry was hailed by the cry 'The Jai Hind has come.' The nationalist salutation had been turned into a noun. Verrier found it 'a rather pleasant variation on the usual Sahib.' Any suspicion that it might instead be a sarcastic comment on Indian hegemony was dispelled when the chief presented the son of the Jai Hind a monkey which slept, ate and played with the teenager. Another chief in another village gave Kumar a wild cat. Kosi's son had a wonderful way with animals; the cat sat purring in his lap though no one else would go near it. But as the cat ate a chicken a day, computed by Elwin as double the boy's school fees, they reluctantly left it behind. Father and son moved on to the Bori tribe, to get to whom they had to 'struggle over great rocks, edge our way along cliff-faces, creep along precipices and landslides.' Most exciting of all were the bridges: long tunnels of cane swinging over the river—one had 'to be an acrobat for NEFA.' The next winter they crossed the Siang river in a bamboo raft, then climbed a cliff by a rickety bamboo ladder. They also crossed illegally into Tibet, where Kumar carved his name on a tree. On this tour they covered 180 miles on foot, climbing up an aggregate of 40,000 feet and climbing down as much. The fifty-four-year-old sahib took 'a certain satisfaction in the sheer physical achievement.'[34]

To the junior officers Elwin successfully conveyed the romance and adventure of work in NEFA. There was his personality, the learning carried with ease and conveyed with wit, its manifestations gleefully passed around the NEFA secretariat, such as this answer to a letter addressed to 'Rev. Elwin:' 'Who has addressed this envelope? The abbreviation "Rev" may, of course, stand for Reverend, Revered or Revolutionary. If the first is intended, it is insulting; if the second, it is undeserved; if the third, it is flattering, but indiscreet.'[35] Then there were the associations with the Father of the Nation and its present ruler, and yet the absence of any feeling of colour or status or rank. There was the example set by his long and difficult tours at his age; and most of all there were his reports, evocative accounts of new and colourful tribes he met each winter. Who would not be attracted to life among the Taraons, hailed for 'the quite wonderful coiffure of the women which would not disgrace a Parisian lady of fashion;' or among the Monpa, a Buddhist tribe 'distinguished for its terraced cultivation, its carpet making and its love of horses' and for being 'quiet, gentle, friendly, courteous, industrious, good to animals, good to children;' or among the Kama Mishmi, whose 'weaving is among the finest in NEFA and is of extraordinary variety,' the designs attributed in legend to butterflies, fish, and snakes.[36]

Elwin was deeply affected by what an educated Mishmi had once told him: 'Remember that we are not by culture or even by race Indian. If you continue to send among us officers who look down on our culture and religion, and above all look down on us as human beings, then within a few years we will be against you.'[37] Under his guidance the Indian Frontier Administrative Service developed a cadre of capable and massively committed young men, almost unique in Indian political history for their readiness to live with and think like the people they had been sent to govern. The officers of the IFAS dwelt in thatched huts, bathed in streams, toured on foot and subsisted on daal and rice for months on end—these were dropped by helicopter, for Elwin insisted that officers not take food from villagers unless it was surplus produce voluntarily sold. Men like Bob Khathing, Rashid Yusuf Ali, Nalini Jayal, Murkot Ramunny, R. N. Haldipur, and Har Mander Singh—to mention just six names, of people belonging to four religions and hailing from diverse parts of India—were taught to practice the intellectual and emotional as well as purely law-and-order side of governance. 'I don't want you to ever give tribals a feeling of inferiority,' Elwin told them, 'Integration can only take place on the basis of equality: moral and political equality.' They must know the people, he said, know what stirred them, moved them, energized them. When on tour they must drink with the tribals . . . drink, he added significantly, from the same *collective* bowl. He asked the POs to write reports on the flora and fauna of the district, the habits, customs, rites, ornaments, and crafts of the people. They sent him drafts which were returned with queries written over in green ink.[38]

There were of course officers who complained of missing the amenities of the 'civilized' plains, others who feared the ritual pollution that came from such close contact with out-of-caste men. Elwin acknowledged that NEFA had 'no railway trains, no limousines, no cinemas, no electricity, no plumbing, no refrigerators, no television,' but then it had 'no Stock Exchange, no colour bar, no caste, no atom bombs, no slums' either. Nor were its people altogether lacking in high culture. In the summer of 1956 Elwin visited the great monastery at Tawang, the epicentre of NEFA Buddhism, which with its narrow streets and great library and 'gentle casual atmosphere which concealed so much formality and protocol' reminded him irresistibly of Oxford. To the monastery came students from the villages around, attached in groups to senior lamas. They worked in the library in an atmosphere of art and learning, books and manuscripts on the tables, paintings and scrolls on the walls. And a 'monastic book is a real book, about the size of half a dozen books of this careless modern world.' The great treasure of the Tawang library was the Getompa, three volumes of which were lettered in gold. This was brought out to the visitor 'in much the same way that an Oxford College librarian would produce a copy of the First Folio of Shakespeare; scarves were offered to it, and it was opened with rather reluctant devotion.'

Another Oxonian trait in Tawang was its reverence for the theatre. The monastery had cupboards full of costumes, masks and other props. The lamas acted in dance-dramas, one of which, the Thutotdam, had the players dressed as skeletons, portraying the journey of the soul after death. All told, the atmosphere was 'almost that of one of the elder European Universities.' The Khempu or Abbot, Gelong Kesang Phuntsog, with his unpretentiousness and 'luminous beauty of character,' reminded

Elwin of a dean of Christ Church he had known long ago. The Khempu was one of the 'few real saints one may meet in a lifetime; . . . he is a completely charming personality and every time I met him I felt the better for it.'[39]

In September 1956, not long after he returned from Tawang, came news from England of his mother's death. His reaction is unrecorded and I wonder what Mrs Minnie Elwin would have made of this latest defection towards Buddhism. Verrier once told Bill Archer of his experience that 'the finest moments in life have been the very reverse of Christian religion and morality.'[40] The rejection of Christianity had been followed by a long period of agnosticism, with him out of sync with all forms of established religion despite a continuing professional interest in them. But after he visited Tawang this former priest, this twice-lapsed Christian, this renegade Gandhian came to pin his faith on 'some form of liberal Buddhism.' In December he was in Delhi, his visit coinciding with that of the Dalai and Panchen Lamas. Elwin spent the best part of a day with them, received their blessings and went along to a great banquet in their honour. This was held at the Rashtrapati Bhavan. The company were fed while seated on the floor, Indian and Christa-Seva-Sangh style. Afterwards Nehru took the Dalai Lama—already a spiritual guide even though a mere lad—for an elephant ride.[41]

Buddhism, and especially its idea of *karuna* or compassion, helped tame and reconcile the conflicts of allegiance that had hitherto dominated Verrier's life. He was no longer concerned, he told a friend, 'whether there was a life after death or whether there was a god or not.' But he knew 'there was a meaning to life, which one can experience in love, in recognition of goodness and in the true appreciation of beauty . . . Heaven and Hell are within ourselves. The key to self-realization is to find peace within us.'[42]

In November 1957 Elwin stayed with the Khamptis, finding to his dismay that Buddhism was losing its sway over the young. The temple at Chowkham resembled an Anglican church in England: 'There were present plenty of old ladies and a few devoted old gentlemen and there were the boys who live in the hostel attached to the Temple who would correspond to the choir-boys in a cathedral school, but except for a few girls in their teens the younger generation was notably absent.' The Indian government was constitutionally wedded to banishing religion from public life, yet

Elwin suggested that it should, at least in the high valleys, 'encourage people in the practice of their traditional faith.' The administration, he thought, should encourage the formation of Temple Committees to repair and maintain shrines; plant trees and plan gardens around them ('so that all who see them may remember the Eternal Beauty'); organize pilgrimages to Tawang; and harmonize in schools the spiritual and secular aspects of education.

The Buddhist area, wrote Elwin, 'presents us with a problem unlike that offered in any other part of NEFA. Elsewhere we have the difficult, indeed vexatious, puzzle of the impact of the atomic age on a Stone Age people. But here we have the conflict between two civilizations, one of which is immensely superior in technological achievement while the other is equally distinguished by spiritual faith, by simple dignity, by compassionate manners.'[43]

Elwin himself carried to the civilization of power a token from this other. The token was a brass figurine of the Buddha, a present from the Khempu of Tawang. From now it was to be found always in his pocket, at home and on tour.

CHAPTER TWELVE

Nehru's Missionary

Far too much has been written on the aboriginal problem. If the measures taken were in any way commensurate with the enquiries, reports, monographs and correspondence about them, the aboriginals would be the happiest people in India.

Verrier Elwin, in a note of November 1944

Convinced that humanity and variety are synonymous, Elwin has always condemned the busybodies who, be it in the name of religion or at the behest of politics, would impose on primitive innocence the standardized sophistications of modern civilization, and just as in the old days he aroused the active hostility of many a British official by his open association with the movement for Indian independence, so now his disapproval of cumulative encroachments on the integrity of primitive culture may seem suspect to champions of militant nationalism.

Sudhindranath Dutta, writing in 1952

If we can develop a NEFA of the Prime Minister's dreams what a marvellous place it would be!

Verrier Elwin, in a note of November 1955

'Whether I shall ever write another book I don't know,' remarked Elwin to Bill Archer nine months after moving to NEFA, 'but perhaps I have written enough.[1] 'You go on producing lovely books and enriching the world with beauty,' he wrote four years later—this a reference to Archer's growing corpus of works on Indian art—'I continue to distract my little world with controversy.

However, both of us are aiming at the preservation of something good and beautiful.'[2]

As it happened Elwin was to write another half dozen books, one of them greatly influential in its time. This was *A Philosophy for NEFA*, first published in 1957 followed by a much expanded edition two years later. *A Philosophy for NEFA* is the book of an anthropologist for the administration, but also of an Englishman for India. The author calls himself a 'missionary of Mr Nehru's gospel,' and a 'very bad "Gandhi man" ' who learnt from the Mahatma to approach the poor through the mind of the poor. In the text Gandhi is quoted no less than fifteen times and Nehru on more than twenty-five occasions. The chapter epigraphs are attributed to other Indian patriots, including G. B. Pant, then home minister of the Government of India, and C. Rajagopalachari, who had been the first Indian governor-general. The most telling quote comes from A. V. Thakkar: 'Separation and Isolation are dangerous theories and strike at the root of national solidarity. Safety lies in union not in isolation.'

No man ever entirely forgets his past, but located as he was between England and India, and between tribe and state, Elwin perhaps forgot less than most. The Thakkar quote stands at the head of a chapter called 'The Fundamental Problem' where the author carefully distances himself from his own prior, 'primitivist' persona of the nineteen-thirties and 'forties. Writing of the policy of Isolation, for instance, he suggests it was a strictly temporary measure for some small tribes under colonial conditions: 'neither I nor any other anthropologist would dream of suggesting such a policy since Independence.' But this assertion of Indian patriotism is also, and intriguingly, a disavowal of his poetic self. It is 'the literary men, the artists, the poets [and] the philosophers,' he now claims, 'who have wanted to keep the tribal people as they were: the artist Gauguin has probably had more influence on the modern attitude to the "primitive" than all the anthropologists put together. In any case, the scientists [among whom he numbers himself] are just not interested in that sort of thing. They are more concerned with developing rather than static societies, with culture-change rather than with culture "as it is" . . .'[3]

Elwin's language in *A Philosophy for NEFA* had to take account of an India restless and on the move, eager to grow, progress, modernize, develop. However, the retreat from protection by no means implied an endorsement of its opposite, that is, the wholesale detribalization of the communities of NEFA and their absorption into the fabric of (Hindu) India. The extremes of Isolation and Assimilation are now both rejected in favour of a Middle Way, the way of Integration. This would foster 'a spirit of love and loyalty for India, without a trace of suspicion that Government has come into tribal areas to colonize or exploit, a full integration of mind and heart with the great society of which the tribal people form a part, and to whose infinite variety they may make a unique contribution.' Phrased in the language of economic development rather than national unity, the great problem is 'how to bring the blessings and advantages of modern medicine, agriculture and education to them, without destroying the rare and precious values of tribal life.'[4]

In a note for official circulation Elwin explained the purpose of the book thus:

> The world is now convinced that India can rule itself; it is less certain that she can do the right thing by her tribal population. All sorts of fantastic misconceptions of our policy in the tribal areas are current abroad: we are supposed to be going in for wholesale Hinduization, we are making them vegetarians and teetotallers, we are allowing merchants and money-lenders to exploit them. I am confident that this book will do a great deal to remove these wrong ideas if we can get it across to the right people. Even in India, it will, as now rewritten, remove many wrong ideas about the NEFA Administration.[5]

The audience of *A Philosophy for NEFA* was, in the first instance, government officials serving in tribal areas. These officials and their wives are urged to rid themselves of any feelings of cultural superiority, to be guided in all their actions by humility—rather than by 'that hard professional inquisitive interference in other people's lives so characteristic of the social worker'—and not to use those awful words 'backward' and 'uplift.' For officers to claim that 'they are "modern" and "advanced" [while] their tribal brethren are lagging behind,' continues Elwin, implies 'a value-judgement, which the conscience of the world may yet reverse. For who is really backward—the honest peasant working in simplicity and truth among the hills, or the representative of modern progress embroiled in the mad race for power and wealth, the symbol of whose achievement is the hydrogen bomb.'[6]

Evidently, allegiance to the Indian government did not imply an endorsement of civilization.

'Make haste slowly' was the leitmotif of *A Philosophy for NEFA* as well as the torrent of reports and memoranda that flowed from Elwin's pen. In 1955, when the Government of India was set to adopt the ambitious Second Five Year Plan, with its charter of rapid industrialization and economic growth, Elwin wished that NEFA had a 'Fifty-Year Plan rather than a Five-Year Plan.' For 'if tribals move too fast,' he explained with his experience in central India in mind, 'they tend to move downwards.'[7]

The NEFA tribals were to be protected; *that* term was also no longer permissible. Thus, in a canny and not altogether insincere manner, Elwin spoke more often of the importance of 'self-reliance.' On tour in the Abor country in March 1957 he came across a bazaar of shops run by Marwari traders from western India, a community noted for cunning and sharp practice. He called the bazaar a 'poisoned arrow aimed at the heart of Abor culture.' The Marwari shops seduced tribals away from self-reliance; moreover, with pictures of gods and goddesses prominently displayed on their walls, they served as centres of Hindu propaganda. He wanted a strict watch on the expansion of shops in NEFA, even supplying a list of commodities they could and could not stock. The import and sale of hurricane lamps, torches, cigarettes, fountain pens and agricultural implements were allowed, but not of 'singlets, sola topis, chauffeur's caps, cosmetics, brassieres, plastic ornaments and belts, expensive and unsuitable shoes.' Shops had to be controlled, he noted, 'to save the tribals from having their taste debased and their money wasted by the import of unnecessary, unsuitable and unartistic goods.'[8]

Here Elwin invoked both Nehru the aesthete's distaste for traders and trading—'we must not encourage the tribal people to get into bad artistic habits which normally follow in the wake of what is called civilization' wrote the prime minister to the NEFA administration—as well as Gandhi, whose swadeshi campaign (the burning and boycott of foreign goods), provided a fine justification. In any case hand-weaving was perhaps 'the chief artistic achievement of the people of NEFA;' were the state to help renew this 'indigenous khadi enterprise,' money that went into the pockets of traders might stay within the community. Unhappily, government weaving centres imposed colours and designs inferior to those that existed already. 'It is absolutely useless,' wrote Elwin after visiting one such centre, 'to bring girls from the villages and spend a lot of money teaching them to weave worse than they weave at home.'[9]

Elwin spoke often of his wish 'to make of the whole of NEFA a work of art.' In 1956 he suggested the creation of a Tagore Memorial Fellowship, for the study of dance and music and the promotion of these in areas where they were absent; and of a Gandhi Memorial Fellowship for the study and guided spread of indigenous traditions of weaving.[10] Two years later, in between the first and second editions of *A Philosophy for NEFA*, he published a volume on the art of the territory. This showcased examples of pottery, mask-making, basketry, jewelry and, above all, weaving. The book was an extended and well illustrated argument on behalf of the artistic traditions of NEFA, traditions now under threat. Here, as elsewhere, folk-artists had increasingly to contend with

> the competition of the cheap oleograph, the commercial calendar, the gaudy mythological reproduction, the political leader in bad print. These are not only easy to obtain but they have the false prestige of modernity, and the village artist becomes haunted by a sense of inferiority and ceases to create. Indeed it is this inferiority complex that is the castrator of the artistic impulse in every field, and unless we can encourage the villager to believe in himself, the folk arts, which cannot be kept alive merely by artificial stimuli, will perish.

These forces could be fought by keeping out the puritans who would abolish much of what was best in tribal expressive traditions, and, more positively, by thoughtful state intervention. His book was written in the belief that 'by encouraging the arts of the tribal people, creating in them a pride in their own products, keeping before them their own finest patterns and designs, and by providing them with raw materials, it will be possible to inspire a renaissance of creative activity throughout the hill areas of India . . .'[11]

Elwin believed that the state must nurture the 'natural good taste' of the tribals and itself blend into the social life of NEFA, growing into the landscape rather than standing in stark contrast to it. As it happened, tribals tended to do things in circles, but the newly built offices and schools followed straight lines. For a people who liked to sit around a fire or gather in a circle around a teacher, he remarked, 'our benches in tidy rows, our dreary rooms with never a fire in them, the regimentation of lines and rectangles is unfamiliar.' He carried this complaint to Nehru, who chastised the chief minister of Assam: 'If a school or dispensary is built in a tribal village in a manner which is completely different from the village style, this is a foreign element which sticks out from the rest of the village . . . If we have to make the tribal people at home with our officers, then our officers should not live in a building which is completely out of keeping with the surroundings.'[12]

The most remarkable of Elwin's proposals was to set up a Sudhaar Kendra, a social rehabilitation centre, for the humane treatment of convicted tribals. Reading the All India Prisons Act he was appalled by its sanction of whipping, fettering and solitary confinement. 'Does anybody know what the prisons of India are really like today?' he asked in June 1956:

> Ten or fifteen years ago, with the flower of the nation in jail, we had every opportunity to discover and men who had themselves languished in prison cells emerged from them with the sincere determination to set things rights when they had the power. But what actually has been achieved? Are our prisons today running on really modern, humane and scientific lines, or are they merely the same prisons with a few reforms and amenities? Has the public attitude to prisons changed, or do we still sheer away from the subject in distaste?[13]

NEFA itself had no jail, so when a group of Tagins were convicted of murder they were sent to a prison in Banaras. Elwin knew the city from his days with the Anthropological Survey—hot, damp and not likely to suit the tribal mind or body. He recommended the Tagins be transferred to Lucknow, and be allowed to spend summers in Almora jail up in the Kumaun Himalaya. Meanwhile he set to work on a plan for a new NEFA prison which was to be as much of a work of art as a prison could.

Elwin viewed the jail as an aspect of 'psychiatric imperialism,' imposing Western ideas of guilt and punishment on a people more worried about shame and status. For the tribal, preoccupied with self-esteem, a fine might work better than incarceration. He thought also that 'the best way of reforming prisons is to put fewer people in prison.' To be sure, some tribals had to be confined, but if Elwin had his way this would be only in a Sudhaar Kendra that would provide the 'healing touch' to individuals momentarily led astray. He identified a site for such a Centre in Lohitpur, among the hills and woods the tribals loved so well. The establishment of the Centre, he told his NEFA colleagues, 'gives us the opportunity of producing something which might be a model to all parts of tribal India and I hope very much that everything connected with it—architecture, food, prison industries, discipline and so on—will be devised on the most up to date and liberal penological principles.'

In Elwin's design the Centre would have high walls for security but would otherwise closely approximate the spirit of tribal life. Inmates would be housed in long dormitories with platforms for sitting out, Abor-style. A community recreation hall, modelled on the morung, would allow people to meet and sing around a fire. A Naga log-drum would summon men to work and meals. The food would be cooked by the tribals themselves. It would have plenty of meat, and the administration would 'be generous with regard to tobacco and the tribal version of betel, and *on special occasion permit even a moderate quantity of rice-beer to be brewed*.'[14]

In Bastar in the nineteen-forties Elwin had been deeply affected by the condition of tribals in Jagdalpur jail.[15] That experience influenced this visionary scheme which, like many others, remained buried in the files.

Both editions of *A Philosophy for NEFA* carried commendatory forewords by Jawaharlal Nehru. The first time around, Nehru directed the reader to a correct understanding of which way the chain of influence ran. 'Verrier Elwin,' he wrote in a foreword dated 16th February 1957,

> has done me the honour of saying that he is a missionary of my views on tribal affairs. As a matter of fact, I have learnt much from him, for he is both an expert on this subject with great experience and a friend of the tribal folk.

> I have little experience of tribal life and my own views, vague as they were, have developed under the impact of certain circumstances and of Verrier Elwin's own writings. It would, therefore, be more correct to say that I have learnt from him rather than that I have influenced him in any way.

Nehru went on to ask officers in NEFA to 'read carefully what Dr Elwin has written and absorb this philosophy so that they may act in accordance with it.' Then he added (and this was Elwin's real triumph): 'Indeed, I hope that this broad approach will be applied outside the NEFA also to other tribals in India.'

Each man's exaggerated deference to the other is in keeping with the north Indian tradition of *taqqaluf* where one must never claim anything for oneself but always hand it to the other fellow. On 25th August 1958 we find Elwin writing to a colleague in Delhi thus:

> As far as *I can understand the Prime Minister's direction* on work in the tribal areas, the four fundamental points are these:
>
> (a) That we should not send too many outsiders into the tribal areas;
> (b) that we should not over-adminster the tribal areas;
> (c) that we should not overwhelm the people by a multiplicity of schemes but aim at doing a few fundamental things really well;
> (d) that we should impose nothing on the people but help them to develop according to their own tradition and genius.[16]

And now move on very quickly to 9th October 1958, the date of Nehru's foreword to the second edition of *A Philosophy for NEFA*. He outlines here 'five fundamental principles' of development in tribal areas:

> 1. People should develop along the lines of their own genius and we should avoid imposing anything on them. We should try to encourage in every way their own traditional arts and culture.
> 2. Tribal rights in land and forests should be protected.
> 3. We should try to train and build up a team of their own people to do the work of administration and development. Some technical personnel from outside will, no doubt, be needed, especially in the beginning. But we should avoid introducing too many outsiders into tribal territory.
> 4. We should not over-adminster these areas or overwhelm them with a multiplicity of schemes. We should rather work through, and not in rivalry to, their own social and cultural institutions.
> 5. We should judge results, not by statistics or the amount of money spent, but by the quality of human character that is evolved.

This foreword was publicized by Elwin as the 'Prime Minister's Panchsheel for tribal development,' the word carrying, he hoped, resonance of the other Panchsheel, the famous five principles for international co-operation offered by Nehru at the Bandung conference of 1955. But did the great man write the foreword himself? Or was this the Elwin gospel being carried, for strategic purposes, through the prime minister's persuasively powerful pen? Jawaharlal Nehru is almost unique among post-war statesmen in writing his own stuff—letters, notes, speeches, books, what-have-you, but an exception seems to have been made here. For the spill-over of words and phrases from the letter of 25th August indicates that the anthropologist must have supplied the first draft. But then that letter was itself advertised as the work of a scribe interpreting the master thinker! Perhaps what matters, in the end, is not proof of authorship but concordance of views between Oxford scholar and Cambridge scientist, the way in which the work of a relatively minor official of a great state was given credence and influence by the support and signature of its head.

That *A Philosophy of NEFA* was both approved and 'forwarded' by the prime minister was calculated to reassure many and enrage some. The Elwin connection, remarked a commentator in the respected *Economic Weekly* of Bombay, was

> further evidence of the schizophrenia of the Nehru mind, the Indian mind. The Prime Minister has not really made up his mind whether he wants the [tribals] to be like himself or remain themselves. He is a great one for civilization, meaning hospitals and refrigerators and automobiles; he is also a romantic of the upper class coloniser type. The quaintness of the [tribal] fascinates him as much as it fascinates Verrier Elwyn [*sic*]; he too is 'gone on' what is so utterly different from him. There is the pathetic Wellsian faith in the march of civilisation, and there is the T. E. Lawrencian fascination for the tribal, the primitive, the elemental. As a personal attitude it is certainly a tenable one. Less so, perhaps, as the begetter of a governmental policy.[17]

In the late fifties the prime minister's bitterest political foe was the brilliant maverick socialist Ram Manohar Lohia, whose numerous interventions in the Indian Parliament had as their main and sometimes sole purpose the discomfiture of Nehru and the ruling Congress party. A political scientist with a Ph.D. from Germany, Lohia was also an extreme

Anglophobe, a trait whose relevance to our story will soon be apparent. For, on 12th November 1958, Lohia arrived at the outpost of Jairampur, on the borders of NEFA. He had come to challenge the policy whereby all outsiders, whether citizens of India or not, had to obtain 'Inner Line' permits to enter the territory. Lohia held that all Indians had the right to wander freely anywhere in their country. But the NEFA guards did not agree: he did not have a pass so he was not allowed to enter. Lohia was enraged. The governor of Assam told him he could get a permit whenever he wished but would first have to come to Shillong and apply for one. Lohia was not prepared to accept this and a year later once again attempted to enter NEFA without a permit. This time he was arrested and brought down to the town of Dibrugarh in Assam, where he was set free. In a press statement he condemned the policy of the NEFA administration as a relic of British colonialism. Lohia insisted that he wished to visit the area only out of a desire to see his land 'in all its various beautiful shapes.' This 'foolish' policy of not allowing other Indians into the territory, he claimed,

> might be partly owing to the fact that a very peculiar type of an erstwhile clergyman, Sri Verrier Elwin, is the adviser of the Governor of Assam in respect of the matters concerning the Adivasis (tribals) of Assam. This former clergyman has carved out a principle of a 'reserved forest' in the same manner as the lions of Gir. But the detachment of these Adivasis with the outer world is all the more greater . . . Until the month of October last year, the photographs of Shiv, Durga, Gandhiji or even Nehru were not permitted to be displayed in the shops, because in the opinion of this former clergyman, there were possibilities of the people of [NEFA] being offended or getting corrupt.[18]

Where some national politicians accused Elwin of separating NEFA from India, the Assamese, the dominant linguistic group in the north-east, suspected him of suppressing the territory's historic links with them. The press in Assam consistently charged NEFA officers with isolating the tribals from their closest neighbours with whom, it was claimed, they had affinities of language, lifestyle and religious belief, as well as associations going back hundreds of years. Months after Elwin moved to Shillong, Assamese journalists sharpened their attacks on NEFA officials, who smelt a mythical 'Assamese imperialism in the tribal areas of the north-east, leading them to weed out Assamese officials from the NEFA Administration.'[19]

The journalists were only taking a cue from their politicians. In November 1955, discussing the report of the States Reorganization Committee, the Assam legislature complained that it failed to recognize their claims to include NEFA in their state. 'We took it for granted,' said one member, 'that [the] North-East Frontier areas are already part of Assam and that their ultimate integration is only a question of time.' A second member clarified what this 'integration' was all about when he called for the free mixing of the tribes of NEFA and the Assamese, which would 'in process of time, leave no difference between Hill people and Plains people.' It seems integration meant many things to many people, for the levelling of difference was precisely what Elwin and his colleagues were working against. The NEFA administration was further condemned in the Assam legislature for demolishing the 'healthy process of gradual integration of all the people of North-East Frontier Agency and the rest [*sic*] of Assam which was developing slowly but surely over centuries . . .' As one politician put it, in a rare flash of wit, a feeling was growing that NEFA now meant 'No Entry For the Assamese.'[20]

The politicians of Assam worked long and hard to absorb NEFA into their state. They sent forth two study teams to the territory; both found what they wished to find, to wit, that the 'people of NEFA desire closer contact with the people of Assam and they consider the people of Assam to be friends and kinsmen.' The legislators asked for the speedy adminstrative integration of NEFA with Assam, the creation of a common secretariat, the formulation of a common plan of economic development for the region as a whole, and the propagation of Assamese in preference to Hindi: all measures stoutly opposed by Elwin and his colleagues.[21]

The first of these delegations remarked that the people of NEFA did 'not want to be kept aloof as specimens of [an] anthropological museum;' the second that 'the Philosophy of NEFA should be reoriented in the light of developing circumstances of the time.' This was perhaps as far as they could go in their criticisms of Elwin; for these were Congress politicians who knew of the anthropologist's closeness to the Supreme Leader, of whom they were in such mortal dread. But the Assamese press was bound by no such inhibitions and often singled out the peculiar type of erstwhile clergyman by name. In a speech in Shillong Nehru had proclaimed, 'I like variety. I like diversity.' The same evening Elwin and Lila were among the guests at a reception for the prime minister. A bitchy journalist, also present, commented on seeing Elwin enter 'with his wife from Bihar [*sic*]:' 'Here comes Nehru's variety.'[22]

Such remarks, in print and otherwise, finally moved Elwin to complain to the governor of Assam. He wrote that he counted himself among those who 'strongly oppose and criticise any idea of isolating the tribal people from their neighbours,' adding that he was himself 'very fond of the Assamese' and an admirer of their culture. He also mentioned in this connection two NEFA calendars designed by him, which had pictorially emphasised 'the importance of the integration of the tribal people with the rest of India and with Assam.'[23]

In that order, of course, for as one of his disciples remembered it, Elwin would not abide in his beloved NEFA any move towards 'Assam-ilation.'[24] Most contentious here was the question of the medium of instruction in NEFA schools. In addition to the tribal dialects, Elwin wanted the national language, Hindi, to be taught, rather than Assamese. Genuflections to Assamese culture in a NEFA calendar were one thing, the language of instruction (and perhaps in time indoctrination) quite another. On this question, at any rate, Elwin and the NEFA administration were unyielding.

A third group which viewed Elwin's work in NEFA with suspicion consisted of his old adversaries, the professional anthropologists. The Anthropological Survey of India wished to assert its own authority over NEFA, claiming a countrywide mandate to commission and supervise research. This was resisted by Elwin, who regarded NEFA as his own bailiwick, a field not open to independent research by other anthropologists, even if they were also in the employ of the Indian state. When the Survey proposed to send a research group into the territory, Elwin advised the governor to forbid them, saying that 'the invasion of NEFA by parties of anthropologists, who may not be trained in our policies, is not desirable. We may remember the P. M.'s directive that we should not allow too many outside bodies into NEFA and finally, the articles produced by the Calcutta anthropologists are sometimes misleading and tend to give a wrong impression of the Administration and its work.'[25]

The territorial imperative aside, Indian anthropologists had other reservations regarding NEFA, as expressed in an April 1957 talk to a conference of social workers by the distinguished Calcutta anthropologist Nirmal Kumar Bose. Like Elwin, Bose was a writer and scholar with a wide range of interests, not a narrow specialist at all; and like Elwin he had for a time been close to Gandhi, whose secretary and interpreter he had been when the Mahatma toured the villages of rural Bengal in 1946–7, dousing the flames of communal passion. Anyhow, for some reason the two men disliked one another, as witness their printed references to the other person's work. Bose, who had also studied the Juangs of Orissa, accused Elwin of photographing the tribe in leaves simply to show a 'vicarious pleasure in the existence of such "natural" savages in midst of India's fast changing economic life;' Elwin, who had also known the Mahatma, accused Bose of totally misunderstanding the man in his 'rather bad book,' *My Days with Gandhi.*[26]

Behind the personal animosity lay two different approaches to the tribal predicament.[27] In his 1957 lecture Bose criticized anthropologists who went 'curio-hunting' and then expresssed an 'unbalanced' romantic concern for tribals. These scholars highlighted aspects of tribal culture which marked them off from their Hindu neighbours, but Bose would rather stress their affinities with other poor Indians. 'Let us not by a special concern for tribal people, as distinguished from other sections of the masses who suffer from very nearly the same disabilities,' he remarked, encourage a 'force endangering social solidarity of the Indian people. Let us unite, not in freeing the tribal people from all bondage, but in devising means which will free all disinherited people from bondage of any kind, whether they are tribal or non tribal in origin.'[28]

Elwin was not mentioned by name in Bose's address, but he and his work were the chief target. Where the Calcutta man spoke for the unity of the poor, other anthropologists attacked Elwin in the name of political unity, or the oneness of India. One such was D. N. Majumdar of Lucknow University, the butcher back in 1952 of the Bondo book. He now took on *A Philosophy of NEFA,* but under a pseudonym. Writing as 'E.T.,' the initials of one of his submissive students, Majumdar charged Elwin with once more trying to pass off his own 'segregation' approach as the so-called anthropological solution to the tribal question. But in the earlier debates too, wrote the Lucknow professor, 'no Indian, no *Indian* anthropologist, toed the line with Elwin.' Indeed, the 'Indian Constitution gave an adequate reply. It was an "intervention therapy" that was recommended and the colossal efforts being made by the Government to rehabilitate the tribes and level them up indicate the dynamic upsurge leading to acculturation and assimilation.' But 'now it is Dr Elwin again [with regard to NEFA] who has reverted to the position of exclusiveness and segregation. If the tribals have a way of life, so they have, and if we have no right to force our way of life on them, are we to suppose that we should concede what the tribals want? We know what they want; the echo of Jharkhand [the movement for a separate tribal province in central India] has reached NEFA—should we follow the philosophy of inaction and intervention? Our stakes are too great . . .'[29]

Preserving the tribes as museum pieces for the sake of science, isolating them from their nearest Hindu neighbours, undermining through his work the prospects for national unity—these criticisms of Elwin's work in NEFA recall for us, as indeed they must have for him, the disputes of the nineteen-forties. The controversialist in him would not keep quiet, but his official status called for a more measured response. References to his critics are scattered through his file notings, but the most public defense was published in the Delhi monthly, *Seminar.* This took up the attacks by Dr Ram Manohar Lohia and that old anthropological Quisling, G. S. Ghurye of Bombay University. In early 1959 Professor Ghurye brought out a revised edition of his book of 1943, *The Aborigines—So Called—and their Future.* The study had a new title, and in several respects had been brought up-to-date, but it retained almost all its original and derisive references to Elwin and his work, without taking account of his writings in the interim.

Elwin took the intellectual more seriously than the politician, for Lohia (who 'seems to have developed a positive complex about me') is disposed off in a couple of paragraphs. He then turned to Ghurye's claim that he remained 'an isolationist, a no-changer and a revivalist,' based on views expressed twenty years previously, and even so, distorted by the Bombay scholar. He quoted from his old studies, *The Baiga* and *The Aboriginals*, to suggest that he had only advocated a temporary policy of isolation for a few vulnerable communities—this too in conditions of colonial rule where social work among the tribes was in its infancy. In any case, with Independence and the 'great awakening throughout the country,' tribal people had found their voice and a place of dignity in free India. No one now, wrote Elwin, 'would advocate a policy of isolation, although it is as important as ever to give some protection to the tribal people in the transition period during which they must learn to stand on their own feet and become strong enough to resist those who would exploit them.' Like everyone else, he was for change and development, with only this caveat: 'what I and those who think with me desire is change for the better and not degradation and decay.'

The tone of the essay, the careful clarification of his own views and his gestures to the dominant mood of 'change' and 'progress,' suggest that Ghurye had once more forced Elwin on to the back foot. And yet, when compared with his sharp interventions of the nineteen forties this is an altogether more assured, less polemical Elwin. Then he stood isolated, with Indian politicians, social workers and scholars all ranged against him. The only men on his side in those controversies were the odd British civil servant and amateur anthropologist: friends who were, in political and strategic terms, distinctly an embarassment.

In his battles in independent India, however, Elwin could call upon a wide array of supporters. Thus praise for *A Philosophy for NEFA* came from all over and from bigwigs of all kinds: from the vice-president of India (Sir Sarvepalli Radhakrishnan), the governor of Bihar (Dr Zakir Hussain), the home minister and the education minister, the high commissioner to the United Kingdom (Vijayalakshmi Pandit, Nehru's sister), the industrialist J. R. D. Tata. Some of these letters, generally from the not-so-mighty, were deeply felt. An Australian scholar, while complimenting the author, noted mournfully that the aboriginals in his country had already been beaten up beyond repair. A British anthropologist wanted him to write a more general work on tribal policy in the underdeveloped world: 'It would be absolutely invaluable in our Colonies and ex-Colonies, especially in Africa, and Pandit Nehru's name would carry enormous weight.

As far as I know nothing of the kind has been written and the fate of African tribals as things are at present is too horrible to contemplate.' The Austrian ethnographer C. von Fürer Haimendorf, who had lived with the Konyaks in the thirties, wrote of reading *A Philosophy* 'with mounting interest and a good deal of nostalgia. I really envy you the opportunity of working among the people of the N. E. Frontier.' Apa Pant, a maharajah-turned-Gandhian-turned diplomat, then serving as Indian ambassador to Bhutan, prayed that Elwin and his philosophy—the 'human, spiritual approach so well expressed in your book'—be granted 'enough time' to succeed. But he wondered 'whether isolated pockets of contented people with vast areas of habitable land would be allowed to exist in this mad world of ours.'[30]

A file in Elwin's papers preserves these letters and others of its kind; they nourished him, but more welcome than private encouragement was the public defense of him and his work. Many of the reviews of *A Philosophy for NEFA* were warmly appreciative, of the book and of the man. 'Great men are rare anywhere,' wrote *The Statesman*, 'in the right place rarer still. It is a question whether India is not exploiting Dr Elwin . . ., but at any rate she is giving both herself and him one of the most magnificent opportunities of recent times.' Tribal policy in NEFA, remarked the newspaper, was 'perhaps the most intelligent and enlightened approach to a terribly complicated problem yet devised.'[31] Another journalist, writing in the *Economic Weekly* after a tour through Elwin's domain, claimed that 'in some ways, NEFA might be considered a paradise. There are no taxes, no money-lenders, no middle men to exploit the people. Most of the officials recruited for service in NEFA have high qualifications and treat the tribesmen with consideration and sympathy . . . One would have to reach far and wide in history to find any comparable parallel to the liberality of the NEFA administration.'[32]

The men who ruled India also went out to bat for Elwin. Nehru's generous praise in print has been noted; nor was he shy of stating, to the press or in Parliament, that he 'broadly agreed with the approach of Dr Verrier Elwin.'[33] The home minister, Govind Ballabh Pant, was another admirer, telling a public meeting in Shillong that 'the great achievement of Dr Elwin in the last twenty years has been to make people all over India regard the tribals with respect. Previously we had looked on

12. The Deputy Director of the Anthropological Survey of India, on the balcony of his Calcutta home, 1949 (Sunil Janah)

13. Lila Elwin, c. 1963 (Sunil Janah/OUP)

14. Kumar Elwin, somewhere on the Frontier, c. 1960 (OUP)

15. The sahib and the scholar—Elwin with Professor C. von Fürer Haimendorf, Shillong, 1954 (OUP)

16. A Konyak Naga girl (Verrier Elwin/OUP)

17. Jawaharlal Nehru visiting Elwin's house and museum, Shillong, 1955 (OUP)

18. Cover portrait of the Indian edition of *The Tribal World of Verrier Elwin* (OUP)

19. Elwin receiving the Padma Bhushan from the President of India, New Delhi, 1961 (Nehru Memorial Museum and Library)

them as savages. But he has shown us that they have a culture and arts of their own.'[34]

The critics would not go away. In a Lok Sabha debate a Member of Parliament from Assam took a swipe at the policies recommended in *A Philosophy for NEFA*. 'Should we cut a frontier into piecemeal entities like this,' asked Hem Barua, or 'should we not have a consolidated entity in the frontier for the sake of our defense?' This was in effect a plea for the creation of a greater Assam, to include, as in colonial times, all the tribal tracts of the north-east. Barua then made a reference to the 'British philosopher-anthropologist' who seemed so influential in the north-east. He was at once contradicted by Jaipal Singh, leader of the Jharkhand movement for a separate tribal state, and also an Oxford contemporary of Elwin. 'Dr Verrier Elwin,' he reminded his colleague, 'is more Indian now than Shri Hem Barua. He is more tribal now than Jaipal Singh.'[35]

CHAPTER THIRTEEN

An Englishman for India

And thus this gentle rebel became the last in the line of Oxford scholar admininistrators in India, with an office in the secretariat.

Ronald Symons on Verrier Elwin, in *Oxford and Empire* (1986)

Sri Madhava Ashish, a venerable Hindu monk of English extraction, once told me that his mentor Sri Krishna Prem and he were the second and third foreigners to be granted Indian citizenship. He believed Verrier Elwin was the first. If true, this was a considerable honour. The evidence to confirm or dispute this claim must exist somewhere in the ministry of home affairs, whose files are not available for public scrutiny.

Verrier himself was now comfortable with his new nationality, the confusions and uncertainties of the early fifties behind him. The job in NEFA had much to do with this, the support in the secretariat and the thrills of the chase besides. After his mother died England became more distant still. He had not been there for years and had no plans to go either.

Almost for the first time Verrier was content at work and at home, free of the torments that had chased him since Oxford. Lila he adored. He was too busy and too old to have as complete a relationship with their sons but he tried as best he could—fortnightly dinners out, alternately at the Pinewood Hotel, Shillong's best, and at a Chinese restaurant, as well as trips to the cinema with blankets and thermos of coffee in tow. What struck the boys most forcibly about their father was his cigar. A drawing by

Wasant, pasted in Verrier's diary, is called 'Daddy with Cigar;' another by Ashok, more inventive, has the little boy smoking the dreadful thing himself, with Mummy ticking off Daddy for allowing him to have one.

On 10th January 1959 Verrier drafted a new will which superseded the old one. This bequeathed 10 per cent of his estate to Kumar, the rest to Lila. If Lila died before him the estate was to be shared equally by Kumar, Wasant, Nakul and Ashok. The lack of any mention of Shamrao also suggests the way in which Verrier closed an earlier chapter of his life. 'I declare,' the will said,

> that in or about the year 1940 I was married to one Kausilya commonly known as Kosi. I have only one child by the said Kosi, namely a son by name Jawaharlal (commonly called Kumar) who was born in or about the year 1941. The said Kosi in or about the year 1947 [*sic*] gave birth to a boy who is named Bijay. The said Bijay is not my child and I have never accepted him as such. Because of the misconduct of the said Kosi, I have divorced her in or about the year 1949 . . . My wife and I have three children, all boys, named Wasant, Nakul and Ashok respectively. Besides [these] there is no living person who has any claim on my estate.[1]

Verrier Elwin was very likely the first Englishman to become an Indian, and most certainly the best known. His official position and proximity to Nehru seemed to many to be just reward for dogged and devoted work for the tribes. Even those who dissented from his views conceded he had stayed the course: twenty-five years in tribal India, twenty-five fine books about them.

An elegantly bound Visitors Book in the possession of Elwin's family in Shillong marks the names of those who came calling. His visitors included maharajahs, generals, and ministers; young Gandhians (Natwar Thakkar, running an ashram for the Nagas at Mokokchung), old Gandhians (Asha Devi Arayanayakam, running a school started by the Mahatma at Sevagram), suspicious Gandhians (D. J. Naik of A. V. Thakkar's Bhil Seva Mandal at Dahod, who allowed that this was 'a wonderful collection, which indicates the love of Dr Elwin for the tribes'), friendly

Gandhians (Kamaladevi Chattopadhyay, Jayaprakash Narayan, and Narayan Desai, son of Mahadev). An old friend who came was Christoph von Fürer Haimendorf, the London professor who rather wished he had Elwin's job. A new friend was Catherine Galbraith, wife of the American Ambassador (her entry: 'A fascinating morning, and I hope we meet again').

Like all of us, Elwin hoarded praise,[2] more so if it came from his ancient enemies—the middle-class Hindus who, now and then, had cavilled at his portraits of their culture; and the professional anthropologists who, over the years, had allowed him in only to throw him out again. But now that he was old and wise and big, the letters came pouring in. Some offered honest praise, others asked for jobs for their kin or forewords for their books. R. N. Gurtu, a Merton man who had not seen Verrier since Oxford, was stirred to write after seeing a collection of his books on display in Allahabad: 'I have led an arid life, though I ended up as a judge of the High Court, arid when I see the works of Elwin which lie before me.' A more recent acquaintance, an officer of the Indian Frontier Administrative Service, wrote of his 'singular luck' in being trained by Elwin, of the 'fatherly affection' he had received from him. 'I have always looked at your life with curiosity and affection,' wrote M. D. Tyagi: 'There are very few persons in this world who have staked their all to live their ideals. You are one of them.'

A young Indian studying in Illinois told Elwin that 'anthropologists in this country refer to you as one of the few great field-workers in anthropology.' Another asked Nehru's confidant to use his 'influence over the power-elite of our country' to help appoint his father (who was teaching in Calcutta University) to the first national professorship in anthropology. One eminent Western scholar, Rodney Needham, begged to be allowed into NEFA—and if that were not possible, for Elwin to send one of his best assistants to be trained in Oxford. A second, Claude Lévi-Strauss, recommended a student for a job and then asked with hopeful interest: 'Are you planning to write any ethnography on the peoples of north-eastern India?' The American Museum of Natural History invited him to spend three months in the United States, introducing and displaying his great collection of tribal artefacts. They would pack and transport his stuff and pay for him, but negotiations broke down when he insisted that they pay for Lila too.

A letter that gave much satisfaction arrived from George Devereux who, long ago, had reviewed *The Agaria* in tones of lofty condescension. The Frenchman then urged Elwin to leave the forest for the graduate seminar; now he completely withdrew his earlier remarks. 'I think you are a very enviable person,' wrote Devereux,

> who has laid out for himself a much wiser and much more gratifying course in life than most of us. Perhaps you do not have a grand piano in your sitting room, nor a Cadillac or a Rolls Royce in your garage—instead, you have chosen to live with people and to work among and with them. I rather think that your human horizons are wider than those of most of us.
>
> I speak of this with some feeling since, in 1935, when I could choose between staying forever among the mountain people of Indochina—who, as you know, are very much like your Gonds and your Nagas—and going back to the hurly-burly of so-called civilization, I underwent a very real inner struggle—and probably chose the wrong solution.

A letter of open admiration also came from Wayland Young, the pacifist, author, and liberal peer. Young, an editor with Jonathan Cape, wrote of having been a 'tremendous admirer' of Elwin's work since reading *The Muria and their Ghotul*, a book which made tribals 'come alive enough for a lot of their sayings and views of the world to pass into the ordinary fabric of life for my wife and me and friends.' 'Will you allow me,' he asked, 'to enter the field of those who are pursuing you for a book? Or are you tied up with the Oxford University Press? Any old thing whether tribal erotics or general observations on the life and lot of those who seek to advise Governments on tribal affairs, or the nature of God and man, or anything else?'

From literary London too came a man whose range of interests and experience matched his. Arthur Koestler had been told of Verrier by Shaun Mandy, and saw in him a likely informant for a book he planned on the religions of the east. He arrived in Shillong in February 1959 and stayed a fortnight with the Elwins. The visitor, wrote Verrier, 'had an electric effect on us all, even the children who loved him. He radiated peace and strength and seemed to like us as much as we liked him.' Koestler was indeed entranced by them all, especially Lila, whom he kissed good-bye in continental fashion. The day before, she had pushed him into a bath he had not entered all week; and when he came out dressed she forcibly cleaned his shoes.

In the evenings the Hungarian-born Englishman and the British-born Indian had 'long enchanting talks.' These fed into *The Lotus and the Robot*, where Koestler's cold-eyed scepticism judged both Gandhism and Zen Buddhism to be unworthy of the modern world. The book, to Verrier's great pride but also some embarrassment, was dedicated to him.[3]

Arthur Koestler, somewhat surpisingly, was to become the recipient by letter of Verrier's confidences, taking the place in this respect of Shamrao—who lived in Madhya Pradesh and never replied in any case—as well as of Bill Archer, whom he had not seen for years, and of Victor Sassoon, who had migrated to Bangkok and disappeared into its fleshpots. After Koestler left Verrier toured the Buddhist uplands, conversing with peasants and visiting their temples. He meditated for hours alone, in front of their exquisite little images of the Buddha. He wrote about his visit to Koestler, the lapsed Zionist-Communist: 'Whether it was the beauty or the love and kindness of the people, I recaptured some of the ecstacy and peace of the days long ago when I found it at the feet of another deity, a god that in my own case later failed.'[4]

Verrier returned with some reluctance to Shillong. Later that month the Dalai Lama himself was seen where Verrier had just been. The monarch of Tibetan Buddhism had dramatically entered NEFA following the failure of a popular uprising against the Chinese. He was first given refuge at the monastery in Tawang, before coming down to Assam.

Elwin was in the plains at the time of the Dalai Lama's entry into India and was disappointed at not being able to go to Tawang to greet him. But he offered *Holiday Magazine* of London an exclusive story, with photographs, of the god-prince's escape from communism. His account was finally published not in *Holiday* but in the more established *Geographical Magazine.* He wrote here of the Tibetan leader feeling immediately at home among the 'simple Buddhist tribesmen' of NEFA, followers of the same faith and devoted to him and his ideals. Here was proof that while great empires such as Communist China will rise and fall, the 'spiritual kingdom endures through exile, hardship and danger.' Elwin smartly gave himself and his government a puff: the Dalai Lama, he noted, had thanked the Indian officers who 'spared no effort in making his stay and journey through this extremely well-administered part of India as comfortable as possible.' The reader, the Western reader, was asked to choose between totalitarianism and democracy, between China's persecution of Tibetans and India's treatments of its minorites who lived, at any rate in NEFA, in 'peaceful, happy villages.'[5]

By now Elwin was being increasingly called to wider duties. In May the home ministry invited him to chair a committee to study the progress of economic development in tribal areas. The assignment was 'rather a triumph,' he told a friend, 'for the home ministry is the centre of Indian puritanism: I shall probably start some furious controversies.'[6] Through its work Elwin renewed contact with the tribes of central India, visiting remote areas of Andhra Pradesh, Orissa and Bihar, 'charging about the country in jeeps like a school inspector.' But for some reason he scrupulously avoided Bastar, despite the warm and repeated invitations of a member of his committee who worked there. I suspect that with his own happy memories of the place he could not bear to find out what civilization had done to Bastar's tribals in the twenty years since he had last seen them.

Elwin saw his report, submitted in March 1960, as a sequel to *A Philosophy for NEFA*, applying its ideas throughout India.[7] Thus shifting cultivation, regarded by foresters as 'almost the essential tribal vice,' was once more defended as a necessary adaptation to a difficult terrain. The state and its officials are asked to acquire the 'tribal touch,' to look at things 'through tribal eyes and from the tribal point of view.' A tribal bias, explained Elwin, 'means that we recognize and honour their way of doing things, *not because it is old and picturesque, but because it is theirs*, and they have as much right to their culture as anyone else in India.' The tribal touch in practice implied a respect for herbal medicine, traditional tribal housing and ways of educating the young, as in the ghotul. Development programmes, it was suggested, might work with and through these institutions rather than in opposition to them.

There is however a sombre and sometimes bitter tone that runs through the home ministry report. For Indian independence, 'which has brought the glories and inspiration of freedom to millions, has given little to these poor people.' The committee, noted its chairman, had 'been deeply shocked by the poverty of the tribal people, the exploitation that they still suffer, the lack of consideration with which they are all too often treated, the burden of fear and anxiety under which they live, the pressure on them of unfamiliar regulations, and the loss of many good elements in their own tradition and culture.' This appears in a prologue: the report's epilogue, meanwhile, explains that much of tribal suffering and deprivation is

> the fault of us, the 'civilized' people. We have driven them into the hills because we wanted their land and now we blame them for cultivating it in the only way we left for them. We have robbed them of their arts by sending them the cheap and tawdry products of a commercial economy. We have even taken away their food by stopping their hunting, or by introducing new taboos which deprive them of the valuable protein elements in meat and fish. We sell them spirits which are far more injurious than the home-made beer and wines which are nourishing and familiar to them, and use the proceeds to uplift them with ideals. We look down on them and rob them of their self-confidence, and take away their freedom by laws which they do not understand.

There is a note of anger here that is by and large missing from Elwin's writings on NEFA, where of course civilization in its many exploitative guises had not yet properly penetrated. Back briefly in central India he challenged head on the commonly accepted meanings of 'primitive' and 'civilized.' 'Primitiveness,' in his view, should be taken to mean 'self-reliance, community work and a spirit of co-operation, artistic creativeness, honesty, truthfulness, hospitality, a highly organized society.' 'Who is backward,' asks Elwin, 'the creative artist at her tribal loom, the gentle mother with her child among the hills, or the inventor of the atom bomb which may destroy her and all the world? Are these self-reliant, co-operative tribes the really backward as against the self-seeking, individualistic, crafty products of our industrial civilization?'[8]

Elwin was next asked to prepare a book on the Nagas, that truculent minority in free India. From 1947 the Indian government had tried with mixed success to control or co-opt an armed struggle for an independent Naga homeland. When in 1960 New Delhi began negotiating with such rebels as were willing to talk, the Western press, and in particular *The Observer* of London, carried a series of reports on 'atrocities' by the Indian army. The government turned to the most fluent and the most credible writer in its ranks, asking him to write a book presenting India's case abroad. Elwin agreed, but most unwillingly. 'I feel that I am entirely the wrong person to do it,' he told a colleague, 'but as it has been allotted to me I must do what I can.' To R. E. Hawkins he described it as 'the most difficult job I have yet done.' The assignment must surely have recalled for him the time of Gandhi's civil disobedience movement, when he had so passionately upheld the right to self-determination of a subject people. Curiously, a British Anglican priest, Michael Scott, was most active in the Naga cause; he was very nearly to the arms-carrying rebels what Elwin had once been to the non-violent Congress.

Jawaharlal Nehru, while certainly affected by the criticisms in the British press, did not count the Nagas among his favourite people. Back in 1953 he was visiting Kohima with the Burmese prime minister U Nu when a Naga delegation wished to present him with a petition asking for a just consideration of their demands. They hoped to hand this over to the prime minister at his public meeting, but some arrogant underlings would not allow them to do this. Nehru was a little late coming to the meeting, by which time the crowd, told of the rebuff, had started dispersing. His daughter Indira Gandhi, speaking unwittingly into the live microphone, said agitatedly, '*Papa, wo jaa rahe hain*' (father, they are all going). Nehru replied, gravely, '*Haan beti, main dekh raha hoon*' (yes, daughter, I can see them go.)[9] Never before had the people's prince been treated so, and Nehru did not forget the slight. He never returned to Nagaland and could not bring himself to trust Naga leaders like Phizo or Naga sympathizers like Scott. Meeting Elwin in July 1960 he professed not to be worried about accusations of rape made against armymen. 'I have gone into the matter very carefully,' he said, 'and I can only find five authenticated accusations of rape by such a large body of troops during the last five years. I do not think that this is really very much.'[10]

Elwin privately described his Nagaland book as attempting 'in as subtle and dispassionate a way as possible to put India's case on all matters about which there has been controversy'—matters such as the treatment of minorities in India as a whole, the legitimacy of India's claims over Naga territory, the representativeness, or lack of it, of the Naga insurgents, and the truth of the allegations regarding army brutality. All the same in presenting India's case Elwin was unwilling to go as far as the foreign ministry wanted him to. He refused to exonerate the Indian army of all the charges brought against it. Critical remarks were necessary not only because they were true but because their absence would raise suspicion: 'from the point of view of readers, especially in England, I believe that if we admit a certain [number of] mistakes we are more likely to convince them of the strength of our case.' He would mention the deaths of tribals as a consequence of their being forced into grouped villages, he said, because he could not 'go against my conscience in these matters.'

Through successive drafts of the book Elwin battled with Indian officials about the use of the word 'rebel.' His superiors prefered 'hostiles' as a characterization of the insurgents; they also complained of his 'tendency to stress the strength of the Naga independence movement.' Elwin held his ground, noting that the best known usage of 'hostiles' was to 'describe a Red Indian who opposed the white settlers in America—hardly a desirable association.' To use 'hostile' as a noun, as he was asked to do, seemed to suggest 'some extra-terrestrial monsters coming from outside space.' His own alternative, 'rebel,' also indicated that the Nagas were 'Indians rebelling against their own legally constituted authority.' 'Rebel' he was finally allowed to retain, but he had however to drop 'rebellion.'[11]

When the Naga struggle began in 1947 his friend Bill Archer had just given up charge of his post at Mokokchung. On the train out of the hills Archer wondered what the future held for the Nagas. 'Would India confuse nationalism with uniformity,' he asked, 'and slowly reduce them to a depressed, unhappy caste? Or would the Indian government swiftly reach some sensible settlement which would allow them to remain Nagas and preserve their vivid way of life?'[12]

What in December 1947 was posed as very much an open question was answered resoundingly in the affirmative by Elwin in 1960. His book on Nagaland is a combination of many things: a breezy survey of the different Naga tribes, a celebration of their artistic traditions, a potted history of the rebellion—but it is above all a claim that the Nagas shall be integrated (as he was) with honour in the Indian nation. The anthropologist most subtly portrays the Nagas as an 'important branch of the great and varied Indian family:' with their production systems like those of other Indian tribes, their religious ceremonials and patterns of sacrifice not dissimilar to Hinduism in its older Vedic forms. If traditional India had something in common with the Nagas, the new India had much to offer them too. The story of India, wrote Elwin,

> has been, in Dr S. K. Chatterjee's words, "a synthesis of races and cultures leading to the creation and characterization of a composite Indian civilization, diverse in its origins but united in its ideals and aspirations—ideals and aspirations which are acceptable to all mankind; while India looks forward to a still greater unification of all mankind, both within her shores and outside."
>
> As Nagaland realizes its position in this great country, of which it is so precious a part, it will share in the fulfilment of this ideal.[13]

All his life Elwin had to work his way between competing allegiances—moral, religious, scientific, sexual, political—yet the Nagaland assignment presented a dilemma of almost unsurpassed painfulness. Long ago, when his publisher had asked him to write a book he did not feel up to writing, he quoted Herbert Paul: 'Seek the prizes of your own calling and be resolutely *hors de combat* to all others.'[14] So long as he was a freelancer he could stand by this, but as an employee of the Government of India he had to bend, slightly. But one thinks that as he wrote his book he espied, watching him, the judgmental shadows of his friends W. G. Archer and J. H. Hutton, men who had known and served the Nagas and were, if anything, prone to overlook the excesses of their side. When Hutton posted him a statement in the London press that was critical of the Indian army, Elwin replied angrily: 'These enthusiastic clergymen, who really know nothing about the subject and whose knowledge of the Nagas is based on a few gentlemen dressed up like members of the YMCA in London, have been talking through their hats and there is little doubt that they have done a lot of harm and have led to a greater loss of life.'[15]

Perhaps the happiest moment in the whole assignment came when Elwin visited a new Gandhian ashram in Mokokchung. To his delight and surprise they served him pork and rice-beer.[16] These Gandhians would accommodate the Naga way of life, but would the government? The conviction carried in his book turns less certain in an anonymous comment he published in *The Statesman.* Reviewing a book on 'Clemency' Canning, the viceroy appointed after the rebellion of 1857, Elwin noted his opposition to the burning of villages and his disregard of the criticisms of the Anglo-Indian press. 'Those who have to deal with the rebel Nagas in the eastern Hills,' he remarked, 'could read this book with profit.'[17]

The unease persisted much after the Nagaland book was printed and published. When R. E. Hawkins passed on a reader's complaint that there seemed some discrepancy between the Elwin of 1930 and the Elwin of 1960, he answered that he had

> consistently behind the scenes, urged the policy of tolerance and compassion; and that I have always pressed for that emancipation from Delhi which has now been achieved for the Nagas by the establishment of Nagaland. I don't myself see much inconsistency between my youth and age, for there is not really any comparison between the Satyagrahis fighting for Freedom and the Nagas and, by and large, I feel that India has given the Nagas a very square deal. But the whole business of any idealist belonging to an official set-up is extremely complicated. On the very day before India marched into Goa [to free it from Portuguese rule] I gave a lecture in Delhi on the importance of non-violence![18]

Since coming to Shillong Verrier had not had a day's holiday. The Government of India had more than its money's worth and knew it. It fell to his friend K. L. Mehta, a former adviser to the governor in NEFA who was now a joint secretary in New Delhi, to convey the 'sanction of the President to the continued appointment of Dr Verrier Elwin as Adviser on Tribal Affairs for a further period of five years from 1/1/1960.' Mehta received in reply a letter asking, 'But who will sanction the continued existence of Dr Verrier Elwin for this period?' It then quoted the Dhammapada:

> Here shall I dwell in the rain, here in winter and summer—thus the fool thinks and does not think of death. Death comes and carries off that man

> boastful of his children and flocks, his mind distracted, as a flood carries off a sleeping village.[19]

Death would call anyway, but there was still work to be done, tours to be made and reports to be written or rewritten. In a profile he wrote as a broadcast to the NEFA outback sometime in June 1960, Elwin remarked of being 'surrounded by floods of galley proofs and reams of paper.' Later that year he was invited to join a high-powered Commission on Scheduled Areas and Scheduled Tribes, eight of whose members were 'teetotal and vegetarian Congress Members of Parliament,' one of these the chairman, U. N. Dhebar, a former chief minister of Gujarat. The opposition consisted of himself and his friend Jaipal Singh, the Jharkhand leader.[20]

Elwin's work with the Dhebar Commission began with a week's tour of Rajasthan in December. This desert state he scarcely knew, and what he saw of its administration he did not much like. A four-page crisply argued report to the governor characteristically combined philosophy with fine detail. Why were Bhil girls, who traditionally wore embroidered skirts, put into white saris, in the manner of Hindu widows, when they entered government schools? Why was the vegetarianism of the rest of the state being imported into Bhil territory? Boys and girls in school hostels from homes where fish and meat were prized foods would be undernourished; moreover, the moralizing bluster of the improving teacher would develop in them a 'sense of guilt so that when they go home they will feel they ought not to eat nonvegetarian food.' Why did school textbooks not speak of Bhil heroes and Bhil myths? 'History lessons bringing in the Bhils would help to preserve their pride in themselves (which seems to be going down). Even in mixed schools it would not do the non-tribal boys any harm to learn something of the history and tradition of their tribal fellow-students and might do something to make them respect them more.' Why couldn't archery be encouraged instead of soccer, wood-carving and mask-making (old Bhil crafts) rather than weaving?[21]

Verrier returned to Shillong in early January; on the 26th (Republic Day) he heard over the radio that he had been awarded the Padma Bhushan. This he described to Eldyth as roughly equivalent to a 'knighthood, but a good knighthood, a GCSI or a GCB.' For the investiture, in April, he took Lila with him. The award was given by the president, Rajendra Prasad; like that old Gandhian Verrier also wore a buttoned-up khadi suit, the first time he'd worn the stuff in years. The next day he had a private lunch with Nehru, where he 'managed to get in a good many points about which I was concerned across to him."

There were however things he could not speak to the great man about. He had no pension and worried about Lila and the children. 'I am finding it extremely difficult to make ends meet,' he told Eldyth, 'taxation is terrible and the price of things is going up almost every month—what will happen when my appointment here comes to an end or I myself go to heaven I really do not know, for the rupee is really losing its value.'[22]

The financial worries apart, Lila and Verrier seemed to have a good thing going, she providing the stability and sustenance, the base from which he would reach out to the outside world and to which he would always return. Shamrao Hivale once wrote of the Pardhan wife that she was 'at once a source of supreme delight and intense anxiety to her husband.'[23] The description, both parts, better fits Kosi, who was of course a Gond. The fires of that union had been swamped by a gush of cold water, but the flame of this one was steady and serene, to be put out only by his death or hers. That at any rate is what the evidence I collected—in letters, in print, and through interviews—would point to. It was therefore a surprise, a shock even, to find in absolutely the last archival collection I laid my hands upon—that of Arthur Koestler—a letter from Verrier of 7th June 1961 that spoke of how

> in the last three months I have fallen into the worst emotional tangle of my life, all the more devastating as it can't come to anything, for I will never do anything to hurt Lila—I am very much in love with her and she is the rock which will go on. But the other person, who is brilliant and has the erotic impact of a dozen atom bombs has introduced me to quite a different kind of love, for all my varied experiences have been tribal, uncomplicated, delicious but non-frustrating. I will adjust myself in time and meanwhile it has done me good, I think, in increasing compassion and understanding of something new to me, and has certainly made me very humble. You are the only person in the world I've told about this.

Her name was Margot, she was married to someone called Bob, and they had children of their own. More details are hard to come by, but they seem to have been British, with Bob probably a planter in the estates around Shillong. She was in love with Verrier too, but her situation made it equally unlikely that they could go further. Letters were exchanged, assignations made, but beyond that it seemed futile. It is no accident that, some weeks after he unburdened himself to Koestler, Verrier had a heart attack. The doctor's report identified a 'ventricle infracted by a coronary thrombosis.' But the patient would make a characteristic joke: it sounded, he said, 'like a young woman describing how she lost her virginity.' He was prescribed eight weeks' rest, but the papers kept coming. U. N. Dhebar brought some of them when he came to Shillong to ask his member to rewrite a draft of their report.

Whatever his reservations about the other teetotaller-vegetarians, Elwin got on well with Dhebar. Their chief disagreement was on the question of prohibition, which Dhebar recommended and Elwin of course opposed. He told his chairman that 'to the tribal people the necessity of liquor in religious and other ceremonies is as real as wine for use in the Mass is to a Catholic.' The analogy was lost to one more familiar with ashrams than cathedrals, but otherwise Dhebar allowed the scribe his way. With the Gandhian looking on, they translated into plain English '600 pages of admirable suggestions but atrocious writing.' It was hard going, but Elwin welcomed the chance of leaving out a good many things he did not like and putting in other things which required more emphasis. The draft quoted a forest botanist as saying, in 1942, that 'of all practices initiated by man, shifting cultivation is the most noxious,' to which the printed report responded, in Elwin's voice: 'The atom bomb had not, of course, been invented at that time.' By the end he had also made sure that this was the first such report which did not have to use those abominable terms, 'backward,' 'uplift' and 'superstition.'[24]

Dhebar finally flew away in September, but the effort had left Elwin tired and irritable. When a young scholar from Nagpur sent him an essay on the old isolation/assimilation debate he replied in somewhat intemperate tones. 'I think,' he wrote, that 'you give rather too much attention to Dr Ghurye who is so prejudiced against his rivals that his work is generally remarkably inaccurate.' The Nagpur scholar had also suggested that Elwin's two marriages 'indicated his appreciation of the tribal people.' The anthropologist did not see this as a compliment. 'I do not quite see what my private affairs have to do with your argument,' he answered, 'the fact that I could marry two or twenty tribal girls would not necessarily give any indication of my appreciation of the tribal people in general but would merely suggest that in erotic matters I was not limited by racial considerations. Moreover the way it is put does not seem to be in very good taste.'[25]

In the last week of 1961 Elwin was due to give the Sardar Patel lectures on All India Radio—India's Reith Lectures, to stretch the analogy a little. Previous lecturers included the writer-statesman C. Rajagopalachari and the great scientists K. S. Krishnan and J. B. S. Haldane. The sponsors hoped he would speak on tribals, but he answered that the subject was by now 'hackneyed and over-written.' This was true in a way, but perhaps he had no wish to become once again the centre of controversy. He finally chose to speak on the theme of love.[26]

The Patel lectures, entitled *A Philosophy of Love*, are a summing-up of the experiences of a scholar-activist, a conspectus of all the men and ideas that came to influence him. The title is from John Donne, to whom he had been introduced by H. W. Flecker at Dean Close. The lectures draw richly on the work of all those Verrier had loved, and what they had to say about love. He revisits here the Christian mystics—Richard Rolle, Catherine of Genoa, John of the Cross—and their Indian counterparts, Kabir and Mirabai. He comes then to Mahatma Gandhi, who brought down the ideal of love 'almost with a bump, to earth, away from abstractions to [the] realities' of human and national friendships; and ends with a bow to compassion, forgiveness and humility, identified by him as the three virtues cherished by all religions.

Only six pages of *A Philosophy of Love* are devoted to love among the tribes. But the lecturer's lifelong engagement manifests itself in other ways. He insists that erotic love does 'not appear as the enemy of what we call the higher love but part of it'—this in contrast to the 'violent reactions of Christian ascetics' and the 'hypocritical outlook of many Puritans.' As both the tribal and classical Indian traditions recognize, sexual love is a 'good beautiful thing,' an art almost. Modern Indians would do well to study ancient techniques of love-making, not 'to extend their lusts outside the marriage-bond but in order to make a greater success of love within it.'

While drafting the lectures Verrier read a news report of the wedding of one of Mahatma Gandhi's grandsons, with a photograph of the couple being blessed by Morarji Desai. He pasted the report in his diary, writing underneath: ' "We must not let our lusts enter into marriage"—Gandhi.' In fact, when Elwin told All India Radio he would speak not on tribals but on love, they asked him to focus on Gandhi. He answered that 'to take the Gandhian philosophy of love as a subject [would] commit me too much to one point of view.'[27] *A Philosophy of Love* can be read as the last of his arguments with Gandhi, albeit an argument conducted with the greatest courtesy. Inspired perhaps by his Buddhism, there is a mellowness to the book as a whole, an uncharacteristic but welcome respect for faiths that he had once held and since rejected.

Psychologists, notes Elwin, have remarked of the frustrated life of the ascetic that 'the mystics or devotees give to their divine lovers what they have been unable to find on earth:' an interpretation that actually well fits his own early intensely personal love for Christ. He now enters into a disagreement with the Christian ascetic and the Gandhian who regard the married life as 'somehow inferior to celibacy.' In 1933, that belief had persuaded Verrier and Mary Gillet to abandon their partnership. Thirty years and two marriages later, Elwin was convinced that the 'danger in marriage is not that we love too much but that we should love too little.'[28]

By a happy coincidence, immediately following the Patel lectures, Elwin presided over a marriage born of love. Amina Yusuf Ali, a Muslim friend who was also the illustrator of his NEFA books, was to marry a Hindu disciple, Nalini Jayal, of the Indian Frontier Administrative Service. The union was opposed by both families, for Amina came from the high Hyderabad aristocracy, Jayal from the equally conservative Brahmin stock of upper Garhwal. The former Christian and priest took it upon himself to arrange this wedding of Hindu and Muslim. He did it with gusto, offering his house, arranging the decorations, even acting as the bride's father.[29]

For some years now Verrier had been as much out of NEFA as within it, so in February 1962 he turned with pleasure to the design of the next year's official calendar. Previous calendars had always illustrated a theme of his choosing—cottage industry, tribal dances, wildlife preservation—and for 1963 he chose 'Integration.' He planned six portraits of how NEFA might be linked with the rest of India. Each picture would capture a group of tribals in a frame of leafy branches—'to give the idea of the forest setting'—looking at, respectively, the Taj Mahal, a hydroelectric project, a statue of Gandhi, a picture of the president with the vice-president and prime minister, one of Sanchi or Bodh Gaya with the Kamengs (themselves Buddhists) doing the viewing, and last of all 'some scene typifying Assam's history and culture.'[30]

There were parts of NEFA he had not seen; the question was whether he would ever get to them. Files in the secretariat took up his days, the writing of his memoirs the evenings. Despite interested letters from Cape and Hutchinson he had decided to publish his autobiography with Oxford University Press. Home to work and back again; that was the routine he now followed, and in June even this was abbreviated. When he complained of breathlessness the doctor confined him to the house for a month. In July he wrote grumpily to his OUP editor, R. E. Hawkins: 'I am getting better slowly but I am still being bullied by my doctor. Yesterday I got the concession that I might go to the cinema once a week and visit an agreeable friend for half an hour once a week. Otherwise I remain under house-arrest.' In time he was allowed to go back to work, but he could not tour that winter.[31] 'The ban on clambering about over the frontier mountains and losing myself in the wilds,' he wrote to Arthur Koestler, 'has been a very severe blow, for I love the remote, the lonely and the obscure. But these are things that happen, I suppose, if one is presumptuous enough to live to the age of sixty.' Koestler's reply was cheerily reassuring: 'I am not unduly worried about your heart attacks. All my medical friends tell me that a few light attacks at the right age are the best life insurance, though nobody can quite explain why. I know of several paradigmatic octogenarian examples.'[32]

In November 1962 the Chinese marched into NEFA and overran the Indian army, an ill-fed, poorly-clothed and completely unprepared soldiery that had been hitherto drilled to think of their northern neighbours as their 'Asian brothers.' Some officials, fearing the worst, fled Shillong for the plains, but Verrier and Lila refused to 'join the pathetic rank of evacuees.' However, Verrier's blood pressure went up twenty points after the fall of Tawang and a further five points after the fall of Bomdi La. He found it 'agonising to hear of places like Tawang or dear little Jang where Lila and I picked wild strawberries long ago, or Wallong where I did an adventurous air-flight with Khemlal Rathee, falling into the hands of the Chinese.' Luckily Kumar, then a trainee with the Assam Rifles, was not close to the fighting.[33]

The Chinese invasion drew fresh criticism of the philosophy for NEFA. A few months before the war a Major Sitaram Johri published a book critical of the NEFA administration. The book and its arguments were now revived. Elwin and his colleagues were accused of isolating their territory from Assam and India, to deadly effect. The 'NEFA official class,' wrote Major Johri, 'is so drugged with adulation that it would never advocate the "open door" policy in the territory lest their privileges might be curtailed. The NEFA . . . must remain an inaccessible Shangrila for the public.' If NEFA had not been kept separate and distinct, it was implied, the Chinese would not have dared come in. The need now was to 'multiply the area of association and contact with the outside world and not keep [the tribals] within their own narrow circle.'[34] It was even suggested by Opposition politicians in Delhi that 100,000 farmers from Punjab be settled in NEFA, both to further the assimilation of tribals and to dissuade the Chinese from coming again.[35]

Elwin was worried by this last proposal. At another time he would have written to Nehru, but the prime minister was deeply disturbed himself, his authority and political standing eroded by the fiasco on the frontier. So he sent in his protest to Indira Gandhi. Her reply is an early indication of how far she was to depart from her father's politics, a presaging perhaps of the state of Emergency she was to impose on India some thirteen years later. 'Thank you for sending me your notes on NEFA,' she wrote: 'I do agree with much that you say but now that the doors have opened, it will be increasingly difficult to keep out undesirable elements or ideas. This is the price we pay for democracy, [which] not only throws up the mediocre person but gives strength to the most vocal howsoever they may lack knowledge and understanding.'[36]

The India-China war also brought a letter from one who had been out of Verrier's life for thirty years—Mary Gillet. She was working at a teacher's training college in Berkshire, still single, still helping and serving. Mary wrote that the news of the Chinese invasion had placed 'India and you and your family and Shamrao in particular in my thoughts . . . The world doesn't seem to have grown much happier since you and I were young in it! I should love to know India now that the barriers between Indians and English are down.'[37]

The Chinese had gone but Verrier's gloom deepened. When R. E. Hawkins suggested that he name his memoirs 'Pilgrim's Way to NEFA,' he replied that 'there is the difficulty that if you are not likely to publish till 1964, by then I will either be dead or turned out or perhaps NEFA itself may have come to an end.'[38] Meanwhile news came from Mandla that Shamrao was desperately short of money and that his wife had fallen in love with a younger man. Verrier was not in a position to help much, for his health continued to decline. 'I am being filled up with antibiotics which make me feel rather miserable,' he wrote to Hawkins in March of 1963. The next bulletin, three weeks later, complained of 'a rather shattering attack when whatever infection was moving around inflamed both my liver and my gall bladder.'[39]

In April Eldyth arrived for a month's holiday. She had not been in India for twenty-five years and had not seen her brother for fourteen. Reading his autobiography in manuscript she complained about the first chapter. The family's faith, she said, was not as dreary as he made out: could he not show mother and Evangelicalism 'real respect'? As for the rest of the book, though, it was a 'wonderful tale,' an 'unfolding of scientific compassion leading to so much. How pitiful it would be if I tried to write my life!' The day she left Shillong Verrier had another attack. He could not sleep night after night, and was finally admitted to the military hospital and put on oxygen. He corrected the proofs of his memoirs amidst mounting depression. 'Everything is very uncertain,' he told Eldyth, 'China and where we will be ourselves and what is going to happen in India itself.' A big blow was Kumar's failure in the matriculation, for had he passed the exam his father's friends had arranged everything to make him an officer.[40]

Through 1963 Verrier was in and out of hospital. His blood pressure remained high and he complained of breathlessness and heaviness in the chest. From May he had been totally sedentary and worked, when not in hospital, out of home. Writing on 12th June, the governor of Assam conveyed his worries and those of his boss: 'I hope you will be careful and not exert yourself for some time. The Prime Minister whom I met the other day was much concerned about your health.'[41]

The same week there arrived a letter from the great man himself. The cares of a defeated state had diminished his interest in the tribals but not it seems in their defender. Nehru came to Assam to open a new bridge over the Brahmaputra but had not time to go up the hill to Shillong. 'My dear Elwin,' he wrote, 'For many years, whenever I have come to Assam I have looked forward to meeting you. If I had gone to Shillong on this occasion, I would certainly have tried to see you.' He went on: 'I have been much concerned to learn of your ill-health and that you have been in hospital for some time. I hope you are getting well there and the rest is doing you good. I hope to meet you when I next come to this part of the world.'[42]

Also in June came Shamrao Hivale. He was broke and unhappy and must have communicated this to his friend, though no record remains. But Lila's son, then a boy of nine, recalls the visit being shot through with tension, for Sham, always proprietorial about Verrier, 'was very arrogant towards my mother.'[43] Quick on Sham's heels arrived his chief tormentor, Jehangir Patel. Before coming he had written to Verrier that he was considering withdrawing support to the school still run by TWARU in Patangarh; Sham, he said, 'is good for another 15 years work but he is one of the laziest human beings in India.'[44] The judgement was deeply unfair and it is difficult to escape the conclusion that the Bombay millionaires would much rather fund a flamboyantly articulate Englishman than a quietly serving Indian. When Elwin left Patan and TWARU the glamour went out of their sponsorship. Even J. R. D. Tata, requested by Verrier to support Sham, granted him a measly one hundred rupees a month.

The summer, and the month of June most particularly, was the time for Verrier's most loved and longstanding friends to call or send word, to bring to him in his bed the memories and associations that had made and unmade his life. On the 19th a lovely letter arrived from W. G. Archer. He thought back

> to those glorious years from 1940 to 1946 when we were running neck and neck and there seemed no end to the tribal poetry which one or other of us would suddenly reveal. . . . I sometimes wonder despite your work for NEFA your own best time was not in Middle India. I still think that the Baiga

> is your finest book and after that, Folk Songs of the Maikal Hills. How proud I am that you dedicated it to me!

Archer was hoping now to get back to his work on the Santals, which he had set aside in 1949 when he joined the Victoria and Albert Museum: 'The Santal book will get done and you must muster all your breath and rally that stupid old heart so that I can dedicate it to you and we can enjoy together my Santal days. . . . Dear Verrier, you should have died so many times in the past. Don't die now.'[45]

In the autumn came two visitors who have left us cameo impressions of Shillong's greatest man. Armand Denis was writing a Baedeker's guide to quaint tribes and quainter customs and wanted to speak to the author of *The Muria and their Ghotul.* He first heard of Elwin from an old Franciscan in England who remembered Brother Verrier as a 'young man of great beauty and sanctity.' The monk also filled him in on the renegade's friendship with Gandhi and his work with the tribes. Denis arrived in Shillong without an appointment and was told that Elwin was not seeing people: indeed, the previous day he had turned away a lady sociologist from America. But when he rang the house Elwin picked up the phone and, in a 'collector's piece among voices—those high pitched, carefully modulated tones you sometimes hear from elderly high church clergymen', invited him over.

Elwin met the visitor in his dressing-gown, puffing one of those smelly Trichnopoly cigars that so infuriated his doctor. (The patient insisted that the damage had already been done, long ago.) They talked of the Muria and other tribes in a

> remarkable room, crammed with pictures, books and objects of folk art. An iron brazier of charcoal glowed in the centre of the floor. Devil masks from Nepal glared across at a regiment of small gilt buddhas on the table opposite, and above Elwin's own battered armchair hung a painting from Tibet in which an azure-bodied Krishna was gently copulating with a female supplicant.[46]

Tara Ali Baig arrived not long after Armand Denis. This diplomat's-wife-turned-social worker had known Elwin years ago in Bombay when they attended the same parties. Now she had come to talk of her work among village children. She asked a man who knew something of poverty and suffering whether he ever regretted leaving the life of an Oxford don. Elwin answered characteristically with a poem:

> Love had he found in huts where poor men lie;
> His daily teachers were the woods and rills,
> The silence that is in the starry sky
> The sleep that is among the lonely hills.[47]

A third caller was the scholar-wanderer Nirmal Kumar Bose, the other Indian anthropologist of towering moral stature. He and Elwin had disagreed on the tribals in print; in conversation they seem to have argued about Gandhi, whom both had followed and then fought with. Elwin wrote dismissively in his autobiography, then in proofs, of Bose's book on the Mahatma, but it seems he had not read it carefully enough, or at all. 'Dear Dr Elwin,' wrote Bose on his return to Calcutta, 'I am sending you a copy of my book "My Days with Gandhi" and I hope to hear from you when you have finished reading it. May I thank you once again for the fine evening I spent in your home?'[48]

Verrier had now turned his guestroom into a sort of Buddhist shrine. To Koestler, who had stayed in that room and who had written dismissively of his religion, he wrote that he got 'a good deal of consolation' from praying there. Buddhism, he said, 'does not seem to be much good as a social gospel but certainly as a psychological cure for anxiety, desire and anger I find it very effective.'[49]

The visitors stimulated the mind, the meditation calmed the spirit, the body continued to decline. Verrier's doctor and some of his friends thought it would do him good if he moved out of Shillong to a lower altitude. But where could he go? In December he was asked by C. D. Deshmukh, vice-chancellor of the University of Delhi, whether he would spend two months teaching there. The implication was that something more promising and permanent might follow.[50]

On the last day of 1963 Verrier completed an abridgement of *The Muria and their Ghotul*, asked for by the OUP. He returned with a certain melancholy to his days in Bastar and Central India. The original book, he wrote in the new preface, was 'a contemporary record,' this version but 'an aspect of India's tribal history.' 'I believe the ghotul survives,' he remarked, although 'it must have known many changes.' The changes are enumerated without their consequences being stated outright: one thousand schools where there had once been half-a-dozen, the 'great schemes of Community Development' spread out over the district, thousands of refugees from East Pakistan in a forest previously reserved for the Murias. He had been fortunate to be able to record, in 1941–2, 'a unique phase of human development about to disappear.' Many friends had helped him in that endeavour; they were fully acknowledged, he said, in the original edition. But in this shortened version he was 'dominated by the necessity to keep within the spatial limits laid on me by my publishers, and that is the only reason why I do not repeat my obligations here.'[51] The *only* reason? Could there be a second, I wonder, the presence in that book and preface, as indeed in the author's life and love, of his first wife, Kosi?

In January Verrier again experienced heartache, a 'mild cerebro-vascular spasm' according to the doctor's report. For a fortnight he could not lift his right arm. On the 26th, Republic Day, he dictated a preface for a source-book on the judicial and political institutions of NEFA. The volume was composed of notes on tribal councils compiled by his colleagues in the NEFA Research Department. In publishing them he hoped that in time 'more and more responsibility for development will be transferred from officialdom to the tribal bodies. There can be no doubt that this will do a great deal to give the people self-confidence, to make them feel that they are masters of their own destiny and that nothing is being imposed on them, and to forward true progress throughout the hills.'[52]

All his life Elwin had urged on the powerful the claims of the powerless and presented to the centre the perspective of the periphery. It was his privilege to move with ease from one sphere to another, to feel equally at home with prime ministers and peasants. The book on political decentralization sent to press, he now prepared to visit the citadel of political power in Delhi. He was due there on the 20th of February to attend a meeting of the Frontier Services Selection Board. On the 8th he wrote to Eldyth that he was not very keen on going, 'but I think as they are now considering the question of my extension in service, it will be a good thing for me to put in an appearance and show myself looking fit and well.' He always liked to help pick young officers for NEFA and hoped also to meet Deshmukh about the Delhi professorship.

Between the 11th and 15th Verrier was not at all well. He was breathing with difficulty and hardly sleeping at night. The heart-specialist examined him and advised against the trip, which was to be in a pressurized aircraft. Verrier argued with him for more than half-an-hour. If he had to go, said the doctor, he must take periodic rest and avoid foods that caused flatulence; he also prescribed five different pills.[53] His personal assistant, S. Lahiri, also asked Verrier not to go. He agreed, but next day sent the P.A. a note saying, 'I think I will defy the doctors after all and go.' He drove down to Guwahati on the 19th to board a plane for Calcutta and thence on to Delhi. When he reached the capital he sent Lila a telegram saying he was fine.

In Delhi Verrier stayed with K. L. Rathee, a former financial adviser to the NEFA administration. On the 20th he spent the whole day with the selection committee. The next morning he called on Jawaharlal Nehru, one supposes to keep him up-to-date on NEFA. Verrier had not met him for more than two years, but it was of books and tribals they must have talked that day. In the afternoon Verrier visited the home ministry. His young colleague Rashid Yusuf Ali now worked there; when Verrier walked into his office he had on his desk a fresh proposal to send sturdy Punjabi farmers to settle in NEFA. It came from a senior politician, a Hindu who complained bitterly that the north-east was run by a Muslim chief secretary of Assam (Kidwai), a Parsi adviser to the governor (N. K. Rustomji), and a Christian (Elwin), who apparently commanded the most influence of all.[54]

The critic was out-of-date, his criticisms unfair and certain to wound. Elwin was back in the home ministry the next morning, the 22nd, it seems to find ways of keeping the intruders out. He returned to the Rathees for lunch. That evening he complained of heartache, and was rushed to Willingdon Hospital. Here he was put on oxygen but his condition deteriorated and within two hours he was dead. As William Paton had predicted many years earlier, Verrier Elwin killed himself in India with overwork.

On the 23rd Nehru was the first to offer a wreath. The next day the body was flown to Shillong. Elwin was cremated here on the afternoon of the 24th, amidst the chanting of Buddhist hymns. The ashes were then taken to a lonely, glorious spot on the Siang river, where they were immersed by his eldest son, Kumar. His P.A. conveyed an apology to his sister Eldyth. 'You may be hurt to hear about his funeral,' wrote S. Lahiri, 'but it was his desire that he should be cremated. He expressed this desire to many people.'[55] The son of the bishop had rebelled to the end.

CHAPTER FOURTEEN

Outsider Within: The Worlds of Verrier Elwin

I understand more clearly today what I read long ago about the inadequacy of all autobiography as history. I know that I do not set down in this story all that I remember. Who can say how much I must give and how much omit in the interests of truth? And what would be the value in a court of law of the inadequate ex parte evidence being tendered by me of certain events in my life? If some busybody were to cross-examine me on the chapters already written, he could probably shed much more light on them, and if it were a hostile critic's cross-examination, he might even flatter himself for having shown up the 'hollowness of many of my pretensions.'

M. K. Gandhi, *The Story of My Experiments with Truth*

How can the autobiographer tell the real truth. . . .? Since he has chosen to write, he is an artist, he is a man who feels, like every artist, the need of escape; and if his narrative is to be a real escape, there must be for the author the pretext of a life more in keeping with his desires than his own life has actually been. To endow himself with this life, he will do what the novelist does; he will create it. The only difference between him and the novelist is that, as he creates it, he will say, and perhaps even believe, that it is his own, whilst the novelist is conscious of his creative act.

André Maurois

How perfect that he wrote this [auto]biography himself, and with such obvious pleasure, before it was too late and when some other hand would have had to write it.

Maeve Scott, friend of Elwin, writing to R. E. Hawkins

The historian David Cannadine once remarked that biography is the only certain form of life after death. He had apparently forgotten about autobiography. For every autobiography is a pre-emptive strike against the future biographer, a formidable and frequently unbeatable challenge to the authenticity of his work. Fortunate the biographer whose subject has not left his own memoirs; he has no carefully crafted record to contend with, to clarify or contest. But here we have to reckon with Verrier Elwin's own remarkable memoirs, finished in his lifetime and published three months after his death.

'What shall I find in your biography that I won't in Elwin's autobiography?' This is a question often asked of me, and with good reason. For *The Tribal World of Verrier Elwin: An Autobiography* is a smooth, coherent, and most readable narrative of a man's life and times. Its plot is exquisite in its simplicity. A young priest out of Oxford meets Mahatma Gandhi and is instantly transformed, reborn as an Indian on Indian soil. His life given over to Gandhi and India, his subsequent missions in central and north-eastern India then follow as exemplifications of this devotion to his adopted land. Elwin's autobiography thus emphasizes the part played by the Mahatma's great lieutenants, Vallabhbhai Patel and Jamnalal Bajaj, in his move to Mandla; so also the significance of the personality and ideas of Nehru in the making of the philosophy for NEFA. So also the urgent desperation with which Elwin scoured the sources for a picture of himself with Gandhi in Sabarmati: and when the original was untraceable, he included nonetheless a 'reprint of a reprint of a reprint of a one-time photograph.'[1] Thus too the scrupulous omission of his controversies with other Indians, whether politicians, social workers, or anthropologists.

The preface to *Tribal World* freely acknowledges that 'much of it is written from the Indian point of view;' indeed, Elwin almost called it the 'Autobiography of a British-born Indian.'[2] Within this organizing principle, the book contains evocative descriptions of Oxford and of his early years in India, crisp accounts of the tribes he worked with in the thirties and forties, and finally an extended treatment of his 'philanthropological' work in the North East Frontier Agency. While the first part of the book makes for marvellous reading, the narrative grows more bland with the autobiographer's rise to prominence. With Elwin determined to name and acknowledge every official he knew, high or low, the NEFA chapters read like a long thank you letter to his Indian friends.

Elwin had in fact first thought of writing his memoirs well before he went to NEFA. In 1949 his friend R. E. Hawkins, who ran the Indian branch of Oxford University Press, received a letter from his counterpart in New York, wondering whether Elwin, clearly a 'remarkable character,' could be persuaded to write his autobiography, which when published 'could be something of a sensation in the good sense.' Knowing his friend to be in dire straits—this was roughly the time Elwin was 'a poor white thinking up unprintable jokes' in Patangarh—Hawkins passed on the suggestion, noting that Jim Corbett had made eight thousand dollars in the first year out of the American edition of his *Man Eaters of Kumaon*, a book that was in its own way the autobiography of a remarkable character.[3]

Then recovering from a bruising divorce, Elwin was not interested. When he did begin his autobiography thirteen years later, the prospect of earning some money for a growing family was one motive; the desire to record his life before anybody else did was a second. The long periods of rest prescribed by the doctor after his heart attack, alongside the ban on touring, enabled him to work almost uninterruptedly on the book, which was sent to Hawkins in March 1962.

Memoirs are made of memories, but as André Maurois once noted the autobiographer's memory 'not only fails, whether by the simple process of time or by deliberate censorship, but, above all, it rationalizes; it creates, after the event, the feelings or the ideas which might have been the cause of the event, but which in fact are invented by us after it has occurred.'[4] Here the correspondence between Elwin and Hawkins provides glimpses of the many pitfalls in the writing of Elwin's memoirs, and of how the writer attempted to negotiate them. Recognizing that it would be 'extremely difficult to be quite sure what to say when writing one's own life,' he asked his editor and friend of twenty years to point out anything that struck the wrong note, 'anything pretentious or pompous or dull.' Hawkins commented that the book revealed very little about Elwin the writer. 'You are chiefly known by your books,' he remarked, 'and I should have expected a much larger part of your autobiography to be concerned with the writing of them—the gathering of material, difficulties of working far from libraries, methods, contacts with other anthropologists, etc.'

Hawkins also complained that the book revealed little of Elwin the man. He could understand Verrier's reluctance to give his *vie amourese*, but not his reticence on the background to the dramatic shifts in his life: the struggle with Christianity, the rejection of civilization, the marriage to a tribal girl, the final adoption of Indian citizenship. The reader, especially the Western reader, wrote Hawkins, 'would like to know far more than you tell him here about the reasons which led you to take these steps, and the mental anguish that must have accompanied many of them.' But as it stood this was a serenely happy book. 'My grouse, indeed,' remarked the publisher who understood Elwin's life better than almost anybody else, 'is that you have omitted nearly all the shadows.'[5]

Elwin knew this too. He wrote to Arthur Koestler saying he had been re-reading his own draft autobiography alongside Koestler's published one: 'What an astonishing different kind of life we each have had! I very much liked your chapter on "Pitfalls for an Autobiographer" but looking at it again yesterday I came to the conclusion that I have fallen into almost all of them.'[6] For all this, he was to disregard R. E. Hawkins' advice. 'My path,' wrote Elwin in the preface to the printed book, 'has sometimes been shadowed by clouds and I have hinted at them in the following pages, but I have not enlarged on them, for I don't think they are very interesting.' A tame apologia perhaps, but whatever it was, the *Tribal World of Verrier Elwin* sidesteps or moves quickly past the major turning points in his life, with the one exception being his break with the Church.

The writing of Elwin's autobiography was shaped by his vulnerability as a British-born Indian, and by his own desire not to rake up or revive controversy. On 9th August 1963, by which time the page proofs were being processed, he sent in what was 'one final—and this is really final—alteration.' In view of the 'rather strained relations between Assam and NEFA at present,' he had added a paragraph 'mentioning my Assam friends.' 'It will not make any difference to the value of the book,' he said, 'but it may make a good deal of difference to me here.'[7] Hawkins accepted the paragraph but then wrote the next week of his wish to sell pre-publication excerpts to the *Illustrated Weekly of India.* Elwin answered to say that the OUP must on no account draw on the NEFA chapters: these were all right when read in the book, but 'if they appear in bits in a periodical they would be bound to cause trouble and I do not want to enter into controversy at this juncture.'[8]

Till the last moment Elwin was editing his text for personal and political rather than literary reasons or the interests of accuracy and greater self-revelation. In the archives of the OUP is a copy of the manuscript almost as it appeared in print, with only a few paragraphs scored out. Excised is a passage describing how he differs from other primitivists in going to the forest without a 'return ticket'—perhaps he thought this did not sit well with the British tradition of self-deprecation. Removed is an innocent joke—'Since I came to India I have never used toilet-paper at home but made do with newspaper—the savings mount up over the years:' he may have thought this would be taken by humourless *lota*-using nationalists as proof that he was never really Indian. Another witty remark taken out at the proof stage pokes fun at Gandhians and *babu* English: 'the Puritan attack is essentially on sex and perhaps the journalist who wrote that the followers of Gandhi are "joy-kills who do not understand the rupture [*sic*] of love" was not far off the mark.'

Most revealing of all is the removal of two comments on his friend Arthur Koestler's book *The Lotus and the Robot.* There had been much hostility to its representation of Indian spiritual traditions and the Government of India had taken typically the stupid and not unprecedented step of banning the book. Elwin, to whom Koestler's book was dedicated, had remarked that the ban was 'an unfortunate and mistaken act.' To 'someone trained in the Oxford tradition of criticism,' it seemed 'almost incredible that a great country should ban a book on religious grounds.'[9]

Elwin's autobiography, in a word, smoothly suppresses the complexity and ambiguities of his life in presenting to the world a mostly happy tale of an Englishman becoming Indian and an Oxford scholar going native. Almost the only indication of the shadows lies in the cover portrait, drawn by the Polish emigré artist Otto Kadlescovics. The artist's interpretation of the man was altogether more complex than the self-portrait in the book itself. Kadlescovics thus explained his drawing:

> The nightmarish masks represent the temptations of the soul. The Naga ones suggest the urge to violence and hatred and among the others are masks of envy and pride. The Eyes represent, in one case the eyes of desire

> lusting for the world and its pleasures, and the large single one is the sardonic, critical eye. [Verrier] looks on the world in three different ways—with spiritual idealistic eyes, slightly masked by tobacco-smoke; with eyes that love beauty; and a last eye that was critical and perhaps slightly sinister.[10]

For all that it leaves out, Elwin's autobiography remains a charming and sometimes moving book. Published so soon after his death, with his memory and work fresh in the mind, it received a wonderful reception. In May 1963, as the book went to press, Hawkins wrote to Eldyth Elwin of his hope that 'Verrier will be alive to see the reviews.'[11] In the event it was left to Elwin's sister, editor and friends to glory in the praise which followed the book's publication.

In India the book was read as an account of an exemplary Indian; in the United Kingdom, where it overcame the disadvantage of being released on Election Day, it was the story of an eccentrically gifted and risk-loving Englishman; in the United States people saw it as the testimony of the brilliant scholar who turned his back on civilization. His sister was to complain that the blurb of the American edition 'twice refers to "natives!" What would Verrier say!'[12] But the word was being used strategically by the publisher even if it was not, by Eldyth's norms and ours, politically correct. In all three countries *The Tribal World of Verrier Elwin* was widely and generously reviewed. To be sure, there were critical remarks. But these tended to be on points of detail. An Indian anthropologist of the younger generation noted that Elwin's policies for the tribes had the logic of 'poetry and romance,' though not always the 'logic of economics and politics.' The British writer Naomi Mitchison, whose brother J. B. S. Haldane became an Indian citizen not long after Elwin, felt the author sometimes saw things 'almost too much from the best Indian point of view.' One reviewer wished the book had more of Shamrao, the lifelong companion whose calm support allowed Elwin to produce 'stupendous work' despite an 'unsteadiness of temperament.' A critic in the *New York*

Times wondered at the absence of a proper account of either of his two marriages. And the smouldering resentments of the Assamese intelligentsia surfaced for one last time in a review which complained that Elwin till the end

> seemed to be very meticulous against the non-tribals coming to NEFA for fear that the latter might exploit [the tribals]. But while this view was appreciated as having some value, it was also pointed out by his critics that if the tribes were allowed to grow and develop [isolated] from the people of the plains [i.e. the Assamese], the task of forging an assimilation at a later stage might have to face formidable difficulties.[13]

All these criticisms, however, only qualified the most extravagant praise of the book as a 'fascinating and remarkable' document; and of the man as one who lived in an 'astonishing and admirable state of near-Christian grace.' Writing of the scholar, the Indian anthropologist S. C. Dube noted that Elwin 'was not a dry-as-dust technician; he was a poet, an artist and a philosopher' who by his 'individual effort produced more and better work than many of the expensively staffed and large research organizations in the country.' Writing of the man, Naomi Mitchison said Elwin 'was one of the small handful of people whom I, in my spiritual arrogance, genuinely respected . . . If there were a few thousand Verrier Elwins about, one would really begin to feel quite hopeful about the world.' An anonymous reviewer in *The Statesman* summed up the loss to literature and to humanity. When news came of Elwin's sudden death, he wrote, 'from secretariat to little mud huts, from NEFA to Madhya Pradesh, in urban artistic, literary and journalistic circles as in remote villages, many thousands who had met or read of him knew that greatness had departed.'[14] A compliment the author would have liked came in the form of the Sahitya Akademi award, only the third time the Indian Academy of Letters had honoured a book written in English. The citation said that *The Tribal World* was 'written with sincerity, courage and charm;' it 'reveals a mind in which Western and Indian idealism were uniquely blended.'

The most remarkable tribute of all was from the pen of the Bombay poet Nissim Ezekiel. Elwin's autobiography was written with 'great charm and persuasion;' one of its great merits, wrote Ezekiel, was that 'his final position on all matters is made absolutely clear. There is not a single ambiguous sentence in [the book] and yet [no] dogmatic pronouncement in it.'[15] That so sensitive a poet was taken in by the smoothness of the narrative is testimony to Elwin's success in banishing from the book the shadows that so relentlessly followed him through his thirty-seven years in India.

It was the pioneer of modern biographical studies, Leslie Stephen, who noted that an autobiography is interesting not so much for what it contains as for what it leaves out. A more contemporary, hence more cynical, critic puts it this way:

> Not all but a fair part of the pleasure of reading autobiography is in catching the autobiographer out in suspicious reticences, self-serving misconceptions, cover-ups, and of course, delightfully clever deceptions. What is he hiding, what's he withholding, why doesn't he talk about his first wife, who's he kidding leaving out his children, odd he never mentions money—such are the questions that roam randomly through your normally licentious reader of autobiography. The intelligent person reads autobiography for two things: the facts and the lies, knowing that the lies are far more interesting than the facts.[16]

One man who appears to have read Verrier Elwin's autobiography in this light was R. E. Hawkins, before it was published; another who certainly did but after it appeared in print was Bill Archer. Asked to review the book by a London newspaper, Archer wrote a handsome tribute, highlighting those aspects of Elwin's work that most appealed to him: the dazzling revelations of the role of love and sex in tribal life, and the marvellous renditions of tribal songs which were quite 'the best translations of Eastern poetry since Arthur Waley.' Elwin, wrote Archer in a claim no one can possibly dispute, had through his thirty-year involvement 'got to know more about India's tribes than any Englishman or Indian before or since.'[17]

Sometimes reviews conceal as much as autobiographies. In a series of scribbled notes he wrote for himself, Archer raised powerful and disturbing questions that he kept out of his printed appreciation of *The*

Tribal World of Verrier Elwin. These notes are a strange mixture of insight and invective. They reveal intimate knowledge as well as unrestrained envy. Bill Archer had wanted to stay on in India. Abruptly posted out of the Naga hills in 1947, he returned to England with some reluctance. Here he carved out a new and successful career as a historian of Indian art, while watching from afar his friend emerge as a figure of high esteem in independent India.

Archer's private comments on Elwin's autobiography first take up some methodological questions: the relationship between 'the writer and his material—the methods and ethics of the freelance do-gooder—but perhaps above all the problem of *whether an Englishman can ever become truly Indian.* Elwin took Indian nationality and his book reveals all the shifts, evasions, compromises that he had to resort to in order to reside as an Indian public figure in the land.' Archer concludes that the book was 'not a declaration of genuine belief' but 'just a bit of propaganda for his continued support by the [Indian] Government.'

Turning from the book's intent to its tone, Archer found it to be 'so effusive that everyone including himself disappears in a haze.' There were

> no personal reactions to anyone or anything
> . . . what made him tick?
> how did he see himself?
> did he believe in anything?
> what made him write?
> what made him become boringly scientific?
> why did he cover up?
> the utter mess and muddle at Patangarh—
> . . . what were his field methods?
> how did he write?
> why did he lose all touch with England?
> on none of these does he say a thing.

Alongside these criticisms Archer's notes contain sharp observations on the man himself. His comments have a peculiar hit-and-miss quality to them, occasionally right on target, at other times wide off the mark. In the first category falls the observation that Elwin 'did not like Hindus and was awkward in their company,' the only Indians he identified with being 'tribals and Westernized ones;' in the second class comes the astonishing charge that Elwin was himself the 'great destroyer' of tribal life who, by publicizing it, 'blew it up on the screen,' attracting the anti-tribal outsider and reformer.

There is a sharpness to Archer's remarks that sometimes borders on the brutal. He claims that Elwin 'never really shed the clergyman's approach—he was always announcing virtues and ideals:' the remark has some truth to it but its manner of expression betrays bitter hostility and prejudice. In the midst of his fusillade Archer pauses briefly to acknowledge what was original about Elwin—this was the 'clear vivid style—the gift for the passionate rhetoric—the neat story—the poet-translator:' his great achievement being 'the discovery of Indian sex and tribal poetry.' All this pertains to Elwin the writer, the pioneering ethnographer of the tribes of central India. Archer disregards or dismisses Elwin's work as an Englishman for India, as well as his claims for applied anthropology advanced in his influential *A Philosophy for NEFA* and in the autobiography itself.[18]

In reading Verrier Elwin's autobiography for its silences and evasions, Bill Archer provided an indirect justification for the present work. Ten years before Archer, the ground had been cleared by Shamrao Hivale, albeit in his own characteristically loving way. While conveying Verrier's decision to wed a second tribal girl to a family traumatized by the fact and failure of the first marriage, he wrote:

> Anyway all these geniuses, poets, prophets and reformers are queer and often quite mad and so why worry? Now that they are telling us truths about these great men like Ruskin, Wordsworth and others—actually one begins to like them much better than before when we felt they were so terribly "proper" or even saints. I wonder what we shall feel if we live to read in cold print the entire truth about Verrier! So my dear Eldyth, if this marriage has upset you or mother Elwin or the rest of the family and friends, I think we ought not let it make *any difference* in our regard or love for him.[19]

I cannot claim to have provided 'the entire truth about Verrier.' But I have tried to do what no autobiographer can: to situate a life and work in context, providing a perspective of their time and place. I have also dogged the shadows which Elwin chose to keep out of his own book and so reveal that his life was more troubled and altogether more interesting than he made it out to be. The life as I see it was marked by paradox, by twist and turn. The son of a bishop who was trained to follow him fought bitterly with the church; the celibate disciple of Gandhi who dissented and left him became a celebrator and chronicler of sex; the once-fervent Indian nationalist who defended the aboriginals against a homogenizing nationalism; the associate of Nehru was loathed, and was loathed by, other Congressmen in independent India; the anthropologist who would much rather be a novelist; the Englishman who lived and loved with the tribes. Of these juxtapositions Elwin himself wrote only of the first and last, and then in a misleading way, as if to go from Christian to anti-Christian, or from Oxford to Patangarh, were moves that were for the most part painless.

But let me end with one of Bill Archer's questions. Can an Englishman ever become truly Indian? Responding to the same book and the same question, but recalling a life spent in sacrifice and service to the Indian poor, another reviewer answered: 'Elwin showed us how to be an Indian, what it is to be an Indian.'[20] Days after his death an editorial in the *Amrita Bazaar Patrika* spoke likewise of India losing 'not only her most eminent anthropologist but another—and perhaps the last—of those liberal-minded Englishmen who had made this country their home and completely identified themselves with its people.' And there was also, in the same issue of the Calcutta newspaper, a poignant insert placed by the staff and actors of a famous Bengali stage company:

> In memory of
> Dr Verrier Elwin
> the best of Indians.[21]

These emphatic endorsements do not of course invalidate Archer's original question, which might in fact be put in other ways. Can an Oxford scholar ever go truly native? Or a novelist become a scientist? Or a political dissenter a high state official?

That, indeed, is the singular theme of Elwin's life. The man was apparently *always* out of place, always where tradition and history least expected him to be: a clergyman with Gandhi, a scholar in a tribal hamlet, a poet in the science of anthropology, a rebel with an office in the secretariat. Placed on the margins, poised uncertainly between two worlds, he would imaginatively interpret one world to another. In his life and in all his work there is visible a passionate desire to make adversaries see the truth in each other: to show Hindus the mystical side of Christianity, for example, or the British the justice of the Indian demand for freedom, or ethnography what it might learn from literature, or the civilized world what it might learn from the tribes.

In this century it has been Verrier Elwin, more than anyone else, who has shown us that the dialogue of cultures need not always be a dialogue of the deaf.

EPILOGUE

Disputed Legacies

On 20th May 1964 the *Times of India* reported that the Government of India wished to endow a fellowship in Verrier Elwin's memory. The award was conceived in the cross-cultural spirit in which he lived his life, for it was to be given to an anthropologist who wished to work 'in remote and inaccessible corners of the world outside India.' The initiative apparently came from Mrs Indira Gandhi and from the education minister, M. C. Chagla, a Bombay jurist who knew or knew of Elwin.[1]

The newspaper report was the first and last thing one heard of the Elwin Fellowship. Jawaharlal Nehru died the following week, and his daughter and their nation went into deep and prolonged mourning. The Nehruvians forgot about the anthropologist but he had meanwhile been rediscovered by the Gandhians. In July 1964 a South Indian follower of the Mahatma came across a copy of one of Elwin's pamphlets in a used bookstore. Elwin had written *Religious and Cultural Aspects of Khadi* in 1931; shortly thereafter he had repudiated both khadi and its most famous proponent. This rebellion was underplayed in Elwin's lately published autobiography, and it was to be thoroughly tamed when the khadi pamphlet was republished towards the end of 1964. Its discoverer and printer procured an admiring preface from Vinoba Bhave, Gandhi's self-appointed spiritual successor. 'The little brochure of Verrier Elwin is ever green,' wrote Bhave, 'I read it through and through. It is so inspiring.' Elwin himself was introduced by the publisher as a

> British anthropologist devoted to Gandhiji. Immediately after his education, he went to Africa to serve the people there. But he came back to India and devoted his whole life to the service of the aborigines in the Madhya

> Pradesh. He identified himself with the aborigines and he married an aboriginal lady and devoted his whole life for their uplift. After India became free, he took the responsibility of a Welfare Officer among the aborigines till he passed away recently.[2]

Thus was the dissident's career refashioned as a life of devoted service to the Mahatma and Mother India, and the opponent of uplift and welfare was thereby turned into its votary. This was a misdescription for which, it must be admitted, *The Tribal World of Verrier Elwin* provided a handy model. Another effective way of dealing with the rebel was found by his old school, Dean Close. Elwin was by any reckoning an outstanding product of a less-than-celebrated institution, but when an Official History was published in 1966 it omitted to mention him, this despite his many contributions to literature and scholarship.[3] The school, unsurprisingly, had long been embarrassed by Elwin's career. Well before the History, an alumni directory had appeared in 1950: this marked the years of Elwin's entry to and exit from Dean Close, listed the academic prizes he won at Oxford, and went on to enumerate the string of acceptable achievements—'Ordained in 1926; Vice Principal, Wycliffe Hall; Chaplain and Lecturer in Theology, Merton College; Examining Chaplain to Bishop of Blackburn,' etc., before abruptly ending, thus: '1928, Poona, India.' Twenty-two years rich in incident and achievement were wiped out.[4] Now, in the nineties, the school continues to regard Elwin as 'something of a black sheep in comparison with his near contemporary Bishop Stephen Neill,' whose career they would rather more willingly memorialize.[5]

What Verrier Elwin did after 1928 could be forgotten by Christians in Cheltenham but not in India. A Naga historian writing in 1974 gently criticized Elwin for his criticism of missionaries, arguing that it was Christianity that pushed the Nagas 'out of the seclusion and isolation from which they were suffering for centuries into [contact with the] open ideas, ideals and civilizations of the peoples of the world.'[6] To be deplored is better than to be ignored: in any case, there are Indian Christians who cheerfully concede that Elwin had a point. A Jesuit theologian of Poona, a spokesman for religious pluralism, wrote in 1984 of the deep-seated intolerance of Christian missionaries working in India, of a history of religious barbarism peppered with 'rare but notable exceptions—a de Nobili, a Rice, a C. F. Andrews, a Verrier Elwin.'[7] The essence of the exception has since been distilled in a fine anthology of Elwin's religious writings published in 1993 by the Indian Society for Promoting Christian Knowledge. This volume's editor suggested, much as Verrier's mother had back in 1936, that the church lost him because it was not tolerant and far-sighted enough.[8] Verrier's former colleague in the Christa Seva Sangh, Leonard Schiff, also felt sorry that his great work was done outside and frequently in opposition to the church. 'The then Bishop of Nagpur must answer for a lot here,' Schiff told an interviewer in 1971: 'The Bishop could only think in terms of the law, and his approach to Elwin was pedestrian.'[9]

One thinks that the church would have lost Elwin anyway. Even if a less dogmatic spiritual director had persuaded him to stay on in 1935, the attractions of the tribal ethos would sooner or later have come in conflict with the imperatives of Christian proselytization. However, the Indian church is *now* more catholic and accommodating of other faiths, perhaps in some small measure due to the labours of Elwin and his ilk. It is also more reliably patriotic, as witness an interdenominational gathering at St Columbus' Cathedral in New Delhi on 15th August 1997. Catholics, Syrian Christians, Baptists, Pentecostals, Methodists, even Anglicans, here offered to the fiftieth anniversary of Indian independence a scroll which pledged to help 'keep the integrity of our beloved country and well being of the people above all narrow and divisive considerations.'[10]

Elwin's rebellion against the third of his churches, Science, was always half-hearted and incomplete. But where the Gandhians and Christians have sought, not always convincingly, to reclaim him, the academics continue to view him with distrust. While he lived, professional anthropologists saw Elwin as a diligent fieldworker and a writer of exceptional sensitivity whose theories, alas, were both inadequate and out of date. One review can stand in for a dozen. Reviewing the *The Religion of an Indian Tribe*, the famous Africanist Victor Turner acknowledged the author's 'vivid and elegant prose,' the 'aesthetic fastidiousness of his photography and illustrations,' while regretting the 'omission of a prior analysis of the social and political structure'—that is, of the rules of property and inheritance, as well as the rights and obligations of different segments of Saora society.

This was written in 1957. A decade later, and with Elwin dead, Victor Turner returned to the book in a long essay commissioned for a research primer on *The Craft of Social Anthropology*. He complained here that Elwin 'does not write as a social anthropologist but as an eclectic ethnographer, and where he interprets, he uses the language of a theologian.' In an essay addressed to the aspiring anthropologist, Turner provides pointers to the 'sociological analysis of the structural relationships within and between Saora villages' that could have provided 'an indispensable introduction to Elwin's study of Saora ritual.' For that study had little to say of the modes of succession and inheritance, the magnitude and mobility of villages, the forms of conflict, the social composition of households and hamlets, and the links between kinship, residence and marriage. Instead of 'the systematic collection of this kind of data,' all Elwin had provided were bare 'morsels of sociological information' interpolated in descriptions of religious custom.[11]

And thus the scientific anthropologist made an example of the eclectic ethnographer who had an eye for an interesting problem, but not the nerve or technique to work towards its successful resolution. A Cambridge scholar, inspired by both Turner and Elwin, has since studied the practice of shamanism among the Saora. This is only one of a series of recent re-studies of Elwin's tribes and themes by professional anthropologists. One aspirant has lived in the Muria ghotul, a second in the Baiga Chak, a third with the Bonda in his highlands. In each case the student has been inspired by Elwin to do fieldwork among a tribe he studied, to provide a fuller and more scientific account of the community and its institutions. By revisting sites studied by Elwin forty years previously, in the hope of proving him wrong or merely half-right, the professionals are (perhaps without knowing it, and certainly without admitting it) paying handsome tribute to the amateur.[12] Would that their books were as readable!

Not all scholars have studied Elwin only to correct or criticize him. A few gathered soon after Elwin's death to bring out a well-rounded *festschrift* in his memory, an unusual honour for a man who did not teach in a university nor who, in a formal sense, ever had students.[13] And a constructive tribute was offered by a group of metallurgists who chanced upon one of Elwin's less-known monographs. They used his evidence and documentation to recreate a functioning Agaria furnace, displayed at the Congress on Traditional Sciences hosted by the Indian Institute of Technology, Bombay, in December 1993.

The people in the places studied by the roving anthropologist have also proposed memorials to remember him by. When Elwin's ashes were sent for immersion to upper Siang, a portion was set aside for safe keeping at the Gompa in Mankhota, it seems for a future memorial asked for by the tribals of the valley.[14] Then in 1979 an official of the Madhya Pradesh government, himself an ethnographer *manqué*, suggested the setting up of an Elwin Memorial Institute in Mandla town—'equipped with an auditorium, a library, and a research unit for social-anthropology'—in tribute to a scholar whose books and essays had made the people of the district known throughout the world.[15] Most recently, a Bastar journalist and social activist, Mohammed Iqbal, has proposed the renovation of Elwin's old house near the Chitrakot falls, and its use as a home and practising exhibition for tribal art and craft.[16] That none of these schemes have thus far borne fruit is because of the Indian culture of memorial-building, in which private initiative must necessarily come to naught in the absence of state sanction and support.

We might remember Elwin as Gandhian, Christian, or anthropologist, but he would want to be remembered most of all as the defender of the aboriginal. What then of the fate of the tribals he lived and loved with? Have the Adivasis of central India been wiped out with the malarial mosquito, and the tribes of the north-east succumbed to the blandishments of civilization? Is there any trace *anywhere* of his philosophy and practice?

Travelling through Elwin's home district of Mandla one sees signs of the continuing struggle between isolation and assimilation. The Gonds still dance and drink—I was lucky to go there during festival time—and retain a proud sense of their identity. In Patangarh now are slogans on the walls calling people to vote for the Gondwana Party, a new formation which stands for a separate province for the tribals. 'Jai Bara Deo jai Gondwana,' the slogan runs, an affirmation of the ancient and distinctly non-Hindu deity of the Gonds. But driving down the valley we saw other and possibly more telling signs. In the village of Chandanghat, by the Narmada river on the pilgrim route, we spied a brand new building, plastered an austere white, advertising a 'Saraswati Savarkar Shishu Mandir.' It was a school promoted by the Rashtriya Swayamsevak Sangh, run to reclaim the tribals to the mother religion, and named both for the Hindu goddess of learning and the most fanatical of Hindu nationalists.

The cultural battle is unresolved, but in independent India, as Elwin feared, it is the pressures of economic development that have told most heavily on the tribals. Their forests have been encroached upon by paper mills, their lands inundated by dams or destroyed by mines. Unhappily, the resources most needed by an industrializing society—water, wood, minerals—are found in India only where tribals live. So the tribals have had to make way for factories and mines, but not without a fight. In this imperfect but not unsubstantial democracy, tribals remain uneducated but not necessarily unrepresented. For one thing, they are assured under law of seven-and-a-half per cent of all jobs in government and of all seats in parliament and state legislatures. For another, the relatively open political system allows for, and even encourages, non-violent protest.[17]

The juxtaposition of economic loss and political voice comes out most clearly in the controversy over the Sardar Sarovar Dam. This dam, being built on a river that Elwin knew so well and lived so close to for so long, will displace some 100,000 people, more than half of whom are tribals. A Narmada Bachao Andolan, led by a forty-year-old woman activist, Medha Patkar—someone from civilization who turned her back on it, like our hero—has won much praise and some hostility by organizing strikes, blockades, and fasts to stop the construction. Patkar and her colleagues speak for the 'victims of development,' but development's beneficiaries have spoken loudly too. The anti-dam movement has been met by an equally strong pro-dam movement, made up of the farmers and politicians of Gujarat, the state where will flow the irrigation water from the project. Picked up by a press that is the most articulate in Asia, the Narmada debate brings back, for the historically minded, the Ghurye-Elwin controversy of the 1940s. Consider these comments of an aggresively modernising economist, speaking to an audience of urban upper-class Indians:

> Those opposed to the dams on the Narmada are . . . outraged by the displacement of tribals from their traditional areas and way of life . . . [But] I would like an India where all tribals are made richer and more sophisticated than me within two generations . . . I believe we must give the tribals education, medicine, roads and the comforts we take for granted. The moment we do so, however, they will cease to be tribals, and become like us. That, I believe, is what we must strive for. . . . Instead of trying to preserve tribals in jungles, let us move to a world where all tribals are taken out of jungles and converted into ex-tribals like us.[18]

And with them, or rather against them, view these remarks from a dissenting report submitted to the World Bank, which had been an enthusiastic sponsor of the dam project:

> Many tribal people in the submergence villages . . . spoke to us about their land and way of life: they often referred to a timeless relationship with the earth, the forest, and the animals. They identified themselves with their land and with the river. . . .
>
> Our opinion is that the evidence demonstrates the tribal status of a large proportion of people to be affected by Sardar Sarovar Projects . . . Concern for such groups is an aspect of the world's increased awareness of how isolated cultures have all too often paid an appalling price for development. The mechanisms by which they become separated from their lands and stripped of their own cultural integrity are all too well known.[19]

The ghost of Elwin is also visible in the report of the Bhuria Committee which was submited to the Indian Parliament in 1995. Tribal societies, suggests this report, 'have been practicing democracies, having been characterized by [an] egalitarian spirit'—this 'communitarian and co-operative spirit visible in many undertakings like shifting cultivation [and] house construction.' And again: 'Tribal life and economy in the not too distant past bore a harmonious relationship with nature and its endowment. It was an example of sustainable development. But with the influx of outside populations it suffered grievous blows.' To reverse this process the Committee recommends that 'tribal communities should be respected as in command of the economic resources,' with Gram Sabhas or village councils placed in charge of land, forests, and minerals, with larger tribal regions given 'sub-state' status, and with 'traditional tribal conventions and laws [to] continue to hold validity.'[20]

One region where these policies had already been followed, to some degree, was the North-east Frontier Agency, now renamed Arunachal Pradesh. There are seven states in India's north-east. All, with the exception of Arunachal, are hotbeds of seccession and insurgency. Nagas, Mizos, Bodos, Kukis and Ahoms wage war on the Indian state, but Monpas and Mishmis do not, or at least not yet. Arunachal Pradesh, notes the journalist George Verghese in a recent book, is an 'island of peace' with a 'degree of political stability not witnessed elsewhere in the Northeast.'[21] In the same vein, Christoph von Fürer Haimendorf writes of Arunachal as the 'best adminstered and most peaceful tribal area in the whole of India.'[22] Officials in the know ascribe the state of comparative calm in good measure to Verrier Elwin's influence. Because he elevated Hindi over Assamese as the 'second' language, they say, a generation brought up to speak Hindi has been bound more firmly to India, not least because it can better appreciate that great cultural unifier, the Bombay film. Because he insisted on restricting outsiders entering the state or owning property, and instilled in officers an attitude of care and compassion, tribals have been able to move into modern life with more assurance and greater stability.[23] The name of the state itself speaks of integration with India: derived from Sanskrit, a 'Pradesh' like other Indian provinces, it contrasts most tellingly with neighbouring Naga-*land*.

Visiting Arunachal in 1994, one reporter spoke to a woman officer born the year Elwin died who nonetheless 'swore' by him and his works. He also met educated Adi tribesmen who revered the anthropologist, for they knew their tradition and myths from what he had collected and printed about them.[24] Two years later, the traveller and writer Bill Aitken made a long motorcycle journey through the state. Arunachal struck him as 'a haven of lost subcontinental values,' with its village life offering 'democratic solutions to problems that the hierarchy of caste in mainstream India would not easily allow.' But to his sorrow he found some government anthropologists who 'opposed Elwin's enlightened mission to allow the tribals to follow their own faith.' Much will depend, he wrote, 'on the maturity of politicians to maintain Arunachal's unique state of tranquility.'[25]

In his darker moments Elwin would have admitted his work was merely to delay the inevitable, to help the Arunachalis hold out and hold their own for a few decades. Civilization would catch up with them or crush them, as it had done in Bastar and Mandla. There it took the form of Christian and Hindu missionaries; but here it has come chiefly in the shape of a chainsaw, which even his beloved 'Inner-Line Permit' was unable to keep out. Aided by corrupt politicians the plywood industry has deforested large parts of Arunachal in the last decade. The axe has been stopped, one hopes more than temporarily, by a recent decision of the Supreme Court in New Delhi ordering all saw mills to shut down. But social harmony has also been disturbed by the settlement within the state of about 50,000 Chakma refugees, leading to conflict over land and jobs. The Buddhist Chakma are theoretically 'outsiders,' but they have come fleeing religious and economic persecution in their native Bangladesh. Their conflict with the Arunachali 'insiders' is thus, as Elwin would have recognized, a struggle of right against right. All the same, to demand that the Chakmas leave the state, the students of Arunachal have taken to the streets, and they might yet take to arms.

Elwin is remembered for his studies of tribal economics and politics, but also for his work on tribal art and aesthetics. When in the early eighties the Madhya Pradesh government started a museum in the state capital, Bhopal, they were imaginative enough to appoint the painter J. Swaminathan as its curator. Besides his prodigious contributions to modern Indian art, Swaminathan was also known as a poet in Hindi and as being steeped in the works of Thomas Hardy—exactly the kind of man who would have admired Elwin. Reading *The Tribal Art of Middle India*, published thirty years earlier, he was inspired to train and send out thirty art students on a search of what remained. The students fanned out into the forests and uplands while Swaminathan himself headed for Patangarh. Here he found one house decorated with the most vivid portraits of birds in flight and tribal deities in zestful mood. These were the work of Jangarh Shyam, 'a young Pardhan artist with an inborn genius for drawing and painting and modelling.' Through these excursions the Bharat Bhavan in Bhopal built up a very fine collection of tribal art, its centrepiece the paintings of Jangarh, a Pardhan from Elwin's village and a kinsman of his wife Lila.[26]

The legacy of Verrier Elwin peeps in and out of dozens of arguments about or within tribal India. To know his work is to better understand the debates of the thirties and the fifties, but also of the seventies and the nineties. He has at times been the object of reverential praise, at other times the target of sudden and unpremeditated attack. A 1972 volume on tribals issued under the auspices of the Vivekananda Kendra—a voice of reform Hinduism based in Kanyakumari in deepest south India—drew heavily from his books, excerpting chunks from his reports and monographs. Elwin himself was described as a 'noted anthropologist' and a 'veteran son of India who rendered life-long service to the cause of the Indian tribes, perhaps as nobody as done . . .'[27] In 1985 a long essay honouring him was published in *The Pioneer* of Lucknow, a town far from anywhere the anthropologist had lived or worked. Elwin deserved to be remembered, it said, 'as the inspirer of burning love [for tribals] in the hearts of Nehru, Indira and all Indians.' 'No academic professional anthropologist,' it noted, 'ever had such a long period of intimate contact with the tribal people.'[28]

Of detractors there have been more than a few. Some showed up at a conference held in Calcutta in December 1966, two years and a bit after Elwin and Nehru were both dead, and in an India eager to shed some part of their legacy. The journalist Harish Chandola complained here that Elwin 'wanted his work to be the law for NEFA. He did not want the NEFA and the Naga people to come closer to the masses of the Indian people. But he is dead now. Who is now obstructing the process of our coming closer to them politically and economically? Is it the administrative progeny of Dr Elwin?'[29] Those who equate patriotism with assimilation have continued to attack Elwin for allegedly undermining the cultural unity of the Indian nation. In the *Economic and Political Weekly* a sociologist spoke dismissively of 'that voluptuously impetuous anthropologist Verrier Elwin who could successfully integrate himself with the Indian powers that be by alluring them for a long time with his neo-colonialist diversionary thought.'[30] This was in 1981; ten years later the Marathi writer Durga Bhagwat, who had once been a friend of Elwin and a fellow student of Gond myths, wrote in her memoirs that he was chiefly responsible for the turmoil in the north-east. She claimed that the prime minister chose Elwin as an adviser because they both studied at Oxbridge. 'For Nehru's love of Oxford,' remarked Bhagwat, 'the Adivasis of India paid dearly.' When he placed the responsibility for tribal policy in Elwin's hands, she argued, the process of systematically separating the north-east from India began. When the writer visited Assam she was asked, 'Are you from India?' Recalling the incident, Bhagwat wrote bitterly and unfairly that this sense of being 'non-Indian' was fathered by Verrier Elwin.[31]

Another *ad hominen* attack was offered in 1985 by Charan Singh, a man who was once prime minister of India for a few months. As a life-long opponent of Jawaharlal Nehru and his progeny, Charan Singh used Elwin as a stick to beat Nehru with. Like several others, he picked on the colour of Elwin's skin and the fact that he had once been a priest. He claimed that 'Nehru went to the extent of appointing a foreign Christian missionary known as Dr Elwin as an adviser to the Governor of Assam and NEFA on matters relating to tribal affairs.' This called for a rejoinder from Murkot Ramunny which explained Elwin's religious history, his willing embrace of Indian citizenship, and the essence of his 'integrationist' philosophy of the tribes: 'We owe it to this great Indian who did so much for the poorest of the poor, for whom so little has been done, by so many.'[32] As an officer of the Indian Frontier Administrative Service Ramunny had once been an associate of Elwin, even a *bhakta* perhaps.

Elwin's ideas have also been ably defended by some who never knew him. One such is Dr H. Sudarshan, a doctor who lives with the Soliga tribals of Karnataka, a selfless social worker who might be described as a Shamrao Hivale with a medical degree. 'The concept of isolation as proposed by Verrier Elwin,' remarks Sudarshan,

> has met with bitter objections by men like Dr Lohia. However, Dr Elwin had a number of progressive ideas about tribal development but he preferred isolation to a *wrong* line of development . . . In fact it appears to us that a religion based isolation is a far better idea than submitting the tribals to dogmatic religious conversions—be it Hindu, Christian or Muslim. Nothing hampers the evolution of culture more than the imposition of an alien religion. Had there been no exploitation of the tribals, there would have been no need for voluntary or governmental intervention and the tribals would have determined their own course of evolution. But intervention

> becomes inevitable due to exploitation. However, if this intervention causes erosion of tribal culture and values, then the purpose of intervention is defeated.

Elwin could not have said it better, and it comes as no surprise that Sudarshan then quotes Nehru's foreword to *A Philosophy for NEFA* as a 'very apt' credo for its time and ours.[33]

We come in the end to that indefatigable critic Professor G. S. Ghurye, the author of weighty attacks on Elwin published in 1943 and 1959. In 1980, aged eighty-seven, Ghurye published *The Burning Caldron of North-East India*, a slimmer and altogether more eccentric book than its predecessors. Elwin was here charged, as a 'British' isolationist who exercised a malevolent influence on the elite of independent India, with contributing to the 'balkanization of Bharat.' Ghurye claimed that the Adviser on Tribal Affairs had been 'the anthropological dictator of NEFA' for a decade, deciding how crores of rupees from the central treasury were to be spent. Or misspent, since it seems the money went on the 'revivalist perpetuation of the habits, dress and customs of NEFA.' Elwin, said the professor, was 'a revitalizer of almost all the cultural complex of those tribes, a complex which was most inconsistent with the cultural complex of the rest of India (Bharat) . . .' The Hindu anthropologist even accused his long dead adversary of aiding the Chinese invasion of 1962, this by encouraging his officers to dance with tribal girls who wormed secrets out of them before passing them on to Mao's men. It seems that while the officers played with the tribals the Chinese came to occupy 24,000 square miles of Indian territory.[34]

As always with Ghurye on Elwin, intellectual criticism is inseparable from personal jealousy. He was furious that it was the amateur and not he who was 'Bombay's pet anthropologist' in the forties, and furious too when Nehru and company listened to Elwin and not him in the fifties and sixties. Now, in 1998, fewer, far fewer, read Ghurye than Elwin, whose books are regularly reprinted by Oxford University Press.[35] There is however one battle that Ghurye has posthumously won. A Shiv Sena government, recently come to power in Bombay, has spent much energy on obliterating Muslim and British names and replacing them with certifiably Hindu ones. The spirit of the professor seems congenial to the chauvinists, for the intersection outside the freshly named Mumbai University has been renamed 'Govind Sadashiv Ghurye Chowk.' In death, if not in life, G. S. Ghurye has become his city's pet anthropologist.

Elwin's personal and familial legacies have been as fiercely contested as his professional and political ones. After he died in February 1964 his friends J. P. Patel (who had funded much of his central India work) and N. K. Rustomji (who was a close colleague in the NEFA administration) took care of Lila's affairs. Patel provided a living allowance and paid the children's school fees, while Rustomji used his official connections to conclude a sale of Elwin's tribal artefacts, which were acquired by the National Museum in New Delhi for Rs 250,000. Lila, a resourceful and remarkably competent homemaker, bought a two-storeyed bungalow with the proceeds, renting out a portion. She was now moderately well placed to bring up her own sons, but she soon fell out with Verrier's. Kumar was in love with a Shillong girl, Hilda; when Lila expressed a certain disapproval he ran away. She met him accidentally in the bazaar and ordered him home. He obeyed but left in a few days. He was also drinking a lot, to the disapproval this time of his commandant in the Assam Rifles. In November 1966 Lila wrote to his aunt, Eldyth: 'God only knows what will happen to him if he goes on like this.'[36]

Not long afterwards Kumar left Assam, to return to Madhya Pradesh. Somehow he located and made up with a mother he had not seen for something like twenty years. Kosi was at this time living with Vijay, her second son. Vijay had taken Elwin's name although—so far as one can be sure in these matters—he was not Verrier's child. Kumar got a job as a compositor in a printing press in Jabalpur, where he lived in a crowded two-room tenement with his wife, his mother, and his half-brother.

Also in Jabalpur, by this time, was Shamrao Hivale. Although Sham had been separated from Verrier for the last ten years of his life, his death affected him deeply. Some of what he felt comes through in a letter written to R. E. Hawkins:

> My dear Hawk,
>
> Its nearly two weeks since the cruel death has taken away Verrier and yet I can't get used to it and I feel as if he would call me 'Sham' from any side. You are one of the very few people of whom I can't think without thinking of Verrier or even think about Bombay without thinking of your unusually quiet and peaceful house where we lived without any awkwardness or inhibitions that was inevitable in Bombay as a result of his or our life in Patangarh or in the Tribal villages. I can hardly sit when I think of you two talking to each other. The sight was almost perfect. And now I shall never see that sight again.
>
> . . . I am anxiously waiting for JP's letter. I can imagine how miserable you two must feel. I wonder if I will ever have the courage to meet the Bombay friends again.
>
> Let me thank you again and again for the wonderful time we used to have in your charming home. . . .[37]

When Verrier died a good part of Shamrao died too. It appears that he soon set into a deep depression. Unfortunately (in view of what was to follow) someone in his family discovered the 1952 will by Verrier bequeathing most of his assets to his dearest friend. On Shamrao's behalf, but we may be certain without his consent, a case was filed in 1968 in the Madhya Pradesh High Court against Lila Elwin who, as Verrier's legal heir, had inherited what he had left. Lila's lawyer now submitted the later will (of 1959) that left 10 per cent to Kumar and 90 per cent to her. Then Kumar, Vijay and Kosi entered a caveat, contending that both wills were forgeries, and arguing that Dr Elwin had died without disposing of his property. In November 1970 the judge finally disposed of the case in favour of Lila, saying that the earlier will had not been attested. He however advised Kumar and Kosi to file separately for the recovery of their share of Verrier's property.

The dispute dragged on. In March 1971 Kosi, Kumar and Vijay filed a fresh suit in the M.P. High Court, naming as respondents Lila as well as Shamrao. Kosi's lawyer argued that at the time of marriage it was agreed that on Verrier's death she and her children would be entitled to his assets: which, in their opinion, included whatever was left in Shillong, the house occupied by Sham's family in Napier Town in Jabalpur (bought in part with Verrier's money), and not least the royalties from his books. Deposing before the court on 21st July 1979, Kosi claimed that by Gond custom a marriage could only be dissolved by customary law, namely, a decision of the village panchayat to whom the person seeking divorce must appeal. But Verrier had instead approached the Calcutta High Court, whose *ex parte* decree of 12 December 1949 Kosi refused to accept since she and her panchayat had no knowledge of it.

The argument by tribal tradition was Elwinesque, but the Jabalpur court would have none of it. For Lila and Kusum Hivale (who was her husband's guardian, Shamrao having been declared of 'unsound mind') maintained that the marriage between Kosi and Verrier had been legally dissolved, that Vijay was not a son of Verrier, and that Kumar had already taken the sum of Rs 5500 in lieu of his share of his father's assets. In his order of 17th April 1980 Justice B. C. Varma found that the Jabalpur house did not belong to Verrier, that Lila and Verrier were lawfully wedded, that Verrier and Kosi had been legally divorced, and that the 1959 will was legitimate.

Kosi, ever the fighter, now filed a special leave petition in the Supreme Court of India. Her lawyer placed emphasis once more on the fact that Verrier and she had been married by tribal custom. He said the Calcutta decree was 'an ex parte proceedings against an illiterate tribal woman who knew nothing about the position of law and was fully dependent for matrimonial obligations as prevalent among the tribals according to their customs.' Kosi also claimed that Lila had been married to a liquor contractor named Bulla, and that *this* marriage too was never dissolved.[38]

Appeal to the Supreme Court was also unsuccessful. Meanwhile in April 1981, in between these various litigations, Dom Moraes arrived in Jabalpur. He had been commissioned by the Madhya Pradesh government to write a book on the state and thought naturally that he would pay tribute to his old hero and reader of his first poems. Moraes came from Patangarh and Amarkantak, where he had met many Gonds who had known Elwin, including a lady who claimed to be his first wife and a man who claimed to be his son. The day after they reached Jabalpur his companion told him that Kumar lived in the town. Moraes arranged to meet him and was devastated by what he saw. He remembered Kumar from their time as fellow-students at St Mary's School in Bombay, as a child full of zest, someone who imitated the monkey in the zoo and jumped up and down on his seat in the cinema. The man was a shadow of the boy. 'His cheeks were sunken, his eyes bloodshot, and there was more grey in his hair than mine. I put my arms round him, and it was like embracing a ghost: there seemed no substance in his body . . . What shocked me most was that a habit of servility seemed to have seized him: at first he refused to sit down in my presence, and after the first few minutes he started to call me sir.'

Kumar told Moraes that the happiest time of his life had been when he went trekking in the NEFA highlands with his father. 'Of course my life has changed terribly since Daddy died,' he said. 'I remember in Shillong, when in the evening Daddy would have his drinks and his cigars and his servants would bring it all to him. Now I can't afford to smoke. I can't afford to drink, and I am a servant myself.' When Moraes asked why he had not written to one of Verrier's friends for help, Kumar replied that he thought 'matters of money are bad between friends. I would never embarass my father's friends by asking them for money.'[39]

Weeks after this meeting Kumar died of a burst ulcer. He was only forty. 'All my thoughts are with your mother,' wrote a friend to Vijay, 'In this life she has moved from tragedy to tragedy.'[40] Dom Moraes used his influence to get Kosi a stipend from the state government. She now lives in the village of Ryatwar, with Vijay, his Gond wife, and their three children. They live off the pension and the earnings from some land they own in the village.

Kosi's break-up with Elwin was as much her doing as his, but her present situation is deeply poignant: a woman once married to a famous scholar and friend of the famous and powerful, herself entertained by them, is spending out her days amidst the poverty and obscurity into which she was born. But in some ways Vijay's situation is more poignant still. He was abandoned by his natural father, disowned with Kosi by his adoptive one, and finally discarded with his mother by the lover (Sahid) who took her up after she left Elwin. And he has lived out his adult life under the fiction, which he must know to be a fiction, that he is the son of Verrier Elwin. He has taken his name, calls him *pitaji* (father), and tells visitors that he only wants his good works to be remembered. He shows some correspondence with the Bodleian Library in Oxford, to whom he had written asking for a list of his 'father's' works. Filed neatly is the Bodleian's reply, with the list it provided Vijay of its holdings under the name of Verrier Elwin.

Lila Elwin stays in Shillong with Ashok, who runs a pharmacy, and with Wasant, who is a teacher. They live in a large, rambling, double-storeyed house, a portion let out, fittingly, to a research centre in Tibetan medicine whose patron is the Dalai Lama. Her third son, Nakul, runs a school in Tura in the Garo Hills. All the boys have married local girls. They have ten children between them. When I met Lila in December 1997 she was accompanying one of her grandchildren to a picnic. The next week, she would be off to visit another in her boarding school in Roorkee. In Shillong she is mostly home-bound, though she dutifully appears for the annual Verrier Elwin Memorial Lecture organized by the North-Eastern Hill University. She remains a lady of great poise, although she would not speak of her husband to the strangers from the plains who keep coming around to ask.

Lila would not talk, but Ashok Elwin did. He is a photographer himself and a careful keeper of Elwin's massive collection of negatives spanning many years and many locations. While we spoke a friend came in to pass on the latest news of a campaign they were involved in. This aimed at protecting the old bridle-path which ran up from the plains to Shillong, which a new and historically insensitive administration wished to demolish: the protection of cultural heritage, an obsession both tribal and English, a struggle that would have met with his father's complete approval.

Back in England Eldyth Elwin remained, till her recent death, devoted to Verrier's memory. To his publishers, John Murray in London and Oxford University Press in Bombay, she wrote a stream of letters asking that this book or that be reissued or reprinted. To a prospective historian of the Christa Seva Sangh, she bravely tried to reconcile her brother's journey of upturned allegiances to her own steady faith. Even after Verrier left the CSS, she told the questioner, his 'life was very arduous and even later he hardly had any possessions and comfort. The tribal people loved him, and I think he lived a life among them that would have delighted

St Francis.'[41] Delighted in some parts, certainly, but one cannot be sure what the saint of Assissi would have made of Kosi and Lila, *The Baiga*, or *The Muria and their Ghotul.*

When I met Eldyth Elwin in 1991, and again in 1992, she lived in a nursing home outside Oxford. She was alone, infirm and blind, but her room was lit up for her by rows of her brother's books and photographs. Underneath her bed was a trunk containing his letters and clippings, the core of what was to become the Verrier Elwin Collection at the India Office Library in London. She complained to me that Verrier's association with Gandhi had been disregarded both in Richard Attenborough's film and a recent biography of the Mahatma by an Oxford historian. She spoke then of 'the poem with which Verrier won the Newdigate;' unfortunately she no longer possessed a copy. The error was wonderfully revealing, for although her brother had won many prizes at Oxford, the Newdigate had not been one of them. As he recalled in his memoirs, he had submitted a long poem on Michelangelo; it came a mere fifth, perhaps because it was, as his teacher H. W. Garrod pointed out, 'too much of a sermon.'[42]

I shall end this account with a fragment of personal experience. In September 1992 I spoke on Elwin at the Nehru Centre in London, newly set up to promote cultural understanding between England and India. The subject attracted an array of men and women from the various worlds which Elwin had touched. To my great good luck, some of these contributed to the discussion. Archbishop Trevor Huddleston (among the foremost British opponents of apartheid) said that the example of Elwin, the brilliant scholar who gave it all up to go overseas and serve the poor, inspired some Oxford Christians of the thirties, such as himself, to do likewise. Charles Lewis of Oxford University Press remembered his first assignment in India, which was to do the publicity for Elwin's last book. The playwright Ebrahim Alkazi recalled how, as a young man, he would direct plays in Bombay to raise money for the Tribal Welfare and Research Unit of Patangarh. The photographer Sunil Janah, Elwin's companion on many journeys through Bastar and Orissa, told a lovely story of their first trip together. In Raipur, on the edge of the Chattisgarh forest, they were directed one evening to the home of a timber contractor who was knowledgeable about the tribals. This man met them in his garden, where they talked, but at regular intervals he would go back into his house. He offered Elwin and Janah no refreshments. Fortunately, they had in their bags a bottle of rum from which they took swigs while their host went in. They later found that to drink rapidly and on the sly was also the purpose of *his* periodic disappearances, for he had been told only of Elwin's sinless past in ashram and church and knew little of his joyful present.

My own talk at the Nehru Centre was altogether more serious. It ended with a discussion of the Narmada controversy. After Huddleston and company had spoken, wistfully and humorously, an intervention of controlled anger came from Maharani Gayatri Devi of Jaipur, one of the great beauties of this century, and even at seventy the most striking woman I had seen. 'I am a tribal,' she dramatically announced: this a reference to the allegedly aboriginal origins of the Cooch-Behar family into which she was born: 'And speaking as a tribal, I charge the Congress goverments which have ruled India with brutally disturbing the cultural ethos of the tribals by taking away their lands, damming their rivers and forcing them into second-rate schools where they are taught to despise their tradition.' Now the Maharani, it needs to be added, had been a political foe of Jawaharlal Nehru and was later jailed by his daughter. I could not answer her charges, but the chairman did. He was C. Subramaniam, at the time the governor of Maharashtra, and in his pomp a senior minister in the cabinets of Nehru and Indira Gandhi. The post-independence Congress, he now rejoined, wished to bring the fruits of modernity to all sections of India, but it respected the culture of the tribals, and designed special and less intrusive policies for them. I listened with attention to the argument between the minister and the maharani, or more accurately perhaps, between Elwin Mark I and Elwin Mark II, between the Protectionist and the Integrationist.

One keeps coming across evidence of Elwin's posthumous influence, instances of his work being attacked or affirmed. The most curious example occurs in a recent biography of P. G. Wodehouse. Seeking to establish the Oxford college which Bertie Wooster graced—if graced is the word—the author cites two essays by Elwin as showing authoritatively that Worster went to Magdalen. Elwin had also established the years Bertie was up, 1918 to 1921, but was stumped as to what he might have read. It could not have been Greats or Classics, for he knew not a word of Latin, and the 'imagination boggled' at the thought of Bertie reading Theology or English, Verrier's own disciplines. The biographer presents Elwin's conclusions approvingly and then refers to *Motley*, the book where the essays appeared, as 'one of the best and scarcest books of literary criticism.'[43] Apparently the Wodehouse scholar, a man of learning and experience (we may assume), knew nothing of Elwin the theologian or novelist, the anthropologist or activist, the Gandhian, Christian, Englishman and Indian. For all this to be forgotten or ignored, and to be remembered only as a student and scholar of English literature! I am certain Elwin would not have been displeased.

APPENDIX ONE

The Social Worker: A Constitution Not Always Honoured

In 1933 or 1934 Verrier Elwin drafted this constitution of the Gond Seva Mandal. The second section, on the Mandal's principles, gives a fascinating insight into his thinking at the time, his delicate juggling of the competing influences of F. W. Green, Mahatma Gandhi, and the Gonds. This version is from a typescript in File R of 1935, Commissioner's Record Room, Jabalpur. I am grateful to Dr Archana Prasad for providing me with a copy.

THE GOND SEVA MANDAL
CONSTITUTION AND RULES

1. The name of this Society shall be the Gond Seva Mandal.
2. The object of the Gond Seva Mandal shall be to serve the Gonds and other forest tribes of the Central Provinces of India.
3. In furtherance of this object, the Mandal shall carry on educational and medical work, and shall undertake any activities—other than missionary and political—which shall contribute to the well-being and enlightenment of the forest-tribes.
4. Membership of the Mandal shall be open to all, men and women, married or unmarried, whatever their nationality or creed, who are ready to devote themselves to the object of the Mandal and observe its rules and principles.
5. There shall be three classes of members:
   (a) Probationary members, who shall work in the Mandal for not less than three months and who may be retained as such for any period not exceeding two years.

(b) Members, who after a probationary period of not less than six months, engage to work in the Mandal for three years, and give a pledge to observe the rules and principles of the Mandal. At the end of the three years period, a member is free either to resign or to offer himself for re-election by the Sabha.

(c) Life-members, who after serving for two periods of three years, profess the intention of serving in the Mandal for life, and are accepted by a unanimous vote of the existing life-members. In the first six years of the life of the Mandal it shall, in exceptional cases, be within the competence of the life-members to accept new life-members before they have completed the full period of their probation.

6. The general direction of the affairs of the Mandal shall be managed by the members and life-members as hereinafter provided.
7. The life members and members shall together compose a Sabha which shall elect one of the life-members as its Mantri or chief servant, to hold office for five years, with the possibility of re-election. It shall elect the same or another life-member as Treasurer on the same terms, and a member to act as secretary of the Sabha to hold office for another year.
8. It shall be competent for the Mandal to acquire and hold moveable and immoveable properties, and such properties shall vest in the Mantri on behalf of the Mandal and he shall deal with them in consultation with the life-members. The funds of the Mandal shall be deposited in a Bank in the name of the Mandal, and the account shall be operated upon by the Treasurer in consultation with the life-members. All the other affairs of the Mandal shall be directed by the members and life-members sitting together in the Sabha.
9. New members will be admitted to the Sabha on obtaining a two-thirds majority vote in their favour. No member can be removed from the Sabha save for grave cause and a two-thirds vote against him.
10. The Sabha shall meet at the headquarters of the Mandal as often as is necessary for the transaction of business, and five members shall form a quorum.
11. The members of the Mandal shall devote themselves entirely to the bona-fide humanitarian service of the poor, and shall not use their

activities as a cloak for religious or political propaganda. They shall neither prepare for, nor ultimately engage in, any campaign of civil disobedience. The Mandal shall not enter into terms of association with any religious, missionary or political body.

12. Not inconsistently with the object of the Mandal, the life-members shall have the power to revise the constitution from time to time by a majority of two-thirds of the members present at a meeting. For the purpose and for the transaction of business relating to property and finance the Mantri may call a meeting of life-members as and when he considers necessary.
13. This constitution shall come into effect as from March 1st 19 . . .

PRINCIPLES

The Mandal is founded on the following principles.

1. TRUTH. There can be no brotherhood and no service without Truth. Only out of a pure transparent heart can there come acts of love and mercy. It is necessary for the spirit of Truth to direct not only our speech, but every aspect of our lives and every detail of our organisation. Then only can we be worthy to serve God who is Truth.
2. LOVE. The servant of the poor must consciously direct all his actions in the spirit of universal love. He will be courteous, gentle, fearless, non-violent in thought, speech and action. Love implies fearlessness, and the members will try to overcome fear of sickness, wild animals, the secular and religious authorities, and death itself. They will try to overcome by love the critics and opponents of their work.
3. PURITY. Purity of personal life is an essential basis of sincere service. Members will therefore endeavour to curb animal passion and fight against every kind of impurity in thought, word and deed. As an aid to purity, control of the palate is advocated. Those who desire to serve the poor, even if they cannot share the actual food of the poor, will regard eating as necessary chiefly for the sustaining of the body and keeping it a fit instrument for service. They will therefore constantly try to regulate and simplify their diet. But as they accept the discipline of fasting, so they will not despise the joy of feasting at the proper time. No food laws may be passed by the Mandal.

4. PRAYER. Communion with God can alone keep the heart transparent and fill the life with love. Without prayer, service becomes lifeless. All members, therefore, will join in the morning and evening prayer (which is of such a character that adherents of all religions can join in it) and they will try to maintain the attitude of prayerfulness in all that they do.
5. SIMPLICITY OF LIFE. The members will try to set an example for the people by the right use of such money as they have. They will gladly accept such small allowance as the Mandal is able to make them for their needs. They will not contract any debt without the permission of the Sabha. They will not waste money, and they will not encourage others to waste money on expensive weddings, funerals, jewellry or caste dinners.
6. RESPECT. The members regard with respect every manifestation of the religious spirit. While they are not committed to any particular theory of the relations of all religions to one another, they refrain from all proselytising. Each member is encouraged to hold firmly and to practise his own religion. But this loyalty to his own faith must only deepen his respect for that of others. In the same way he will treat with equal respect rich and poor, Indians or foreigners, friends or foes.
7. KNOWLEDGE. Knowledge, art, music, etc are not to be despised by the lover of the poor. Knowledge, by purifying and enlarging the mind, actually equips him with the means of better service. Members will be encouraged to make research in the customs and ancient traditions of the people, and to give some time at least daily to general study.
8. UNITY. The members aim at a sincere unity of spirit. The Mandal desires to embrace in one fellowship Hindu and Christian, Mussalman and Parsi, Gond and Panka, Brahmin and Harijan. It will try to co-operate with all men of good will, whatever their political or religious opinions, who are endeavouring to ameliorate the lot of the poor.
9. DISCIPLINE. No organisation can exist without discipline. The members will aim at exact punctuality, the loyal fulfilment of the tasks alloted to them, and the perfect cleanliness of the land and buildings where they live.

10. BREAD-LABOUR. The ideal of identification with the poor is meaningless unless it finds expression in some form of bread-labour. Moreover the servant of the poor who comes not to be ministered to but to minister must reduce to a minimum the service that he receives from others. Sacrificial spinning is a perfect symbol of love for and identification with the poor. Members will not be ashamed to do their own cleaning, wood-cutting, cooking, grinding and rice-pounding.
11. HINDI. The educational work of the Mandal, which will be in the national language, will aim at fostering a truly national spirit: it will try to recreate the national self-respect of the forest tribes and to foster pride in their ancient heritage. The official language of the Mandal is Hindi, which every member will undertake to learn and use.
12. INTERNATIONALIST. The outlook of the Mandal will never be merely nationalist. As it aims at binding together in one fellowship of service members of different religions, so it desires to unite those of different races. Its members will ever strive to make their love more universal, their sympathies more catholic.

The Author: An Unwritten Book

In the Verrier Elwin Papers in the Nehru Memorial Museum and Library there are two files (numbers 160 and 161) containing his notes on the Kondhs. These run to some five hundred pages, and were to be used in a book he planned to write on the tribe. His work in NEFA meant that the book was never written, but a chapter scheme left by him tells us how it was to have been structured.

THE ECONOMICS OF THE KUTTIA KOND

INTRODUCTION

The people
The country and climate
Village
House
Dress and ornament

THE ECONOMICS OF RELIGIOUS OBLIGATION

The cost of customary worship
The medicine-man and fees of the gods
Obligations to the dead

THE ECONOMICS OF SOCIAL DUTY

Corporate enterprise
Payments to the State
Payments to the Patro
Payments to tribal priests and headmen
Tribal justice and its cost

THE ECONOMICS OF FAMILY RELATIONSHIPS

The Family
Reciprocal obligations
Birth
Marriage
Death

THE SUPPLY OF FOOD

Axe-cultivation
Forest products
Hunting and fishing
Domestic animals
Liquor

THE CONSUMPTION OF FOOD

The Store-room
The Kitchen
The Dining Room
The Tavern

PROPERTY AND DEBT

Income
Expenditure
Property
Debt
The Disposal of Surplus Goods

POVERTY AND 'CRIME'

The Kond in revolt
The Kond dacoit
The Kond murderer

Also in the notes on the Kondhs is this checklist of questions to ask on tribal hunting, a fine illustration of the field-methods of this ostensibly 'amateur' anthropologist.

Ceremonial hunt
Any stories of Forest Guards interfering
Guns?
Traps
Slings

How do they beat?
How divide? Carry home?
Where do they deposit it?
How cook?
Rites?

Methods of stringing bow
Pits

Eating of bear, monkey, bison
crow, kite
frogs, snakes, lizard
rats, birds, porcupine

APPENDIX THREE

The Public Official: Policies 'Rejected or Forgotten'

Two-and-a-half years after Verrier Elwin joined the NEFA Administration, he wrote a note asking 'how far the various suggestions [made on the basis of his tours in the interior], many of which have been generally approved, have actually been implemented.' Striking in its comprehensiveness and attention to detail, the note is dated the 10th of April, 1956, and is reproduced here from File 133, Elwin Papers, NMML, New Delhi.

[Abbreviations: G = Governor; AG = Adviser to Governor; DAG = Deputy Adviser to Governor; DC = Development Commissioner; EO = Educational Officer; PO = Political Officer; ATA = Adviser on Tribal Affairs; PM = Prime Minister]

The following points arise for discussion and implementation from suggestions made by the ATA in his various tour notes:

1. The problem of slavery. Can we accelerate the liberation of slaves? Should we pay compensation?
2. The problem of opium in Tirap and Lohit. Should we try to move faster?
3. Dress for school-children. What has been finally decided? Has a directive actually issued? Has any progress been made in the production of suitable clothes?
4. The promotion of weaving. What has been decided? Can we distribute yarn at subsidised rates, and if so how much? What progress has been made about getting 'weaving organisers?' Or starting itinerant weaving schools? Should we or shouldn't we close down some of the weaving sections in places like Teju and Dambuk, where the people

already weave well? What can we do about the bad designs coming in to the Pasighat weaving centre?

5. Political presents. Is our directive being followed with regard to the kind of things being given? Should we not call for a report?
6. Relief. AG some time ago suggested a directive; has one issued? If not, what action can we take? What actually is the present policy?
7. Has any report come in about the political situation in the neighbourhood of Roing (as apart from enquiry into specific allegations)?
8. Has any action been taken about the Supervisor who so offended the Mishmi boys at Pasighat?
9. What action has been taken about the Lohit schools?
10. What can we do to improve the morale and discipline of the Army Supply Corps boys and stop them (a) black-marketing in cloth, cigarettes etc and (b) introducing bad habits like card-playing to the tribal people?
11. The Adviser suggested that there should be a directive about the propaganda used by teachers to persuade children to go to school, e. g., that they would then get Government jobs, and to stress that there must be no forcing of children to attend. Has this been done?
12. School architecture. Has any decision been made about this? Can we improve it and make it more tribal, especially when buildings are put up on a self-help basis and are thus not tied down by the engineering rules?
13. What is the final decision about the rules for [officials'] learning tribal languages and passing the exams?
14. Cottage Industry Training and Production Centres. What are DC's reactions to my suggestion to cut out the 'training' and make them 'production' centres?

    Has the suggestion of having small museums been approved and has Finance agreed?

    What of the suggestion that instructors and supervisors should make short tours to acquaint themselves with the realities of tribal life? Has it been possible to employ tribal wood-carving instructors in Teju, Mon and Tuensang?

15. Has a directive about the control of shops been issued, and have we any information as to how it is being implemented?
16. What about sweepers? DC and I have both noticed a certain lukewarmness in implementing our directives on this subject. Is there any way whereby we can eliminate sweepers from the hospitals?
17. Has any action been taken to capture for Government the trade (a) in Lama coats and ornaments in Lohit and (b) the trade in Khampti and Tangsa bags etc in Tirap?
18. I suggested for schoolboys in Lohit and Siang the attractive small coat made of the 'Abor rug' material, a specimen of which is in my Museum. Has that commended itself to the EO? If so, has anything been done about it?
19. Variety shows. I am afraid I have myself held up the DC's directive on 'instructional entertainment' until we could discuss the matter fully and issue a comprehensive directive on what I have called the NEFA Theatre. We should take this up now.
20. Venereal disease. I have already suggested that we might have the C[hief] M[edical] O[fficer]'s advice on this. I feel it is a most important matter.
21. Has the PO Tirap been asked to enquire about the alleged visit of Burmese officials across the border, and if so has any reply been received?
22. What are DC's views about a BS [Boys School?] at Laju?
23. What progress has been made towards solving the porter problem? Has anything been done to obtain animal transport?
24. AG has asked for action with regard to getting good portraits of the PM and President. What has been done?
25. What are DC's views about an N[ational] E[ducation] S[cheme] block for the upper Tirap valley, which would have the special aim at eliminating opium by substituting other interests?
26. Orders have already issued regarding hair-cutting of children in Tangsa schools and the wearing of the Tangsa lungi.
27. Are the PO's implementing the instructions, based on the PM's wishes, regarding the singing of Ramdun etc?
28. Has any progress been made in the way of adapting our architecture generally to tribal models?

29. Can we do something about having a Cleanliness Week?
30. DAG has noted that he would correspond with the PO Tirap about the Tangsa girls and what action has been taken to improve the situation. Has this been done and has any reply been sent?
31. I would be very grateful if the EO could let me have a report on the progress made in encouraging tribal games.
32. I would also be grateful for a note on progress made in combating dermatitis in northern Subansiri. I have noticed the same infection in northern Siang: it seems to affect the Tagins and certain groups of Galongs and not other tribes. This is a most urgent human problem and I do hope that real progress has been made.
33. G. made certain suggestions about training Tagin girls in weaving. Have we had any success in this?
34. G. noted on my Subansiri report last year that 'we should take systematic steps to develop the fibre cloth industry in our Divisions. Kameng has a good tradition of it.' What has been done about this?
35. G. further noted that he had issued instructions 'long ago' for the development of the wool and yarn industry in the Monpa area. Has this made progress?
36. I have also raised the question of providing wool for the weavers in northern Siang (for Boris, Pailibos and Bhokars etc). What can we do about this?
37. I suggested last year, and G issued orders approving the suggestion that, in G's words, 'we may correspond with Kalimpong authorities for the supplies of deo-ghantis [bells?] if the rates are reasonable. I think we can easily order 100 for each division.' Was this ever taken up?
38. What progress has been made in developing Sherdukpen agriculture in the area around Rupa and Shergaon, as I suggested last year? AG asked the A(gricultural) O(fficer) to make 'a personal study' of the local plough with a view to its improvement. Has he done this?
39. Have we been able to make progress in the introduction of cash crops such as pepper and cardamom, especially in areas near the plains where the people could market their wares?

40. AG has noted on my Kameng report that it will be 'well worth examining' whether we can utilise temple or monastic buildings for our schools as is done in Siam. Has anyone examined this?
41. Charts and pictures in schools. I have frequently drawn attention to the poor quality of these, and on my first visit to Margherita in 1954 the DC (then PO) and I spoke very strongly about it to the education people. Yet I still see exactly the same pictures and charts which we both condemned so heartily displaying their dreary inappropriateness on the walls of our schools. Why?
42. AG notes that it is a 'good idea' to have a few pictures illustrating the life of Buddha and a simple life of Buddha and his teachings to be used in our schools in the Buddhist-tribal areas. Has anything been done?
43. AG also notes that my suggestion about the repair of prayer-wheels in the Buddhist parts of Kameng 'should be attended to right away.' Has it been?
44. I made suggestions about a special hat for leading men with a badge of the Asoka pillar. Has this been rejected or just forgotten?
45. *ATA's notes on his tour in Siang 1956.* The suggestions in this note have only just been put up, and I have not seen AG's notings. The following points may be considered.
    (a) I would much appreciate a copy of DC's views and DAG's on roman script and use of Assamese.
    (b) Flowers are suggested for the Leprosy Home at Along, and better implements for the smithy tiers.
    (c) Designs for Galong weaving.
    (d) A possible rule that instructresses in Weaving Schools should wear khadi if not local hand-woven cloth.
    (e) The provision of large quantities of yarn at subsidised rates. We also have to discover the right kind of yarn as well as right colours.
    (f) Encouragement of shopkeepers on the positive side to stock the right kind of useful goods.
    (g) The making available of cheap but good books for purchase by our people.
    (h) The substitution of undesirable pictures and calendars in shops by our own NEFA calendars and other pictures.
    (i) This is not included in my original suggestions, but I feel it is

imperative to engage at least two artists, one for the Research Department, when Shri Dholling leaves us, and the other for the Development group of departments on a *much higher* salary than approved at present. How can we guide tribal taste in text-books, charts, pictures etc if we can only engage mediocre artists who will not put their hearts into the job on the miserable pittance which Government seems to think suitable for anyone who works for art, good taste and beauty?

(j) The production of small books of songs.

(k) Prizes in NEFA

(l) The engagement of one or two dance experts, themselves tribals, to encourage and teach dancing in areas where it does not exist.

(m) Stepping up of provision of wire ropes for bridges in Siang.

46. What is being done about Interpreters?
47. I suggest it is time now that we get reports on the Divisions about the implementation of the directives on Religion. How in fact are the festivals of Durga, Holi and Christmas being celebrated? Is anyone taking seriously the encouragement of tribal religions?
48. We also need a report as to how far directives have actually reached all our officers, especially those in outposts.
49. I had suggested (a) importing a stock of Manipuri shawls, some cheap and some of better quality, but all colourful, into Tirap, and if possible some of the Ao and other Naga shawls; (b) the importation of Mishmi coats into Tirap and the starting of weaving black coats of the Mishmi type but with Wancho or Nocte or Tangsa designs for the usual Mishmi or Abor decoration.
50. Could not the excellent chairs being made at Namsang be made in other carpentry sections also? And the Kampti or Singhpo loom?

Acknowledgements

I first heard of Verrier Elwin in the monsoon of 1978, from a kindly Oriya veteneraraian named Das. We were both in the hills of Koraput, he running a government clinic, me studying, on behalf of the Delhi School of Economics, the 'assimilation of tribals into industrial society.' For weeks prior to our meeting I had pored over the productivity records of an aircraft factory situated in that unlikely location, and concluded, at the 1 per cent level of significance, that tribal workers were as efficient as non-tribal ones. The work complete, on my last Sunday I was taken by my host, a Mr Patro, on a courtesy tour of a Gadaba village where I met Dr Das. 'Many years ago,' he remarked, 'a scholar like you came from far away to study the tribals of Koraput. Do you know of Verrier Elwin?' I did not, so the doctor told me a little, enough for it to be clear that the parallels between Elwin and myself ended rather abruptly.

Back in Delhi I picked up *Leaves from the Jungle* from the library. In print six decades after its first publication, *Leaves* has been many things to many people: it was to send me away from economics towards social anthropology and history. Verrier Elwin has since been a visible and occasionally invisible presence in my life. That it has taken so long for this work to come to a close is in part due to other commitments, and in part due to the man's fanatically prodigious output. I can see why Kosi Elwin thought she had married a typewriter, for a reasonably comprehensive bibliography of her husband's works by the Japanese scholar Takeshii Fuji runs to some forty closely printed pages. It lists more than thirty books and almost four hundred articles. There are also the letters sent and received, as well as intelligence reports, newspaper reports, church and college records, school records, Gond Seva Mandal records, government records. . . .

But I protest too much, for the chase has been rich and invigorating and abetted by conscientious record-keepers, tolerant employers, loving friends. In the first category fall the staff of the following libraries and archives, ordered roughly according to the burdens placed upon them: the Oriental and India Office Collections (formerly the India Office and Records), London; the Nehru Memorial Museum and Library, New Delhi; the National Archives of India, New Delhi; the National Library, Calcutta; Oxford University Press, Mumbai; Merton College, Oxford; the Centre for South Asian Studies, Cambridge; Bishop's College, Calcutta; John Murray, London; the Bodleian Library, Oxford; the Christa Seva Sangh, Pune; Hilfield Priory, Dorset; the Society for the Propagation of the Gospel, London; Dean Close Memorial School, Cheltenham; the British Library Newspaper Collection, Collindale; the *Church Times* Record Office, London; the Institute of Social Anthropology, Oxford; Wycliffe Hall, Oxford; the United Theological College, Bangalore; Green Library, Stanford; Friends House, London; and St Stephen's College, Delhi.

Then come the institutions who have paid the bills in my itinerant career. Some of their money has gone unjustifiably, one could say unaccountably, towards understanding Elwin. I thank the Indian Institute of Management, Calcutta; the Centre for Studies in Social Sciences, Calcutta; Yale University, New Haven; the Indian Institute of Science, Bangalore; the Institute of Economic Growth, Delhi; St Antony's College, Oxford; the University of California at Berkeley; and the Ford Foundation, New Delhi. I must acknowledge above all two centres that know about collegiality precisely because they are not colleges in the formal sense. The first is the Nehru Memorial Museum and Library, which gave me a fellowship with a long rope, privileged access to its records, and to cap it an office overlooking the back lawn of Teen Murti House, so that I might write of Elwin as if he were in sight of me, walking and talking with his hero—also one of mine. The second is the Wissenschaftskolleg zu Berlin, where this book was conceived in its present form, and whose Fellows urged me cheerfully and consolingly along.

The last category is the most spacious and is itself subdivisible. First, the true believers in knowledge as common property, those people who generously and selflessly gave me access to original records in their possession. These good souls are Ashok Elwin, Daniel O'Connor, Paul Newton, Benedict Green, Archana Prasad, Nandini Sundar, William Emilsen, Jacques Pouchepadass, Arvind Khare, Michael Young, and Amit Baruah.

Then there are the colleagues and strangers who passed on tips and sources or subjected themselves to interviews or sermons or chapters or sections. I thank Mildred Archer, Ravi Bhagwat, Richard Bingle, Stanley Brandes, David Brokensha, Shareen Brysac, Mahendra Desai, Vasudha Dhagamwar, F. W. Dillistone, the late Shyama Charan Dube, the late Eldyth Elwin, Anjan Ghosh, Ann Grodzins Gold, Chris Gregory, S. J. Gunn, R. N. and Krishna Haldipur, Zoya Hasan, J. R. F. Highfield (of Merton College), Rivka Israel, Pico Iyer, Sunil Janah, Amina Jayal, Mukul Kesavan, Sunil Khilnani, Elizabeth Krishna, Charles Lewis, Alan Macfarlane, T. N. Madan, Hans Medick, Arvind Krishna Mehrotra, Karl Meyer, Shibani Mitra, Prabhu Mohapatra, O. K. Moorthy, Dom Moraes, Santosh Mookherjee (of Oxford University Press), K. K. S. Murthy (proprietor of the Select Bookshop, Bangalore), Bansi Narmada (son of Elwin's longtime research assistant Sunderlal Narmada), Humphrey Osmond (of Dean Close School), the late G. Parthasarathi, Gyanendra Pandey, Vivek Rae, N. Raghunathan, Satish Saberwal, Savyasachi, Vikram Seth, Har Mander Singh, Khushwant Singh, James Scott, K. Sivaramakrishnan, M. N. Srinivas, Ramaswamy Sudarshan, the late J. Swaminathan, Adil Tyabji, Khalid Tyabji, and C. S. Venkatachar. I have benefited much from comments on the penultimate version by Kirin Narayan, a friend, and from Wendy Doniger and Lee Siegel, two no longer anonymous readers.

I grieve that two friends who encouraged me for many years did not live to see this book in print. One was the journalist P. K. Srinivasan, an admirer of English culture and, with discrimination, of Englishmen; the other the scholar and democrat C. V. Subba Rao, who in a brief life did as much as anyone since Elwin to draw attention to the problems of India's tribes.

A few debts, the most consequential perhaps, remain to be acknowledged. T. David Brent of the University of Chicago Press has been a wonderfully supportive editor. My 'Wiko' colleague Nicholas Boyle taught me aspects of the biographer's craft, gently squeezing out the residues of my sociological training (some remain, alas). Both David and Nicholas prodded me, as a pious agnostic, to more seriously explore the faiths of my subject. Keshav Desiraju and Gopal Gandhi, sahibs sometimes in the secretariat, both steeped in Indian history and world literature, saved me from numerous errors of fact and interpretation. They also brought me back to Elwin whenever I strayed too far from him. And Rukun Advani has read drafts and half-drafts with a novelist's eye and a friend's concern. As with my other books, Rukun directed this one from pen to paper and finally to print.

Savaging the Civilized is dedicated to my wife, Sujata. 'At the bottom of his heart,' wrote Raymond Chandler, 'every decent man knows that his approach to the woman he loves is like an approach to a shrine.' It has been that way for some time now, for I first heard of Sujata the week I first heard of Elwin. Her goodness and tranquillity have sustained me since.

Notes

NOTES TO PROLOGUE

1. Tamara's dispatches are reproduced in Shamrao Hivale, *Scholar Gypsy: A Study of Verrier Elwin* (Bombay 1946), pp. 212–14.
2. Romain Rolland, foreword to Elwin's *Leaves from the Jungle: A Diary of Life in a Gond Village* (London 1936).
3. *TLS*, 20 January 1950.
4. E. P. Thompson, *No Alien Homage: Edward Thompson and Rabindranath Tagore* (New Delhi 1993), p. 10.
5. Cf. correspondence in File E10, Oxford University Press Archives, Mumbai.

NOTES TO CHAPTER ONE

1. Anon., *Wycliffe Hall, Oxford, 1877–1927* (privately printed pamphlet, issued on the occasion of the seminary's Golden Jubilee).
2. F. S. Johnson, *The Story of a Mission: The Sierra Leone Church: First Daughter of the C. M. S.* (London 1953).
3. James Denton, 'An African College: Its Story,' *Church Missionary Review*, August 1905; Christopher Fyfe, 'Royal Charter for Fourah Bay College,' *West African Review*, March 1960.
4. W. Vivian, 'The Missionary in West Africa,' *Journal of the African Society*, vol. 3, 1903–4, pp. 100–3; also H. R. Fox Bourne, 'Sierra Leone Troubles,' *The Fortnightly Review*, August 1898.
5. E. H. Elwin, 'The Temne Mission after the Revolt,' *Church Missionary Intelligencer*, October 1899, pp. 837–40.
6. Verrier Elwin, *The Tribal World of Verrier Elwin: An Autobiography* (Bombay and New York 1964), p. 2 (hereafter *Tribal World*).
7. Quoted in T. J. Thompson, *The Jubilee and Centenary Volume of Fourah Bay College* (Freetown 1930), pp. 106–7.
8. As reported in the *Sierra Leone Weekly News*, 22 February 1902 (based on an earlier report in *The Times* of London).
9. To the distance in years was added an emotional and intellectual distance, such that in later life Verrier had almost nothing to do with Basil. He will not appear again in this biography.

10. The verdicts, respectively, of Reverend F. W. Dillistone in an interview with this writer in June 1991, of Shamrao Hivale in *Scholar Gypsy: A Study of Verrier Elwin* (Bombay 1946), p. 3, and of Frank Moraes in his *Witness to an Era* (Bombay 1973), p. 22.
11. *Tribal World*, pp. 9–12.
12. Many years later, and aided by her granddaughter Eldyth, Flora Holman wrote down these and other tales from the Raj. See 'A true story of Indian life in the days of John Company,' typescript in Mss. Eur. D. 950/27, Elwin Papers, India Office Library, London (hereafter IOL).
13. As reported in *Church Missionary Review*, April 1909.
14. Archer, 'Notes on Verrier Elwin,' Mss. Eur. F. 236/228, IOL.
15. Hivale, *Scholar Gypsy*, p. 2.
16. *Tribal World*, pp. 2–3, 9–10.
17. Close's life and work are described in R. J. W. Evans, 'Town, Gown and Cloth: An Essay on the Foundations of the School,' in M. A. Girling and Sir Leonard Hooper, editors, *Dean Close: The First Hundred Years* (Cheltenham 1986).
18. This sketch of H. W. Flecker draws on books by a student, grandson and friend respectively: *God's Apprentice: The Autobiography of Stephen Neill*, edited by Eleanor M. Jackson (London 1984); John Sherwood, *No Golden Journey: A Biography of James Elroy Flecker* (London 1973); Charles Williams, *Flecker of Dean Close* (London 1946).
19. Geraldine Hodgson, *The Life of James Elroy Flecker, From Letters and Materials Provided by his Mother* (Oxford 1925); also Verrier Elwin, 'The Poetry of J. E. Flecker,' *The Statesman* (Calcutta), 28 June 1953.
20. R. F. McNeile, compiler, *A History of Dean Close School* (privately printed in 1966).
21. Quoted in Archer, 'Notes on Verrier Elwin.'

NOTES TO CHAPTER TWO

1. From a letter of January 1923 written by Robert Byron in Lucy Butler, editor, *Robert Byron: Letters Home* (London 1991), pp. 17–18.
2. Rowse, *Friends and Contemporaries* (London 1989).
3. 'Professor Garrod,' *The Postmaster*, vol. 1, no. 1, 1952; also the entry on Garrod in the *Merton College Register, 1900–1964* (Oxford 1964).
4. George Mallaby, *From my Level: Unwritten Minutes* (London 1965), p. 240.
5. *John Betjeman's Oxford* (reprint, Oxford 1990), p. 27; also D. J. Palmer, *The Rise of English Studies* (London 1965), pp. 115–30.
6. *Tribal World*, p. 22.

7. Letter of 12 March 1914, Kuruvilla Zachariah Papers, Merton College Archives, Oxford.
8. This last a phrase used in an paper presented by Verrier to the Bodley Club, a study of the range of geographical allusions in the plays and poems of Shakespeare. Verrier Elwin, 'Topographical Anachronisms,' manuscript in Mss Eur. D. 950/26, IOL.
9. Cf. Martin Green, *Children of the Sun: A Narrative of 'Decadence' in England after 1918* (London 1977); Cyril Connolly, 'The Twenties,' in his *The Evening Colonnade* (New York 1971); Robert Graves and Alan Hodge, *The Long Week-end: A Social History of Great Britian, 1918–39* (revised editon, New York 1963).
10. *Myrmidon Club Minutes, 1909—*, Merton College Archives.
11. Sykes, *Four Studies in Loyalty* (London 1946), p. 80.
12. F. M. Turner, 'Religion,' in Brian Harrison, editor, *The History of the University of Oxford: Volume VIII: The Twentieth Century* (Oxford 1994).
13. S. C. Ollard, *The Anglo-Catholic Revival: Some Persons and Principles* (London 1925).
14. Obituary in *Church Times*, 23 January 1953; letter from Benedict Green (F. W. Green's son) to the author, 21 June 1995.
15. See *Registrum College Mertonensis, 1915–36.*
16. *Bodley Club Minutes, 1914–23*, Merton College Archives.
17. Quoted in Turner, 'Religion,' p. 307.
18. Minutes of meetings of 16 March and 8 May 1922, in *Church Society Minutes, 1907–22*, Merton College Archives.
19. *Tribal World*, pp. 29–30.
20. Oliver Fielding-Clarke, *Unfinished Conflict: An Autobiography* (London 1970), p. 149f.
21. Bryan Beady, 'A Gandhi Disciple at Oxford,' *The Evening News*, 21 January 1932. Duns Scotus was a famous Franciscan of the fourteenth century, and the subject of Donne's poem "Duns Scotus' Oxford."
22. Church Society minutes of meetings held on 25 May 1923, 3 December 1923 and 3 March 1924, *Church Society Minutes, 1922—*, Merton College Archives.
23. *Tribal World*, pp. 24–5.
24. *Church Times*, 3 October 1924.
25. Cf. *The Decanian*, December 1924, p. 73.
26. Beady, 'A Gandhi Disciple at Oxford.'
27. Verrier Elwin, *Onward Bound* (pamplet printed in 1926 by the Oxford University Church Union), p. 10.
28. Untitled poem in Mss. Eur. 950/26, IOL.
29. *Tribal World*, p. 23.

30. Cf. Brian Harrison, 'College Life, 1918–39,' in Harrison, editor, *The History of the University of Oxford: Volume VIII: The Twentieth Century* (Oxford 1994).
31. Hivale, *Scholar Gypsy*, p. 9.
32. *Tribal World*, pp. 31–4.
33. J. C. Winslow, *The Indian Mystic: Some Thoughts on India's Contribution to Christianity* (London 1926), pp. 7–9.
34. J. C. Winslow, *Christa Seva Sangh* (London 1930).
35. Barbara Noreen, *A Wheat Grain Sown in India* (privately printed by the author, Wantage 1988).
36. *Tribal World*, p. 28.
37. Poem reproduced in Verrier Elwin, *Desiderium* (London 1926).
38. Minutes of meetings of 28 October 1926, 17 May 1927 and 3 June 1927, *Church Society Minutes, 1922—*, Merton College Archives.
39. Quoted in *Scholar Gypsy*, p. 11.
40. Cf. picture postcard with handwritten caption, 'Where Verrier got his call for India,' in Mss. Eur. D. 950/24, IOL.
41. *Tribal World*, p. 36.
42. Elwin to F. W. Green, 31 July 1927 (addressed, significantly, to 'My dear Guru'), letter in the possession of Benedict Green.

NOTES TO CHAPTER THREE

1. Quoted in J. C. Winslow, *The Eyelids of the Dawn: Memories, Reflections and Hopes* (London 1954), pp. 89–90.
2. *The Church Times*, 21 October 1927.
3. Oliver Fielding-Clarke, *Unfinished Conflict: An Autobiography* (London 1970), pp. 153–4.
4. H. V. E(lwin), 'A Passage to India,' in *The Servant of Christ* (newsletter of the Christa Seva Sangh), Feast of the Purification, 1928, copies held in the archives of Hilfield Priory, Dorset.
5. *Tribal World*, pp. 40–1.
6. Elwin to his mother, 22 November 1927, Mss. Eur. D. 950/1, IOL.
7. Quoted in Alexa Grace Cameron, 'Christian Missions and the Social Reform Movement in the City of Poona in Western India (1880–1920),' unpublished D.Phil. dissertation, Department of Education, New York University, 1973, p. 143.
8. Muriel Lester, *My Host the Hindu* (London 1931), pp. 128–9.
9. Father J. Sadananda, 'The aims and aspirations of the CSS,' unpublished typescript in W. Q. Lash Papers, Hilfield Priory, Dorset.
10. Chattopadhyay, *Inner Recesses, Outer Spaces: Memoirs* (New Delhi 1986), pp. 92–3.

11. Nehru, *An Autobiography* (1936: reprint London 1949), p. 375.
12. Letter of 5 December 1927, F. W. Green Papers, in the possession of Benedict Green.
13. 'Discussion on Fellowship,' in *Collected Works of Mahatma Gandhi*, vol. 35, p. 461.
14. H. V. E(lwin), 'The Friendly Road,' *The Servant of Christ*, Feast of St Barnabas, 1928, Hilfield Priory, Dorset.
15. *Young India*, 19 January 1928.
16. *Tribal World*, p. 42.
17. Elwin to George, 24 May 1928, Green Papers.
18. Ibid.
19. Roderick M. Bell to Brother John Charles, 8 November 1971, in 'File of Interviews and Correspondence with Brother John Charles,' Hilfield Priory, Dorset.
20. *Tribal World*, pp. 43–4.
21. H. V. E(lwin), 'The Library,' *The Servant of Christ*, Feast of St Francis, 1928.
22. Elwin to his mother, 6 September 1928, Mss. Eur. D. 950/1.
23. As recounted in *Tribal World*, p. 44.
24. Elwin to his mother, 31 August 1929, Mss Eur. D. 950/1.
25. Verrier Elwin, *Christian Dhyana, or Prayer of Loving Regard: A Study of 'The Cloud of Unknowing'* (London 1930).
26. Cf. the reference to the book in H. A. Popley, *K. T. Paul: Christian Leader* (Calcutta 1938), p. 189.
27. Verrier Elwin, *Richard Rolle: A Christian Sanyasi* (Madras 1930), preface and pp. 3, 7, 29, 67–73, 75–9, etc.
28. Ibid., p. 5.
29. Elwin to Sorella Amata, 12 March 1929, Mss. Eur. D. 950/7, IOL.
30. Idem., 27 June 1929.
31. Idem., 6 October 1929 (emphasis in original).
32. See Denis Dalton, *Mahatma Gandhi: Non-Violent Power in Action* (New York 1993), chapter IV.
33. Verrier Elwin, *Christ and Satyagraha* (Bombay 1930), pp. 3–4.
34. Circular letter from J. C. Winslow, Feast of St Francis, 1930, in L/P/J/6/2013, IOL.
35. Elwin to Sorella Amata, 30 April 1930, Mss Eur. D. 950/7, IOL.
36. Note of 22 July 1930, File 338 of 1930, Home (Political) department, National Archives of India, New Delhi (hereafter NAI).
37. 'Minutes of the Special Chapter of the CSS held on 18th June, 1930,' Folder 1, CSS/CPSS Record Room, Poona.
38. Reginald Reynolds, *To Live in Mankind: A Quest for Gandhi* (London 1951), pp. 72–7.

39. 'Minutes of the General Sabha held on 7th July 1930,' Folder 1, CSS/CPSS Record Room, Poona.
40. *Christ and Satyagraha*, pp. 5, 17, 18, 23, 47, etc.
41. Elwin to J. C. Kumarappa, letters of 26 June and 7 July 1930, Kumarappa Papers, Nehru Memorial Museum and Library, New Delhi (hereafter NMML). The *Bombay Chronicle* series, published in ten parts under the running title 'Studies in the Teaching of Gandhiji,' appeared between 24th September and 8th November 1930.
42. Notes of 4 September and 29 September 1930, both in L/P/J/6/2013, IOL.
43. *Servant of Christ*, no. 9, copy in File 338 of 1930, Home (Pol.), NAI.
44. Circular Letter (hereafter CL) from Elwin, written from Matheran, Ash Wednesday 1931, in W. Q. Lash Papers, Hilfield Priory, Dorset.
45. Verrier Elwin, 'A Fortnight in Gujerat: What Personal Investigation Revealed,' in three parts, *Bombay Chronicle*, 12, 13 and 14 January 1931.
46. Elwin to Sorella Amata, 30 April 1930, Mss. Eur. D. 950/7, IOL.
47. 'Copy of a speech delivered by Father Elwin at Shivaji Mandir, Poona, on 23 May 1931,' in File 11/II/1931, Home (Pol.), NAI.
48. Verrier Elwin, 'A Darshan of Bapu,' *The CSS Review*, vol. 1, no. 4, June 1931.
49. CL from Elwin, Labour Day 1931, in Lash Papers.
50. *Young India*, 21 May 1931.
51. Elwin to Mirabehn, 7 May 1931, copy in File 11/II/1931, Home (Pol.), NAI.
52. Cf. *Tribal World*, pp. 54–6.
53. Verrier Elwin, 'Ten Days with Mahatma Gandhi,' *The CSS Review*, vol. 1, no. 6, August 1931; also Elwin to Sorella Amata, 31 May 1931, Mss Eur. D. 950/7, IOL.
54. 'Extracts from the confidential weekly diary of the District Superintendent of Police, Surat, for 8 June and 13 June 1931;' 'Translation of a speech delivered by Father Elwin at Rayan, 4 June 1931,' both in File 11/II/1931, Home (Pol.), NAI.
55. Elwin to F. W. Green, 11 May 1931, Green Papers.
56. Elwin to Sorella Amata, 31 May 1931, Mss. Eur. D. 950/7, IOL.
57. Thakkar's life, work and writings are well covered in T. N. Jagadishan and Shyamlal, editors, *Thakkar Bapa Eightieth Birthday Commemoration Volume* (Madras 1949).
58. Quoted by Elwin in a note of 17 November 1961, File 69, Elwin Papers, NMML.
59. H. P. Desai, 'A. V. Thakkar: The Man and his Work,' *The Modern Review*, January 1928.

60. CL dated The Visitation, 1931, in Mss. Eur. 950/12, IOL.
61. Ibid.
62. Elwin to Sorella-Mother, 18 August 1931, Mss. Eur. D. 950/7, IOL.
63. CL from Elwin, Labour Day 1931, in Lash Papers.
64. Source cited in footnote 60 above.

NOTES TO CHAPTER FOUR

1. J. C. Winslow and Verrier Elwin, *The Dawn of Indian Freedom* (London 1931); Elwin to his mother, undated letter (August 1931?), in Mss. Eur. D. 950/1, IOL.
2. As recounted in a profile of Shamrao Hivale published in the *Times of India*, 29 April 1956.
3. Elwin to Sorella Amata, letters of 14 September and 18 September 1931, Mss. Eur. D. 950/7, IOL.
4. *Collected Works of Mahatma Gandhi*, vol. 48, p. 125.
5. *Tribal World*, p. 58f.
6. These paragraphs draw on the letters and notes in file 150/CDM, 1932 ('Correspondence regarding the activities of Father Verrier Elwin in the Central Provinces'), Political and Military Records, Madhya Pradesh Secretariat Record Room, Bhopal (hereafter MPSRR).
7. Elwin to Bishop Wood, 12 December 1931, copy in 'Personal' Box no. 2, Bishop's College Archives, Calcutta.
8. Wood to Bishop Foss Westcott, 15 December 1931; Wood to Elwin, 15 December 1931, both in Personal Box no. 2, Bishop's College Archives, Calcutta.
9. Elwin to 'My dear little Mother,' 2 January 1932, Mss. Eur. D. 950/7, IOL.
10. Elwin to 'My dear little Mother,' 2 January 1932, Mss. Eur. D. 950/7, IOL
11. *Tribal World*, p. 67.
12. Intercepted letter from Elwin to Brijkrishna Chandiwala, 7 January 1932, in File 5/7/1932, Home (Pol.), NAI.
13. *Tribal World*, pp. 70–3; *The Hindustan Times* (New Delhi), 27 January 1932.
14. Verrier Elwin, *What is Happening in the Northwest Province* (January 1932). This pamphlet was banned and confiscated by the government as soon as it was printed; for years even the author did not have a copy. The copy I have consulted, marked 'proscribed pamphlet,' is in File 29/9/1932, Home (Pol.), NAI.
15. Quoted in *District Gazetteer of Mandla* (1929), p. 2.

16. CL dated 28 January 1935, Mss. Eur. D. 950/12, IOL.
17. Verrier Elwin, *Leaves from the Jungle: A Diary of Life in a Gond Village* (1936; reprint New Delhi 1990, hereafter *Leaves*), pp. 31–3.
18. Elwin to Sorella Carisimma, letters of 7 February and 23 February 1932, Mss Eur. D. 950/7, IOL.
19. Letter of 24 February 1932, in file 150/CDM, 1932, Political and Military Records, MPSRR.
20. Verrier Elwin, *Truth about India: Can we Get it?* (London 1932); notice in *The Indian Review*, November 1932, p. 794.
21. *Leaves*, p. 40f; Elwin to Nonna, 30 March 1932, Mss Eur. D. 950/7, IOL.
22. Elwin to Sorella Amata, 30 March 1932; Shamrao to Sorella Amata, 16 April 1932, both in Mss. Eur. D. 950/7, IOL.
23. Shamrao Hivale, *Scholar Gypsy: A Study of Verrier Elwin* (Bombay 1946), p. 40.
24. Elwin to Wood, 1 March 1932, in Personal Box no. 2, Bishop's College Archives, Calcutta.
25. Wood to Elwin, 16 March 1932, in ibid.
26. Wood to Westcott, 9 April 1932, ibid., on which the next few paragraphs are based.
27. *Leaves*, p. 45.
28. Elwin to Westcott, 29 April 1932, in Personal Box no. 2, Bishop's College Archives, Calcutta.
29. Gandhi to Elwin, 25 April 1932, in the *Collected Works of Mahatma Gandhi*, vol. 49, p. 367.
30. Gandhi to Elwin, 27 May 1932, ibid., pp. 485–6.
31. Verrier Elwin, *St Francis of Assissi* (Madras 1933), pp. 3–5, 21, etc.
32. Elwin to 'My dear, dear friend,' 17 May 1932, Mss. Eur. D. 950/7, IOL.
33. Clipping from *The Times of India* and Elwin's letter to Naraindas Gandhi, 20 July 1932, both in File 25/38/1932, Home (Pol.), NAI; also *Tribal World*, pp. 79–80.
34. Elwin to 'My dear, dear friend,' 23 July 1932, Mss. Eur. D. 950/7, IOL.
35. Verrier Elwin, 'India Today,' *The India Review*, 9 July 1932, with attached note by Sir Malcolm Seton, both in L/P/J/6/2013, IOL.
36. Letter from Elwin to Secretary of State, 30 July 1932, in File 25/89/1932, Home (Pol.), NAI.
37. Note on meeting between Lord Snell and William Paton, dated 9 July 1931; Paton to Snell, 20 July 1931, both in L/P/J/6/2013, IOL.
38. Paton to Sir Findlater Stewart, letters of 3 August and 2 September 1932, in ibid.
39. Elwin to Lady Graham, letters of 31 July and 6 August 1932, File 25/89/1932, Home (Pol.), NAI.

40. Note by H. G. Gowan of 18 August 1932; note by C. M. Trivedi of 8 August 1932, both in ibid.
41. Hallett's notes of 23 August and 26 September 1932, in ibid.
42. Elwin to Nonna Amata Carissima, 26 August 1932, Mss Eur. D. 950/7, IOL.
43. Elwin to R. T. Peel, Under Secretary of State, dated 3 October 1932, in L/P/J/6/2013, IOL.
44. CL, dated Folkstone 10 October 1932, Mss. Eur. D. 950/12, IOL.
45. Bombay Government's notes of 13 September and 29 September 1932; Hallett's note of 6 October 1932; Haig's note of 8 October 1932; telegram from Home Department, Simla, to Secretary of State, 11 December 1932; and reply from Secretary of State, 12 November 1932, all in File 25/89/1932, Home (Pol.), NAI.

NOTES TO CHAPTER FIVE

1. *Bombay Chronicle*, 4 November 1932.
2. Bajaj to Elwin, dated Dhulia jail 10 November 1932, in File No. E1, Bajaj Papers, NMML.
3. Elwin to Gandhi, 7 January 1933, in Bhabagrahi Misra, *Verrier Elwin: Pioneer Indian Anthropologist* (London 1973), Appendix II ('Gandhi—Elwin correspondence'), pp. 116–17.
4. Barbara Noreen, *A Wheat Grain Sown in India* (Wantage 1988), pp. 52, 140, 142; Mary Gillet, 'Impressions of CSS and Hopes for the Future,' and 'Christ and Justice,' *The CSS Review* (Poona), issues of February 1932 and February 1933 respectively.
5. Mary Gillet to Sorella Maria, 14 January 1933, in Mss Eur. D. 950/8, IOL.
6. Elwin to Giovania, 25 January 1933, Mss Eur. D. 950/8.
7. Verrier Elwin and Mary Gillet, circular letter to friends, Candlemass 1933, ibid.
8. Elwin to Sorella Amata, Candlemass 1933, in Mss. Eur. D. 950/8.
9. Elwin to Gandhi, 12 February 1933, in Misra, op. cit., pp. 118–19.
10. *Tribal World*, pp. 56–7.
11. Quoted in Elwin to Sorella Amata, Candlemass 1933, Mss Eur. D. 950/8.
12. Gandhi to Elwin, 23 February 1933, *Collected Works of Mahatma Gandhi*, vol. 53, pp. 376–7.
13. Elwin to Gandhi, letters of 27 February 1933 and 18 March 1933, in Misra, op. cit., pp. 120, 123–5.
14. Elwin to Sorella Amata, 4 March 1933, Mss Eur. D. 950/8, IOL.
15. Mary Gillet to Sorella Maria, 4 March 1933, ibid.

16. Gandhi to Andrews, 7 April 1933, *Collected Works of Mahatma Gandhi*, vol. 54, pp. 328–9.
17. Gandhi to Elwin, 11 March 1933, in ibid., pp. 59–60.
18. Mary Gillet to Sorella Maria, 5 August 1933, Mss Eur. D. 950/8, IOL.
19. As quoted in Frank Moraes, *Witness to an Era* (New Delhi 1973), p. 33.
20. Entries for 15 & 16 July 1933, in Verrier Elwin, *Leaves from the Jungle: A Diary of Life in a Gond Village* (London 1936: reprint New Delhi 1990), pp. 67–9.
21. Circular Letter (hereafter CL) from Elwin, 20 July 1933, Mss Eur. D. 950/8, IOL.
22. CL of 28 July 1933, ibid.
23. Elwin to Sorella Maria, 2 September 1933, ibid.
24. 'The Gond Seva Mandal: Constitution and Rules' (1933–4), in File R of 1935, Commissioner's Record Room, Jabalpur.
25. Quoted in Hugh Tinker, *The Ordeal of Love: C. F. Andrews and India* (Delhi 1979), pp. 270–1.
26. Verrier Elwin, 'The Gond Seva Mandal,' *Hindustan Times*, 14 May 1934.
27. CLs by Elwin of Easter 1933, Epiphany 1934 and Easter 1934, Mss Eur. D. 950/12, IOL.
28. Elwin to Sorella Maria, 13 April 1934, Mss Eur. D. 950/9.
29. Clipping from the *News Chronicle* (undated, probably 1933 or 1934), Mss Eur. D. 950/14.
30. Elwin to Sorella Amata, 24 June 1933, Mss Eur. D. 950/8; CLs of 28 January and 12 May 1935, Mss Eur. D. 950/12.
31. A. V. Thakkar, 'My Tour Diary,' *Harijan*, 28 November 1934.
32. CL of 17 March 1935, Mss Eur. D. 950/9; *Leaves from the Jungle*, pp. 53–4, 139.
33. CL of 3 March 1934, Mss Eur. D. 950/9; Shamrao Hivale, *Scholar Gypsy: A Study of Verrier Elwin* (Bombay 1946), p. 153; *Leaves from the Jungle*, p. 103.
34. *Leaves from the Jungle*, pp. 6, 11, 12–13, 38, 41, 62, 65, 83, 114.
35. CL of 8 September 1934, Mss Eur. D. 950/9.
36. Elwin to Bill Lash, 22 May 1934, Lash Papers, Hilfield Priory, Dorset.
37. Elwin to his mother, 26 July 1935, and to his sister, 2 August 1935, Mss Eur. D. 950/1; Elwin to Sorella Maria, 10 April 1935, Mss Eur. D. 950/9; William Emilson, *Violence and Atonement: The Missionary Experiences of Mohandas Gandhi, Samuel Stokes and Verrier Elwin before 1935* (Frankfurt 1994), p. 341.
38. Verrier Elwin, review of Stephen Neill's *Builders of the Indian Church*, in *The Ashram Review*, September 1934, pp. 71–2.
39. CLs of 21 April and 4 August 1934, Mss Eur. D. 950/9.

40. CL dated 24 January 1936, Mss Eur. D. 950/13.
41. Wood to Temple, 4 February 1937; Carey to Foss Westcott, 27 September 1937, both in Personal Box no. 2, Bishop's College Archives, Calcutta.
42. Mrs M. O. Elwin to Foss Westcott, 13 December 1935, in ibid.
43. Foreword to the second edition of *Leaves from the Jungle* (Bombay 1958), pp. xxviii.
44. Verrier Elwin, *Studies in the Gospel* (Madras 1929), p. 56.
45. W. G. Archer, 'Notes on Verrier Elwin' (no date, probably from the 1940s), Mss Eur. F. 236/228, IOL; Dharmendra Prasad, 'Elwin in Mandla,' *India Cultures Quarterly*, vol. 34, nos. 1 and 2, 1979, the two sources on which this account relies.
46. Marguerite Milward, *Artist in Unknown India* (London 1948), pp. 155–6; *Leaves from the Jungle*, p. 146.
47. *Leaves from the Jungle*, pp. 3 to 10.
48. Verrier Elwin, 'In Baiga Land,' *The Modern Review* (Calcutta), April 1934.
49. CLs of Easter 1934 and 12 May 1935, Mss Eur. D. 950/12, IOL; Verrier Elwin, 'The Gond Seva Mandal,' *Hindustan Times*, 14 May 1934; news report in the *Bombay Chronicle*, 26 September 1935.
50. Elwin to the Deputy Commissioner, Mandla District, 14 May 1934, File 33 of 1937, District Record Room, Mandla.
51. Verrier Elwin, 'Gonds,' *Modern Review*, November 1933, pp. 547–8.
52. Shamrao Hivale and Verrier Elwin, *Songs of the Forest: The Folk-Poetry of the Gonds* (London 1935).
53. CLs of 17 March and 13 April 1934, Mss Eur. D. 950/9, IOL.
54. Lawrence Housman to Mrs M. O. Elwin, 21 October 1934, Mss Eur. D. 950/1, IOL.
55. *Leaves from the Jungle*, pp. 31, 118, 27.
56. *TLS*, 19 September 1936; other quotes from publicity material in John Murray Archives, London.
57. CL of 25 June 1936, Mss Eur. D. 950/13, IOL.
58. Marguerite Milward, *Artist in Unknown India*, pp. 152–68.

NOTES TO CHAPTER SIX

1. Elwin to Malinowski, letters of 3 November and 13 November 1936, Malinowski Papers, London School of Economics and Political Science; *Tribal World*, pp. 113–14.
2. The rest of this section is based on the notes and correspondence in L/P & J/2013, IOL.
3. The *Observer* interview was reproduced in *The Bombay Sentinel*, 21 December 1936.

4. Cf. *Bombay Chronicle*, 22 December 1936.
5. Elwin to E. S. Hyde, 17 February 1937, Box III, Hyde Papers, Centre for South Asian Studies, Cambridge.
6. Elwin to H. C. Greenfield, Divisional Commissioner, Jabalpur, 15 November 1937, Jabalpur Collectorate Records.
7. Elwin to Hyde, 20 June 1937, Hyde Papers.
8. Elwin to his mother, 11 September 1937, in Mss Eur. D. 950/1, IOL.
9. Elwin to his mother, 5 October 1937, Mss Eur. D. 950/1; Shamrao Hivale, *Scholar Gypsy: A Study of Verrier Elwin* (Bombay 1946), pp. 142, 153.
10. CL from Elwin dated 8 April 1937, Mss Eur. D. 950/13.
11. Elwin to S. C. Roy, 18 November 1938, in File No. DM 2, John Murray Archives, London.
12. Interview with Sahib Lal, Patangarh, January 1998.
13. Margaret Moore, 'A Visit to the Ashram,' in Temp Mss 4619, Agatha Harrison Papers, Friends House, London.
14. CL of June 1938, in *Scholar Gypsy*, pp. 149–50.
15. Eldyth's letters home, on which the following paragraphs are based, are in Mss. Eur. D. 950/18, IOL.
16. Verrier Elwin, *Phulmat of the Hills: A Tale of the Gonds* (London 1937).
17. Verrier Elwin, *A Cloud That's Dragonish: A Tale of Primitives* (London 1938).
18. CL of 4 January 1937, Mss. Eur. D. 950/13, IOL.
19. Elwin to Lord Gorell, 26 December 1937; John Murray to Elwin, 20 January 1938; Elwin to John Murray, 10 March 1938, all in File DM2, John Murray Archives.
20. Verrier Elwin, *The Baiga* (London 1939), Preface, chapters IV and VIII.
21. *The Baiga*, especially pp. 76–130.
22. *The Baiga*, pp. 511, 515–17.
23. *The Baiga*, p. xxx.
24. Sir John Squire, 'The Charm of the Aboriginal,' *Illustrated London News*, 23 December 1939.
25. Report by Alan Watts, dated 12 May 1938, File DG 40, John Murray Archives, London.
26. *TLS*, 9 December 1939.
27. J. H. Hutton to John Murray, 19 August 1938, File No. DG 40, John Murray Archives; W. V. Grigson, review of *The Baiga* in *Man*, March–April 1941, pp. 38–40; Beryl de Zoete, quoted in *Scholar Gypsy*, p. 186.
28. C. G. Chenevix Trench, review of *The Baiga*, *International Review of Missions*, no. 114, April 1940, pp. 283–6.
29. Elwin to his mother, letters of 13 September, 26 September, 25 November and 12 December 1939, Mss Eur. D. 950/2. Elwin did in due course win the Wellcome medal.

30. CL from Elwin dated 4 January 1940, Mss Eur. D. 950/14.
31. William and Mildred Archer, *India Seen and Observed* (London 1994); *Scholar Gypsy*, pp. 178, 186.
32. Elwin to Archer, 13 March 1940, Mss. Eur. F. 236/259, IOL.
33. Verrier Elwin, *The Agaria* (Bombay 1942).
34. Elwin to Barbara Smith, 19 July 1942, in File E 5, Oxford University Press Archives, Bombay.
35. Review by George Devereux in *The American Anthropologist*, vol. 48, no. 1, 1946, pp. 110–11.
36. M. N. Srinivas, 'The Observer and the Observed in the Study of Cultures,' in his *The Cohesive Role of Sanskritization and Other Essays* (New Delhi 1987).
37. Verrier Elwin, *The Muria and their Ghotul* (Bombay 1947), pp. viii–ix.
38. *The Agaria*, p. xxi.
39. Lovejoy and Boas, *Primitivism and Related Ideas in Antiquity* (Baltimore 1935).
40. Todorov, *On Human Diversity: Nationalism, Racism and Exoticism in French Thought*, translated by Catherine Porter (Cambridge, Mass. 1993).
41. See Lovejoy and Boas, *Primitivism*, pp. 7–8; Todorov, *On Human Diversity*, pp. 312, 316, etc.
42. 'The Tribal World of Verrier Elwin: An Autobiography,' manuscript copy in the archives of the Oxford University Press, Bombay, pp. 68–9, emphasis added.

NOTES TO CHAPTER SEVEN

1. *Tribal World*, p. 138.
2. Elwin to Archer, 12 June 1940; Note entitled 'I Married a Gond,' both in Mss Eur. F. 236/259, IOL.
3. Elwin to Archer, 2 May 1940, Mss Eur. F. 236/259.
4. Verrier Elwin, 'I Married a Gond,' *Man in India*, vol. 20, no. 4, 1940.
5. Elwin to his sister, 20 January 1940, Mss Eur. D. 950/2, IOL; Elwin to Archer, 2 May 1940, Mss Eur. F. 236/259.
6. Elwin to Archer, letters of 21 April and 12 June 1940, Mss Eur. F. 236/259.
7. *The Evening News of India*, 17 March 1939.
8. Verrier Elwin, 'With a Camera in the Indian Jungle,' *Sunday Statesman* (Calcutta), 1 March 1942.
9. Archer, 'Notes on Verrier Elwin,' Mss Eur. F. 236/228; Elwin to Archer, 3 April 1940, Mss Eur. F. 236/259, IOL.
10. Circular letter (hereafter CL) from Elwin of 1 May 1940, Mss Eur. D. 950/14, IOL.

11. Elwin to E. S. Hyde, 12 April 1940, Box III, Hyde Papers, Centre for South Asian Studies, Cambridge.
12. CL from Elwin of 24 December 1940, Box III, Hyde Papers (emphasis added).
13. Elwin to Archer, 23 August 1940, Mss Eur. F. 236/259.
14. Krishna Hutheesingh, 'Verrier Elwin,' *National Herald* (Lucknow), 13 September 1940.
15. *The Times of India*, 31 July 1940.
16. As reported in the *Bombay Chronicle*, 6 August 1941.
17. Saguna Karnad, 'A Gond Girl Looks at Bombay,' *The Illustrated Weekly of India*, 8 September 1940.
18. Archer, 'Notes on Verrier Elwin;' Elwin to Archer, 23 August 1940, Mss Eur. F. 236/259.
19. quoted in D. F. Karaka, *This India* (Bombay 1944), p. 92.
20. Elwin to Archer, November 1942, Mss Eur. F. 236/259.
21. Elwin to Archer, 2 May 1940, ibid.
22. Quoted in Tim Hilton's obituary of Hutchinson, *The Guardian* (London), 6 June 1991.
23. W. G. Archer, 'Notes on Verrier Elwin.'
24. John Miles (former Warden of Merton College, Oxford) to Warden of Merton, 17 August 1949, File No D 1-46, Merton College Archives, Oxford.
25. Cf. Nandini Sundar, *Subalterns and Sovereigns: An Anthropological History of Bastar, 1840–1995* (New Delhi 1998).
26. Elwin to E. S. Hyde, letters of 9 February 1936, 20 June 1937, 28 October 1937, 31 December 1938, 7 August 1939, 11 February 1940, 12 April 1940 and 15 April 1940, all in Box III, Hyde papers; Elwin to his sister Eldyth, 26 October 1940, Mss Eur. D. 950/2, IOL.
27. Shamrao Hivale, *Scholar Gypsy: A Study of Verrier Elwin* (Bombay 1946), p. 187.
28. Elwin to his mother, 14 December 1940, Mss Eur. D. 950/2.
29. Untitled note by Verrier Elwin on the administration of the Bastar State (written in 1941 or 1942), File A, Box VIII, Hyde Papers.
30. Elwin to E. S. Hyde, 8 February 1941, Box III, Hyde Papers.
31. Verrier Elwin, *Loss of Nerve: A Comparative Study of the Contact of Peoples in the Aboriginal Areas of the Bastar State and the Central Provinces of India* (Bombay 1941); Elwin to R. E. Hawkins, 28 August 1940, File E 5, Oxford University Press (OUP) Archives, Bombay.
32. The Bastar Dassera festival is described in D. N. Majumdar's classic essay, 'Tribal Cultures and Acculturation,' Presidential Address to the Section of Anthropology, printed in *Proceedings of the Twenty-sixth Indian Science Congress, Lahore, 1939* (Calcutta 1940), pp. 179–224.

33. Elwin to Archer, 8 November 1941, Mss. Eur. F. 236/259, IOL; Elwin to E. S. Hyde, 8 November 1941, Box III, Hyde Papers, Cambridge.
34. Elwin to his sister, 9 December 1940, Mss Eur. D. 950/2, IOL.
35. Jerome Menzies, letter to the editor, *Indian Express* (Bombay), 28 December 1978.
36. Entries for 4 December and 5 December 1941, and for 3 January, 6 February, 9 February, 9 March and 10 March 1942 in 'Journal of Tour in South Maria country, November 1941 to March 1942,' Mss Eur. D. 950/15, IOL.
37. Verrier Elwin, *The Muria and their Ghotul* (Bombay 1947), pp. ix, 292, 334, 419, 431, 475, 614–16, 620, 633, 636, 655–6, 659, etc.
38. Ibid., pp. 420, 656.
39. Elwin to Hawkins, 8 February 1943, File E6, OUP Archives.
40. Cf. *Illustrated Weekly of India*, 9 July 1942.
41. Elwin to Hawkins, 18 June 1944, File E 6, OUP Archives. 'Miss Mayo' was the American writer Katherine Mayo, whose book *Mother India* was an attack on caste and the suppression of women in India: although not quite dismissed by Gandhi as a 'drain-inspector's report'—Gandhi thought it deserved attention for pointing out Indian indifference to hygiene—the book nonetheless had called forth nine book-length rejoinders by lesser Indians.
42. Alfred Kinsey, et. al., *Sexual Behavior in the Human Female* (Philadelphia 1953).
43. Cf. Simeran Man Singh Gell, *The Ghotul in Muria Society* (London 1992).
44. *The Listener*, 9 December 1948; *Man*, vol. 49, November 1948.
45. Evelyn Wood, quoted in *Scholar Gypsy*, p. 193.
46. Translator's preface, in M. K. Gandhi, *An Autobiography or the Story of my Experiments with Truth* (second edition: Ahmedabad 1940).
47. Verrier Elwin, 'Mahadev,' in D. G. Tendulkar, M. Chalapathi Rau, Mridula Sarabhai and Vithalbhai K. Jhaveri, editors, *Gandhiji: His Life and Work* (Bombay 1944).
48. Elwin to Archer, 17 September 1946, Mss. Eur. F. 236/264, IOL.
49. Conversation with K. Rangachari, February 1994.
50. Verrier Elwin, *Maria Murder and Suicide* (Bombay 1943), pp. ix–x, xxv, 3–5, 36–8, 51, 53, 81, 98–9, 207–9, 215, 219–20, etc.
51. Elwin to E. S. Hyde, 26 February 1939, File A, Box VIII, Hyde Papers.
52. Elwin to Archer, 18 July 1942, Mss Eur. F. 236/260, IOL.
53. Elwin to R. E. Hawkins, 6 December 1942, File E6, OUP Archives; Verrier Elwin, 'Notes on the Juang,' *Man in India*, vol. 28, no. 1, 1948.
54. Elwin to Archer, 6 December and 19 December 1942, Mss Eur. F. 236/260.
55. Verrier Elwin, *Report of a Tour in the Bonai, Keonjhar and Pal Laharia*

States (1943, privately circulated, printed at The British India Press, Bombay).

56. Cf. Elwin's letters to J. H. Hutton quoted in A. C. Sinha, 'Indian Social Anthropology and its Cambridge Connections,' *The Eastern Anthropologist*, vol. 44, no. 4, October–December 1991.
57. 'Dr Verrier Elwin's report on tribals of Ganjam and Koraput,' dated April 1945, in File No. 145, Elwin Papers, Nehru Memorial Museum and Library, New Delhi.
58. *The Baiga*, p. 235.
59. Verrier Elwin, *The Aboriginals* (Bombay 1943), pp. 18–19.
60. *The Aboriginals*, p. 8; *The Muria and their Ghotul*, p. 368.
61. Elwin, *Loss of Nerve*, pp. 9–27; *Maria Murder and Suicide*, pp. 35–6.
62. *Loss of Nerve*, p. 44; Note on education by Elwin reproduced in W. V. Grigson, *The Aboriginal Problem in the Central Provinces* (Nagpur 1943), pp. 399–403.
63. Elwin to Sorella Maria, 15 March 1938, Mss Eur. D. 950/10, IOL.
64. *The Muria and their Ghotul*, p. xii.

NOTES TO CHAPTER EIGHT

1. *Tribal World*, pp. 137–8.
2. S. C. Dube, review of *Tribal World*, in *The Eastern Anthropologist*, vol. 12, no. 2, 1964, pp. 134–6.
3. *Bombay Chronicle*, 17 October 1941.
4. D. F. Karaka, *I've Shed my Tears: A Candid View of Resurgent India* (New York 1947), pp. 100–1.
5. D. F. Karaka, 'Verrier Elwin,' *Bombay Chronicle*, 7 August 1940.
6. Krishna Hutheesingh, 'Verrier Elwin,' *National Herald* (Lucknow), 13 September 1940.
7. Cf. Correspondence between Elwin and Thakkar in P. Kodanda Rao Papers, NMML; P. Kodanda Rao, 'Aboriginalisthan: Anthropologist's Imperium,' *Social Science Quarterly*, vol. 30, no. 2, October 1943.
8. Most recently in Vinay Srivastava, 'The Ethnographer and the People: Reflections on Field Work,' in two parts, *Economic and Political Weekly*, 1–8 and 15 June 1991, an account of a 1987 visit to the Baiga Chak in the tracks of Elwin.
9. Bhumijan Seva Mandal, Bulletin Number 1, 1 March 1942, Mss Eur. D. 950/17, IOL.
10. Verrier Elwin, 'Do We Really Want to Keep Them in a Zoo,' typescript in Subject File no. 7, P. Kodanda Rao Papers, Nehru Memorial Museum and Library, New Delhi, p. 2.
11. Cf. G. S. Ghurye, *I and Other Explorations* (Bombay 1973); Dhirendra

Narain. 'Govind Sadashiv Ghurye: Reminscences,' in A. R. Momin, editor, *The Legacy of G. S. Ghurye: A Centennial Festschrift* (Bombay 1996); 'Prof. G. S. Ghurye: An Introduction,' in K. M. Kapadia, editor, *Professor Ghurye Felicitation Volume* (Bombay 1955).

12. G. S. Ghurye, *The Aborigines—So Called—and their Future* (Poona 1943).
13. M. N. Srinivas, review of *The Aboriginals*, in *Journal of the University of Bombay* (History, Economics and Sociology), New Series, vol. 12, no. 4, January 1944, pp. 91–4.
14. Interview with M. N. Srinivas, Bangalore, August 1994.
15. Hivale, *Scholar Gypsy: A Study of Verrier Elwin* (Bombay 1946), pp.187, 194.
16. Elwin to W. G. Archer, 6 January 1944, Mss Eur. F. 236/262, IOL.
17. Verrier Elwin, 'Truth in Anthropology,' Presidential address to the Section of Anthropology and Archaeology, in *Proceedings of the 31st Session of the Indian Science Congress* (New Delhi 1944), pp. 91–107.
18. Elwin to his mother, 28 May 1944, Mss Eur. D. 950/3, IOL.
19. Verrier Elwin, *Folk-Tales of Mahakoshal* (Bombay 1944).
20. Verrier Elwin and Shamrao Hivale, *Folk-Songs of the Maikal Hills* (Bombay 1944).
21. Verrier Elwin, *Folk-Songs of Chattisgarh* (Bombay 1946).
22. Verrier Elwin, 'Epilogue,' *Man in India*, vol. 23, no. 1, March 1943 (Folk-Song number), p. 88; *Folk-Songs of the Maikal Hills*, pp. xvi, xix–xx, xxviii.
23. Undated typescript entitled 'Bhumijan Seva Mandal,' in Elwin correspondence, Bhulabhai Desai papers, NMML; Elwin to E. S. Hyde, 6 July 1944, Box III, Hyde Papers, Cambridge.
24. Verrier Elwin, 'Missionaries and Aboriginals,' undated typescript (probably written in 1944), in Bhulabhai Desai Papers, NMML.
25. 'Report of Some Catholic Priests of Mandla District in Connection with the Questionnaires Issued by the Aboriginal Tribes Enquiry Officer,' Box II, Hyde Papers.
26. Elwin to W. V. Grigson, 6 December 1940; Elwin, 'Note on the Gond "Karma" ' (undated ts., prob. from early 1940s), both in Box II, Hyde Papers.
27. *The Hindustan Times* (New Delhi), 14 June 1944.
28. *The Hindustan Times*, 8 July 1944.
29. Ibid.
30. As reported in *The Guardian* (Madras), 7 December 1944.
31. Simon Bara, *Aboriginals and Missionaries: A Rejoinder to Verrier Elwin* (Ranchi 1944).
32. See correspondence in L/P & J/6919 of 1944, IOL.
33. Amery to Wavell, notes of 9 August and 28 September 1944, L/P & J/6787, IOL.

34. Wavell to Amery, 3 December 1944, in Nicholas Mansergh, editor, *The Transfer of Power, Volume V* (London 1974), pp. 263–4.
35. Undated circular letter (prob. 1945 or 1946) from Elwin; Elwin to P. Thakurdas, 2 January 1945; circular letter from P. Thakurdas of 15 January 1947, all in File 337, Purshottamdas Thakurdas Papers, NMML.
36. Elwin to Sir Francis Wylie, 8 November 1944, in L/P & J/6787, IOL.
37. Quoted in *The Guardian* (Madras), 23 November 1944.
38. Elwin to Archer, 30 November 1941, Mss Eur. F. 236/259, IOL.
39. *The Aboriginals* (Bombay 1943), pp. 31–2.
40. *The Aboriginals* (second edition: Bombay 1944), pp. 29–31.
41. Verrier Elwin, 'Notes on a Kondh Tour,' *Man in India*, vol. 24, no. 1, March 1944; 'Notes on the Kondhs,' in File 160, Elwin Papers, NMML; Felix Padel, *The Sacrifice of Human Being: British Rule and the Konds of Orissa* (New Delhi 1995).
42. Verrier Elwin, *Bondo Highlander* (Bombay 1950), Preface; 'Tribal Life in Middle India,' *Geographical Magazine*, February 1950; 'My Worst Journey,' *Geographical Magazine*, October 1954.
43. Based on a handwritten, untitled narrative of 34 pages in File 64, Elwin Papers, NMML.
44. Verrier Elwin, 'Saora Pictographs,' *Marg*, vol. 2, no. 3, Summer 1948.
45. Elwin to Archer, 7 July 1945, Mss Eur. F. 236/263, IOL.
46. Elwin to John Murray, 11 July 1945, File DG 40, John Murray Archives, London.
47. Untitled note of 1945, File 160, Elwin Papers, NMML.
48. Entries by Shamrao for 14 May and 15 May 1942, Journal for April–August 1942, Mss. Eur. 950/16, IOL.
49. Archer, 'Notes on Verrier Elwin,' Mss. Eur. F. 236/228, IOL.
50. Elwin to his mother, 7 May 1944, Mss. Eur. D. 950/3, IOL.
51. Elwin to Archer, letters of 9 January 19 April, and 29 April 1946, Mss. Eur. F. 236/264, IOL.
52. Elwin to S. S. Khambata (of Wadia and Ghandy, Solicitors, Bombay), 31 July 1946, Verrier Elwin Papers, Shillong.
53. Diary entry of 30 November 1946, ibid.
54. Tata to Patel, 23 September 1946, ibid.
55. Elwin to his mother, 5 November 1947, Mss. Eur. D. 950/3, IOL.
56. Shamrao Hivale, *The Pardhans of the Upper Nerbudda Valley* (Bombay 1946).
57. Shamrao Hivale, *Scholar Gypsy*, pp. 9, 216, 217, etc.
58. Quoted in the *Bombay Chronicle*, 29 September 1941.
59. Shamrao's work is described in Elwin to E. S. Hyde, 24 July 1943, File A, Box VIII, Hyde papers; Elwin to Hyde, letters of 23 May 1941 and 6 July 1944, Box III, Hyde Papers; CL from Elwin of 1 October 1941, Mss Eur.

D. 950/14; Bhumijan Seva Mandal Bulletins dated March 1942, August 1943 and September 1945, in Mss Eur. D. 950/17.

60. *The Muria and their Ghotul*, p. xiii.
61. Entries of 5 August and 6 August 1942 in Journal for April–August 1942, Mss. Eur. 950/16, IOL.
62. CL of 29 September 1946, Mss Eur. D. 950/17.
63. Cf. correspondence in L/P & J/6787, IOL.
64. Elwin to Archer, 17 September 1946, Mss. Eur. F. 236/264, IOL. His father, of course, was another kind of D.D., a Doctor of Divinity.
65. Elwin to his mother, letters of 12 May and 28 May 1947, Mss. Eur. 950/3, IOL; diary entries of 8 June, 22 June and 30 June 1947, Elwin Papers, Shillong.
66. Verrier Elwin, 'The Anthropological Survey of India: Part I, History and Recent Development: Part II, The Five Year Plan,' *Man*, vol. 68, June and July 1948, pp. 68–9, 80–1.
67. CL from Elwin of 1 October 1941, Mss Eur. D. 950/14, IOL; Bhumijan Seva Mandal Bulletins dated March 1942, July 1942, August 1943 and October 1944, all in Mss Eur. D. 950/17, IOL.
68. 'Anthropology and the Ordinary Man.' Typescript of two talks by Verrier Elwin on All India Radio, in File No. IV, G. E. Mallam Papers, Centre for South Asian Studies, Cambridge.

NOTES TO CHAPTER NINE

1. Letter from Thompson to Gandhi, 2 October 1931, quoted in William W. Emilsen, *Violence and Atonement: The Missionary Experiences of Mohandas Gandhi, Samuel Stokes and Verrier Elwin in India before 1935* (Frankfurt 1994), p. 141.
2. Circular letter (hereafter CL) from Shamrao Hivale, 15 November 1947, Mss Eur. F. 236/265, IOL.
3. 'Extracts from the evidence given by Dr. Verrier Elwin before the Excluded and partially Excluded Areas sub-committee of the Constituent Assembly of India at New Delhi on 13 August 1947,' in Mss Eur. F. 236/265, IOL.
4. Elwin to Archer, 16 December 1947, Mss Eur. F. 236/265, IOL.
5. These two paragraphs are based on Elwin's diary for 1947–8, Verrier Elwin Papers, Shillong.
6. Entry for 5th February, ibid.
7. Elwin to Archer, letters of 16 December 1947 and 12 January 1948, Mss Eur. F. 236/265, IOL.
8. Elwin to Archer, 8 January 1949, Mss Eur. F. 236/266, IOL.
9. Interview with Sunil Janah, London, September 1992.
10. Interview with Jivan Lal, Patangarh, January 1998.

11. W. G. Archer, 'Notes on Verrier Elwin,' Mss. Eur. 236/228, IOL.
12. Elwin to Archer, 8 January 1949, Mss Eur. F. 236/266, IOL.
13. Interview with Kosi Elwin, Ryatwar, January 1998.
14. Cf. letters from George Kennedy (of Fowler and Sons) to Elwin, 11 March and 19 November 1949, Elwin Papers, Shillong.
15. Elwin to Archer, 27 October 1948, Mss Eur. F. 236/265, IOL.
16. Letters from Elwin to Archer of 17 August 1948, 8 January 1949, 25 January 1951 and 29 August 1951, Mss Eur. F. 236/266, IOL.
17. Adrian Brent, *The Snares of Death*, typescript in File 148, Elwin Papers, NMML.
18. Adrian Brent, *The Five Men*, typescript in File 70, Elwin Papers, NMML.
19. Diary entry of 30 May 1949, Elwin Papers, Shillong.
20. Elwin to Mildred Archer, 3 June 1949, Mss Eur. F. 236/266, IOL.
21. As recalled by a distinguished British anthropologist and former student of Evans-Pritchard, in a conversation with me in June 1991.
22. Cf. correspondence in File D. 1. 46, Merton College Archives.
23. Diary entry of 5 June 1949, Elwin Papers, Shillong.
24. Elwin to his mother, letters of 27 October and 10 December 1950, Mss Eur. D. 950/3, IOL.
25. Elwin to his mother, letters of 5 December, 10 December, and 18 December 1950 and 4 January 1951, Mss Eur. D. 950/2.
26. Diary entry for 31 December 1950, Elwin Papers, Shillong.
27. Elwin to his mother, 30 January 1951, Mss Eur. D. 950/3.
28. Elwin to his mother, 11 June and 30 June 1951, Mss Eur. D. 950/3.
29. Archer to Elwin, 12 November 1951, Mss. Eur. F. 236/266, IOL; Elwin to his mother, 22 October 1949, Mss Eur. D. 950/3, IOL.
30. Diary entries of 14 July and 23 July 1951, Elwin Papers, Shillong.
31. Diary entries for 13 October and 14 October 1951, ibid.
32. Gerald Sparrow, *Land of the Moonflower* (London 1958), pp. 140–51.
33. *Tribal World*, pp. 220–2.
34. These poems are reproduced from the diary for 1951, Elwin Papers, Shillong.
35. Diary entry for 4 January 1952, Elwin Papers, Shillong.
36. *Tribal World*, p. 85.
37. See M. K. Gandhi, *Satyagraha in South Africa* (second English edition: Ahmedabad 1950), Translator's Note.
38. Pp. 62–3 of 'The Snares of Death,' typescript in File 148, Elwin Papers, NMML.
39. Elwin to Victor Sassoon, 26 January 1951, copy in Elwin Papers, Shillong.
40. Cf. Elwin to his mother, 6 May 1951, Mss Eur. D. 950/3, IOL; Elwin to his sister Eldyth, 5 May 1953, Mss Eur. D. 950/4, IOL; Elwin to Barbara

Smith, 15 May 1952, File 434E, OUP Archives, Bombay; Elwin to Archer, letters of 25 January 1949 and 11 February 1950, Mss Eur. F. 236/266, IOL.

41. TWARU Newsletter No. 5, July 1953, in File 337, Purshottamdas Thakurdas Papers, NMML.
42. CL from Shamrao Hivale, 15 November 1947, Mss Eur. F. 236/266, IOL.
43. Printed appeal for TARU, enclosed with VE's letter to Sir Purshottamdas Thakurdas of 8 December 1949, in File 337, Thakurdas Papers, NMML.

NOTES TO CHAPTER TEN

1. R. D. Acland to Q. Q. Lash, 30 May 1936, in Lash Papers, Hilfield Priory, Dorset.
2. Elwin to Hawkins, 8 August 1947, File 509, OUP Archives, Mumbai.
3. Letter of 8 April 1951, Mss. Eur. D. 950/3, IOL.
4. Elwin to Devendra Satyarthi, 22 February 1952, File 509R, OUP Archives.
5. Verrier Elwin, *The Tribal Art of Middle India: A Personal Record* (Bombay 1951).
6. Marion W. Smith, review of *Myths of Middle India*, in *American Anthropologist*, vol. 50, no. 3, 1950, pp. 535–6.
7. Verrier Elwin, *Myths of Middle India* (Bombay 1949).
8. Verrier Elwin, *Bondo Highlander* (Bombay 1950), pp. 5, 7, 22, 87, etc.
9. Elwin to P. J. Chester, 25 September 1947, File E7, OUP Archives.
10. Interview with S. C. Dube, New Delhi, January 1994.
11. See *Illustrated Weekly of India*, 25 November 1951.
12. D. N. Majumdar, review of *Bondo Highlander*, *Man in India*, vol. 32, no. 1, 1952, pp. 43–6.
13. Elwin to his mother, 8 January 1951, Mss Eur. D. 950/3, IOL.
14. Elwin to Archer, 29 August 1951, Mss. Eur. F. 236/266, IOL. Elwin's place in the history of anthropology is discussed more fully in my essay, 'Between Anthropology and Literature: The Ethnographies of Verrier Elwin,' *Journal of the Royal Anthropological Institute (incorporating Man)*, vol. 3, no. 2, June 1998.
15. Verrier Elwin, *Tribal Myths of Orissa* (Bombay 1954).
16. Elwin to his mother, 6 May 1948 and 29 November 1950, Mss Eur. D. 950/4, IOL.
17. Elwin to P. J. Chester, dtd 15 October 1951, File 509R, OUP Archives.
18. Verrier Elwin, 'Forest People 4: The Gadabas,' *Illustrated Weekly of India* (hereafter IWI), 30 July 1950.
19. Review of *The Religion of an Indian Tribe* by C. von Fürer-Haimendorf in *Bulletin of the School of Oriental and African Studies*, vol. 19, part 3, 1957, pp. 602–3.

20. Verrier Elwin, *The Religion of an Indian Tribe* (Bombay 1955), pp. 8, 10, 141, 171, 559, 561, 571, etc.
21. Elwin to Archer, 31 July 1952, Mss. Eur. F. 236/266, IOL.
22. Elwin to his mother, 7 July 1952, Mss Eur. D. 950/3, IOL.
23. Cf. Elwin to his mother, letters of 29 November 1950 and 19 October 1952, ibid.
24. From File 64, Elwin Papers, NMML.
25. Verrier Elwin, 'Comic Strips of Rural India,' in three parts, *Illustrated Weekly of India* (hereafter IWI), 15, 22 and 29 June 1952.
26. Verrier Elwin, 'Forest Peoples,' in six parts, IWI, 9 July, 16 July, 23 July, 30 July, 6 August, and 13 August 1950.
27. 'The Dance in Tribal India: Part V,' IWI, 19 June 1955.
28. Verrier Elwin, 'Forest Peoples: Part IV: the Gadabas,' IWI, 30 July 1950; also his 'Aboriginals in Free India,' *The March of India*, May 1952.
29. Verrier Elwin, 'Children of the Forest at Play,' IWI, 26 October 1952.
30. Cf. 'The Dance in Tribal India: Part I," IWI, 22 May 1955; 'The Carved Totems of the Uraons,' IWI, 5 April 1953.
31. CL of 15 November 1948, Mss Eur. D. 950/17, IOL.
32. Verrier Elwin, 'Ancient and Modern Man,' in *Nehru Abhinandan Granth: A Birthday Book* (New Delhi 1949).
33. Elwin to Archer, 4 January 1948, Mss Eur. F. 236/266, IOL.
34. Elwin to Archer, 10 July 1950, ibid.
35. Shamrao Hivale to Mrs M. O. Elwin, 28 June 1951, Mss. Eur. D. 950/4, IOL.
36. Elwin to Archer, 6 October 1950, Mss. Eur. F. 236/266, IOL.
37. Elwin to his mother, letters of 20 January and 29 January 1952, Mss. Eur. D. 950/3, IOL.
38. Dom Moraes to Elwin, 30 October 1953, Miscelleaneous Correspondence, Elwin Papers, NMML.
39. Dom Moraes, *Answered by Flutes: Reflections on Madhya Pradesh* (Bombay 1983), p. 158; *idem, My Son's Father: An Autobiography* (London 1968), pp. 82–3; interview with Dom Moraes, Bombay, December 1990.
40. Interview with Sahib Lal, Patangarh, January 1998.
41. Elwin to Archer, letters of 14 September and 15 November 1951, Mss. Eur. F. 236/266, IOL.
42. Diary entry of 27th January 1952, Elwin Papers, Shillong.
43. Elwin to his mother, letters of 20 January, 29 January and 4 February 1952, Mss. Eur. D. 950/4, IOL.
44. Elwin to Archer, 11 February 1952, Mss. Eur. F. 236/266, IOL.
45. Cf. *Bondo Highlander*, chapter V, 'The Establishment of Love.'
46. quoted in Archer, 'Notes on Verrier Elwin,' in Mss Eur. F. 236/228, IOL.
47. Elwin to Sassoon, 2 May 1952, Elwin Papers, Shillong.

48. 'The Tribal Folk,' in *Jawaharlal Nehru's Speeches, Volume II* (New Delhi 1954), pp. 576–83.
49. Elwin to Archer, 31 July 1952, Mss Eur. F. 236/266, IOL; Elwin to Sassoon, 23 June 1952, Elwin Papers, Shillong.
50. Elwin to his mother, 31 August 1952, Mss Eur. D. 950/3, IOL.
51. Elwin to his sister, 29 September 1952, ibid.
52. Elwin to Nehru, 21 September 1952, copy in Miscelleaneous Correspondence, Elwin Papers, NMML.
53. Copy of will dated 10th November 1952, in the possession of Arvind Khare.
54. Elwin to his mother, letters of 27 November, 3 December, 15 December, and 30 December 1952, and 6 January and 12 January 1953, Mss Eur. 950/3 & 4, IOL.
55. Verrier Elwin, 'Impressions of Assam,' in Satis Chandra Kakati, editor, *Discovery of Assam* (Gauhati 1954), p. 177.
56. *Tribal World*, p. 229.
57. Elwin to Jairamdas Daulatram, 24 January 1953, Elwin Papers, NMML.
58. Elwin to Sassoon, 18 February 1953, Elwin Papers, Shillong.
59. Diary entry of 28 February 1953 (Holi), ibid.
60. Elwin to his mother, 19 June 1953, Mss Eur. D. 950/4, IOL.
61. Mrs M. O. Elwin to Mrs K. Hivale, 22 August 1953, Elwin Papers, Shillong.
62. Shamrao to Eldyth, letters of 5 September and 22 October 1953, Mss Eur. D. 950/4.
63. Cf. Elwin to Archer, 23 October 1953, Mss Eur. F. 236/266, IOL.
64. Jehangir Patel to Elwin, 12 July 1953, Elwin Papers, NMML.
65. Diary entry of 20 September 1953, Elwin Papers, Shillong.
66. Elwin to his mother, 21 September 1953, Mss. Eur. D. 950/4, IOL.
67. A. A. Noronha, 'Dr Verrier Elwin: Reminscences,' in W. Q. Lash Papers, Hilfield Priory, Dorset.
68. Elwin to his mother, 6 June 1953, Mss Eur. D. 950/4, IOL.
69. Letter of 1 March 1953, in *Jawaharlal Nehru: Letters to Chief Ministers, Volume III* (New Delhi, n.d.), pp. 247–8.
70. The circumstances of Elwin's NEFA appointment are described in letters to his mother of 6 June and 26 November 1953, Mss. Eur. D. 950/4, IOL; *Tribal World*, pp. 229–33.
71. Elwin to his mother, letters of 12 December and 19 December 1953, Mss. Eur. D. 950/4.
72. Elwin to his mother, 12 December 1953, Mss. Eur. D. 950/4.
73. Elwin to T. N. Kaul, 11 December 1953, File 8, Elwin Papers, NMML.
74. J. R. D. Tata to Verrier Elwin, 4 January 1954, Elwin Papers, Shillong.
75. Elwin to Hawkins, 12 January 1954, File 434E, OUP Archives.
76. Diary entry of 22 December 1953, Elwin Papers, Shillong.
77. Elwin to Jairamdas Daulatram, 12 December 1953, Elwin Papers, NMML.

NOTES TO CHAPTER ELEVEN

1. Elwin to K. L. Mehta, 15 May 1955, File 7, Elwin Papers, NMML.
2. Elwin to his mother, letters of 12 January, 17 January and 25 January 1954, in Mss. Eur. D. 950/5, IOL.
3. Elwin to Jairamdas Daulatram, 2 January 1954, File 151, Elwin Papers, NMML.
4. Elwin to the Deputy Commissioner, United Khasi and Jaintia Hills, 20 February 1954, File 141, Elwin Papers, NMML.
5. T. N. Kaul, 'A brief note on NEFA, Manipur State, Naga Hill District (Kohima) and Lushai Hills' (Secret), dated 21 April 1953, File 8, Elwin Papers, NMML.
6. Elwin to his mother, letters of 10 March and 25 March 1954, Mss. Eur. D. 950/5, IOL.
7. Unless otherwise mentioned, the quotes in the rest of this section are taken from the unpublished 'Tour Notes of Dr Verrier Elwin for the months of March–April, 1954 on the Tuensang Frontier Division,' in File 139, Elwin Papers, NMML.
8. Elwin to his mother, 29 June 1954, Mss. Eur. D. 950/5, IOL.
9. Elwin to his mother, letters of 20 February and 19 June 1955, ibid.
10. Interview with Amina Jayal, New Delhi, April 1994.
11. Diary entry of 9 July 1954, Elwin Papers, Shillong.
12. Page 363 of manuscript version of *Tribal World*, OUP Archives, Bombay.
13. Elwin to his mother, 5 July 1954, Mss. Eur. D. 950/5, IOL.
14. Verrier Elwin, *Gandhiji: Bapu of his People* (Shillong 1956), pp. 44–5. The book was translated into several languages, including Tibetan, Hindi and Assamese.
15. Shamrao to Eldyth, 20 September 1954, Mss Eur. D. 950/5, IOL.
16. Elwin to Archer, 28 September 1954, Mss. Eur. F. 236/266, IOL.
17. Diary entries of 30 December and 31 December 1954, Elwin Papers, Shillong.
18. Elwin to his mother, letters of 22 January, 7 February and 20 February 1955, Mss Eur. D. 950/5, IOL.
19. Diary entry of 17 January 1955, Elwin Papers, Shillong.
20. 'Touring among the Sherdupkens in April 1955,' in File 138, Elwin Papers, NMML.
21. Elwin to his mother, 14 May 1955, Mss. Eur. D. 950/5, IOL.
22. Elwin to his mother, letters of 6 May, 8 May, 9 July, 7 August and 14 August 1955, Mss, Eur. D. 950/5, IOL.
23. Elwin to his sister, 20 August 1955, ibid.
24. Jawaharlal Nehru, confidential note on NEFA of 28 August 1955, File 149, Elwin Papers, NMML.

25. Cf. Elwin's notes of 1 November 1955 and of 19 April 1956, and his report of a tour between 23 October and 3 December 1958, in Files 116, 133 and 139 respectively, Elwin Papers, NMML.
26. Note in File 7, Elwin Papers, NMML.
27. Quoted in Shamrao Hivale's letter to Elwin, 26 February 1954, Elwin Papers, Shillong.
28. Elwin to his sister, 10 October 1955, Mss Eur. D. 950/5, IOL.
29. Elwin to R. E. Hawkins, 8 August 1959, File E (parts 7 and 8), OUP Archives, Bombay. Also *Tribal World*, pp. 249–50.
30. Elwin to K. L. Mehta, 12 December 1955, File 119, Elwin Papers, NMML.
31. 'Report on a Tour of Mishmi Hills, November 1955,' Mss. Eur. D. 950/5, IOL.
32. Elwin to Sir Robert Reid, 30 November 1955, Mss. Eur. E. 278/16, IOL.
33. Diary entries for 31 November 1955 and 1 January 1956, Elwin Papers, Shillong.
34. Elwin to his mother, letters of 29 December 1955, 9 January, and 14 January 1956; Elwin to his sister, letters of 8 December 1956 and 28 January 1958, Mss Eur. D. 950/6, IOL.
35. Quoted in K. L. Mehta, *In Different Worlds* (New Delhi 1985), pp. 159–60.
36. Verrier Elwin, 'The People of NEFA' (in six parts), *The Illustrated Weekly of India*, 30 September to 4 November 1956.
37. Quoted in his 'Report of Tour in Lohit Frontier Division in November 1955,' File 138, Elwin Papers, NMML.
38. This paragraph draws on interviews with Har Mander Singh, New Delhi, February 1994; with R. N. Haldipur, Bangalore, September 1997; and with Rashid Yusuf Ali, Shillong, December 1997.
39. Verrier Elwin, 'The People of NEFA: VI: Tawang' *The Illustrated Weekly of India*, 4 November 1956.
40. Quoted in 'Notes on Verrier Elwin,' Mss. Eur. F. 236/228, IOL.
41. Elwin to his sister, 8 December 1956, Mss. Eur. 950/5, IOL.
42. Interview with O. K. Moorthy, New Delhi, August 1992; Mehta, *In Different Worlds*, pp. 161–2.
43. 'Report of Tour in Lohit Frontier Division in November 1957,' File 139, Elwin Papers, NMML.

NOTES TO CHAPTER TWELVE

1. Elwin to Archer, 28 September 1954, Mss Eur. F. 236/266, IOL.
2. Elwin to Archer, 10 January 1959, ibid.
3. Verrier Elwin, *A Philosophy for NEFA* (second edition: Shillong 1959), p. 46. All quotes are from this edition.

4. *A Philosophy for NEFA*, pp. 53–60.
5. Note dated 23 August 1958, File 23, Elwin Papers, NMML.
6. *A Philosophy for NEFA*, pp. 131, 146–7, 152–3, 246, etc.
7. Elwin to K. L. Mehta (Adviser to Governor), 16 September 1955, File 7, Elwin Papers, NMML; 'Comment on a Memorandum on the Impact of Modern Civilization on the Tribal People of Madhya Pradesh,' in File 8, Elwin Papers, NMML.
8. 'A Critical Survey in 1957,' File 139, Elwin Papers, NMML; note by Elwin of 24 October 1955, File 116, Elwin Papers, NMML.
9. Elwin to Commissioner of NEFA, 4 October 1962, File 46; tour diary, entry for 5 March 1962, in File 139; report of a trip made to Tripura in 1958, File 133; correspondence and notes in file 116 (all files in Elwin Papers, NMML).
10. Elwin to Adviser to Governor, 2 March 1956, File 130, Elwin Papers, NMML.
11. Verrier Elwin, *The Art of the North East Frontier of India* (Shillong 1958); also Elwin, 'Introduction,' in Anon., *Folk Paintings of India* (New Delhi 1961).
12. Undated note by Elwin on architecture in Tirap; Nehru to B. P. Chaliha, 1 August 1958, both in File 47, Elwin Papers, NMML ('Architectural Designs, 1955–61').
13. Verrier Elwin, review of John Bartlow Martin, *Break Down the Walls* (a book on Australian prisons), *Illustrated Weekly of India*, 3 June 1956.
14. Cf. notes and correspondence in File 69, Elwin Papers, NMML.
15. Verrier Elwin, *Maria Murder and Suicide* (Bombay 1943), esp. chapter XVIII.
16. Elwin to M. C. Nanavatty, 25 August 1958, File 91, Elwin Papers, NMML, emphasis supplied.
17. 'Flibbertigibbet' (pseudonym, possibly of the left-wing commentator Ashok Mitra), 'Going Gaga over the Nagas,' *The Economic Weekly*, 7 September 1957.
18. Onkar Sharad, *Lohia: A Biography* (Delhi 1972), pp. 269–71.
19. Translation of news report in *Natun Assamiya*, 15 May 1954, Elwin Papers, NMML.
20. *Discussion on the Motion to consider the recommendations of the States Reorganization Commission relating to Assam (extracts from the proceedings of the Assam Legislative Assembly at its meeting held on the 17th November, 1955)* (Shillong 1955).
21. *A Report on the Visit to North-East Frontier Agency by the Delegation of the Assam Legislative Assembly in the Month of December, 1962* (Shillong 1963); *A Report on the Visit of North-East Frontier Agency by the Second*

Delegation of the Assam Legislative Assembly in the Month of April, 1963 (Shillong 1963)

22. Press cutting in Elwin Papers, Shillong.
23. Elwin to Vishnu Sahay (Governor of Assam), 13 June 1963, quoted in K. S. Singh, *Ethnicity, Identity and Development* (Verrier Elwin Memorial Lectures of 1985, published in 1990 by Manohar, New Delhi), pp. 13–14.
24. Interview with Rashid Yusuf Ali, Shillong, December 1997.
25. Note by Elwin of 19 February 1957, File 18, Elwin Papers, NMML; Elwin to K. L. Mehta, 15 October 1957, File 113, Elwin Papers, NMML.
26. Cf. N. K. Bose, 'Tribal Economy' (first published in 1955), reprinted in his *Culture and Society in India* (Bombay 1967), p. 174; *Tribal World*, p. 317.
27. Cf, in this connection, Bose's important essay, 'The Hindu Method of Tribal Absorption,' first published in *Science and Culture*, 1941, and reprinted in his *Culture and Society in India*, pp. 203–15.
28. N. K. Bose, 'Anthropology and Tribal Welfare,' *Man in India*, vol. 37, no. 3, 1957 (based on the address to the Fourth Tribal Welfare Conference, Koraput, 30 April 1957). In a later essay Bose criticized Elwin for his 'sentimental approach to a rather serious problem.' N. K. Bose, 'Change in Tribal Cultures before and after Independence,' *Man in India*, vol. 44, no. 1, 1964.
29. Review of *A Philosophy of NEFA* by 'E.T.' (pseudonym used by D. N. Majumdar), in *The Eastern Anthropologist*, vol. 12, no. 3, 1959 (emphasis added).
30. Letters in File 49, Elwin Papers, NMML.
31. *The Sunday Statesman*, 10 May 1959.
32. Gertrude Emerson Sen, 'Sortie over NEFA,' *Economic Weekly*, Annual Number, January 1960.
33. Cf. *The Statesman*, 9 October 1959.
34. Diary entry of 1 November 1955, Elwin Papers, Shillong.
35. *Lok Sabha Debates*, 18 August 1960.

NOTES TO CHAPTER THIRTEEN

1. Will dated 10 January 1959, copy in the possession of Arvind Khare. Bijay was, of course, born in 1946, not 1947.
2. In four files in his papers (Files 19, 23, 39 and 62, Elwin Papers, NMML), on which the following paragraphs draw.
3. Elwin to his sister, letters of 5 February, 17 February and 3 March 1959, Mss. Eur. D. 950/6, IOL.
4. Elwin to Koestler, 3 March 1959, Koestler Papers, University of Edinburgh.

5. Verrier Elwin, 'The Dalai Lama comes to India,' *The Geographical Magazine*, July 1959.
6. Elwin to Koestler, 14 May 1959, Koestler Papers.
7. Elwin to Nehru, 27 August 1960, File 89, Elwin Papers, NMML; Elwin to Major General A. S. Guraya, Inspector General of the Assam Rifles, undated, File 74, Elwin Papers, NMML.
8. *Report of the Committee on Special Multipurpose Tribal Blocks* (New Delhi 1960), pp. i, 14–17, 21, 25, 29, 31, 45–6, 48–9, 178, etc.
9. As recalled in P. D. Strachey, *Nagaland Nightmare* (Bombay 1968), pp. 58–60.
10. Diary entry of 18 July 1960, Elwin Papers, Shillong.
11. These paragraphs are based on the letters and notings in Files 20, 59 and 120, Elwin Papers, NMML.
12. W. G. Archer, 'In the Assam Mail,' typescript dated 4 December 1947, Mss Eur. F. 236/275, IOL.
13. Verrier Elwin, *Nagaland* (Shillong 1960), p. 104.
14. Elwin to R. E. Hawkins, 28 August 1940, File E5, OUP Archives, Mumbai.
15. Elwin to Hutton, 20 October 1962, Elwin Papers (personal correspondence files), NMML.
16. Elwin to Murkot Ramunny, 3 September 1960, File 59, Elwin Papers, NMML.
17. Unsigned, undated typescript in File 4, Elwin Papers, NMML.
18. Elwin to Hawkins, 20 September 1962, File E10, OUP Archives, Mumbai.
19. As recounted by K. L. Mehta in a letter to *The Statesman*, 9 April 1964.
20. Elwin to J. H. Hutton, 5 November 1960, Elwin Papers (personal correspondence files), NMML.
21. Undated 'Aide Memoire' in File 28, Elwin Papers, NMML.
22. Elwin to his sister, letters of 1 February, 20 April and 27 April 1961, Mss. Eur. D. 950/6.
23. *The Pardhans of the Upper Nerbudda Valley* (Bombay 1946), p. 149.
24. Elwin to his sister, 3 August 1961, Mss Eur. D. 950/6, IOL; *Report of the Scheduled Areas and Scheduled Tribes Commission* (New Delhi 1962).
25. Elwin to T. S. Wilkinson, 22 September 1961, Elwin Papers, Shillong. The essay was published, without the references to Elwin's marriages, as T. S. Wilkinson, 'Isolation, Assimilation and Integration in their Historical Perspective,' *Tribal Research Institute Bulletin*, vol. 2, no. 1, June 1962—it is a little-known but remarkably fair account of the Elwin-Ghurye controversy.
26. Cf. correspondence in File 41, Elwin Papers, NMML.
27. Elwin to P. C. Chatterjee, 30 May 1961, File 41, Elwin Papers, NMML.
28. Verrier Elwin, *A Philosophy of Love* (Delhi 1961).

29. Interview with Amina Jayal, New Delhi, April 1994.
30. Cf. File 68, Elwin Papers, NMML.
31. Elwin to Hawkins, 25 July 1962; Elwin to Hutton, 20 October 1962, personal correspondence files, Elwin Papers, NMML.
32. Elwin to Koestler, 17 October 1962; Koestler to Elwin, 24 October 1962, Koestler Papers, Edinburgh.
33. Elwin to his sister, letters of 29 November and 11 December 1962, Mss. Eur. D. 950/6, IOL.
34. Major Sitaram Johri, *Where India, China and Burma Meet* (Calcutta 1962), pp. 16, 78–9, 106, 110, 277, etc.
35. Elwin to R. N. Haldipur, 26 December 1962, File 104, Elwin Papers, NMML.
36. Indira Gandhi to Elwin, 14 January 1963, Elwin Papers, Shillong.
37. Mary Gillett to Elwin, 19 November 1962, Elwin Papers, Shillong.
38. Elwin to Hawkins, 21 December 1962, File E10, OUP Archives, Mumbai.
39. Elwin to Hawkins, letters of 13 March and 14 April 1963, Elwin Papers (personal correspondence files), NMML.
40. Elwin to his sister, letters of 15 May, 27 May and 10 July 1963, Mss. Eur. D. 950/6, IOL.
41. Vishnu Sahay to Elwin, 12 June 1963, File 6, Elwin Papers, NMML.
42. Nehru to Elwin, 8 June 1963, Elwin Papers, Shillong.
43. Interview with Ashok Elwin, Shillong, December 1997.
44. Patel to Elwin, 29 June 1963, Elwin Papers (personal correspondence files), NMML.
45. Archer to Elwin, 12 June 1963, Mss. Eur. F. 236/266, IOL.
46. Armand Denis, *Taboo* (London 1966), chapter XI.
47. Tara Ali Baig, *Portraits of an Era* (New Delhi 1988), p. 45f. The lines are from Wordsworth's 'Song at the Feast of Brougham Castle;' the next stanza, also a favourite of Elwin's, runs thus:

    'In him the savage virtue of the Race,
    Revenge, and all ferocious thoughts were dead;
    Nor did he change; but kept in lofty place
    The wisdom which adversity had bred.'

    The two stanzas had been prophetically invoked by Elwin in his early essay, 'Mahatma Gandhi and William Wordsworth,' *The Modern Review*, February 1931.
48. Bose to Elwin, 28 November 1963, in File 39, Elwin Papers, NMML.
49. Elwin to Koestler, 28 December 1963, Koestler Papers, Edinburgh.
50. Cf. Sourin Roy to Elwin, 17 February 1964, Elwin Papers, NMML.
51. Preface dates 31 November 1963, in Verrier Elwin, *The Kingdom of the Young* (Bombay 1968).

52. Verrier Elwin, editor, *Democracy in NEFA* (Shillong 1965), Preface and p. 23.
53. Medical report of Lt. Col. (Dr) C. R. Gopinath, Military Hospital, Shillong, 14 February 1964, in File 140, Elwin Papers, NMML.
54. Interview with Rashid Yusuf Ali, Shillong, December 1997.
55. Lahiri to Eldyth, 28 February 1964, Mss. Eur. D. 950/21, IOL.

NOTES TO CHAPTER FOURTEEN

1. As characterized by Sunil Janah, the friend who finally touched up the photograph for publication. Cf. Elwin–Janah correspondence, Elwin Papers, NMML.
2. *Tribal World*, p. viii. In a letter to an editor at the OUP, Elwin wrote that 'it was only when I came to write this book that I realized how Indianized I have grown.' Elwin to Toyne, 12 (?) 1961, File E10, OUP Archives, Bombay.
3. Philip Vaudin to R. E. Hawkins, 13 October 1949; Hawkins to Elwin, 25 November 1949, both in File E10, OUP Archives.
4. Andre Maurois, 'Autobiography,' in his *Aspects of Biography* (Cambridge 1929), p. 145.
5. Hawkins to Elwin, 9 April 1962; also Elwin to Hawkins, letters of 15 March and 17 March 1962, all in File E10, OUP Archives.
6. Elwin to Koestler, 11 April 1962, Koestler Papers, Edinburgh.
7. Elwin to Hawkins, 9 August 1963, File E10, OUP Archives, Mumbai.
8. Elwin to Hawkins, 16 August 1963, File 62, Elwin Papers, NMML.
9. Manuscript copy of *Tribal World*, OUP Archives, Mumbai, pp.161, 165–6, 492–3, 521.
10. As described in Elwin to Hawkins, 24 June 1963, File E10, OUP Archives.
11. Letter of 28 May 1963, in ibid.
12. Eldyth Elwin to R. E. Hawkins, 9 August 1964, ibid.
13. Cf. reviews by K. S. Mathur in the *International Journal of Comparative Sociology*, vol. 8, 1965, pp.127–8; by Naomi Mitchison in the *Glasgow Herald*, 31 October 1964; by Bool Chand in *Kurukshetra*, July 1964; and by Robin White in the *New York Times Book Review*, 21 June 1964; unsigned review in *The Assam Tribune*, (Gauhati), 30 May 1964.
14. S. C. Dube, review in *The Eastern Anthropologist*, vol. 17, no. 2, 1964; Mitchison, op. cit.; *The Sunday Statesman*, 5 April 1964.
15. Review in *Imprint*, March 1965.
16. Joseph Epstein, 'First Person Singular,' *The Hudson Review*, 45 (3), Autumn 1992, p. 370.

17. W. G. Archer, 'Converted by India,' *The Daily Telegraph* (London), 10 October 1964.
18. Untitled, undated notes by W. G. Archer in Mss. Eur. F. 236/266, IOL.
19. Shamrao Hivale to Eldyth Elwin, 5 September 1953, Mss Eur. D. 950/4, IOL.
20. SVV, 'Marginalia,' *The Illustrated Weekly of India*, 3 May 1964.
21. Inserted by the Little Theatre Group and the Minerva Theatre in the *Amrita Bazaar Patrika*, 25 February 1964.

NOTES TO THE EPILOGUE

1. *The Times of India*, 20 May 1964.
2. Verrier Elwin, *Religious and Cultural Aspects of Khadi* (1931: reprinted by Sarvodaya Prachuralaya, Thanjavur, 1964).
3. R. F. McNeile, compiler, *A History of Dean Close School* (printed by the School in 1966). A reviewer in *The Decanian*, Summer 1966, was sensibly 'puzzled by the absence from chapter XIII of the name of Verrier Elwin, for instance, the only O.D. to take a double first from Oxford and who became one of the world's foremost anthropologists.'
4. *Dean Close School Alumni, 1886 to 1948* (Winchester 1950).
5. Cf. Humphrey Osmond to Paul Newton, 19 April 1991.
6. Asoso Yonuo, *The Rising Nagas: A Historical and Political Study* (Delhi 1974), p. 120.
7. George M. Soares-Prabhu, *Incultural Liberation Dialogue: Challenges to Christian Theology in Asia Today* (Pune 1984).
8. Daniel O'Connor, editor, *Din-Sevak: Verrier Elwin's Life of Service in Tribal India* (Delhi 1993).
9. Leonard Schiff, interview with John Charles, 2 July 1971, in Archives of the Hilfield Priory, Dorset.
10. Reported in *The Times of India*, New Delhi, 16 August 1997.
11. Victor Turner, Review of *The Religion of an Indian Tribe, in Man*, article 50, May 1957; Turner, 'Aspects of Saora Ritual and Shamanism: An Approach to the Data of Ritual,' in A. L. Epstein, edited, *The Craft of Social Anthropology* (London 1967). See also Ramachandra Guha, 'Between Anthropology and Literature: The Ethnographies of Verrier Elwin,' *Journal of the Royal Anthropological Institute (incorporating Man)*, vol. 3, no. 2, June 1998.
12. Piers Vitebsky, *Dialogues with the Dead: Intimations of Mortality among the Sora of Eastern India* (Cambridge 1993); Simeran Man Singh Gell, *The Ghotul in Muria Society* (London 1993); Bikram Narayan Nanda, *Contours of Continuity and Change among the Bonda of Koraput* (New Delhi 1994);

Vinay Srivastava, 'The Ethnographer and the People: Reflections on Fieldwork,' in 2 parts, *Economic and Political Weekly*, 1–8, 15 June 1991.

13. M. C. Pradhan, R. D. Singh, P. K. Misra and D. B. Sastry, editors, *Anthropology and Archaeology: Essays in Commemoration of Verrier Elwin* (Bombay 1969). The essays ranged from a study of tribal assertion in modern Bihar to party conflict in a Kerala village: the publishers were Elwin's own, the Indian Branch of Oxford University Press.
14. Note by B. Das Shastri, 12 March 1964, File 158, Elwin Papers, NMML.
15. Dharmendra Prasad, 'Elwin in Mandla,' *India Cultures Quarterly*, volume 34, nos 1 and 2, 1979, pp. 19–21.
16. Personal communication from Nandini Sundar.
17. This paragraph brutally summarizes a history told in more detail in Madhav Gadgil and Ramachandra Guha, *Ecology and Equity: The Use and Abuse of Nature in Contemporary India* (London 1995). Also see Amita Baviskar, *In the Belly of the River: Tribal Conflicts Over Development in the Narmada Valley* (New Delhi 1996).
18. Swaminathan S. Anklesaria Aiyar, 'We are all Tribals,' *The Sunday Times of India*, 11 October 1992.
19. Bradford Morse, et al., *Sardar Sarovar: Report of the Independent Review* (Ottawa 1992), pp. 68–9, 78.
20. Quotes from *Report of the High Level Committee to Make Recommendations on the Salient Features of the Law for Extending Provisions of the Constitutional (73rd) Amendment Act 1992, to Scheduled Areas* (New Delhi 1995).
21. B. G. Verghese, *India's Northeast Resurgent: Ethnicity, Insurgency, Governance, Development* (New Delhi 1997), chapter XI.
22. Haimendorf, 'The Example of Verrier Elwin,' *Anthropology Today*, vol. 11, no. 4, August 1985.
23. Interviews with Vivek Rae, New Delhi, January 1991, and with R. N. Haldipur, Bangalore, August 1997.
24. Reports by Parsa Venkateshwar Rao Jr. in *The Indian Express*, 18 and 20 April 1994.
25. Cf. the three-part series by Bill Aitken in *The Telegraph* (Calcutta), 25 May and 1 and 8 June 1996.
26. Cf. introduction and paintings reproduced in J. Swaminathan, ed., *The Perceiving Fingers* (Bhopal 1987); interview with J. Swaminathan, New Delhi, March 1992. An anecdotal and affectionate account of the Swaminathan–Patangarh–Jangarh–Elwin connection can be found in Mark Tully's *No Full Stops in India* (London 1991).
27. *Vivekanda Kendra Patrika*, vol. 1, no. 2, 1972, special issue on Hill India.
28. Uma Shanker Misra, 'Remembering the Scholar Gypsy,' *The Pioneer*, 21 April 1985.

29. *A Common Perspective for North-East India: Speeches and Papers of National Seminar on Hill People of North-Eastern India, held in Calcutta from December 3 to 6, 1966* (Calcutta 1967), pp. 158–9.
30. A. R. Kamath, 'Rural Sociology in the Fifties,' *Economic and Political Weekly*, 4 April 1981.
31. Durga Bhagwat, *Athavale Tase* (As I Remember It) (Bombay 1991), pp. 160–5.
32. *The Hindu*, 29 October 1985.
33. *Soliga: The Tribe and Its Stride* (published by Vivekananda Girijana Kalyana Kendra, B. R. Hills, Mysore 1991), p. 18.
34. G. S. Ghurye, *The Burning Caldron of North-East India* (Bombay 1980), pp. 6–7, 17, 22, 26–7, 53, 100, etc.
35. Books republished in the last decade include *Leaves from the Jungle*, *The Agaria*, *Maria Murder and Suicide*, *The Muria and their Ghotul*, *Myths of Middle India*, and *The Tribal World of Verrier Elwin*.
36. Lila to Eldyth, 18 November 1966, Mss. Eur. D. 950/21, IOL.
37. Shamrao to Hawkins, 12 March 1964, File E10, OUP Archives, Mumbai.
38. This account is based on papers held by Arvind Khare, who assisted Kosi and Kumar in the cases.
39. Dom Moraes, *Answered by Flutes: Reflections from Madhya Pradesh* (Bombay 1983), pp. 158–165; also interview with Dom Moraes, Mumbai, December 1990.
40. Dharmendra Prasad to Vijay Elwin, dated 22 June 1981, letter in the possession of Arvind Khare.
41. Eldyth Elwin to John Charles, 23 April 1971, Archives of the Hilfield Priory, Dorset.
42. *Tribal World*, p. 20.
43. Barry Phelps, *P. G. Wodehouse: Man and Myth* (London 1992), p. 201. Also Verrier Elwin, *Motley* (Calcutta 1954), and Elwin, 'The College Life of Bertie Wooster,' *The Sunday Statesman*, (?) November 1953.

Index

Except for the entry under his own name, Verrier Elwin has been abbreviated to VE throughout. Entries marked with an asterisk denote tribal communities visited or studied by Verrier Elwin.